The Multisensory
Museum

The Multisensory Museum

Cross-Disciplinary Perspectives on Touch, Sound, Smell, Memory, and Space

Edited by Nina Levent and Alvaro Pascual-Leone

ROWMAN & LITTLEFIELD

Lanham • Boulder • New York • Toronto • Plymouth, UK

Published by Rowman & Littlefield
4501 Forbes Boulevard, Suite 200, Lanham, Maryland 20706
www.rowman.com

10 Thornbury Road, Plymouth PL6 7PP, United Kingdom

British Library Cataloguing in Publication Information Available

Library of Congress Cataloging-in-Publication Data

Multisensory museum : cross-disciplinary perspectives on touch, sound, smell, memory, and space / edited by Nina Levent and Alvaro Pascual-Leone.
pages cm
Includes bibliographical references and index.
ISBN 978-0-7591-2354-0 (cloth) — ISBN 978-0-7591-2356-4 (electronic)
ISBN 978-0-8108-9535-5 (pbk:alk. paper))
1. Museums and people with visual disabilities. 2. Museum techniques. I. Levent, Nina Sobol, 1971– editor of compilation. II. Pascual-Leone, Alvaro, editor of compilation. III. Lacey, Simon (Neurologist), author. Please do touch the exhibits!
AM160.M85 2014
069'.17—dc23   2013042555

∞™ The paper used in this publication meets the minimum requirements of American National Standard for Information Sciences—Permanence of Paper for Printed Library Materials, ANSI/NISO Z39.48-1992.

Printed in the United States of America

Dedication

To my children, Edis-Alexander and Isabelle, for accompanying me on many trips to museums around the world. They did so from the time they could barely walk, and most times without a fight. They almost always found ways to enjoy the experience—by stuffing a sibling headfirst into an ancient sarcophagus, racing up and down the stairs, or engaging in some other hijinks. They also made sure every museum trip was a sensory experience by never skipping the museum café.

—NL

I would like to dedicate this book to my father, Alvaro Pascual-Leone Pascual, who introduced me early to the joy of visiting museums. Without his early influence, I would not have developed a delight and appreciation for the importance of the appropriate display and presentation of art such that all might enjoy and learn from it. I would also like to dedicate this book to my wife Elizabeth and my children, Ana, Nico and Andres, who keep reminding me what is important.

—APL

Contents

PART I: MUSEUMS AND TOUCH

PART II: MUSEUMS AND SOUND

PART III: SMELL AND TASTE IN MUSEUMS

PART IV: MUSEUM ARCHITECTURE
AND THE SENSES

Acknowledgments

This book would not have been possible without Elisabeth Axel's initiative and vision for such a publication. On the neuroscience side, the late Paul Bach-y-Rita was a strong influence in our thinking about a multisensory experience of the world and the value and challenges of sensory substitution. The influence of his pioneering work and thinking permeates many of the chapters of this book.

We want to thank Joan Muyskens Pursley for her patient and sage advice; David Howes for his generosity and a truly collegial spirit; Kaywin Feldman, for helping to lead the conversation about the future museum; our editors, Marissa Parks, Charles Harmon, and Robert Hayunga, for bearing with us and believing in this book; Andrea Vatulas for keeping all things organized and moving; Jared Horvath for helping with the language of cognitive science articles; Tina Breckwoldt, who reads cuneiform; and Jan Mark. The following artists and curators have kindly shared their expertise, thoughts, and time: Deborah Butterfield, Sebastian Chan, John Connelly, Jan-Lodewijk Grootaers, Ann Hamilton, Rafael Lozano Hammer, Heather Knight, Geoffrey Mann, Frederick John Lamp, Yukio Lippit, Jen Mergel, Lawrence Rinder, Peter Sellars, Annalisa Trasatti, and Julián Zugazagoitia.

This book was made possible with the support of Art Beyond Sight's Board of Directors: Elisabeth Axel, president and creative director; Nick Williams, chairman of the board; Cheryl Rosario, vice president; John T. Donnellan, treasurer; Nancy Aronson, Robert H. Duckman, Freda Gimpel, Carole Gothelf, Tahra Lore Grant, Amy Salzhauer McMarlin, Richard Donald Smith, Sheldon Tannen, Jennifer Teich, and Harold Wenning.

Last, but not least, we would like to thank Elisabeth Axel, Joan Muyskens Pursley, Marie Clapot, Rebecca McGuiness, Norihiro Sadato, Leonardo Cohen, Mark Hallett, Hugo Theoret, Amir Amedi, Lotfi Merabet, Marina Bedny, Alfonso Caramazza, Rebecca Saxe, Peter Meijer, Franco Lepore, Maryse Lessonde, Robert Zatorre, Barry Stein, M. Alex Meredith, Jon Kaas, Michael Merzenich, Norman Doidge, and Vincent Walsh for our rich conversations. The synergy of these conversations was an inspiration, and we are looking forward to where the dialogue will take us next.

Introduction

Nina Levent and Alvaro Pascual-Leone

Today's museums are much more than repositories of ancient artifacts to be preserved for the future, although collection care remains a critical function in any museum. They are centers of learning, community centers, social hubs, even places of healing and contemplation. Museums reach out to their communities by facilitating important and relevant conversations through their collections and exhibits, and by making the objects in their collections accessible and meaningful to a wide variety of visitors. Many exhibits focus on the materiality of a single object and help visitors connect with the sensory properties of historic artifacts, their context, and the stories behind them. Other museums, with the use of technology, create immersive learning experiences that have no artifacts at all.

We now understand that a museum visit is not simply an encounter between an eager visiting public who soaks up the knowledge articulated by the curatorial team. The museum experience is a multilayered journey that is proprioceptive, sensory, intellectual, aesthetic, and social. The end result might be learning, wonder, reflection and relaxation, sensory stimulation, conversation with friends, new social ties, creation of lasting memories, or recollection of past events.

At the same time as the meaning and purpose of museums is being redefined, the study of the human brain and its function has profoundly modified our understanding of perception, cognition, and knowledge. Modern neuroscience has come to view the brain as a creator of expectations and hypotheses of reality, which then get contrasted against experience. The brain is not a passive recipient of information through the senses but instead an active seeker of information to confirm or refute predictions. Human neuroscience has taught us that our internal representations of reality, and thus the predictions we approach experience with and the nature of such experiences themselves, are intrinsically multisensory (Pascual-Leone and Hamilton, 2001). Therefore, museums need to consider the combined and complex interactions between visual, auditory, olfactory, spatial, and other aspects of the visitors' experience. Human neuroscience has also taught us that the brain is intrinsically plastic, dynamically changing to respond to changes in environment, activity, demands, and so forth (Pascual-Leone et al., 2005). As a result, museums need to consider their potential impact on visitors and the opportunity they represent to literally shape visitors' brains.

This book seeks to open a dialogue between modern museum science and human neuroscience. We aim to highlight today's best multisensory practices and reflect on how new research and technology will influence museums of the future. We hope to inspire museum staff to develop layered museum experiences and try to provide practical information on how to do so. We challenged the book's contributors—experts in various disciplines—to take a critical look at current trends in designing multimodal museum experiences and exhibits and to think about the sensory dimensions of museum learning, contemplation, and dialogue. We are most fortunate to have the contributions of leading neuroscientists, cognitive researchers, architects, anthropologists, historians, artists, curators, and educators to shape a framework of ideas. This book is thus a cross-disciplinary effort to create a conceptual framework for thinking about present and future sensory experiences in museums.

COGNITIVE RESEARCH SENSES AND MUSEUM PRACTICE: A BIT OF HISTORY

Art Beyond Sight (ABS, formerly Art Education for the Blind) has been fostering a dialogue between museum practitioners and cognitive researchers since the organization's inception in 1987. Because Art Beyond Sight's original goal was to make museums and visual culture accessible to people who are blind, much of its effort was initially focused on developing multisensory tools for blind audiences, such as tactile images, verbal descriptions, touch collections, and sound images. ABS founder Elisabeth Axel and her team pioneered tactile book printing and developed a tactile language of lines and patterns; they created the first tactile art history encyclopedia, *Art History through Touch and Sound*. Axel and her team also developed the first guidelines for verbal descriptions of art and museum objects in 1996 and periodically update these guidelines.

In the 1990s, ABS, led by Axel, established itself as a think tank and clearinghouse for the latest research on multisensory perception, including tactile images for people who are blind, haptic perception of forms and shapes, auditory perception, verbal description, sonification, and art education through the senses. One of ABS's first national conferences focusing on research done by cognitive psychologists, including John M. Kennedy (*Drawing and the Blind*, 1993) and Morton Heller (*Psychology of Touch*, 1991), was held in 1990 at the Metropolitan Museum of Art. Over the next two decades ABS became a hub for cutting-edge research and best practices in museum pedagogy. One of the most critical partnerships formed early on was with Alvaro Pascual-Leone and his colleagues at Berenson-Allen Center for Non-Invasive Brain Stimulation at Beth Israel Deaconess Medical Center and Harvard Medical School. Pascual-Leone and his colleagues collaborated with ABS on a study involving a congenitally blind figurative artist, Esref Armagan (Amedi et al., 2008). The group worked together to identify new research areas that held particular relevance for museum and art practice.

ABS began partnering with the Metropolitan Museum of Art on a biennial international conference, Art Beyond Sight: Multimodal Approaches to Learning. With creative input from Rebecca McGinnis at the Metropolitan Museum of Art, the conference expanded to address larger issues around multisensory learning for all museum audiences. The four such conferences that have taken place in the last ten years have brought together researchers and practitioners from disciplines as varied as neuroscience, social psychology, museology, education, art history, computer science, and art therapy.

The conversation about art, senses, and cognition connects to museum practice through a number of recent innovative collaborations between museums, artists, and neuroscience research labs. In 2010 the Walters Art Museum announced a major collaboration with John Hopkins University's Mind/Brain Institute. The same year, the renowned performance artist Marina Abramović, during her retrospective at New York City's Museum of Modern Art, was inspired to collaborate with neuroscientists from New York University on a project that looks at the art and science of the mutual gaze. A growing number of museums on both sides on the Atlantic are sponsoring lectures and presentations on the neuroscience of sound, visual attention, learning, aesthetics, creativity, and other aspects of the museum experience.

NEUROSCIENCE AND PERCEPTION OF OBJECTS TODAY

Confronted with the question of how we perceive objects in the world, we are often taught that we have a series of distributed systems structured according to the sensory modalities that they process. We talk about a visual system, a somatosensory or tactile system, an auditory system, and so forth. Certainly, the existence of specialized detectors or receptors for different sensory modalities grants us the opportunity to process different forms of energy and hence capture different views of the world in parallel. Some experiences are uniquely unimodal. Hue can only be experienced by sight, tickle can only be felt by touch, and pitch can only be differentiated by audition. Nevertheless, our perceptual experience of the world is richly multimodal, as eloquently elaborated by Barry Stein and Alex Meredith (Stein and Meredith, 1993). We are able to integrate into a richer percept the impressions generated by different sensory modalities. Furthermore, we routinely extract information derived from one sensory modality and use it in another; we can, for example, know a shape by touch and subsequently identify it correctly by sight. This raises the broad issue of internal versus experiential influences in the organization of the brain, and in that context modern neuroscience increasingly emphasizes the importance of internal representation. Our brain is not a passive recipient of sensory inputs, but rather an active source of expectations—hypotheses about the world and its objects—that we can then contrast with and refine by experience.

In this role of creator of expectations and predictions about the world and its objects, the brain might in fact have a metamodal representation of reality (Pascual-Leone and Hamilton, 2001). The brain appears to be made up of metamodal operators, local neural networks defined by a given computation that is applied regardless of the sensory input received. This does not mean that there are not preferred sensory modalities for specific computations (and hence operators). Indeed, this is the case and the reason that the cortex gives the illusion of being built around sensory modalities rather than operators. However, internal representation of reality appears to effectively transcend specific sensory modalities. If this is so, it would imply a multisensory experience of the world as default.

SENSORY STUDIES, MULTISENSORY
LEARNING, AND MUSEUM STUDIES

The field of sensory studies has flourished in the last two decades as a result of researchers from across the humanities and social sciences turning their attention to the sensorium and delving into the cultural life of the senses. Much of this research has been generated or inspired by the work of anthropologist David Howes and historian Constance Classen who, together with sociologist Anthony Synnott, formed the Concordia Sensoria Research Team in 1988. They and their colleagues have published a range of books, beginning with *The Varieties of Sensory Experience* (Howes, 1991) and continuing with investigations of the five canonical senses (for example, Classen, Howes, and Synnott, 1994; Bull and Back, 2003; Classen, 2005, 2012; Korsmeyer, 2005; and Edwards and Bhaumik, 2008), as well as other studies that focus on the shifting relationships among the senses in history and across cultures (Classen, 1998; Howes, 2005; M. Smith, 2007). (Literary scholars and medical historians have also joined this movement to "culturalize" our understanding of the sensorium [B. Smith, 1999; Bynum and Porter, 1993; Jütte, 2005; *pace* Ackerman 1991].) There is much material of both general and particular interest to museum professionals in this literature, such as the chapter on visitor experience in the early museum in *The Book of Touch* (Classen, 2005). In this chapter, Classen relates how in the late seventeenth and eighteenth centuries, visitors to the Ashmolean and British Museum would rub, pick up, shake, smell, and even taste the artifacts on display. Other historians have documented how the restrictions on the senses, which we take for granted today, emerged gradually (Leahy, 2012) and culminated in only conservators and connoisseurs being permitted to enjoy the intimate interaction with museum objects that had once been the norm (Candlin, 2010).

In the wake of this "sensory turn," contemporary museum professionals have started rethinking the multiple restrictions on the use of the senses in the museum and begun actively soliciting the senses instead (to the extent that the competing demand for conservation will allow). The role of touch in the museum has been expanded significantly as more and more studies have pointed to the social, cognitive, and even therapeutic value of handling objects (Pye, 2008; Chatterjee, 2008). A new emphasis on "experiencing the properties of things" directly has taken shape (Dudley, 2010, 2012), which has revolutionized the ways in which the material legacy of the past and other cultures is now being interpreted. Museum educators are also benefiting from a growing body of research on multisensory learning strategies that address the needs of not only young children but school-age and adult learners as well. Education researchers and practitioners point to the success of multisensory methods used in learning math, language, and reading (Birsch, 2005; Campbell et al., 2008; Kerry and Baker, 2011; Shams and Seitz, 2008; Scheffel et al., 2008). Among the benefits of multisensory learning are increased student engagement, better information retention, improved native and foreign language skills, better performance on reading tests, enhanced mathematical skills, and improved ability to multitask. Such multisensory teaching approaches could be particularly effective when working with learners with disabilities (Malatesha Joshi et al., 2002; Axel and Levent, 2003; Al-Hroub, 2010).

The sensory turn that has been sweeping the academy has also inspired artists to explore the aesthetic potential of the nonvisual senses. Over the past few decades, artists have abandoned the easel and started incorporating sound, smell, touch, movement, and also taste into their creations. Thanks to advances in technology, it has become possible to better control sound and smell experiences, as well as use complex digital and robotic technologies to amplify touch and movement. Multisensory immersion has taken the place of disinterested contemplation as the goal of much art (Jones, 2006; Schwartzman, 2011) and has in turn led art critics and philosophers to challenge the restrictive sensory politics of the modern museum (Drobnick, 2004, 2006; Voegelin, 2010; Serres, 2009; Kelly, 2011; Bacci and Melcher, 2011). Breaking down the barriers to and among the senses and the drive to include rather than exclude populations, such as the visually impaired, has opened up an exciting new terrain for museum studies, which this book seeks to extend even further.

SENSORY EXPERIENCES AND CONSUMER TRENDS

Multisensory museum experiences are still few and far between. There are only rarely attempts to attend to the different senses and design museums to promote the multisensory experience. This is important because, whether addressed explicitly or not, modern neuroscience teaches us that basically all experience of the world is multisensory. Therefore, museum curators and directors ought to understand the importance of explicitly designing multisensory museum experiences. Essentially, the museum experience will be multisensory, whether we want it or not—thus it is better to pay attention to achieve desired effects rather than allowing for incidental and potentially undesirable effects.

With that in mind, let us go back to the situation nowadays. Touch and smell in museums, as many of this volume's contributors remark, are still subject to the "sense hierarchy" that elevates and privileges sight above other senses. When many of the exhibits are under glass and art is still often arranged in salon style, sensory experiences may get into the museum culture through the "back door" of museum shops and restaurants that are eager to respond to consumer trends towards more sensory merchandise. Dahesh Museum, which is dedicated to European academic art, used to have its galleries on Madison Avenue and 57th Street in New York City. The museum's gift shop, featuring Victorian jewelry, silk and cashmere shawls, fine art objects, and furniture celebrating nineteenth-century orientalism, rivaled any other commercial venue on Madison Avenue. Many visitors and hurried tourists never made it past Moroccan stools, Turkish pillows, Parisian pill boxes, and Indian shawls into the downstairs galleries.

Neue Galerie is a small jewel of a museum on New York's Upper East Side devoted solely to early-twentieth-century German and Austrian art and design. This museum houses not one but two restaurants in its relatively small space, Café Sabarsky and Café Fledarmaus, both featuring traditional Viennese menus. In these cafes patrons are seated in chairs designed by the modernist Austrian architect Adolf Loos, and in the restaurant spaces are other period objects, including lighting fixtures by Josef Hoffmann and banquettes upholstered with a 1912 Otto Wagner fabric. Thus, as you dine on Viennese classics you are offered the most authentic experience of Viennese Café Kultur in New York City. The restaurants are almost always packed, whether the upstairs galleries are crowded or not. To the naked eye it seems that Café Sabarsky's sensory experience is getting many more new and repeat visitors than the museum galleries.

SENSORY MUSEUM OF THE MIND

Museums are places where we have a chance to explore and contemplate objects—curious and bewildering objects, functional objects, and elegant art objects. Museums are also places where we encounter each other, create social bonds, share stories, gauge our opinions, and debate ideas. Our experience in the physical space of a museum, however, is colored by our previous knowledge, motivations, and background (Falk, 2009). In fact, as discussed above, modern neuroscience reveals this role of the brain as predictor of experience to be pervasive. We enter a museum like we travel through life, with our brains creating frameworks of expectations that determine what we perceive (we only see what we look for) and influence our experience (we feel more comfortable when our brains' models map onto our experience).

Young and not-so-young visitors are reminded about the museum of the mind by brilliant British children's author Jan Mark, who wrote this about the ultimate museum collection:

It is in your head. Everything you have ever heard, smelled, tasted, or touched is in there. Most of it has been pushed to the back, like things in a real museum, but an enormous amount is still there when you need it. You can get it out and have an exhibition whenever you want; you can spend as long as you like wandering around it. As you get older, many things that you did not understand when you first stowed them away suddenly start making sense. Bring them back from the basement. . . . Memory is your museum, your cabinet of curiosities, your Wunderkammer. It will never be full; there is always room for something new and strange and marvelous. (Mark, 2007)

As if following Mark's advice, a blind New Yorker in her seventies walked us through her museum of the mind. One of the first things she described vividly was her childhood experience of a ninety-foot whale at the American Museum of Natural History. She did not have vision to see the whale, nor could she touch it, as the model is on the ceiling of the gallery, but she had carried around for decades a vivid mental image that was created through verbal description and the dynamic and joyous experience of measuring ninety feet with a yardstick to understand the scale of this giant animal (Reich et al., 2011, p. 95). When we leave a museum, we leave behind the giant blue whale, Ben Franklin's walking stick, Lincoln's top hat, the Mona Lisa; what we take home is a mental image of the object or work of art, a dynamic image that is colored by our own preconceptions, the atmosphere of the museum, enthusiasm of the gallery guide, conversations we overhear standing in front of the object. Museums of the mind are universal; adults and children, those who can see and those who are blind, collect mental images of objects they encountered. This multisensory museum of the mind is a context for most of the experiences we have in a physical museum space.

BOOK STRUCTURE: A CROSS-DISCIPLINARY FRAMEWORK FOR THE FUTURE MUSEUM

We want to acknowledge the paradox of this book in which we attempt to create a discourse about rich sensory experiences through narrative only. We applaud the many authors who tackled the task of describing complex multisensory museum encounters and recreating the essence of subtle and intense sensory object experiences on these pages.

The book is organized around the overarching themes of touch, sound, space, smell, taste, and the future museum. However, its goal is to emphasize the fact that such a separation, while practically useful, is in fact ultimately artificial given the interwoven, multisensory (metamodal) reality of our brains' representation of reality, and of our experience of the world.

Each thematic section opens with a chapter that gives a broad overview of current research and the science behind tactile, auditory, spatial, and olfactory perception. These opening chapters shed light on what we know about the workings of the brain, including how it processes information through different sensory pathways and how it creates mental images and memories based on different sensory inputs. All of the thematic sections include examples from current museum practice and reviews of trends in museum programming, studio art, and exhibition design. For the purpose of this book we define museums broadly, as does the American Alliance of Museums; this definition includes living collections such as botanical gardens, zoos, aquariums, science museums, history museums, and historic sites, as well as art museums. Also included are cultural centers that preserve Native American traditions and artifacts.

Part 1, Museums and Touch, opens with a chapter by Krish Sathian and Simon Lacey, who give us a neuroscientific perspective on tactile perception and similarities between touch and vision in object recognition. They discuss that exploration of objects through touch is not unisensory and distinctly separate from the experience of seeing the object, but that haptic processing in fact employs many of the same visual brain regions. In chapter 2, Francesca Bacci and Francesco Pavani suggest that "there is more to touch than meets the hand" and take a broader perspective on touch that is inclusive of whole body proprioceptive and interoceptive experiences, for example, the physical experience of empathy when looking at a work of art, and a sense of one's body position and scale in relationship with the work of art. Francesca Rosenberg and Carrie McGee explore programming possibilities involving handling artists' materials and tools based on their experience at the Museum of Modern Art in New York. Molly Steinwald, Melissa A. Harding, and Richard V. Piacentini from Phipps Conservatory and Botanical Gardens explore new exhibit and programming trends of using touch and other sensory experiences around living collections of botanical gardens. They give examples of how museums and gardens can address community social and learning needs by providing green spaces and nature-based education that puts their visitors "in touch" with real plants. Nina Levent and Lynn McRainey review diverse current museum and artistic narratives that are developed around touch experiences.

Stephen R. Arnott and Claude Alain, whose chapter opens part 2, Museums and Sound, look at how auditory neuroscience may inform the development of a sound gallery and acoustic museum experiences. Research in the past two decades has focused on understanding how the brain processes entire soundscapes, and how it is able to separate and identify the various sounds in the environment by allocating attention to auditory objects of interest. Seth Cluett, composer, artist, and performer, reviews sound as curatorial theme in the last fifty years. His review includes not only sound artworks but other multisensory art pieces and exhibits where sound emerges as one of the themes. He takes us on a journey in three parts: from the initial awareness of the ephemeral phenomenon of sound as a component of art in the late 1960s, to the full immersion in the medium of sound art in the 1970s and 1980s, and finally to the twenty-first century, when curators use acoustic art and sound consistently and constantly re-evaluate its potential as a medium. Salomé Voegelin brings the practice of soundwalking—walking the landscape with a focus on listening to one's environment—to the museum—and takes us on a sound journey through London's museums. She highlights how sound connects spaces, illuminates unseen relationships between museum objects, invites a different appreciation of its architecture, and encourages different curatorial strategies.

Part 3, Smell and Taste in Museums, is dedicated to the use of olfaction and taste in a museum context. Richard Stevenson's chapter on "forgotten sense" highlights the unusual properties of olfaction, which include its capacity to act as a retrieval cue for early childhood memories, to induce strong affective states that are often negative, such as disgust and fear, to manipulate mood, and to generate a sense of becoming part of what is being smelled. Stevenson concludes with a few suggestions regarding the use of olfaction to enhance the museum experience for all visitors, including those with sensory disabilities. Andreas Keller, another neuroscientist, analyzes challenges and opportunities faced by artists, exhibition designers, architects, curators, and educators, who consider incorporating smells in a museum exhibit. In particular, Keller focuses on fundamental differences between olfaction and vision. This discussion addresses museum professionals who are used to working with visual objects and plan to incorporate odors in exhibits. Keller notes that olfactory art can be difficult to control in space, often has strong subliminal effects, and can trigger strong emotional responses. Jim Drobnick, an art critic and a curator of olfactory art, takes us on a tour of olfactory art and other smells in museums and galleries; he begins with pleasurable smells in the gift shop and ends with artists who deal with cultural and social taboos through smell and odor. Drobnick shows how olfactory artworks and exhibitions turn the museum into an animated smellscape. He also points out some complex challenges that these works pose for the curators who mediate this experience. The final chapter in the section is about the sense of taste and notable trends in taste-related educational experiences at museums. Irina Mihalache explores the ability of taste to perform a pedagogical role and to inspire critical thinking by discussing food cultures and cultural stereotypes, as well as food as a marker of identity, including collective meanings and values .

Part 4, Museum Architecture and the Senses, opens with an overview of the cognitive aspect of navigating a museum by Hugo Spiers, Fiona Zisch, and Steven Gage, who focus on recent discoveries about how the brain represents and remembers the space defined by architecture. Based on this state-of-the-art research, the authors suggest possible implications for architects who design exhibits and museum spaces. Finnish architect and architecture theorist Juhani Pallasmaa builds on the argument that he first developed in his 1996 volume, *The Eyes of the Skin.* This book, which has since become a classic of architectural theory, laid the foundation for a multisensory architecture. Here, Pallasmaa suggests that museum architecture at its best has to enhance perception, activate the senses of the visitor, and facilitate an intense dialogue between the exhibits and the viewer. Pallasmaa demonstrates this idea using some of his own recent museum exhibit designs to show how design can heighten the presence of the exhibits. Joy Malnar and Frank Vodvarka write about the multisensory architecture that can appropriately house the living artifacts of the Native peoples of Canada and the United States. Native cultures seldom like the term "museum," as it implies "dead" things. Their traditions and objects require a space that will perceptually resonate with a particular culture and its sensory, symbolic, spiritual, and mythological concerns—and their spatial manifestations.

Part 5, Future Museums, offers ideas that will shape our understanding of tomorrow's museums and interactions between visitors and objects. We included perspectives from cognitive research, anthropology, museum education, digital technology, and robotics alongside the voices of artists, curators, and engineers. Jamie Ward offers a look at how memories are constructed and the role sense might play in facilitating remembering in certain circumstances. He concludes with the implications of these scientific findings on museum learning and other museum experiences. David Howes, a cultural anthropologist, invites us to reexamine the conventional Western definition of the aesthetic that is linked to the visual, and the protocols of museums, which enforce that definition. He suggests that sensory aesthetic experience in non-Western cultures can help us to start imagining a new *intermodal* definition of the aesthetic. Howes proposes that the secret of aesthetics lies in the conjugation of the senses, and he compares the future museum to a sensory gymnasium where aesthetic experience is structured across a range of cultures and involves multiple modalities. The discussion of aesthetics continues with a chapter by Salvatore Aglioti, Ilaria Bufalari, and Matteo Candidi, who focus on psychological and cognitive processes underlying aesthetic perception and how aesthetics might be linked with the viewer's sense of embodiment. Their argument is built on the embodied cognition theories, and suggests that the way we feel our body and use it in interacting with the art objects and people in museums likely plays an important role in aesthetic perception. When contemplating a work of art, our brain simulates states that are linked to the object of art and the artist; such an empathetic link and mental imagery might be at the heart of our aesthetic judgment.

Rebecca McGinnis opens her chapter with a unique perspective on museums as seen through the eyes of visitors who are blind and partially sighted. She then considers these visitors' insights alongside current trends in museum education and how they might inform future programing and curation. McGinnis's experience with visitors in the galleries supports the ideas of situated cognition, where the position of our bodies in space, the museum environment, and interaction with facilitators shapes our thinking and understanding of museum objects and collections. McGinnis describes a range of present and future museum experience that encompass the intellectual, aesthetics, the social, relaxation, contemplation, and mindfulness. Finally, the Future Museums section concludes with a discussion of current and future technologies, including the digitalization of collections and robotics. Samantha Sportun, from the Manchester Museum in the United Kingdom, explores the present and the future of high-resolution 3D scanning of museum collections and the use of these scans for printing 3D replicas, as well as virtual access through haptic devices that allow visitors a virtual touch experience. These technologies could potentially mean that museums will be without borders, as visitors will have access to millions of objects and artifacts without ever being physically close to them. The section concludes with a conversation between Nina Levent, curator Sebastian Chan, artist Rafael Lozano Hammer, and roboticist Heather Knight on the role emerging technologies can play in transforming the museum in the years to come. We especially focus on the technologies' capacity to amplify senses and facilitate interactive, whole-body, immersive, and multisensory experiences in the galleries.

REFERENCES

Ackerman, Diane. (1991). *A Natural History of the Senses*. New York: Vintage.

Al-Hroub, Anies. (2010). Programming for mathematically gifted children with learning difficulties. *Roeper Review*, 32(4), pp. 259–71.

Amedi A., Merabet, L. B., Camprodon, J., Bermpohl, F., Fox, S., Ronen, I., Kim, D. S., and Pascual-Leone, A. (2008). Neural and behavioral correlates of drawing in an early blind painter: A case study. *Brain Res*, 252–62.

Axel, Elisabeth, and Levent, Nina. (2003). *Art Beyond Sight: A Resource on Art, Creativity and Visual Impairment*. New York: AFB Press.

Bacci, Francesca, and Melcher, David (eds.). (2011). *Art and the Senses*. Oxford: Oxford University Press.

Birsch, Judith. (2005). *Multisensory Teaching of Basic Language Skills*. Baltimore: Paul H. Brookes Publishing Co.

Bull, Michael, and Back, Les, eds. (2003). *The Auditory Culture Reader*. Oxford: Berg.

Bynum, W. F., and Porter, Roy, eds. (1993). *Medicine and the Five Senses*. Cambridge: Cambridge University Press.

Campbell, Monica, Shawmla Helf, and Nancy Cooke. (2008). Effects of adding multisensory components to a supplemental reading program on the decoding skills of treatment resisters. *Education & Treatment of Children*, pp. 267–95.

Candlin, F. (2010). *Art, Museums and Touch*. Manchester: Manchester University Press.

Chatterjee, Helen J., ed. (2008). *Touch in Museums: Policy and Practice in Object Handling.* Oxford: BERG.

Classen, C. (1998). *The Color of Angels: Cosmology, Gender and the Aesthetic Imagination.* London: Routledge.

Classen, Constance, ed. (2005). *The Book of Touch.* Oxford and New York: Berg.

Classen, Constance. (2012). *The Deepest Sense: A Cultural History of Touch.* Urbana: University of Illinois Press.

Classen, Constance, Howes, David, and Synnott, Anthony. (1994). *Aroma: The Cultural History of Smell.* London: Routledge

Drobnick, Jim, ed. (2004). *Aural Cultures.* Toronto: YYZ Books.

Drobnick, Jim, ed. (2006). *The Smell Culture Reader.* Oxford: Berg.

Dudley, S., ed. (2012). *Museum Objects: Experiencing the Properties of Things.* London: Routledge.

Dudley, Sandra H., ed. (2010). *Museum Materialities. Objects, Engagements, Interpretations.* Routledge.

Edwards, Elizabeth, and Bhaumik, Kaushik, eds. (2008). *Visual Sense: A Cultural Reader.* Oxford: Berg.

Falk, John H. (2009). *Identity and the Museum Visitor Experience.* Walnut Creek, CA: Left Coast Press.

Howes, David, ed. (1991). *The Varieties of Sensory Experience.* Toronto: University of Toronto Press.

———. (2005). *Empire of the Senses: The Sensual Culture Reader.* Oxford: Berg Publishers.

Jones, Caroline A., ed. (2006). *Sensorium: Embodied Experience, Technology, and Contemporary Art.* Cambridge, MA: The MIT Press.

Jütte, Robert. (2005). *A History of the Senses. From Antiquity to Cyberspace.* Cambridge: Polity Press.

Kelly, Caleb, ed. (2011). *Sound.* Whitechapel: Documents of Contemporary Art. MIT Press.

Kerry, Jordan, and Baker, Joseph. (2011). Multisensory information boosts numerical matching abilities in young children. *Developmental Science*, 14(2), pp. 205–13.

Korsmeyer, Carolyn, ed. (2005). *The Taste Culture Reader: Experiencing Food and Drink.* Oxford: Berg.

Leahy, Helen Rees. (2012). *Museum Bodies: The Politics and Practices of Visiting and Viewing.* Farnham, Surrey: Ashgate.

Malatesha Joshi, R., Dahlgren, Mary and Boulware-Gooden, Regina. (2002). Teaching reading in an inner city school through a multisensory teaching approach. *Annals of Dyslexia*, 52, pp. 229–42.

Mark, Jan. (2007). *The Museum Book: A Guide to Strange and Wonderful Collections.* Candlewick.

Pallasmaa, Juhani. (1996). *The Eyes of the Skin.* London: Academy Press.

Pascual-Leone, A., and Hamilton, R. (2001). The metamodal organization of the brain. *Progress in Brain Research*, 134, pp. 1–19.

Pascual-Leone, A., Amedi, A., Fregni, F., and Merabet, L. B. (2005). The plastic human brain cortex. *Annual Review of Neuroscience*, 28, pp. 377–401.

Pye, Elizabeth, ed. (2008). *The Power of Touch: Handling Objects in Museum and Heritage Context*. Left Coast Press.

Reich, Christine, Lindgren-Streicher, Anna, Beyer, Marta, Levent, Nina, Pursley, Joan, and Mesiti, Leigh Ann. (April 2011). Speaking Out on Art and Museums: Study on the Needs and Preferences of Adults who Are Blind or Have Low Vision. Report. http://www.artbeyondsight.org/new/speaking-out-on-art-and-museums.shtml.

Scheffel, Debora, Shaw, Jack, and Shaw, Rose. (2008). The efficacy of a supplemental multisensory reading program for first-grade students. *Reading Improvement*, 45(3), pp. 139–52.

Schwartzman, Madeline. (2011). *See Yourself Sensing. Redefining Human Perception*. London: Black Dog Publishing.

Serres, M. (2009). *The Five Senses: A Philosophy of Mingled Bodies*. London; New York: Bloomsbury Academic Press.

Shams, Ladan, and Seitz, Aaron. (2008). Benefits of multisensory learning. *Trends in Cognitive Sciences*, 12(11), pp. 411–17.

Smith, Bruce. (1999). *The Acoustic World of Early Modern England*. Chicago: University of Chicago Press.

Smith, Mark M. (2007). *Sensing the Past. Seeing, Hearing, Smelling, and Touching in History*. Berkeley and Los Angeles: University of California Press.

Stein, B. E., and Meredith M. A. (1993). *The Merging of the Sense*. Cambridge, MA: MIT Press.

Voegelin, Salome. (2010). *Listening to Noise and Silence: Towards a Philosophy of Sound Art*. Continuum.

Part I

MUSEUMS AND TOUCH

1

Please DO Touch the Exhibits!

Interactions between Visual Imagery and Haptic Perception

Simon Lacey and K. Sathian

Shifting from a unisensory to a multisensory perspective characterizes both neuroscientific studies and the museum experience. Until recently, the museum or gallery visit was predominantly a unisensory visual experience (Candlin, 2008), with exhibits behind glass or otherwise out of reach, and stern injunctions from notices and attendants to "look, but don't touch!" More recently, these restrictions have been relaxed in some cases: For example, the British Museum's (London, UK) "Hands On" project allows visitors to handle selected objects from their back-collection. Appeals to the other senses are still rare, although the Yorvik Viking Center (York, UK) famously recreates the smells and sounds of a Viking settlement. However, such examples mainly arise from outreach and educational initiatives rather than being directly informed by neuroscience.

Our previous conception of brain organization was that it processed sensory inputs in separate unisensory streams, with the predominant research emphasis on visual processing. However, many brain regions previously considered to be specialized for various aspects of visual input are now known to also be activated during analogous tactile or haptic (passive or active touch, respectively) tasks. For example, the region that processes visual motion is also activated by tactile motion (Hagen et al., 2002; Summers et al., 2009); haptic texture perception activates visually texture-selective areas (Stilla and Sathian, 2008; Sathian et al., 2011); and the lateral occipital complex (LOC) is shape-selective during both visual and haptic perception (Amedi et al., 2001, 2002; Zhang et al., 2004; Stilla and Sathian, 2008). As a result, the old consensus is giving way to the concept of a "metamodal" brain with a multisensory task-based organization (Pascual-Leone and Hamilton, 2001;

Lacey et al., 2009a; James et al., 2011); for example, shape-selective regions respond whether the task is visual or haptic. An intuitively appealing idea is that the activation of classical visual regions during haptic perception reflects visual imagery (Sathian et al., 1997): When feeling an object, one naturally imagines what it might look like. In this chapter, we review the evidence concerning the potential role of visual imagery in haptic shape perception and outline a process model. By way of background, we begin with a review of the similarities between vision and touch in object recognition and mental imagery before moving on to the brain regions involved in visuo-haptic shape processing and the inferences that can be drawn from this evidence about the underlying representation of object shape.

SIMILARITIES BETWEEN VISION AND TOUCH IN OBJECT RECOGNITION

Object recognition is said to be view-dependent if rotating an object away from its original orientation impairs subsequent recognition; this is true for both vision and touch (see Peissig and Tarr, 2007, and Lacey and Sathian, 2011, respectively for reviews). The latter finding is surprising, given that the hands can explore an object from different sides simultaneously and therefore might be expected to acquire information about different "views" at the same time. As objects become more familiar, however, rotation is less disruptive and both visual and haptic recognition become broadly view-independent (Peissig and Tarr, 2007; Lawson, 2009). In contrast to within-modal recognition, visuo-haptic cross-modal recognition is view-independent even for unfamiliar objects, whether visual study is followed by haptic test or vice versa (Lacey et al., 2007a). Cross-modal recognition of familiar objects is also view-independent when haptic study is followed by visual test, but not vice versa (Lawson, 2009), although the reason for this asymmetry is not clear.

Based on these findings, we concluded that the same object representation likely underlies both cross-modal recognition and view-independence. In a perceptual learning study (Lacey et al., 2009b), we showed that view-independence acquired by learning in one modality transferred completely and symmetrically to the other. Cross-modal learning (whether haptic-study:visual-test or vice versa) also resulted in both visual and haptic within-modal view-independence. Thus, we concluded that visuo-haptic view-independence, whether within-modal or cross-modal, relies on a single multisensory representation that directly integrates the unisensory, view-dependent representations.

VISUAL IMAGERY AND TOUCH

If vision and touch engage a common representational system, then we would expect to see similarities in processing of visually and haptically derived representations; this, in fact, turns out to be the case. For example, the time taken to scan both visual images (see Kosslyn, 1980, chapter 7; 1994, chapter 10) and haptically derived images (Röder and Rösler, 1998) increases with the spatial distance to be inspected. Also, the time taken to judge whether two objects are the same or mirror images increases nearly linearly with increasing angular disparity between the objects for mental rotation of both visual (Shepard and Metzler, 1971; Kosslyn, 1980, chapter 8; 1994, chapter 10) and haptic stimuli (Marmor and Zaback, 1976; Carpenter and Eisenberg, 1978; Dellantonio and Spagnolo, 1990). The same relationship was found when the angle between a tactile stimulus and a canonical angle was varied, with associated activity in the left parietal cortex (Prather et al., 2004) in an area also active during mental rotation of visual stimuli (Alivisatos and Petrides, 1997). Similar processing has been found with sighted, early-, and late-blind individuals (Carpenter and Eisenberg, 1978; Röder and Rösler, 1998). These findings suggest that spatial metric information is preserved in representations derived from both vision and touch, and that both modalities rely on similar, if not identical, imagery processes (Röder and Rösler, 1998).

COMMON IMAGERY DIMENSIONS IN VISION AND TOUCH

Mental imagery is not a unitary ability and recent research has shown that there are two different kinds of visual imagery, with individuals varying in their preference. "Object" imagers tend to generate images that are pictorial and deal with the actual appearance of objects in terms of shape and surface properties such as color and texture. By contrast, "spatial" imagers tend to generate more schematic images dealing with the spatial relations of objects and their component parts, and with spatial transformations (Kozhevnikov et al., 2002, 2005; Blajenkova et al., 2006).

In recent work, we investigated whether object and spatial imagery dimensions exist in haptic and multisensory representations, in addition to the visual domain (Lacey et al., 2011). We exploited the idea that object imagers encode information about surface properties while spatial imagers do not and employed tasks that required shape discrimination across changes in texture and texture discrimination across changes in shape. In both vision and touch, we found that shape discrimination was impaired by texture changes for object imagers but not spatial imagers, while texture discrimination was impaired by shape changes for spatial imagers but not object imagers. A similar pattern occurred in the cross-modal conditions when participants were accessing the multisensory view-independent representation discussed above (see Lacey et al., 2009b): object imagers were worse at shape discrimination if texture changed, while spatial imagers could discriminate shape whether texture changed or not (Lacey et al., 2011). Thus, it is probably beneficial to explore the roles of object and spatial imagery rather than taking an undifferentiated visual imagery approach. This distinction is relevant because both vision and touch encode spatial information about objects—for example, size, shape, and the relative positions of different object features—and such information may well be encoded in a modality-independent spatial representation (Lacey and Campbell, 2006). Support for this possibility is provided by recent work showing that spatial, but not object, imagery scores were correlated with accuracy on cross-modal, but not within-modal, object identification (Lacey et al., 2007a).

CORTICAL REGIONS INVOLVED IN VISUO-HAPTIC SHAPE PROCESSING

The principal cerebral cortical region involved in visuo-haptic shape processing is the lateral occipital complex (LOC) (figure 1.1), originally identified as a visual object-selective region (Malach et al., 1995). However, part of the LOC responds selectively to objects in both vision and touch (Amedi et al. 2001, 2002). The LOC is active during both haptic 3D (Amedi et al., 2001; Zhang et al., 2004; Stilla and Sathian, 2008) and tactile 2D shape perception (Stoesz et al., 2003; Prather et al., 2004). The LOC is thought to be a processor of geometric shape, since it is not activated during object recognition triggered by object-specific sounds (Amedi et al., 2002), but does respond, after appropriate training, when auditory object recognition is mediated by a visual-auditory sensory substitution device (Amedi et al., 2007). Such devices convert visual shape information into an auditory stream, or "soundscape," conveying the visual horizontal axis through auditory duration and stereo panning, the vertical axis by varying auditory pitch, and brightness by varying loudness. Extracting shape information from these soundscapes, after considerable training, enables object recognition and generalization to untrained objects; note that this happens only when individuals (whether sighted or blind) are trained using the rules described above and not when merely arbitrary sound-shape associations are taught (Amedi et al., 2007). Altogether, these findings strongly suggest that the LOC is concerned with shape information, regardless of the input sensory modality.

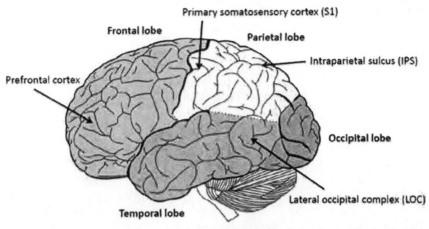

Figure 1.1. Schematic diagram of the left hemisphere of the human brain showing lobar divisions and the main cortical areas referred to in the text.

Several parietal cortical regions also show multisensory shape selectivity, including the posterior part of primary somatosensory cortex (S1, figure 1.1) (Stilla and Sathian, 2008), which was not usually thought to be multisensory, although neurophysiological studies in monkeys do suggest that parts of S1 are visually responsive as well (Zhou and Fuster, 1997; Iwamura, 1998). Visuo-haptic shape selectivity has also been widely reported in various parts of the human intraparietal sulcus (IPS, figure 1.1) in the parietal lobe, which is squarely in classical multisensory cortex (Grefkes et al., 2002; Saito et al., 2003; Stilla and Sathian, 2008).

A crucial question about haptic or tactile activation of supposedly visual cortical areas is whether this is merely a by-product or, in fact, necessary for task performance. Two lines of evidence indicate that the latter is the case. First, case studies of patients with damage to the LOC indicate that it is necessary for both haptic and visual shape perception. For one patient, such damage resulted in both tactile and visual agnosia (an inability to recognize objects), even though basic somatosensory cortex and function were intact (Feinberg et al., 1986), while another was unable to learn new objects either visually or haptically (James et al., 2006). Second, some studies have employed transcranial magnetic stimulation (TMS) to temporarily disrupt various visual brain regions shown to be involved in tactile tasks. For example, TMS over a parieto-occipital region activated during tactile discrimination of grating orientation (Sathian et al., 1997) interfered with performance of this task (Zangaladze et al., 1999). A recent study reported that TMS over left LOC disrupted object categorization (Mullin and Steeves, 2011), suggesting that object processing cannot be carried out without a contribution from this area. Similarly, TMS over the left intraparietal sulcus (IPS) impaired visual-haptic, but not haptic-visual, shape matching using the right hand (Buelte et al., 2008), but TMS over the right IPS during shape matching with the left hand had no effect on either cross-modal condition. The reason for this discrepancy is unclear, and emphasizes that the exact roles of the somatosensory and parietal regions and LOC in multisensory shape processing have yet to be fully worked out.

VISUAL IMAGERY OR MULTISENSORY CONVERGENCE?

An obvious possibility is that haptically evoked activation of visual cortex is mediated by visual imagery (Sathian et al., 1997). Many studies have shown that the LOC is active during imagery tasks: for example, mental imagery of familiar objects previously explored haptically by blind individuals or visually by sighted individuals (De Volder et al., 2001) and recall of both geometric and material object properties from memory (Newman et al., 2005). Interestingly, individual differences in ratings of the vividness of visual imagery strongly predicted the magnitude of activation in the right LOC during haptic shape perception (Zhang et al., 2004). Some researchers have argued against a visual imagery explanation on the basis that the congenitally blind show shape-related activity in the same regions as the sighted. Since the congenitally blind do not have visual imagery, such imagery, it is felt, cannot account for the activations seen in the sighted (Pietrini et al., 2004). However, the fact that the blind cannot employ visual imagery during haptic shape perception is certainly no reason to exclude this possibility in the sighted, particularly given the extensive evidence for neural differences between sighted and blind individuals (Sathian, 2005; Sathian and Stilla, 2010). A further objection has been that the magnitude of activity in the LOC during visual imagery is only about 20 percent of that seen during haptic object identification, suggesting that visual imagery is relatively unimportant during haptic shape perception (Amedi et al., 2001; and see Reed et al., 2004). However, these studies generally did not monitor performance on the visual imagery task, and so the low LOC activity during imagery could simply mean that participants were not performing the task consistently or were not maintaining their visual images throughout the imagery scan.

An alternative to the visual imagery hypothesis is that incoming inputs in both vision and touch converge on a multisensory representation, which is suggested by similarities between visual and haptic processing (see above). By "multisensory," we mean a representation that can be encoded and retrieved by multiple sensory systems and which retains the modality "tags" of the associated inputs (Sathian, 2004). The multisensory hypothesis is supported by studies of effective connectivity derived from functional magnetic resonance imaging (fMRI) data indicating the existence of bottom-up projections (that is, from primary sensory regions) from S1 to the LOC (Peltier et al., 2007; Deshpande et al., 2008) and also by electrophysiological data showing early propagation of activity from S1 into the LOC during tactile shape discrimination (Lucan et al., 2010). However, both Peltier et al. (2007) and Deshpande et al. (2008) also found evidence for top-down projections (that is, from regions involved in higher cognitive functions such as imagery), indicating that shape representations in the LOC may be flexibly accessible by either bottom-up or top-down pathways.

A PRELIMINARY MODEL OF VISUAL IMAGERY IN HAPTIC SHAPE PERCEPTION AND REPRESENTATION

An important goal of multisensory research is to model the processes underlying visuo-haptic object representation. In pursuit of this, we investigated the cortical networks involved in visual object imagery and haptic perception of both familiar and unfamiliar objects (Deshpande et al., 2010; Lacey et al., 2010). As a result, we are able to outline a preliminary process model of visual imagery in haptic shape perception that draws together the various findings reviewed above.

In one experiment (Lacey et al., 2010), a visual imagery task required participants to listen to word pairs and to decide whether the objects designated by those words had similar (for example, snake-rope) or different (for example, spoon-fork) shapes. Thus, in contrast to earlier studies, participants engaged in a task requiring visual imagery that could be verified by monitoring their performance. In a separate session, participants performed a haptic shape task in which they felt a series of unfamiliar objects with their right hand and made a same-different shape discrimination. Each of these tasks was paired with a suitable control task (see Lacey et al., 2010, for details). We were particularly interested in brain areas that were activated in both the imagery and the haptic tasks and whether activation magnitudes in these overlap zones were correlated between the two tasks. There were only four such overlap zones, only one of which showed a significant, positive intertask correlation. These results therefore offered only weak, if any, evidence for the visual imagery hypothesis, perhaps reflecting only transient imagery of basic shape elements of the unfamiliar objects. However, while the haptic shape task involved unfamiliar objects, the visual imagery task obviously involved retrieving images of familiar objects from long-term memory. Reasoning that this discrepancy in familiarity might have accounted for our findings, we conducted a second experiment in which the visual imagery and haptic shape tasks were exactly the same as before, except that we substituted a set of familiar objects in the haptic task. Thus both tasks were now matched for familiarity. This yielded an extensive network of overlap zones in which activation magnitudes were significantly positively correlated between tasks in bilateral LOC, parietal, and prefrontal regions. We should also note that the visual imagery and familiar haptic shape tasks probably engaged visual object imagery rather than visual spatial imagery (see discussion above). Thus, putting both experiments together, we demonstrated that while visual object imagery was only weakly associated with haptic perception of unfamiliar objects, it was strongly linked to haptic perception of familiar objects.

Having found support for the visual imagery hypothesis, we then wished to place this on a stronger footing by examining the connectivity within the cortical networks involved in visual imagery and haptic shape perception (Deshpande et al., 2010). In addition, examination of connectivity could distinguish between the visual imagery and multisensory convergence hypotheses. We had previously suggested that vision and touch share a common shape representation that is flexibly accessible both top-down and bottom-up (Lacey et al., 2007b). Visual imagery involves top-down paths from prefrontal and posterior parietal areas into visual cortex (Mechelli et al., 2004) and so, if LOC activity were mediated by visual imagery, we would expect to find similar, top-down paths into the LOC during both the visual imagery and haptic shape tasks. Alternatively, LOC activity might reflect convergence on a multisensory representation, in which case we would predict bottom-up pathways into the LOC from somatosensory cortex. The existence of paths relevant to both these possibilities was suggested by earlier studies of effective connectivity (Peltier et al., 2007; Deshpande et al., 2008), but these only employed unfamiliar objects and did not analyze task-specific connectivity. During both visual imagery and haptic perception of familiar shape, the LOC was primarily driven top-down by prefrontal areas; moreover these two networks were strongly correlated with each other. During haptic perception of unfamiliar shape, however, a very different pattern emerged, in which bottom-up pathways from somatosensory cortex dominated LOC inputs. Furthermore, the haptic unfamiliar shape network was uncorrelated with either the visual imagery or the familiar haptic shape network.

Based on these findings and on the literature reviewed earlier in this chapter, we proposed a conceptual framework for visuo-haptic object representation that integrates the visual imagery and multisensory approaches (Lacey et al., 2009a). In this model, the LOC contains a representation that is independent of the input sensory modality and is flexibly accessible via either bottom-up or top-down pathways, depending on object familiarity (or other task attributes). For familiar objects, global shape can be inferred more easily, perhaps from distinctive features that are sufficient to retrieve a visual image, and so the model predicts important top-down contributions from parietal and prefrontal regions on the basis that haptic perception of familiar shape utilizes visual object imagery via these regions. By contrast, because there is no stored representation of an unfamiliar object, its global shape has to be computed by exploring it in its entirety. Haptic perception of unfamiliar shape may therefore rely more on bottom-up pathways from somatosensory cortex to the LOC. Since parietal cortex in and around the IPS has been implicated in visuo-haptic perception of both shape and location (Stilla and Sathian, 2008; Sathian et al., 2011), the model also predicts that, in order to compute the global shape of objects, these parietal regions would be involved in processing the relative spatial locations of object parts and would reflect increased use of spatial imagery.

In a further test of the model, we recently compared visual spatial imagery to familiar and unfamiliar haptic shape perception (Lacey et al., 2012). This study showed that there are parietal regions common to spatial imagery and both haptic shape tasks, some of which demonstrated correlations of activation magnitude between the spatial imagery task and one or other haptic shape task. These results suggest that in fact, spatial imagery appears to be implicated in haptic shape perception regardless of object familiarity, possibly related to assembling a global shape representation from component parts (Lacey et al., 2012).

CONCLUSIONS

In this chapter, we have reviewed evidence for the involvement of visual cortical areas in touch. Focusing on the LOC, a visual object-selective area, we discussed its role in haptic shape perception and outlined a process model in which this involvement reflects visual object and spatial imagery, depending on object familiarity. Both activation and connectivity analyses suggest that object imagery is associated with familiar, more than unfamiliar, objects while spatial imagery may be associated with both. Further work is required to examine individual differences as they relate to this model and to investigate how it interfaces with earlier models of visual imagery.

In the light of these findings, we recommend that programs allowing visitors to handle objects should be extended. Clearly, this must be restricted to original artifacts whose archaeological context has been lost, and which therefore have minimal historical value, or to detailed replicas.

However, it need not be restricted to historical objects but could include replica sculptures or tactile line drawings (see Heller, 2006) for art exhibits. Doing so may lead to more elaborate processing, thus enabling better understanding and improved recall of the museum experience and its intellectual content. It would also open many exhibits to the blind and visually impaired who would otherwise be excluded from engaging with historical objects except through Braille text or audio devices. Most importantly, perhaps, such multisensory approaches could encourage a deeper public engagement with history. Recently, the remains of Richard III, lost since he died in battle in 1485, have been unearthed, showing the grisly evidence of multiple wounds from bladed weapons (University of Leicester, 2013). How thrilling it would be to feel the heft of a medieval sword and imagine, as never before, the king's final moments.

ACKNOWLEDGMENTS

The authors' research was supported by the NEI, the NSF, and the Veterans Administration.

REFERENCES

Alivisatos, B., and Petrides, M. (1997). Functional activation of the human brain during mental rotation. *Neuropsychologia*, 35, 111–18.

Amedi, A., Jacobson, G., Hendler, T., Malach, R. and Zohary, E. (2002). Convergence of visual and tactile shape processing in the human lateral occipital complex. *Cerebral Cortex*, 12, 1202–12.

Amedi, A., Malach, R., Hendler, T., Peled, S. and Zohary, E. (2001). Visuo-haptic object-related activation in the ventral visual pathway. *Nature Neuroscience*, 4, 324–30.

Amedi, A., Stern, W. M., Camprodon, J. A., Bermpohl, F., Merabet, L. et al. (2007). Shape conveyed by visual-to-auditory sensory substitution activates the lateral occipital complex. *Nature Neuroscience*, 10, 687–89.

Blajenkova, O., Kozhevnikov, M. and Motes, M. A. (2006). Object-spatial imagery: a new self-report imagery questionnaire. *Applied Cognitive Psychology*, 20, 239–63.

Buelte, D., Meister, I. G., Staedtgen, M., Dambeck, N., Sparing, R. et al. (2008). The role of the anterior intraparietal sulcus in crossmodal processing of object features in humans: An rTMS study. *Brain Research*, 1217, 110–18.

Candlin, F. (2008). Museums, modernity, and the class politics of touching objects. In H. J. Chatterjee (ed.), *Touch in Museums: Policy and Practice in Object Handling*, pp. 9–20. Oxford, UK: Berg.

Carpenter, P. A. and Eisenberg, P. (1978). Mental rotation and the frame of reference in blind and sighted individuals. *Perception & Psychophysics,* 23, 117–24.

Dellantonio, A. and Spagnolo, F. (1990). Mental rotation of tactual stimuli. *Acta Psychologica,* 73, 245–57.

Deshpande, G., Hu, X., Lacey, S., Stilla, R. and Sathian, K. (2010). Object familiarity modulates effective connectivity during haptic shape perception. *NeuroImage,* 49, 1991–2000.

Deshpande, G., Hu, X., Stilla, R. and Sathian, K. (2008). Effective connectivity during haptic perception: A study using Granger causality analysis of functional magnetic resonance imaging data. *NeuroImage,* 40, 1807–14.

De Volder, A. G., Toyama, H., Kimura, Y., Kiyosawa, M., Nakano, H. et al. (2001). Auditory triggered mental imagery of shape involves visual association areas in early blind humans. *NeuroImage,* 14, 129–39.

Feinberg, T. E., Rothi, L. J. and Heilman, K. M. (1986). Multimodal agnosia after unilateral left hemisphere lesion. *Neurology,* 36, 864–67.

Grefkes, C., Weiss, P. H., Zilles, K. and Fink, G. R. (2002). Crossmodal processing of object features in human anterior intraparietal cortex: An fMRI study implies equivalencies between humans and monkeys. *Neuron,* 35, 173–84.

Hagen, M. C., Franzen, O., McGlone, F., Essick, G., Dancer, C. et al. (2002). Tactile motion activates the human middle temporal/V5 (MT/V5) complex. *European Journal of Neuroscience,* 16, 957–64.

Heller, M. A. (2006). Picture perception and spatial cognition in visually impaired people. In M. A. Heller and S. Ballesteros (eds.), *Touch and Blindness: Psychology and Neuroscience.* Mahwah, NJ: Lawrence Erlbaum Associates.

Iwamura, Y. (1998). Hierarchical somatosensory processing. *Current Opinion in Neurobiology,* 8, 522–28.

James, T. W., James, K. H., Humphrey, G. K. and Goodale, M. A. (2006). Do visual and tactile object representations share the same neural substrate? In M. A. Heller and S. Ballesteros (eds.), *Touch and Blindness: Psychology and Neuroscience,* 139–55. Mahwah, NJ: Lawrence Erlbaum Associates.

James, T. W., VanDerKlok, R. M., Stevenson, R. A. and James, K. H. (2011). Multisensory perception of action in posterior temporal and parietal cortices. *Neuropsychologia,* 49, 108–14.

Kosslyn, S. M. (1980). *Image and Mind.* Cambridge, MA: Harvard University Press.

———. (1994). *Image and Brain: The Resolution of the Imagery Debate.* Cambridge, MA: MIT Press.

Kozhevnikov, M., Hegarty, M. and Mayer, R. E. (2002). Revising the visualiser-verbaliser dimension: evidence for two types of visualisers. *Cognition & Instruction,* 20, 47–77.

Kozhevnikov, M., Kosslyn, S. M. and Shephard, J. (2005). Spatial versus object visualisers: A new characterisation of cognitive style. *Memory & Cognition,* 33, 710–26.

Lacey, S. and Campbell, C. (2006). Mental representation in visual/haptic crossmodal memory: Evidence from interference effects. *Quarterly Journal of Experimental Psychology,* 59, 361–76.

Lacey, S., Campbell, C. and Sathian, K. (2007b). Vision and touch: Multiple or multisensory representations of objects? *Perception,* 36, 1513–21.

Lacey, S., Flueckiger, P., Stilla, R., Lava, M. and Sathian, K. (2010). Object familiarity modulates the relationship between visual object imagery and haptic shape perception. *NeuroImage,* 49, 1977–90.

Lacey, S., Lin, J. B. and Sathian, K. (2011). Object and spatial imagery dimensions in visuo-haptic representations. *Experimental Brain Research,* 213, 267–73.

Lacey, S., Pappas, M., Kreps, A., Lee, K. and Sathian, K. (2009b). Perceptual learning of view-independence in visuo-haptic object representations. *Experimental Brain Research,* 198, 329–37.

Lacey, S., Peters, A. and Sathian, K. (2007a). Cross-modal object representation is viewpoint-independent. *PLoS ONE,* 2, e890. doi: 10.1371/journal.pone0000890

Lacey, S. and Sathian, K. (2011). Multisensory object representation: insights from studies of vision and touch. *Progress in Brain Research,* 191, 165–76.

Lacey, S., Stilla, R., Porath, M., Tipler, C. and Sathian, K. (2012). *Spatial imagery in haptic shape perception.* Abstract, Society for Neuroscience, New Orleans, October 13-17, 2012.

Lacey, S., Tal, N., Amedi, A. and Sathian, K. (2009a). A putative model of multisensory object representation. *Brain Topography,* 21, 269–74.

Lawson, R. (2009). A comparison of the effects of depth rotation on visual and haptic three-dimensional object recognition. *Journal of Experimental Psychology: Human Perception and Performance,* 35, 911–30.

Lucan, J. N., Foxe, J. J., Gomez-Ramirez, M., Sathian, K. and Molholm, S. (2010). Tactile shape discrimination recruits human lateral occipital complex during early perceptual processing. *Human Brain Mapping,* 31, 1813–21.

Malach, R., Reppas, J. B., Benson, R. R., Kwong, K. K., Jiang, H. et al. (1995). Object-related activity revealed by functional magnetic resonance imaging in human occipital cortex. *Proceedings of the National Academy of Sciences USA,* 92, 8135–39.

Marmor, G. S. and Zaback, L. A. (1976). Mental rotation by the blind: does mental rotation depend on visual imagery? *Journal of Experimental Psychology: Human Perception & Performance,* 2, 515–21.

Mechelli, A., Price, C. J., Friston, K. J. and Ishai, A. (2004). Where bottom-up meets top-down: neuronal interactions during perception and imagery. *Cerebral Cortex,* 14, 1256–65.

Mullin, C. R. and Steeves, J. K. E. (2011). TMS to the lateral occipital cortex disrupts object processing but facilitates scene processing. *Journal of Cognitive Neuroscience,* 23, 4174–84.

Newman, S. D., Klatzky, R. L., Lederman, S. J. and Just, M. A. (2005). Imagining material versus geometric properties of objects: An fMRI study. *Cognitive Brain Research,* 23, 235–46.

Pascual-Leone, A. and Hamilton, R. H. (2001). The metamodal organization of the brain. *Progress in Brain Research,* 134, 427–45.

Peissig, J. J. and Tarr, M. J. (2007). Visual object recognition: Do we know more now than we did 20 years ago? *Annual Review of Psychology,* 58, 75–96.

Peltier, S., Stilla, R., Mariola, E., LaConte, S., Hu, X. et al. (2007). Activity and effective connectivity of parietal and occipital cortical regions during haptic shape perception. *Neuropsychologia,* 45, 476–83.

Pietrini, P., Furey, M. L., Ricciardi, E., Gobbini, M. I., Wu, W.-H. C. et al. (2004). Beyond sensory images: Object-based representation in the human ventral pathway. *Proceedings of the National Academy of Sciences USA,* 101, 5658–63.

Prather, S. C., Votaw, J. R. and Sathian, K. (2004). Task-specific recruitment of dorsal and ventral visual areas during tactile perception. *Neuropsychologia,* 42, 1079–87.

Reed, C. L., Shoham, S. and Halgren, E. (2004). Neural substrates of tactile object recognition: An fMRI study. *Human Brain Mapping,* 21, 236–46.

Röder, B. and Rösler, F. (1998). Visual input does not facilitate the scanning of spatial images. *Journal of Mental Imagery,* 22, 165–81.

Saito, D. N., Okada, T., Morita, Y., Yonekura, Y. and Sadato, N. (2003). Tactile-visual cross-modal shape matching: A functional MRI study. *Cognitive Brain Research,* 17, 14–25.

Sathian, K. (2004). Modality, quo vadis?: Comment. *Behavioral & Brain Sciences,* 27, 413–14.

Sathian, K. (2005). Visual cortical activity during tactile perception in the sighted and the visually deprived. *Developmental Psychobiology,* 46, 279–86.

Sathian, K., Lacey, S., Stilla, R., Gibson, G. O., Deshpande, G. et al. (2011). Dual pathways for haptic and visual perception of spatial and texture information. *NeuroImage,* 57, 462–75.

Sathian, K. and Stilla, R. (2010). Cross-modal plasticity of tactile perception in blindness. *Restorative Neurology and Neuroscience,* 28, 271–81.

Sathian, K., Zangaladze, A., Hoffman, J. M. and Grafton, S. T. (1997). Feeling with the mind's eye. *NeuroReport,* 8, 3877–81.

Shepard, R. N. and Metzler, J. (1971). Mental rotation of three-dimensional objects. *Science,* 171, 701–3.

Stilla, R. and Sathian, K. (2008). Selective visuo-haptic processing of shape and texture. *Human Brain Mapping,* 29, 1123–38.

Stoesz, M., Zhang, M., Weisser, V. D., Prather, S. C., Mao, H. et al. (2003). Neural networks active during tactile form perception: Common and differential activity during macrospatial and microspatial tasks. *International Journal of Psychophysiology,* 50, 41–49.

Summers, I. R., Francis, S. T., Bowtell, R. W., McGlone, F. P. and Clemence, M. (2009). A functional magnetic resonance imaging investigation of cortical activation from moving vibrotactile stimuli on the fingertip. *Journal of the Acoustical Society of America,* 125, 1033–39.

University of Leicester. (2013). *University of Leicester announces discovery of King Richard III.* Press release retrieved February 4, 2013, from http://www2.le.ac. uk/offices/press/press-releases/2013/february/university-of-leicester-announces-discovery-of-king-richard-iii.

Zangaladze. A., Epstein, C. M., Grafton, S. T. and Sathian, K. (1999). Involvement of visual cortex in tactile discrimination of orientation. *Nature,* 401, 587–90.

Zhang, M., Weisser, V. D., Stilla, R., Prather, S. C. and Sathian, K. (2004). Multisensory cortical processing of object shape and its relation to mental imagery. *Cognitive, Affective, & Behavioral Neuroscience, 4*, 251–59.

Zhou, Y.-D. and Fuster, J. M. (1997). Neuronal activity of somatosensory cortex in a cross-modal (visuo-haptic) memory task. *Experimental Brain Research, 116*, 551–55.

2

"First Hand," Not "First Eye" Knowledge

Bodily Experience in Museums

Francesca Bacci and Francesco Pavani

FROM FORBIDDEN TO INADEQUATE: LONGING FOR THE RIGHT TOUCH IN MUSEUMS

In museums all around the world it is assumed, even when there is no written rule to that effect, that touching the exhibits is forbidden. Institutions invest significant amounts of money to enforce this rule in visible and invisible ways: through a simple rope, with sensors that beep when one comes too close to the art, through a change of level in the floors, or by placing the exhibit behind a glass. The reason is simple: The most recurrent damages to artworks, aside from those caused during transport, are the result of the public's disregard of the rule to refrain from touching the art—and repairing this type of damage is very expensive. To summarize the most common interventions required, it suffices to read this instruction given by the Getty Museum to its visitors: "DON'T touch pictures: fingers and fingernails scratch varnish and paint. DON'T touch picture frames: fingers dislodge fragile gliding and very old wood. DON'T touch furniture and sculpture: oils from your fingers stain wood and stone and etch your fingerprints into metals. DON'T enter the museum with crayons or pencils. DON'T open furniture drawers, lift tops, or sit on chairs and tables. If you're in a wheelchair, be careful that your footrest doesn't bump into furniture or walls" (Classen, 2005).

All these measures speak loud and clear of a deep-rooted need that is instinctual in mankind: that of touching objects to acquire information about them. Early museums, which originated in the seventeenth and eighteenth centuries from private collections, catered to this need by encouraging visitors to touch the exhibits. As sociologist Constance Classen writes, "the museum tour led by a curator matched the house tour that might be offered by a host. The curator, as gracious host, was expected to provide information about the collection and offer it up to be touched. The museum visitors, as polite guests, were expected to show their interest and goodwill by asking questions and by touching the proffered objects" (Classen, 2005). The switch toward our current touch-less museum experience was brought on for several reasons: the impossibility of controlling uncultured masses of visitors; improvement of display techniques and electric lighting, which reduced the need to handle the object in order to see it better; and the new prominent role of sight in nineteenth-century cultural discourse (see the works of Charles Darwin, Max Nordau, and Sigmund Freud, for example).

So, has touch disappeared from the museum experience? If touch means only the contact between one specific body part (the hand) and the object, then the answer is affirmative. But there may be more to touch than meets the hand.

First, although surface touch has been banned from museums, other bodily sensations are not. We are taught in school that the senses are five, but a quick introspection can easily reveal that our body is a much richer source of sensations than just surface touch. While reading this book, your body has a specific posture. Whether you are sitting on an armchair with your legs crossed one over the other, or you are laying down on a sofa, you know exactly the posture of your trunk, your head, your upper and lower limbs, your fingers and your feet. You know all this despite the fact that your eyes are busy reading the words on this page, and you likely see very little of your body parts. The body sensation conveying this information to your brain is termed proprioception and results from specialized sensory receptors in our muscles and tendons. Through proprioception we derive information about the angles of our joints, the static or moving state of our own body parts and—to some extent—the extension of our body segments in space (Longo et al., 2009). Proprioception, however, cannot inform the brain as to the overall orientation of the body with respect to gravity (upright, horizontal, or tilted). For this we rely on a different bodily sensation, termed vestibular sense, which depends on specialized receptors that rest within our inner ear, next to the sensory organ for hearing. Finally, a number of visceral sensations contribute to our body experience: from the rhythmic changes of chest volumes caused by breathing to the beats of our heart, from the feeling of the digestion processes in our stomach to some diffuse pain inside our body. These inputs associated with the physiological conditions of our own body and with the autonomic nervous system are known as interoceptive sensations, and are distinguished from touch, from proprioception, and from vestibular sensations (Craig, 2009). All of these body senses continuously provide information during our museum visits, albeit not through our hands.

The second reason why touch has not disappeared from the museum experience is more subtle and has to do with the multisensory nature of our perceptual experience. Prohibiting touch does not halt the constant and unavoidable tendency of the visitors to represent a multisensory environment. Even when we are forced to keep distant from a painting or a sculpture, and thus seemingly allowed only a visual experience, our brain builds a representation of the observed object that goes beyond each single sensory modality. This occurs because our perceptual experience is fundamentally integrative, binding together in a seamless way inputs from multiple sensory stimuli with motor plans and action executions. At any given moment our brain processes multisensory and motor inputs, and forges a representation of the environment in which each contribution is weighted as a function of its reliability (the so-called optimal integration theory of multisensory perception; Ernst and Banks, 2002; Alais and Burr, 2004). Thus, we can evoke touch through sight or audition and our bodies anticipate the sensation of touch when we are particularly close to the object that we are about to stroke. We can activate our vestibular sensations through sight, or feel a sensory-motor impulse when confronted with moving artworks (or even just artworks which refer to or imply motion). Finally, as detailed above, we constantly experience other bodily senses while in the museum environment.

Extending the concept of touch to bodily sensations and to multisensory perception has at least two implications: First, museum restrictions to one's ability to touch do not necessarily imply a complete absence of some alternative bodily experience of art; second, permission to touch does not necessarily imply a more accurate perception of the work of art. In this chapter we will address each of these implications, exploring also the consequences of this perspective for the experience of blind people in museums.

THE EXPERIENCE OF ART THROUGH
PROPRIOCEPTION AND INTEROCEPTION

One of the qualities of art that makes it worthwhile to experience is its power to elicit empathetic emotions. In figurative art, we often find ourselves identifying with the protagonist of a painting or sculpture, wondering how it would feel to be in the same place, time, or situation of the sitter portrayed. It is an intense way to vicariously feel what our fellow humans feel, of exploring—as Rothko once said—"tragedy, ecstasy and doom" safely and painlessly. This empathic process, which most frequently occurs as the visitor takes in the artwork through sight, is felt in one's body. The response is as physical and physiological as it is intellectual. When visual routes are not available, we propose that one meaningful way to convey this sensation is posing the visitor as the figures in the painting or the sculpture, along with a verbal description of what the artist represented. To know and to feel that one's body is in exactly the same position as that of the person portrayed eliminates the gap between public and artwork, thus throwing one's body (as the phenomenologist Merleau-Ponty would say) in the space and time of art itself.

Proprioception (that is, the body position sense) is at the core of a series of works by Erwin Wurm—the "one-minute sculptures," an ongoing project started in the late 1980s. In these works the artist asked passers-by to pose with one or more everyday objects for approximately one minute. The living sculpture is photographed and, in its stillness and volumetric solidity, it becomes equivalent to more traditional sculpture forms. Aside from all the considerations on Wurm's project as a critical commentary to notions of permanence and materiality in sculpture, this work gives visitors a chance to feel the sculpture's position in their own muscles and skeleton, making their identification with the work something that you can feel, rather than think about. Similarly, in 2009 sculptor Anthony Gormley presented "One and Other," which consisted of having ordinary people occupy, for one hour each, the empty fourth plinth in the northwest corner of Trafalgar Square in London. A total of 2,400 people took the stage, becoming a living sculpture and a collective portrait of contemporary Great Britain. Once again, embodying what is on display can provide a new self-awareness, which in turn has the power to deeply affect our experience of art. We are not made to be only viewers but rather fully sentient entities with a personal understanding of the art—not only at a high cognitive level but also at a more basic, yet rich sensory level.

Another example of art that relies on body sensations other than touch is art based on biofeedback. In the last decade, sensors capable of recording physiological signals have become noninvasive, cheap, and reusable. In sports equipment, a simple metal handle can serve to capture the heartbeat, a band around the chest can measure breathing, and a few reusable surface electrodes can measure skin conductance response (that is, the electrical conductance of the skin, which varies with its moisture level). These indicators capture private interoceptive experiences, and initially attracted attention because they are indices of psychological and physiological arousal. One example of such artworks is "Emergence," a mixed-media sculpture by Sean Montgomery. In the words of the artist,

> when a viewer touches the installation, the electrical impulses generated by each beat of the viewer's heart propagate throughout the viewer's body and are detected and digitized by the installation. During this interaction, Emergence synchronizes its own electrical pulses with the viewer's heart to create a synco-

pated light and sound-scape that reflects its intimate experience with the viewer. (Montgomery, 2012)

This type of art is designed from the body and for the body and certainly has the potential to be interesting to members of the public with different sensory abilities.

One recent theory in cognitive neuroscience suggests that the implications of biofeedback art can go much beyond manifesting some otherwise private arousal states. Anil Seth and colleagues at the University of Sussex (Seth et al., 2012) have suggested that interoception could contribute to one's sense of the reality of the world and of the Self within the world (that is, the sense of "presence," nowadays used also to describe the degree of realism of virtual environments or avatars). Specifically, they propose a framework termed "interoceptive predictive coding," which postulates that a successful sense of presence results from the brain's capability of predicting the interoceptive signals from the body. Vice versa, pathologically imprecise prediction of interoceptive signals could be at the basis of psychiatric disorders of presence, such as depersonalization (the loss of the subjective sense of reality of the Self) or derealization (the loss of the subjective sense of reality of the world). Within this framework, amplification of interoceptive sensations in art may elicit particularly strong sensations by modulating the sense of presence of the visitor. Notably, this type of art does not need to be visual, as the amplified heartbeat or the modulation of skin conductance can be (and in medical biofeedback devices typically is) conveyed through sounds.

TAKING ADVANTAGE OF MULTISENSORY PERCEPTION IN ART

One powerful case of touch sensations elicited by sight is offered by body art. Let us consider a famous performance by Gina Pane, titled "Sentimental Action" (1973), in which the artist bled as she pricked her arm skin by pressing rose thorns into it and concluded by etching a rosebud in the palm of her hand with a blade. The sense of pain and danger experienced by viewers was palpable, so much so that visual displays similar to those originally adopted by Pane have now become the standard way of studying evoked empathic responses in cognitive neuroscience research. For instance, Avenanti and colleagues (2005) measured the excitability of the sensorimotor system of people while they observed video of a needle penetrating deeply into the hand of a stranger. This scene evoked a reduction of sensorimotor excitability, similar to that observed when people experience pain directly (Urban et al., 2004), which was not observed when participants observed a needle penetrating into a tomato or the scene of a harmless cotton bud touching a stranger's hand. Using a brain imaging technique (functional magnetic resonance imaging, fMRI), Singer and colleagues (2004) measured brain activity in female partners of couples while they experienced pain directly or when they saw their male partner being hurt. The results showed that the circuit of brain areas typically involved in the affective processing of pain (that is, bilateral anterior insula, anterior cingulate cortex, brain stem, and cerebellum) was active both during the personal experience of pain and also during the empathic experience of pain. In sum, the mere viewing of someone else being hurt can evoke in us an empathic sensory and affective experience of pain, which is likely mediated by the activation of the same brain circuits we activate when we experience pain directly (Singer and Lamm, 2009).

In the case of Pane's art, all that remains from her actions are photographs; thus, visually impaired visitors could not find touching the art useful. However, hearing a verbal description with appropriate noise from this action while being touched on the arm and possibly smelling the odor of blood would surely cause a strong reaction. Recent findings from neuroimaging research again suggest that such a strategy can prove very effective. Lang and colleagues (2011) tested whether empathy for pain can also be evoked by pain-related exclamations. Compared to control conditions in which participants heard human utterances with positive (for example, laughing) or negative (such as snoring) valence but not associated with suffering, pain-related exclamations modulated brain activation in auditory areas as well as in the regions associated with affective pain (for example, secondary somatosensory cortices, anterior cingulate cortex, cerebellum). This suggests that similar brain circuits are involved in hearing and seeing others' pain, suggesting a truly multisensory processing of this sensory and affective empathic experience.

Clearly, multisensory experience of pain in body art is only one of the many examples of how multisensory processing of art can evoke bodily sensations. In Anthony McCall's exhibition "Five Minutes of Pure Sculpture" (2003–2012), on view at the Museum für Gegenwart–Hamburger Bahnhof in Berlin in August of 2012, a dark room full of a fine water mist hosts numerous light installations. Simple white drawings are projected from the ceiling onto the floor, and the beams of light form what appears to be a solid shape in the air. Visitors invariably try and strike the boundary between darkness and light, as if the edges of the shapes were solid. The awareness that these sculptures are immaterial is reinforced by the fact that people walk through them in the exhibition space, yet the sensation that one must be able to feel the forms is too strong to resist extending a hand to touch. It would be interesting to create a similar sensory play for visually impaired visitors, using immaterial perceivable elements such as directional hot air streams in place of the light beams, which can be felt but do not offer a material resistance to the hand. Research suggests that such implied experience of touch can be wired in the brain, and even encoded at the level of single neurons. In the 1970s Finnish neurophysiologists working with macaque monkeys discovered neurons in the brain that responded in a multisensory fashion (Hyvärinen and Poranen, 1974): They were activated by tactile stimuli on specific regions of the skin but were also activated by visual stimuli that occurred in the immediate vicinity of the same region of the skin that triggered the tactile response. Thus, for instance, if the neuron responded to a touch to the dorsum of the right hand, it also responded when the experimenter approached the right hand dorsum, without touching it, provided the stimulation was near enough to the hand (approximately 12 inches). This initial evidence has been extensively confirmed, with bimodal visuo-tactile neurons documented in many regions of the brain (Graziano and Gross, 1994; Rizzolatti et al., 1981), and with behavioral and neuroimaging studies in humans pointing in the same direction (Makin, Holmes and Zohary, 2007). Most interesting for blind people, these anticipatory touch experiences have also been documented between hearing and touch. In monkeys (Graziano et al., 1999) and humans (Làdavas et al., 2001) nearby sounds (compared to sounds farther away from the body) interact strongly with processing of tactile stimuli, as if they were already treated by the brain as bodily events. In brief, our brain represents space near the body in a special manner, anticipating visual and auditory events as if they were already in contact with the skin. It is touch before touch and likely serves as an interface that permits us to anticipate the contact of an approaching object in order to program avoidance or defense movements. In addition, it can allow better planning of our voluntary actions toward the surrounding objects. Neuroscientists call this space "peripersonal" (Rizzolatti et al., 1981).

The implications of multisensory coding of peripersonal space for behavior and for art likely extend beyond anticipation of touch. Behavioral scientists are now exploring the possibility that peripersonal space may play a role in how much a space can be perceived as suffocating or restrictive. Stella Lourenco from Emory University and colleagues examined the relationship between peripersonal space and claustrophobic fears, and found that people with larger peripersonal space showed stronger phobic reactions to enclosed spaces (Lourenco et al., 2011). To explore these sensations, Austrian artist Erwin Wurm recently presented his installation of a "Narrow House" (2010) at the CAC in Malaga, Spain, as part of his wider project titled "Am I a House?" In this work Wurm reconstructed his childhood house in full scale, but altered the width of the construction so that the walls progressively close in on the visitors. When walking across its length, one feels the progressive narrowing of the space around one's body, starting to feel uncomfortable when the peripersonal space is invaded by the objects and furniture, and experiencing a true claustrophobic sensation when, once arrived in the bathroom, one needs to turn his/her body sideways to avoid being touched (or rather, sandwiched) by the house walls. It is precisely in the unpleasant anticipation of the moment in which the space will be too narrow and we will be touched by the house that the work releases all of its expressive potential and meaning.

Walls and objects around us are not just external stimuli that can enter our peripersonal space, they are also powerful visual cues about the orientation of our body. Sculptor Richard Serra is famous for his monumental-scale steel installations, a good example of which is the Guggenheim Bilbao series titled "The Matter of Time," comprising eight large sculptures measuring 12 to 14 feet in height and dating from between 1998 and 2005. In positioning huge slabs of corten steel loosely parallel to each other (but not quite so), often tilted as to be nonperpendicular to the ground and according to an irregularly curved trajectory, Serra places us in an architecture that defeats our perceptual assumptions and habits on the shape of human-built spaces. Walking through these canyons or narrow corridors, one feels the need to hold onto the artwork in order to maintain one's erect posture and equilibrium, as a slight sense of vertigo and confusion take hold. Clearly Serra is interested in the "physicality of the space [. . .] [s]hifting in unexpected ways as viewers walk in and around them, these sculptures create surprising experiences of space and balance, and provoke a dizzying sensation of steel and space in motion" (FMGB Guggenheim Bilbao Museoa, 2013). It would be crucial to the inclusion of all audiences if sculptors such as Serra and Wurm would provide specific information regarding permission to touch their work, since it seems that such art would well withstand gentle stroking; the aesthetic consequences of touching may even be of interest to the artists who created these pieces. The artworks' correct interpretation would benefit enormously from such a practice, since it is in the dynamic relationship between the visitors' bodies and the sculpture that the meaning is conveyed.

One final aspect that must be emphasized when discussing the bodily sensation evoked by multisensory art experiences is the close link between our sensory perceptions and the motor system. During the last two decades the notion that vision and the other senses evoke responses in our motor system, as well as the related notion that we recruit our motor circuits while experiencing the environment, has become primarily linked with the well-known notion of mirror neurons and mirror systems (Rizzolatti and Craighero, 2004). However, the theoretical notion of a constant interplay between perception and action predates the important neuroscientific discovery of mirror neurons and mirror systems by several decades. The psychologist James J. Gibson, for instance, was among the first scientists to note that the afferent input from the receptors serves motor exploration of the environment and is constantly changed by this process (Gibson, 1966). Even before Gibson, the French psycho-physiologist Henri Piéron argued that the reason why we believe we have five senses is because our approach to active exploration of the environment is centered around five actions: seeing, touching, hearing, smelling, and tasting (Piéron, 1953). Other authors have stressed the role of the motor system in art perception (for example, Gallese, 2011). Along these lines, here we suggest that sensory-motor appraisal of art can exist even in the absence of visual input. Many sound artists exploit this human ability to create art of compelling intensity and beauty, as in the case of the installation "FOREST (for a thousand years . . .)" (2012) by Janet Cardiff and George Bures Miller. Placed in a real forest, it blurs the boundaries between the noise coming from the environment and that from the speakers, which play a variety of sounds that are meant to evoke a temporal journey through history, such as "sounds of war: whistling screeches, big explosions, the rat-a-tat of machine gun fire. There is a brief but shocking scream, a crashing tree, sounds of a mother and child, clanging metal. Singers come close, but then leave. You hear the trees and the wind again, and the crickets and birds" (Volk, 2012).

The ability to appraise art through our sensory-motor system works just as well in unnatural situations. One such paradoxical example is Dave Cole's large-scale installation, "Cranes Knitting," presented at MASS MoCA (North Adams, Massachusetts) in 2005. It featured two cranes facing each other that were electronically controlled to knit an enormous American flag through needles as big as lampposts. One of the reasons for the work's great appeal to the public was the fact that two machines, normally used for heavy-duty tasks such as digging soil or lifting cement, implausibly performed the feminine yet mechanical operation of knitting. Those of us who have tried our hands at this work know that there is a rhythm and a repetitiveness that characterizes the act of knitting, which has the power to virtually transform the knitter into a human machine (and vice versa—in "Cranes Knitting," the machines appear almost humanized). Beyond the critical interpretation of this work as addressing the passage of time and the concept of national identity, it is precisely this sensory-motor knowledge that informs the public of the message of this artwork—so much so that organizing a knitting class before confronting the work may be a good way to convey the core concept through a bodily experience, rather than leaving this aspect to a descriptive verbal approach. Also, trying to maneuver the big poles to knit may prove an interesting way to capture the surreal dimension of this piece.

TOUCHING IS NOT ALWAYS THE SOLUTION

If bodily sensations cannot be reduced to touch, and they are part of our overall multisensory-motor experience, then touching alone may not necessarily be the best approach to experience art for the blind. It is undeniable that persons who do not have the use of the sense of sight are accustomed to deploy their training in touching to acquire the desired information. But it is important to remember that the experience of art is something radically different from any other experience of everyday life, and as such it requires specifically tailored forms of communication in order to convey its meaning. When confronted with an everyday object, we can predict in most cases how the visual characteristics will feel when touched, as we have accumulated several experiences with that type of object. In the case of art, this predictability, this consistency across different sensory modalities is rarely maintained. It is therefore not enough to permit visually impaired audiences to touch the art, as this may often not be the best way to convey the artwork's meaning. Finding new ways to translate across sensory modalities requires passion, creativity, and a deep understanding of the senses, along with an undefeatable will to pass on the artwork's meaning and message.

Let us provide an example of a common situation in which the touch of the hand may fail in allowing full appreciation of an artwork. Sculptor Duane Hanson is deservedly celebrated for his hyperrealistic representations of everyday persons. His sculptures of housewives pushing a shopping cart or tourists sightseeing are visually stunning, as they can easily be mistaken for real people (and were indeed made through casting from live models). If approached visually, they elicit touch only as a strategy to reassure the viewer that, surely enough, the figures are not alive. But the attempt to render this uncanny sense of life-likeness through touch alone would hardly be effective. The sculpture's visual clues, such as its rosy cheeks and convincing skin tone, would translate under the fingers into something very different from the feel of a real human face. Although perfectly faithful to their originals in shape, these figures are made of fiberglass, bronze, or sometimes polyester fibers, which surely do not feel, when touched, like human flesh would. Mimesis, the crucial characteristic of this work, must find ways other than mere touch to reach the awareness of the visually impaired visitor.

CONCLUSIONS: BIG CHANGES CAN START SMALL

When museums acquire works of contemporary art, it would be useful if they would implement the good curatorial practice of collecting from the artist some indication of whether it is acceptable to touch the piece. It would be simple enough to adopt a form with some standard questions to attach to the other technical information customarily provided with the work: Is touching allowed? If yes, to everyone or just to the visually challenged visitors? Are there any exceptions to this prescription? If not, how would the artist wish to convey the essence of his/her artwork through alternative modalities?

If standardized, this procedure would present two advantages. First, artists would become responsible for the modality of fruition of their works which, if decided by museum officers, is by default restrictive rather than permissive. After all, most contemporary art is privately owned and, as such, is constantly touched—and, when needed, repaired. Second, it would gradually augment the presence of touchable works in public collections, thus increasing awareness of the different needs of diverse museum populations.

Another helpful hint that could prove useful to museum educators is to acquire a deeper knowledge of the many senses gathered under the umbrella term "touch" and think about how each of these senses is called to contribute to our understanding of the pieces on show, as we detailed with several examples above. This could lead to more effective nonvisual communication of the key aspects of the artworks to be experienced.

REFERENCES

Alais, D., and Burr D. (2004). The ventriloquist effect results from near-optimal bimodal integration. *Curr. Biol.*, 14, 257–62.

Avenanti, A., Bueti, D., Galati, G., and Aglioti S. M. (2005). Transcranial magnetic stimulation highlights the sensorimotor side of empathy for pain. *Nature Neuroscience*, 8, 955–60.

Classen, C., ed. (2005). *The Book of Touch*. Oxford and New York: Berg, 274.

Craig, A. D. (2002). How do you feel? Interoception: The sense of the physiological condition of the body. *Nat. Rev. Neuroscience*, 3(8): 655–66.

Ernst, M. O., and Banks, M. S. (2002). Humans integrate visual and haptic information in a statistically optimal fashion. *Nature*, 415, 429–33.

FMGB Guggenheim Bilbao Museoa. (2013). http://www.guggenheim-bilbao.es/en/exhibitions/richard-serra-2/.

Gallese, V. (2011). Mirror neurons and art. In Bacci, F. and Melcher, D., *Art and the Senses*. Oxford: Oxford University Press, 455–63.

Gibson, J. J. (1966). *The Senses Considered as Perceptual Systems*. Boston, MA: Houghton Mifflin.

Graziano, M. S., Reiss, L. A. and Gross, C. G. (1999). A neuronal representation of the location of nearby sounds. *Nature*, 397, 428–30.

Graziano, M. S., Yap, G. S. and Gross, C. G. (1994). Coding of visual space by premotor neurons. *Science*, 266, 1054–57.

Hyvärinen, J. and Poranen, A. (1974). Function of the parietal associative area 7 as revealed from cellular discharges in alert monkeys. *Brain*, 97, 673–92.

Làdavas, E., Pavani, F. and Farnè A. (2001). Auditory peripersonal space in humans: A case of auditory-tactile extinction. *Neurocase*, 7, 97–103.

Lang, S., Yu, T., Markl, A., Müller, F. and Kotchoubey, B. (2011). Hearing others' pain: Neural activity related to empathy. *Cognitive Affective Behavioral Neuroscience*, 11, 386–95.

Longo, M. R., Kammers, M. P. M., Gomi, H., Tsakiris, M., and Haggard, P. (2009). Contraction of body representation induced by proprioceptive conflict. *Current Biology*, 19, R727–R728.

Lourenco, S. F., Longo, M. R. and Pathman, T. (2011). Near space and its relation to claustrophobic fear. *Cognition*, 119, 448–53.

Makin, T. R., Holmes, N. P. and Zohary, E. (2007). Is that near my hand? Multisensory representation of peripersonal space in human intraparietal sulcus. *Journal of Neuroscience*, 27, 731–40.

Montgomery, S. M. (2012). http://produceconsumerobot.com/emergence/ (accessed December 2012), where photos of the piece are also available.

Piéron, H. (1953). *La Sensation*. Paris: Presses Universitaries de France.

Rizzolatti, G. and Craighero, L. (2004). The mirror-neuron system. *Annual Review of Neuroscience*, 27, 169–92.

Rizzolatti, G., Scandolara, C., Matelli, M. and Gentilucci, M. (1981). Afferent properties of periarcuate neurons in macaque monkeys. II. Visual responses. *Behavioral Brain Research*, 2, 147–63.

Seth, A. K., Suzuki, K., and Critchley, H. D. (2012). An interoceptive predictive coding model of conscious presence. *Front Psychol.* 2, 395.

Singer, T. and Lamm, C. (2009). The social neuroscience of empathy. *Annals of the New York Academy of Science*, 1156, 81–96.

Singer, T., Seymour, B., O'Doherty, J., Kaube, H., Dolan, R. J. and Frith, C. D. (2004). Empathy for pain involves the affective but not sensory components of pain. *Science*, 303, 1157–62.

Umiltà, M. A., Berchio, C., Sestito, M., Freedberg, D., and Gallese, V. (2011). Abstract art and cortical motor activation: An EEG study. *Front Hum. Neuroscience*, 6, 311.

Urban, P. P., Solinski, M., Best, C., Rolke, R., Hopf, H. C. and Dieterich, M. (2004). Different short-term modulation of cortical motor output to distal and proximal upper-limb muscles during painful sensory nerve stimulation. *Muscle Nerve*, 29, 663–69.

Volk, G. (2012). A Walk in the Park. Documentary. *Art in America*, June 15, 2012.

3

Art Making as Multisensory Engagement

Case Studies from The Museum of Modern Art

Carrie McGee and Francesca Rosenberg

The Museum of Modern Art (MoMA) in New York City has a long history of incorporating hands-on experiential learning into its educational programs. In the 1940s and '50s the museum's Department of Education became a laboratory where new techniques and methods for teaching art making were developed. MoMA became a link connecting the worlds of art and education. Between 1937 and 1969, under the pioneering leadership of Victor D'Amico, MoMA's first director of education, the museum offered interactive spaces and activities including the Young People's Gallery, The People's Art Center, and the Children's Art Carnival. The educational philosophy guiding these spaces and events espoused an experiential, child-centered approach to learning. In 1944, the War Veterans Art Center was developed to serve thousands of returning World War II veterans through rehabilitative and prevocational training through the arts. Classes were taught by fine artists in disciplines ranging from painting and sculpture to pottery, jewelry, and design. In 1952 and 1953 the museum co-produced a television series called *Through the Enchanted Gate*, in which D'Amico led both children on the set and those at home through open-ended art-making explorations using simple materials that could be found around the home.

Today MoMA's Department of Education builds on this legacy with a commitment to offering opportunities for visitors to explore artists' materials and processes through art making. One of the most multisensory experiences you can have in a museum, art making is physical, social, emotional, and intellectual. It engages the body and the mind—the senses of touch and sight but also often sound, smell, and sometimes even taste. It also complements looking and enhances learning about works of art. Understanding how and why a work of art was made helps make it relevant and exciting.

Furthermore, exploring artistic processes nurtures a skill that translates into many other areas of life. Recently, experts in the fields of education and economics have described the importance of cultivating the creative potential of both individuals and communities. As we increasingly spend more and more time staring into screens, the opportunity for creative engagement that is physical, as well as social and intellectual, is more important than ever, and we believe that art museums have a unique opportunity to facilitate that engagement. Many museums are rising to the challenge, finding new and exciting ways to be more participatory—through public programs, hands-on workshops, exhibitions that encourage audience participation, interactive spaces for children, and social events.

Museums are recognizing that there are different types of visitors with varying goals for their experiences. More than ever, museums need to be nimble, flexible, and creative about meeting the demands of their audiences, who are increasingly seeking more than contemplative experiences. To this end, at MoMA we have worked to create programs and interactive spaces in which individuals of all ages and abilities can engage in hands-on exploration of artistic materials and processes. The following three case studies will demonstrate how such multisensory museum experiences can enable visitors to understand and enjoy modern and contemporary art through social, emotional, physical, and intellectual participation.

CASE STUDY 1:

Creating an Art-Making Workshop for Adults Who Are Blind or Have Low Vision

MoMA has a long history of serving individuals who are blind or have low vision. Since offering the first Touch Tours of original sculptures in 1972, the museum has worked to establish itself as a leader in the field of accessible programming. While we continue to offer Touch Tours, over the years we learned from our blind and partially sighted visitors that they wanted access to all aspects of MoMA's collection and special exhibitions, including two-dimensional paintings, drawings, prints, and photographs that could not be touched. In the 1990s we began offering eight-week in-depth art appreciation courses that employed the use of tactile diagrams, visual description, and art making. These courses took place in one of the museum's classrooms and focused on a particular artist or theme. Through program evaluation we learned that many participants wanted to spend less time in the museum's classroom and more time in the museum's galleries. They also wanted the opportunity

Figure 3.1. An Art inSight participant creates a sculpture out of white paper clay. Photo by Kirsten Schroeder.

to explore temporary exhibitions. At the same time, MoMA's Department of Education was moving away from programs based on a traditional lecture format and toward discussion-based programs that encourage close looking and dialogue. In 2003 we began piloting discussion-based programs for blind and partially sighted visitors through collaborations with community-based organizations, and in 2005 we launched the Art inSight program as a monthly offering to the general public. In the program, specially trained art historians provide detailed verbal descriptions to help paint a picture in the mind's eye and also share art historical information to promote discussion. Each month, we focus on a different theme or special exhibition. Individuals listen to descriptions of the works of art and then engage in lively conversation, sharing their own interpretations and ideas. The program includes touching sculptures or design objects when possible. If we are visiting an exhibition without works that can be touched we often bring other objects related to an artist's process (such as a painted canvas replicating a particular method or texture, a partially carved printmaking block, or a piece of plaster) for participants to handle. Due to the program's popularity, we offer two groups at the same time, accommodating up to forty people each month.

Over the past couple of years, several Art inSight participants expressed an interest in making art. While we were eager to meet our audience's demands, we were also intimidated. What would a successful art-making workshop for blind and partially sighted adults look like? There were several challenging parameters. First of all, the participants varied greatly in terms of their previous art experience, enthusiasm for hands-on activities, and level of vision. The program regularly welcomes individuals who are just beginning to experience sight loss, individuals who have been blind since birth, and many others in between. In terms of art-making experience, our long-time participants range from a professional jewelry designer with an extensive knowledge of art practice to a woman who has never made a piece of art in her life. The "regulars" also include several participants who are very knowledgeable about art history but skeptical of art-making programs. On top of all this, each month we welcome new participants about whom we know very little. The challenge was to develop a plan for an art-making workshop that would be sophisticated enough not to feel childish but accessible enough that it would allow individuals of all levels of vision and experience to feel successful.

As two hours is hardly enough time to finish a sketch, much less a masterpiece, we had to be realistic about what could be accomplished in the time we had. We decided that the workshop should focus on the exploration of artistic ideas and processes rather than finished products. We hoped this would allow all participants to leave the experience with a greater understanding of some aspect of contemporary art practice, regardless of their level of satisfaction with their physical creation. We decided to focus on a theme of "Symbolic Self-Portraits" and to create sculptural objects out of white paper clay. We chose paper clay because it is virtually odorless, has a pleasing texture that is not overly sticky, is easily manipulated, and can be used to create fine detail. Specifically, we looked for a bright white paper clay with a decent weight to it. Some paper clays are gray and very lightweight, and we wanted a version that would more closely approximate the color and weight of porcelain. We chose to create symbolic self-portraits in clay for several reasons. First of all, we didn't want participants to get caught up in trying to create a physical likeness, especially given our time constraints. Rather, we wanted to elucidate some of the more complex ways that artists translate ideas into objects and employ symbolism in their work. Also, we wanted to encourage self-expression and have participants share aspects of their personalities and interests with one another. Finally, we wanted participants to make works that were small and sturdy enough to be passed around and handled by others in the group. We planned to begin the workshop with a warm-up exercise, then move into the main project, and finish the workshop touching and discussing the objects that had been created.

We recognized the importance of using high-quality supplies and displaying them in an organized and professional way. We have learned that preparing the studio space creates the atmosphere for the workshop, and small details can make a big difference. For this workshop we covered the tables with black paper and used white paper and white clay for the projects, ensuring the highest possible level of contrast for those with some residual vision. We arranged the materials uniformly at each position: a short stack of sheets of thick white drawing paper on the table to the left of each chair and a slab of white paper clay wrapped in plastic to the right. Having the supplies laid out consistently for each participant meant that we could orient the participants and guide them with verbal directions by saying things such as "on the table in front of you and to your right you will find a stack of paper; grab one sheet."

Understanding that some of the participants might be intimidated, we wanted to make sure the workshop was infused with a sense of fun. After welcoming participants, we reminded them that we had a limited amount of time together and let them know what to expect, that the workshop would not be technical instruction but rather an exploration of an artistic process and a chance to exercise our own creativity. We began with an icebreaker that would get the participants thinking creatively about their identities. We asked them to describe themselves through the metaphors of an animal, a smell, and a moving vehicle. As various participants went on to describe themselves as "a monkey," "the smell of freshly baked bread," and "a top-of-the-line Mercedes," the mood lightened and we began to see each other in new ways.

Since we'd warmed up our minds, we explained that we would need to warm up our hands. We explained that this was just an exercise, that we were not going to make anything to keep during this warm-up, and that the idea was to work quickly and intuitively. Then, we briefly described and discussed Richard Serra's *Verb List* (1967–68) and the way that actions can translate into art objects. We asked the participants to take one sheet of paper from the stack in front of them. Once everyone was ready, we shared a verb from the list and asked the participants to demonstrate it with their sheet of paper. Once finished, we asked them to exchange with the person sitting across from them and examine what the other person had done. Then we moved on to another verb from the list. As the participants handled each other's creations they expressed surprised at how differently one could interpret such simple phrases as "to fold," "to tear," or "to roll." As the group got warmed up, we moved on to slightly more complex directives, such as "surround," "arrange," and "expand," sharing after each. Occasionally we would give a verbal description of a particularly original interpretation one participant had created, sharing it with the entire group.

Once the group was warmed up, we moved on to the main project. We asked everyone to remember the metaphors they had used to describe themselves during the icebreaker. We explained that we would be making small, symbolic self-portraits out of clay and that they might consider using one of their metaphors as a starting point, or they might prefer to work intuitively, kneading the clay and seeing where the material took them. Finally, we suggested that if anyone felt unsure about how to begin, they could perform one of the actions from the verb list to get started. Clay was a great material to use, as it's satisfying to touch and easy to manipulate. It was fascinating to watch the group begin, as each participant had a different approach. Because we had spent time getting to know each other through the icebreaker and warming up with the verb list exercises, everyone began experimenting with their slab of clay immediately. We explained that they would have about thirty minutes to make their sculpture and then we would ask them to share it with the three other people sitting at their table through touch and verbal description.

Their creations were as different as their personalities. One woman made three musical notes and we learned that she is a jazz singer who has recorded an album. Another woman created a tall pair of legs to symbolize her height. One man created a web inspired by his nickname, Spider. The participants seemed to enjoy the opportunity to share their creations and to see and feel the sculptures that others had made. The high contrast between the black paper covering the tables and the white clay was successful; one participant with low vision remarked that she could not believe she could actually see her sculpture. Several participants asked for extra clay to take home to make more sculptures. Even the few participants who seemed less enthusiastic about making art at the beginning of the workshop expressed their satisfaction with the experience. Everyone agreed that they would sign up for another workshop.

Things to keep in mind:

- Keep the group small (eight to twelve people per educator) to ensure everyone receives one-on-one attention.
- Focus on a conceptual theme that will elevate the project beyond craft and help to elucidate art in your museum's collection.
- Use high-quality, adult-level art-making materials.
- Utilize materials that will be appropriate for the audience. Choose supplies that are especially tactilely appealing. Avoid sharp tools.
- Make use of materials with high contrast when possible.
- Organize supplies in a consistent arrangement at each workspace.
- Orient the participants to familiarize them with the workspace with verbal directions, such as "To your left you will find a slab of clay."

- Manage expectations—remind participants the goal is to have fun and to explore a creative process, not to make the next museum masterpiece.
- Begin with an icebreaker to create a sense of fun and community among the group members.
- Move on to a warm-up art-making exercise that is easy, ephemeral, and unintimidating to ease participants into the art-making experience.
- Share visual descriptions of works made by participants with the group.
- Encourage participants to share their creations with one another through touch and verbal description.

CASE STUDY 2:

Exploring Performance Art with Individuals with Developmental or Learning Disabilities

The Museum of Modern Art is committed to providing a variety of programs and services to ensure that our visitors' different needs and abilities are recognized and met. Our Create Ability program serves children and adults with learning or developmental disabilities, including autism spectrum disorders, and their families. Through conversations with members of this audience, as well as organizations that advocate for them, we learned that often there are not many meaningful leisure activities designed for them to enjoy together as a family. We also became aware of the lack of access to the arts in general for adults living with such disabilities, an audience underserved by many cultural institutions. We decided to create a monthly program that would be accessible, enjoyable, informative, and creative. We met with colleagues from other museums who provided programming for this audience to discuss their challenges and successes and decided that we wanted the program to be both a forum for discussion and a hands-on learning environment. As we knew that some participants were coming from considerable distances to attend and that many of the parents worked during the week, we decided to hold the programs on a weekend and to have each session last two hours, allowing us to spend time in both the museum's gallery and studio spaces. After a successful pilot program in collaboration with the Metropolitan Museum of Art, we were ready to launch Create Ability to the general public in early 2006.

Create Ability now takes place one Sunday each month at the museum. There is a two-hour session in the morning for children ages five to seventeen and their families, and a two-hour session in the afternoon for adults and their families. Each session includes one hour of art-looking and discussion in the museum's galleries and a one-hour art-making workshop in our studio space. Participants are encouraged to explore the various facets of their artistic ability through experimentation with diverse materials and processes. The goals of the program are intellectual, emotional, and social. Of course we want participants to learn new things about art, but we also want them to have fun and learn new things about themselves and each other. We create a supportive environment and encourage participants to challenge themselves to try new things and explore new ideas. Often, they discover new talents and interests in the process, which helps build self-esteem. The program is also meant to be social. We want to bring people together—both families and individuals—to create a creative community.

Since the program's inception, we have branched out to explore different types of art. Over the years participants have done many painting, sculpture, collage, drawing, and printmaking projects in workshops led by MoMA educators (who are professional artists themselves). In 2009 the museum renamed a curatorial department to focus on the acquisition and exhibition of performance art, and we began to think about how we might make this complex art form accessible and appealing to the Create Ability audience—a diverse group of individuals with a range of background experience, areas of interest, and physical and cognitive abilities.

In our planning each month, we begin by choosing a specific theme for inspiration. Working thematically provides a lens through which to explore complex ideas. It also helps to keep us focused and guides our decision-making as we plan which works of art to discuss and the content of the hands-on art-making workshop. The theme we chose within the realm of performance art was "Everyday Objects, Everyday Actions." We chose this theme for several reasons. First, it aligned with several works on view in the galleries at the time. We felt it would be relatable and also help the group wrestle with the question, "What makes a performance a work of art?" Perhaps the most integral ingredients to the Create Ability program's success are the educators who lead the workshops. All Access Programs at MoMA are taught by professional artists and art historians with interest in and experience working with audiences of varying abilities. For this program we chose two educators who are performance artists to facilitate the workshops, as we knew their vast knowledge of and genuine enthusiasm for the medium would ensure a high-quality experience.

On the day of the program, as we do every month, we began by gathering in the studio to go over the plan for the day, writing the steps on a large sheet of paper. We have learned that it is important for some of the participants of this program to know exactly what to expect to happen throughout the workshop. We let the participants know that we would first have a brief discussion about performance art, then head into the galleries to discuss some works in the museum's collection. Then, we would then return to the studio and create our own performances. Finally, those who wanted would be invited to share their performance piece with the group.

Before viewing specific works, the educators began with an introductory discussion about performance art in general. They asked participants to discuss previous performances they had seen. Most participants had seen musical, theatrical, or dance performances, but many had never given much thought to the idea of performance art. As a group we began to question what differentiates the two, acknowledging that sometimes it's hard to say. The educators asked the group to think about artists' tools and materials. For instance, "If you want to make a painting, what materials do you need? What if you want to make a sculpture?" Based on their previous experiences, the participants discussed the necessary supplies. One educator then shared the information that today we would be creating performances and explained that we would use our bodies and our voices as our materials.

He then introduced "Everyday Objects, Everyday Actions" as the theme for the day, and led the group into the museum's galleries. We looked at works such as Martha Rosler's *Semiotics of the Kitchen* (1975) and Trisha Brown's *Man Walking Down the Side of a Building* (1970) and discussed what makes them art. We began thinking about the materials, processes, and familiar objects and actions used in each piece and the effect they had on us. Back in the studio, we began with a warm-up exercise. The educators had the group form a large circle and told us they wanted us to scream for one minute. At first, the participants weren't sure if it was really okay to scream in the museum, but once a couple people began, others joined in and soon the room was abuzz. Participants smiled as their sounds filled the space. When the minute was over we discussed how it felt to scream and hear the other participants screaming. Several participants felt it was cathartic. One spoke of a feeling of freedom in doing something you're not really supposed to do in a museum. With the mood lightened, we were ready to move on.

The educators led the group in a discussion about "What makes performance art?" writing the question on a big piece of paper. The group threw out many ideas and eventually all agreed that two of the components were a performer and an action. The educator wrote these words on paper and hung it where all could see. Next, he introduced the parameters for the performances the participants were going to create. He told the group that they could include one or more of the everyday objects we'd placed in the studio in their performance in any way they'd like. He said individuals could create performances on their own or work in small groups with their family members or other participants.

Next, the two educators took turns presenting a performance to the group. The studio space we were using had a piano and the educators had brought an assortment of smaller everyday objects as well. One educator's performance included using the objects to make sounds on the piano, rather than playing it with his fingers. The other's required audience participation: she picked up an object from the space and began to tap it to make noise and invited others to pick up objects and join her. The participants ended up parading through the space, making sounds as they went.

After the demonstration performances, participants were told that they had approximately twenty minutes to develop their performance piece, and then there would be an opportunity for those who wanted to share their piece with the group. The educators encouraged participants to play and experiment with different objects and actions. They offered suggestions of ways to transform everyday actions—by repeating them, slowing them down, or speeding them up. We had several volunteers with art teaching experience on hand to assist the educators and work one-on-one with participants who needed support or encouragement. At first, the space became a bit chaotic, but soon things settled as each participant became focused on exploring different movements and actions. Many worked silently and others enjoyed making as much noise as possible with the piano and objects at hand. The educators went from one participant to the next, offering suggestions and praise. They encouraged the participants to think about how long their performance would last and how it would end.

Soon it was time to share. Nearly every participant wanted to perform in front of the group. One teenage boy with dreams of being a newscaster took on the role of the emcee, introducing each piece. As participants performed one at a time in front of the group, their faces transformed. Even those who often have flat expressions lit up as they presented their pieces. Their performances were as diverse as their personalities. One woman did a silent lyrical dance between a spotlight and a wall, so you could see her shadow copying her every move. Another boy with a great sense of humor began his performance buried under a heap of crumpled construction paper and had a fellow participant dig him out. A father called out different natural elements and phenomena while his son silently interpreted them through movement. Each was met with loud applause. After the program, we made a compilation video of all the performances and sent a copy to each family.

The program was a success because it was both structured and flexible. The educators were able to meet participants where they were, and the project offered opportunities for many different styles of expression and levels of participation. Participants could use different modes of creating movements or sounds to create something that fit their abilities and personalities. The opportunity to share with the group (something we include every month) lets participants know that they are valued members of the community and builds self-esteem. We aim to create an atmosphere of respect and dignity, infused with positive emotion.

Each year at the museum, we mount an exhibition of art made in the Create Ability program. The experience of seeing their art on the walls of MoMA delights the participants and their loved ones. They bring siblings, friends, teachers, and extended family members to see their art and meet their friends from Create Ability. At each opening we give the participants the opportunity to deliver remarks. This can be intimidating as some have limited verbal ability and many have no experience with public speaking. Still, many choose to share something with the audience, some with the help of assistive technology. Their words have reinforced our belief that individuals with disabilities desire challenges, opportunities to be creative, and the chance to grow. We often hear how much these families desire access to new people and ideas, and how much they appreciate being challenged within the safe and welcoming environment that our program provides. As people with disabilities often report that negative attitudes are one of the largest barriers they face in society, such an environment can be transformative.

Things to keep in mind:

- See people with disabilities as people first. Become knowledgeable about learning and developmental disabilities without focusing on stereotypes.
- Employ artists with experience working with diverse audiences and personal interest in the art form you're exploring.
- Have skilled volunteers on hand to provide one-on-one attention and support where needed.
- Let participants know what to expect at the beginning of the workshop. List the sequence of activities.
- Create a relaxed atmosphere; make sure the workshop is structured but not rigid.
- Break a process down into manageable steps. List the steps for participants to see.
- Use clear, literal language and demonstrate what you mean.
- Offer a variety of ways to participate (big, small, loud, silent).
- Use and pay attention to nonverbal communication; employ humor and read facial expressions and body language.
- Document the process through photographs and video recordings that you can share with participants.
- Mount a professional-looking exhibition and host an opening reception where participants can share their work with the wider community.

CASE STUDY 3:

Designing an Accessible Interactive Space for Families

MoMA Art Labs are interactive spaces developed by Family Programs staff in collaboration with designers from the museum's Graphic and Exhibition Design departments. They are drop-in spaces, open to all visitors during museum hours. In each lab, children and adults experiment, play, and create as they make connections between their own creative explorations and the ideas, tools, and techniques of modern and contemporary artists. Between 2008 and 2013, there were five different labs, each with a unique focus. All MoMA Art Labs aim to create a safe, inclusive, and welcoming environment where all visitors, especially families with young children, can engage in art making. Through a thematic lens, visitors are encouraged to make connections between their experiences in the lab, in the museum galleries, and in their own lives. All MoMA Art Labs are staffed by trained facilitators who assist and encourage visitors as they explore the various art-making activities in the space. In addition to the trained facilitators, a roster of dedicated volunteers assist in managing the spaces by greeting all guests, providing quick orientation tours of the space, and giving explanations of the various activities.

In developing each lab, the team wanted to ensure the space had a clear connection to MoMA's collection, rather than exist solely as a play or craft

Figure 3.2.   Children explore the "Discovery Boxes" in MoMA Art Lab: Material Lab. Photo by Michael Nagel

space. In Material Lab, the fourth lab in the series, visitors were invited to touch, explore, and create with both traditional and nontraditional art-making materials. As with previous MoMA Art Labs, the challenge was to create a drop-in space open enough to encourage exploration, play, and discovery, while being structured enough so that families could work independently. We also wanted to ensure that the lab would be accessible and interesting to children (and adults) of all abilities and nationalities, understanding that some participants would not speak English and others would have limited verbal skills and/or limited mobility or dexterity. We aimed to create a multisensory environment in which hands-on engagement would foster independent learning about artists' materials and processes, ultimately building understanding about modern and contemporary art. While previous MoMA Art Labs had been designed with an audience of children five to twelve years old in mind, we had observed many toddlers in the space, so in Material Lab, another goal was to provide more opportunities that would be appropriate for younger children.

In order to ensure the space was as universally accessible as possible, staff from Access Programs were included in the design team at the outset of the project to ensure the maximum inclusiveness of both the physical space and the content of the activities throughout the conceptual, design, and implementation phases. We knew that the adaptations we were making with individuals with disabilities in mind would benefit all visitors. The designers created tables for art making that would be accessible for wheelchair users and step stools for smaller visitors that could also be used as seats. In addition to stools at workstations, which were easily moveable to make room for wheelchairs and strollers, we provided comfortable seating on a flexible cardboard bench that could be extended to a longer couch in order to fit more visitors or compressed to take up less space. We installed carpet tiles on top of the hard floors to create a softer cushion for visitors' comfort and to make the space safer for children just learning to walk. All text on the walls and activity cards was printed in a large-print, bold, sans-serif font. While all text was translated into multiple languages with international visitors in mind, we strove to limit the use of text, instead using pictures and symbols and developing activities that would be intuitive.

A broad range of content was developed. We wanted to offer tactile, sensory experiences in order to engage a wide audience of varying ages, abilities, interests, and learning styles. Through specially designed "Discovery Boxes," visitors were invited to discover one material at a time—exploring its physical properties and more. Materials such as paint, rubber, cardboard, resin, velvet, and spices each had their own box, containing examples of the material that could be handled, a suggestion for an activity, and information about a work of art made of the material in MoMA's collection. Families were invited to open multiple boxes and explore the ways artists use different materials to create works of art. For instance, one box asked visitors to smell an assortment of spices, some of which Brazilian artist Ernesto Neto has used in his large-scale installations.

Beyond the Discovery Boxes, there were art-making stations for collage, assemblage, sculpture, drawing, and digital painting. Each station had a simple open-ended prompt that encouraged innovation with particular materials. The art-making prompts changed every few weeks to accommodate return visitors. For example, "Make a musical instrument" and "Create a structure" were two of the prompts used at the sculpture station. We have learned that limiting the number of supplies used in a particular art-making activity encourages experimentation and innovation with the materials at hand. At the sculpture station, the only materials provided were cardboard, papers of various colors and textures, and colored tape. As scissors were not available, children were encouraged to tear, fold, scrunch, and layer the paper, freeing them from worrying too much about "getting it right." We wanted visitors to use their imaginations and improvise without concern about their level of skill or previous experience. Adult companions helped children as needed by offering support and suggestions and often made their own creations. Art created by previous visitors was on display to offer inspiration for those unsure of how to get started.

Another station for the duration of the lab offered digital painting. We wanted to present opportunities to try some of the traditional materials that artists use, such as charcoal and oil paint, but our space did not have sinks so using actual paint and charcoal was not possible. We decided to explore options for a digital painting experience and learned that Microsoft was developing a digital painting application. They generously donated touchscreen monitors featuring Microsoft Digital Art technology and agreed to preview the application in the lab. The program is particularly impressive in its ability to simulate the effects of different types of painting and drawing media. Visitors could select to draw or paint with a virtual pencil, piece of charcoal, pastel, or paintbrush. There were various virtual brushes and papers available as well, allowing visitors to understand the qualities and nuances of various materials and tools. For instance, painting wet on wet would cause colors to blend differently than layering different colored pastels. In terms of accessibility, the monitors were attached to adjustable arms so that they could be lifted, lowered, and tilted to be reachable by small children, individuals using wheelchairs, or visitors with limited use of their arms or hands. Also, the touchscreens were sensitive enough to react to the light touch of a visitor with limited dexterity, and children as well as adults with low vision benefited from a magnifying feature that enabled them to zoom in on their onscreen creations.

While the space was designed to be inclusive of people with disabilities during public hours, the lab was also open for private group visits for individuals with disabilities during nonpublic hours. During these special sessions, children and adults with learning or developmental disabilities, as well as students who are blind or partially sighted, were able to engage in the lab's activities with the support of educators from MoMA's Access Programs.

During its eighteen-month run, over 72,000 children and adults visited Material Lab. Throughout that time, visitor research that included both interviews and observations was conducted. We learned that 96 percent of visitors surveyed felt that the lab had a positive impact on the way they and their children experienced the museum. Forty-eight percent explained that exploring materials through touch and art making helped them and their children better understand the art and artistic processes represented in the collection at MoMA. One grandmother said, "The lab reinforces what we saw. In the galleries kids see what artists have done and this gets them closer to thinking about the hand of the artist, what materials they work with, and how they work with those materials. This helps us to connect to the art after we've looked at it." Another adult visitor pointed out, "Art is no longer just a spectator sport but something that all can participate in."

Things to keep in mind:

- Trained facilitators and volunteers can create a welcoming atmosphere and offer further explanations of the opportunities available in the space.
- Make do and be creative with the space and resources that you have.
- Close physical proximity of the space to the galleries is ideal.
- Think about accessibility throughout the conceptual, design, and implementation phases of the project.
- Go beyond compliance with the Americans with Disabilities Act—the accommodations that you make for individuals with disabilities benefit all visitors.
- Don't forget nonverbal and non-English-speaking visitors. Limit the use of text, include translations of all texts, use pictures or symbols when possible, and develop activities that are intuitive.
- Interactive spaces need to endure a great deal of wear and tear—choose durable furnishings and materials.
- Offer a mix of exploratory activities and projects that can be made and taken home.

- Keep in mind that tactile, sensory experiences appeal to a wide audience, especially kinesthetic learners, very young visitors, and children with certain disabilities.
- Limiting the number of supplies and tools for an art-making project encourages experimentation and creative problem solving.

ACKNOWLEDGMENTS

We would like to acknowledge our colleagues Liz Margulies, Cari Frisch, and Kirsten Schroeder, whose hard work, creativity, and vision led to the development of Material Lab; educators Andrew Ondrejcak and Rebecca Goyette, who led the Create Ability performance art workshop; and the many educators and volunteers who work tirelessly to create accessible multisensory experiences at The Museum of Modern Art.

4

Multisensory Engagement with Real Nature Relevant to Real Life

Molly Steinwald, Melissa A. Harding,
and Richard V. Piacentini

E. O. Wilson's theory of biophilia posits that all humans have an "urge to affiliate with other forms of life"; that is, the desire to interact with nature is strongly innate in everyone. This theory is in agreement with years of research that reveal that people strongly and positively respond to nature. There is also a growing recognition that the human need for nature is not only material but emotional, spiritual, and cognitive (Louv, 2005; Townsend and Weerasuriya, 2010). The field of eco-psychology finds that people experience many positive and therapeutic effects when exposed to nature. Whether from just looking out a window or actually being outside, exposure to nature has been shown to lead to positive mental health outcomes, decreased risk of mental illness, and longer life expectancy (Louv, 2005; Pretty et al., 2009). Access to nature has also been associated with reduced stress levels, higher levels of physical activity outdoors, a greater sense of well-being, increased community involvement, and increased social connections. Many studies also show that direct experiences with nature help in the formation of conservation attitudes and active care for the environment (Louv, 2005, Chawla, 2009).

Open green space and access to nature are especially important for children; free play in nature has been shown to create a sense of freedom and independence (Pretty et al., 2009). The freedom to explore and play outdoors is thought to allow children to test their boundaries, take risks, and activate their potential. Free outdoor play also affects physical strength: Research shows that children who play in natural areas test better for motor fitness, especially agility and balance, than their peers. Additionally, outdoor play allows for greater self-discovery; education that takes place in natural spaces can lead to greater connectedness to nature and environmental knowledge, as well as increased creativity and ability to learn. Besides these cognitive benefits, children also benefit emotionally from being outside. Children who live near nature tend to have a higher sense of self-worth than their corresponding peers; nature exposure bolsters children's resilience against stress and adversity. Green spaces also have been shown to foster social interaction, as well as nurture solitude, both of which are important to emotional development (Louv, 2005).

Unfortunately, we are living in a time of isolation from nature. Children and adults spend much of their daily lives in buildings; physical activity has been decreasing, while screen time has been increasing. Overall, people are less connected to the natural world and its systems than they were even a generation ago. As author Richard Louv writes, we are living in a time of "nature deficit disorder," which he defines as "costs of alienation from nature: among them diminished use of the senses, attention difficulties and higher rates of physical and emotional illnesses" (Louv, 2005). This problem can be detected in the individual and the community, where both are challenged with increasing rates of obesity, disease, social isolation, and sedentary behavior. For communities, these problems are often coupled with shrinking health care and social spending budgets. A growing body of evidence suggests that increasing access to nature and natural areas for people of all ages and social spheres can alleviate some of these complex social and health problems (Chawla, 2009; Louv, 2005). Museums can make a difference in their communities and help to address these social needs by providing necessary green spaces and experiences through exhibits and innovative nature-based education.

THE SENSORY IMPORTANCE OF PLANTS

One of the easier ways for museums to connect their visitors to nature is through the use of plants. Not only are plants relatively easy to care for and predictable in their behavior, but they are incredibly sensory. Fragrant, textured, and sometimes even tasty, a single plant can stimulate a person's senses in multiple ways.

Digging further down, interaction with plants is also shown to confer similar benefits to those of nature exposure. Studies on the effects of plants in the workplace suggest that people feel more relaxed and recover faster from stress when plants are present. Seeing natural objects reduces work-related stress and influences overall well-being (Shibata and Suzuki, 2002). The positive effects of gardening are also widely recognized. It was more than 2,000 years ago that Taoists believed that gardens and greenhouses were beneficial for human health. Fast-forward to the present day and now there is an entire field of certified horticulture therapists who use gardening as a tool to treat chronic diseases in their patients. Plants have been integral in research showing that nature is instrumental in people healing from physical ailments. A ten-year study of surgery patients showed that those whose rooms faced a grove of trees recovered more quickly from their surgery than those whose rooms faced a brick wall (Louv, 2005). In a related study, prison inmates whose cells faced a prison courtyard had 24 percent more illnesses than those whose cells faced farmland (Louv, 2005). This research suggests that exposure to plants can foster a connection to nature in both children and adults, making plants a useful medium for museums to enhance the experience of visitors and program participants through sensory stimulation.

The idea of using plants and real nature to stimulate the senses is an increasing trend in informal learning institutions such as museums. Within the museum sector, botanic gardens are a great resource to look toward for ideas and trends in sensory exhibits and education programs using plants and nature as a medium for learning—botanic garden, plant-based multisensory exhibits are not only well established but growing in breadth and depth. Naturally immersive, botanic gardens allow visitors to encounter plants with their whole bodies: visitors smell, see, and, in many cases, touch plants as they walk through the gardens. The visitor experience is only that much more augmented by the addition of interactive displays and programs. Even without large-scale plant habitats, however, most museums still can provide people–plant multisensory experiences.

At first glance, incorporating plant–people experiences into traditional museums may not seem possible, but there are a multitude of areas in which living plants and plant concepts can be incorporated. Consider first exploring the landscape immediately around the museum building itself as a potential exhibit and programmatic space for connecting people to plants. Next, take advantage of atriums and any other space that has access to natural light for indoor plantings. These areas are often available and underutilized to this end. Another opportunity involves using simple, inexpensive fluorescent lighting to turn a windowless space into an environment capable of housing a lush plant exhibit.

Drawing from established examples in the botanic garden world, here we focus on basic areas in which museums can incorporate components that connect people to nature through plants. The four basic areas in which museums have opportunities to incorporate multisensory plant experiences include: 1) exhibits, 2) docents or interpretive staff, 3) classes and programming, and 4) community outreach to engage people beyond the museum property. The main gardens we draw examples from here are the Chicago Botanic Garden (CBG), the Minnesota Landscape Arboretum (MLA), the New York Botanical Garden (NYBG), and the Phipps Conservatory and Botanical Gardens (PCBG).

ENCOURAGING EXPLORATION

The CBG presents itself as a place where "classrooms can be without desks or walls, and where students can discover the ways and wonders of plants, in and out of doors" (CBG website). Its mission is to promote enjoyment, understanding, and conservation of plants in the natural world. Patsy Benveniste, the CBG's director of education, believes that "sensory learning is an indispensable feature of environmental education and reflects what we believe is how all people learn" (personal communication, November 21, 2012). The MLA's motto of "Create. Engage. Grow. Restore." describes perfectly its commitment to sensory-based education.

The NYBG educates learners of all ages about the "science, function, and beauty of plants to generate awareness, inspire appreciation, and provide an understanding of the importance of plants to all life on Earth." Its education division offers a wide range of sensory-and inquiry-based programs for both children and adults. James Boyer, director of children's education, says that "nature play and science learning—using the senses—are the initial gateway in which we get kids excited about nature and then we layer on the science skills" (personal communication, November 21, 2012). The NYBG believes that touch and observation are crucial aspects for teaching science skills, prompting both parents and children to engage (J. Boyer, personal communication, November 21, 2012). And the PCBG's mission, "to inspire and educate with the beauty and importance of plants, to advance sustainability and foster human and environmental well-being through action and research," has as its ultimate goal to connect people to the important role plants play in their lives.

Focusing on the area of exhibits, trends such as the creation of sensory gardens are encouraged. These gardens allow interaction between guests and plants for educational and therapeutic purposes, use multidisciplinary approaches to teaching science and other knowledge areas, and use food-based concepts as a medium for teaching healthy lifestyle choices. These methods are all fast being adopted by some of today's most venerable museums and public gardens. Sensory garden exhibits, it is important to note, can be located either indoors or outdoors; this recognition can expand opportunities to take advantage of plant–people sensory experiences.

The MLA educational facility's Please Touch Greenhouse is filled with a variety of plants of assorted shapes, sizes, colors, textures, and smells, and has signage that enthusiastically prompts visitors to explore the plants with all their senses. The greenhouse simultaneously serves as an entry point to explore the MLA's full gardens, model-landscapes, and natural areas, with several of these gardens specifically dedicated to free play and sensory exploration.

MLA's Green Play Yard is a 15,000-square-foot outdoor play space for families with young children to experience "nearby nature" through plantings and natural play features. With zones for infants, toddlers, and preschoolers, the play yard has such features as stumps for jumping, a crawl-along garden for the very young, plant tunnels, fort-building, and sand, dirt, and water play. Also full of walking paths, dramatic play areas, and bridges, the play yard lets young ones "dig in" with all their senses to fully experience the natural world and offers adults simple ideas that are easily replicable at childcare centers, preschools, and backyards. Another sensory garden, Under the Oak, is a rustic natural play area for all ages set under the oldest oak on the MLA property. Using primarily salvaged wood and branches from the MLA's wooded areas, and designed and constructed in collaboration with a local artist and on a small budget, this is an area where children are invited to "move things around, build forts and dens, hold tea parties and puppet shows, clamber on fallen logs and generally re-create things to suit their fancy." Full of "loose parts" like sticks, cones, branches, and leaves, and small pieces of tarp, children have a supply of base materials for their imaginative play.

Following on the same theme of encouraging exploration, at the NYBG, the Everett Children's Adventure Garden is a twelve-acre sensory garden filled with features meant for exploration, including plant-based mazes, a "touch tank" filled with aquatic plants, boulders for climbing, giant flowers, and even an indoor laboratory where learners can participate in science experiments. This garden is a safe, enclosed space where caregivers can let their children play freely.

CBG's Children's Growing Garden is the perfect place for budding scientists; children can work in child-size raised-bed gardens and engage in experiential learning activities that use music, art, and cooking to share plant science with visitors. Families visiting the CBG can check out backpacks that include magnifiers, binoculars, field guides, journal, and pencils to record discoveries while interacting with plant exhibits. These backpacks, which are available on a first-come, first-serve basis and are checked out in exchange for the caregiver's driver's license, make exhibits suddenly much more engaging and interactive by challenging backpack users to observe aspects of the plants more closely.

Though not nearly as large as other children's gardens, the PCBG's Outdoor Discovery Garden is tucked in a small area between several greenhouses, and allows children to immerse themselves in a child-size garden built for exploration and play. Originally based on exploring the question of why plants have flowers, the garden comprises several smaller, themed gardens and large play sculptures. Capitalizing on the idea of expanding the sensory and learning experiences for visitors, the themed gardens include

Figure 4.1. Photo by Cory Doman

a small stream and connected bog garden, butterfly and pollinator beds, a sensory garden, bird gardens, and more. Amid these gardens are large play sculptures that include a giant stump, play house, maze of living walls, watering can center, stream, and a pond with child-controlled fountains. Full of directional prompts, child-size displays and lots of wildlife to observe, the Discovery Garden can entertain and fascinate children for hours.

In an attempt to allow for more free play and sensory exploration, as well as increase adult engagement, PCBG recently built a second children's garden called the Nature Play Area. The Nature Play Area is an open play space containing a fort building area, digging pit, arbor tunnel, maze, and play house; PCBG supplies building materials such as sticks, wood cookies, stumps, and other loose parts to facilitate imaginative play. As a companion to the Discovery Garden, the Nature Play Area allows parents to let their children play more freely; this unrestricted play is not only fun but important to child development. Children can use the primarily plant-based materials in the garden in any manner they like, providing a more connecting and meaningful outdoor experience. They can spend hours digging in the dirt and stacking logs and sticks. Unlike in the Discovery Garden, children can be freer and wilder in their play. While parents still need to be engaged, there is a decreased likelihood that children will be injured. The additional space also provides a greater area for all of the children, reducing the density of bodies in both gardens and making it easier for parents to monitor their children. In these two gardens combined, children can experience the outdoors with their whole bodies and minds, being totally unrestricted to learn and play.

THE SENSORY EXPERIENCE OF FOOD AND GARDENING

Another multisensory means of connecting people to nature through plants is with food. At the PCBG, the important role plants play in people's lives is likely most apparent in the Edible Garden exhibit, where vegetables are grown in raised beds on a green roof. The space is not only used for viewing, touching, and reading informational signage about vegetables used in daily life and their importance in a balanced diet but it also serves as a site for more participatory programming. Children can roam freely in the enclosed garden space and are encouraged to explore the plants in the beds. Staff interact with visitors in the form of tastings, scavenger hunts, and other informal programming. Such engagement can both stimulate multiple senses and engage adults who are interested in growing their own edible gardens. Part of the Edible Garden is also now used in camps and internship programs, where youth are able to interact for much longer periods of time than single visits, and participate in the stimulating process of growing and cooking their own food.

In deliberately close proximity to the vegetable garden, PCBG's Children's Public Market, an interactive public market display filled with removable plastic fruits and vegetables, is one of the most popular parts of the PCBG for small children. Many of the "play" fruits and vegetables in the Children's Public Market can be found in the Edible Garden exhibit. Children can use child-size shopping carts to "shop" for "organic" fruits, vegetables, meats, dairy, and baked goods, mimicking a visit to a real farmer's market. The exhibit also contains recipe cards for older children, a register for "checking out," and scales for weighing. Visitors of all ages enjoy the hands-on and visually stimulating aspects of the market. Not only does it allow learning through dramatic play but it also teaches children what real food looks like and the types of foods that can be combined for a healthy meal.

Exhibits are not the only place where sensory involvement can be incorporated. The NYBG's Ruth Rea Howell Family Garden allows participants to learn about plants through a hands-on gardening experience. Guided by education staff, participants plant, tend, and harvest fresh produce. They also have the chance to prepare and taste these plants through family cooking classes, soon to be taught through the Edible Academy. The Edible Academy, a new building for "edible education," will realize the NYBG's vision of expanding its nutrition and gardening-based classes to twelve months a year and increasing participation for families, children, and teachers.

Often in museums, including botanic gardens, many displays do not necessarily allow for sensory experiences beyond viewing or may not be utilized to their fullest extent due to visitors' perception that museums, including botanic gardens, are traditionally hands-off. In these cases, creating smaller learning stations that can accompany a nonparticipatory exhibit and/or training interpretive staff to engage visitors through alternate modes can help welcome sensory engagement and learning.

At PCBG, Discovery Carts are small, movable learning stations throughout the Conservatory, staffed during peak hours and containing short lessons related to the exhibits, the seasons, and general plant science. These lessons take the form of books, crafts, and hands-on discovery of plants and insects. Staff at the carts can teach these short lessons to anyone who approaches, as well as help direct visitors to explore certain exhibits further. Staff can act as facilitators of displays where touching is encouraged and gently redirect visitors when it is not.

Additional informational signs encourage visitors to interact with the exhibits, and displays help the visitors explore deeper. Some signs are permanent, while others change with the seasons and the exhibits. For children, many signs have learning prompts related to the observation of plants, birds, and pollinators. For adults, these signs can help to broaden the scope of the related display, as well as help visitors take the knowledge that they learn at PCBG home to their own gardens.

PROGRAMMING THAT ENGAGES THE SENSES

At NYBG, through its Explainer Program, youth ages fourteen to seventeen participate in a competitive internship program to work as volunteer educators, or "Explainers," in the Adventure Garden. Explainers help children to use their senses as tools for exploring and learning about the garden. Not only is this program beneficial to families but to the Explainers themselves, many of whom report an increase in confidence and connectedness to nature as a result of their participation.

As well as free play and exploration, the NYBG provides sensory education programs for children and families that explore plants, horticulture, seasonal change, and ecological cycles through hands-on and inquiry-based classes. Camp and school programs, as well as drop-in programs for busy families, allow the garden to reach learners through many different means (J. Boyer, personal communication, November 21, 2012).

At the PCBG, many of its formal youth programs, including seasonal camps, school and youth group field trips, and scout groups, take a hands-on

Figure 4.2.   Photo by Cory Doman

approach to learning as well. While camp is a naturally multidisciplinary way to teach, PCBG has increased its ability to reach new participants by adding art, cooking, fitness, and photography-based programs. Offering nature photography, for example, is a great way to attract participants who are interested in photography to a camp that also contains quite a bit of botanical teaching. PCBG's photography camps, focusing on the sense of sight, teach concepts like composition and lighting, while also teaching about flower structure, rainforest strata, and plant adaptations. Another example of multidisciplinary learning is cooking camps; these camps consist of planting, harvesting, and cooking produce from the Edible Garden while simultaneously teaching about healthy food choices. By hiding botany and science in multidisciplinary camps, PCBG has been able to interest nontypical youth participants in engaging with nature. Eating, smelling flowers, drawing, and cooking are all very sensory ways to explore plants. These camps not only teach participants skills in the subject matter but they also foster a connection to the natural world through their hands-on components.

More museums, including botanic gardens, are moving toward incorporating multidisciplinary components to revive previously minimal sensory engagement programs, which standardly relied heavily on lecture or one-way presentation programs based in a classroom separate from the main exhibit spaces. While directly teaching a lecture program is inexpensive and sometimes easier for staff, it does not necessarily provide as meaningful an experience for participants. Though moving group programs to be primarily based out of exhibit spaces is a large step toward increasing engagement, smaller steps of incorporating experiments and hands-on components with real nature in the museum classroom and evolving class content to be more inquiry-based are extremely beneficial as well.

For PCBG, its preschool program, Little Sprouts, involves caregivers and children together engaging multiple senses in nature-based crafts, stories, songs, and games to learn about simple science concepts. The program takes place in the middle of PCBG's Tropical Forest exhibit, immersing campers and caregivers in the sights, sounds, and smells of the rainforest. Not only do participants learn a lesson but they also enjoy exploring the forest around them. Based in the classroom, programs for older youth teach, in a hands-on manner, how to make healthy snacks, nature-based beauty products, and recycled jewelry.

The MLA offers hands-on classes for all ages. For children and families, the MLA offers myriad multidisciplinary programs for children to be "hands-on scientists, artists, chefs, and explorers" while they connect with plants in an experiential way. From parent-child programs to scout and school programs, the MLA offers many different avenues for groups and individual learners to explore the world of plants.

Similarly to the NYBG, the MLA also offers family cooking classes where participants taste, touch, and smell plants on their way into healthy, seasonal recipes. MLA includes a sensory garden made up of a series of demonstration schoolyard plantings called Learning Habitats for Schools. Used as both a place for inspiration and on-site field trips, each "learning habitat" allows participants to experience seasonal changes through observation and data collection.

At CBG, in addition to youth, teachers and other adults also benefit from experiential plant education. Through its Professional Development program, teachers gain increased knowledge of plants and ecology while learning to create more engaging lessons that meet state and federal science standards, and even receive their very own living plants. By disseminating this information to teachers, the NYBG is moving plant-based learning to classrooms all over the region. Finally, the NYBG offers over 500 courses and lectures for adult learners through their certificate programs, including a nationally accredited School of Professional Horticulture, with a broad range of hands-on learning with living material.

THE THERAPEUTIC POWER OF PLANTS

Multisensory, multidisciplinary, plant-based programming in museums can go beyond traditional audiences of children, families, school groups, and so forth, to audiences that can benefit from the experience in a different way. Horticulture therapy is a form of therapy in which plants and gardening are used to help people with all manner of mental or physical illnesses. Specialists work both on- and off-site, using the sensory nature of plants to direct their participants' attention away from pain, alleviate depression, and relieve stress.

The CBG is an example of one botanic garden that has its own horticulture therapy department. The simple act of planting a bulb off-site or working in the CBG's Buehler Enabling Garden, a special barrier-free on-site sensory garden, both connects participants to the natural world through their senses and improves the effects of other treatment from their health care providers. Of special concern to the CBG are returning veterans, many of whom have varying degrees of post-traumatic stress disorder; their ability to accommodate normal life patterns is compromised. The soothing nature of plants and gardening helps these patients to engage their senses and reintegrate their feelings (B. Kreski, CBG director of horticulture therapy services, personal communication, November 16, 2012).

The MLA also helps visitors to engage their senses through their horticulture therapy department. The MLA's Center for Therapeutic Horticulture and Recreation Services provides participants with the opportunity to explore accessible garden techniques and the use of horticulture as a means to relaxation and the elimination of physical and mental barriers. Both on- and off-site programs reach people with a variety of sensory input disorders and those with mental and physical illnesses. The center also goes so far as to provide professional support for those looking to plan their own therapeutic landscapes and a certification program to help those wishing to enter the horticulture therapy profession.

The CBG is heavily involved in community gardening, including work with both youth and adults. The Green Youth Farm program offers students the opportunity to be a part of the process of food production, from planting seeds to cooking and selling the food they grow. Every year, sixty high school students work twenty hours a week from mid-May to mid-October on one of three organic farms; students learn not only horticulture but also teamwork, job skills, the importance of community service, and a new outlook on food. For adults, the Windy City Harvest program trains participants in sustainable vegetable production and business skills, including planning, sales, marketing, and pricing; students exit the program prepared to enter the "green collar" job sector. Another adult program, the Vocational Rehabilitation Impact Center (VRIC), works with inmates to teach horticulture skills. Participants in the program grow and harvest organic vegetables to be used in the prison mess hall, all while learning useful skills to help them find meaningful work upon their release. All of these hands-on horticulture programs give participants the time to be quiet and reflect while enjoying the sensory pleasures of digging in the dirt, working in the sun, and cooking and eating their harvest (P. Benveniste, personal communication, November 21, 2012).

MLA offers an extensive gardening outreach program for youth called the Urban Gardening Program. Started as a neighborhood garden site for underserved children, the program now includes an experience-based garden curriculum, a garden-based employment program to develop leadership skills in urban youth, and opportunities for exposure to higher education environments. This program gives children and youth the opportunity to grow and tend their own gardens, use the produce to prepare fresh foods, and learn the important role plants play in our lives through interaction with caring and encouraging adult educators who model positive behavior.

A major way schools can engage in sensory learning through PCBG is the Fairchild Challenge, a multidisciplinary, standards-based environmental education program based out of the Fairchild Tropical and Botanic Gardens in Florida. Since 2008, PCBG has been a satellite partner in this program and offered the Fairchild Challenge to local middle and high school students. In the Fairchild Challenge, which takes place over the course of the entire school year, both middle and high school students participate in a variety of environment-based challenges. All of these challenges are different and designed to appeal to a variety of students; they are based in art, writing, music, acting, science, community activism, and civic engagement. Schools can choose to participate in one or all of the challenges offered them over the course of the school year. At the end of the school year, monetary awards are given to the winning schools for use in their environmental projects on-site. Before the addition of the Fairchild Challenge to PCBG, programs offered to older students were very limited. For students who love visual and musical arts, this may be a way to get involved in a conservation-based art project, where there may have been no opportunity or interest in it before. This program also engages participants with the environment and plants, though they never have to come to PCBG.

THE CHALLENGES AND REWARDS OF IMPLEMENTING PARTICIPATORY ELEMENTS

While there is much excitement and many marked successes in incorporating multisensory, plant–people experiences into exhibits, among docents and interpretive staff, in classes and programming, and in community outreach, it is important to acknowledge that each of these areas involve their own challenges. Based on each museum's constraints, some areas may be more promising or feasible to pursue than others. Here we review some of the common challenges encountered.

While it can increase visitor engagement and learning, adding a hands-on exhibit has its drawbacks. Maintaining exhibits that are manipulated daily can be difficult, especially when the objects being used are living plants. Children can be rough on interactive exhibits, as can adults. These exhibits also often require extra staff to maintain and clean them; for instance, if an exhibit contains smaller, portable pieces, those pieces will inevitably migrate to other areas of the museum unless someone is responsible for making sure they remain with the exhibit. Living plants and exhibit pieces are also likely to require replacement on a regular basis, depending on the frequency and duration of the use. All of these issues combined can make hands-on, sensory exhibits more expensive than less interactive ones.

One challenge that PCBG faces regarding the hands-on nature of its exhibits and programs is being able to change visitor perceptions. Established in 1893, the PCBG has functioned primarily as a display garden with viewing rooms, where touching of exhibits was not encouraged. Over the years it has evolved, particularly recently, and has incorporated more informative signs, interactive exhibits, and sensory-based programs into its existing structure and operations. While the evolution toward a more multisensory experience at the PCBG may be evident to staff, it may not always be evident to visitors, especially those who have visited the PCBG over the course of their own lifetime.

When considering the creation or modification of a children's nature play space, there are many factors to consider. Children can sometimes love the space too much, taking it upon themselves to climb into the pond or walk in the stream created for visual, tactile, but not likely full-body experiencing. Stone pathways are also very inviting to running feet, but running on sometimes slippery and uneven paths could end in an accident. Lack of parental involvement, especially in small play spaces, can be challenging; signage and staff encouraging parental involvement can help overcome this.

When in small play spaces, children are likely not able to play freely, and running and wild behavior is unsafe in crowded areas. Similarly, crowding can actually make it challenging at times for parents to keep track of a single child. Having enclosed areas where children cannot leave without the notice of a caregiver can help to alleviate that stressor. These problems can sometimes arise from inconsistent supervision.

When considering creating a new or modifying an existing exhibit to allow for more tactile participation through moveable loose parts, keep in mind that exhibit pieces will likely gradually disappear. In a play market, for example, children fill carts with pretend food items, and then may leave the exhibit space without putting them away or simply take them when they leave, whether on purpose or accidentally. It is not uncommon to find pieces of one exhibit in another space in the museum. Additionally, exhibit pieces that are being touched and carried regularly will often break down over time; anticipating this and planning to have back-ups is essential. When working with live plants as the "touchable" pieces, regularly having several of the same plant type is important to move forward when one plant is injured or needs time to recover from overuse.

With exhibit pieces that receive a lot of tactile interaction, it is important to regularly clean them and provide a hand-cleansing station nearby with signage prompting participants to wash hands in order to reduce spread of germs.

When combining hands-on interactive components that are located near exhibits that are considered hands-off, it is important to make the message clear to visitors which items welcome interaction and which do not. For example, at the PCBG, the living plant exhibit space surrounding the children's market space is primarily a hands-off exhibit. This has the potential to confuse visitors, and children particularly; while playing with the market items, visitors can in turn be relatively rough with the plants. It is imperative that a staff person be at the market during peak visitor hours. Combined with replacing items regularly, this extra staff time has the potential to compound the expense of such an exhibit space.

In addition to expense associated with staff time and exhibit maintenance, a more hands-on approach has the challenge of attempting to engage adults and children at the same time. In the case of the market, adults are not always engaged along with their child. This can result in accidents or damage from unsupervised children, which is another reason for staff to be present. Creating exhibits that engage both adults and children together is a useful way to curb this drawback.

There are also challenges related to docents or interpretive staff. In a setting where more multisensory engagement has not traditionally been encouraged, visitors are not the only people at museums that can be confused or resistant to changes. Staff and volunteers who have spent many years at a museum that is moving toward being more immersive can also be difficult. A reworking of docent and volunteer programs overall, including more frequent and varied trainings and a strengthened relationship with education staff, has helped to create better tours for visitors of varied backgrounds and interests and enable more sensory participation throughout.

The following are some specific challenges related to classes and programs: While making programs more experiential and multisensory is a great boon for participants, it is more typically expensive in terms of both staff time and materials costs. For example, cutting open a cactus to illustrate its photosynthesizing stem is a dramatic and exciting part of PCBG's desert program, but purchasing cacti in quantity is an increased expense. While the majority of the programs do have participant fees, the staff time it takes to develop and prepare for even a short camp may negate the income generated. At museums where the education department is expected to generate revenue, this can be a difficult balance to strike.

Developing and preparing for a program, only for it to be cancelled due to lack of participation is not uncommon among education departments. Any education department that wants to expand and grow will have to find a way to deal with these setbacks. One way that PCBG has dealt with this dichotomy is to begin by offering more multidisciplinary programs to wider age ranges, and later hone in on certain topics and age groups once interest levels have been gauged.

While the projects, successes, and challenges of these botanic gardens are meant to provide readers from museum institutions with ideas on what to consider trying in their own institutions, these are only examples of a broad array of work being done in the botanic garden world to that end. Like all organizations across the museum sector and beyond, gardens are continually working to modernize and engage visitors and community members in new ways that address both societal and environmental issues, create relevancy to daily life, and provide stability for the organizations. Creating multisensory plant-based experiences is certainly worth pursuing, in varying degrees, by many museums. Looking deeper into the botanic garden world is a great source for ideas and connections. We are just at the beginning of what is possible. Below are some basic tips and ideas to get started.

- Start small; add a touch tour or taste- and scent-guessing games to an already established program. Once you have tried this approach, move on to bigger goals.
- Try adding sensory components to an otherwise noninteractive exhibit to engage your audience; a touch table or docent-guided tasting activity are easy things to include.
- Add a simple plant potting station; this allows participants to experience the sensory joy of gardening on a small scale and take home a bit of nature.
- Create linkages across the entire museum experience. For example, do a taste testing in the café of a plant type that is located in an exhibit in another part of the museum.
- Add a multidisciplinary on-site or off-site program to your offerings; create a program that uses art, music, food, or planting to explore botany from a whole new viewpoint.
- Use participant feedback to guide your decisions; there is no sense in spending money or time on continuing an avenue that is unsuccessful.

REFERENCES

Chawla, L. (2009). Growing up green: Becoming an agent of care for the natural world. *Journal of Developmental Processes* (4)1, 6–20.

Louv, Richard. (2005). *Last Child in the Woods: Saving our Children from Nature-Deficit Disorder.* Chapel Hill, NC: Algonquin Books.

Pretty, J., Angus, C., Bain, M., Barton, J. Gladwell, V., Hines, R. and Sellens, M. (2009). *Nature, Childhood, Health and Life Pathways.* University of Essex: Interdisciplinary Center for Environment and Society.

Shibata, Seiji and Suzuki, Naoto. (2002). Effects of the foliage plant on task performance and mood. *Journal of Environmental Psychology, 22*, 255–72.

Townsend, M. and Weerasuriya, R. (2010). *Beyond Blue to Green: The Benefits of Contact with Nature for Mental Health and Well-Being.* Melbourne, Australia: Beyond Blue Limited.

5

Touch and Narrative in Art and History Museums

Nina Levent and D. Lynn McRainey

Touch and proprioception were once appropriate and accepted ways of relating to art and ritual objects, from Aphrodite of Knidos to medieval icons and Early Modern sculpture (Cannon, 2011; Johnson, 2002). Although touch has always been contrasted with sight, in most cases to rationalize the supremacy of sight (Jutte, 2005; Johnson, 2002), it is only in modern times that senses were sanitized and regulated in public spaces (Classen, 2012; Candlin, 2008; Smith, 2007, 93). Anthropologists and historians have revived the sensory discourse in the last decade, due in large part to the Sensory Studies program at Concordia University, which has conducted, fostered, and inspired much of this research. Constance Classen, one of the program's founders, writes about the early days at the Ashmolean Museum of Oxford, when tours included lifting, shaking, and handling objects, and travelers remarked on the weight, smell, and feel of the pieces in the collection. Handling seemed to be essential for acquiring information, aesthetic pleasure, and establishing a connection to the object (Classen, 2005).

A lot has been written about the "sanitation" of the senses in modern Western culture and how it affected museums (Classen, 2012, 136). It is telling that in most museums today the sensory experience is confined to museum stores: This is where we touch small stone sculptures, handle jewelry, admire the texture of luxurious textiles, handle pottery and wood, run our hands over fabrics and pottery glazes, smell weaving and incense. This might account for the crowds in museum stores, and why some visitors spend a good deal of their "museum" time there. In our recent research, blind museum visitors told us that it was in the museum store where they did most of their learning about Kachina dolls after visiting an exhibit where all of the dolls were under glass (Reich et al., 2011).

Here, we will look at the re-introduction of meaningful touch and handling of museum objects into the mainstream museum experience. We will provide an overview of different curatorial, educational, and artistic narratives and strategies that use touch and proprioception as a learning tool, a means of aesthetic appreciation and exploration, and a way of engaging with an audience on a deeper level.

Touch and handling are part of many artistic narratives, from those by performance artists who avail their bodies and various objects for touch by viewers, to new media works that are activated through touch or movement. Sculptors from Rodin to Richard Serra valued touch and created works of art that dare a viewer to touch. Felix Gonzalez-Torres's beaded curtains, small mountains of candy, and stacks of paper might be a way of disrupting the institutional hierarchy through touch. Patrick Dougherty's and Deborah Butterfield's sculptures connect to touch through the natural elements that inspire their art; they seek to convey the physicality and poetry of their connection to nature through their art.

To attract new audiences, history museums are turning to alternative interpretive approaches that challenge visitors' assumptions and consumption of history. History museums must engage their audiences with the unknown and unseen—places and buildings that no longer exist, people they have never met, and events that more than likely occurred before they were born. The teaching and interpretation of history is, in part, making the somewhere, someone, and something of the past relevant, meaningful, and to some extent, believable. To transform visitors' perceptions of this somewhat remote discipline, history museums are broadening their interpretation and presentation of the past. Oral histories have added multiple perspectives to the once solitary voice of the curator, and the integration of emerging technologies has transformed once quiet galleries into interactive spaces that invite participation and meaning-making. Whereas touch was once sequestered to hands-on galleries for children, tactile and other sensory encounters have found their way into core exhibitions.

These and other changes have given history a contemporary voice, raised new questions and interpretations of past events, and redefined venerable "historical societies" into history museums and centers. The ongoing transformation of history museums makes them as much about the present and the future as about the past.

Collectively, the narratives of history exhibitions and programs cited in this chapter are trying to change visitors' passive consumption of facts, dates, and names of historical events, as well as challenging their "been there, done that" attitudes that one visit to a local history museum should last them a lifetime. Touch and narrative emerge as a complementary duo in their abilities to provide physical and cognitive access as well as affective engagement with history—making the past visible, doable, and real.

TOUCH, AESTHETIC PLEASURE, AND ART COLLECTING

Ritual and devotional handling of sculpture, icons, and other representations were widespread in the Middle Ages and the Renaissance. The signs of wear on statues and paintings testify to the practice of devotional touch and kissing (Cannon, 2011). Devotional touch might not be an experience that can be easily or authentically recreated in a secular museum environment, but The Walters Art Museum in Baltimore made a remarkable attempt to explore the value of aesthetic touch and tactility in Early Modern Europe in an exhibit space.

In 2011, The Walters Art Museum premiered an exhibit titled Touch and the Enjoyment of Sculpture: Exploring the Appeal of Renaissance Statuettes. Joaneath Spicer, The Walters' curator of Renaissance and Baroque sculpture, focused the curatorial narrative on small sculpture and its tactile appeal to collectors and art connoisseurs. As a Renaissance scholar she knew that art objects were touched to register qualities of the surface and appreciate volume, and that many statuettes fit comfortably in a palm of a hand. Through its exhibit, The Walters Art Museum offered visitors a similar experience of touching replicas of the originals in the museum's collection. Visitors were then asked to provide feedback to researchers who were studying the tactile appeal of certain forms.

Spicer's exhibition narrative was built around the idea of the satisfaction that is gained from touching and handling small bronze statuettes. Such satisfaction and pleasure gained from handling these intricate bronzes might have been the reason for collecting and commissioning this art form. Sixteenth-century art patrons who owned and commissioned statuettes were rewarded with the pleasure of cradling these works in the palm of their hand. Now museum visitors are offered some access to this experience.

TOUCH AS A DEMOCRATIC MEDIUM

Perhaps one of the reasons why touch is so rare in museums is that in modern, commodity-driven consumer culture touch has been linked with ownership. Mark Smith sums up the discussion of touch and possession by saying: "If you want to touch what you do not currently own go to a store, not a museum" (Smith, 2007, 116). Felix Gonzalez-Torres's works, which are now a

Figure 5.1.   Felix Gonzalez-Torres, "Untitled" (Golden), 1995; strands of beads and hanging device, dimensions vary with installation; installation view of Passages: Felix Gonzalez-Torres. Museum of Fine Arts, Boston. 17 September 2011–January 2015. Cur. Jen Mergel, © The Felix Gonzalez-Torres Foundation. Courtesy of Andrea Rosen Gallery, New York

part of almost every major contemporary art collection, are an example of an artist engaging in a critical conversation about touch, ownership, and the experience of art. When exhibited in galleries, more often than not, Gonzalez-Torres's works are the most accessible and the only touchable pieces in the gallery, whether a pile of candy at New York City's Museum of Modern Art, a beaded curtain that leads into the galleries at the San Francisco Museum of Modern Art, or a stack of papers at The Baltimore Art Museum. These pieces are often referred to as democratic; they can be understood as coming to life and becoming a work of art the moment a museum visitor realizes that he is welcome to the candy or the papers arranged in a stack on the floor, and that going through the curtain and touching beads is part of the museum experience (Chambers-Letson, 2010).

When the Museum of Fine Arts, Boston, opened its first contemporary art wing in 2011, Jen Mergel, the Museum's curator of contemporary art, included Gonzalez-Torres's beaded curtain titled "Untitled (Beginnings)" in the doorway of the first gallery. This curtain was the first part of a five-year-long survey exhibition curated by Mergel; the exhibition includes all of the five beaded curtains created by the artist during his life. The artist stipulated that the curtains be hung in a natural doorway where visitors walk through rather than just look at them.

The curtains are installed in a gallery that explores the range of contemporary art experiences; each curtain is a critical part of the conversation about expanding the definition of art. While the gallery features photographs of land art or body art, Gonzalez-Torres's curtains provide actual physical contact with art and an experience of becoming part of the work of art as one passes through the doorway.

The artist speaks of his work and himself "as a virus, an imposter, an infiltrator" that always replicates himself with a museum that owns his art (Gonzalez-Torres, 1993). Gonzalez-Torres's works are designed to be replicated and replenished; they can be touched, consumed, and taken out of the museum. Gonzalez-Torres directly addresses power structures and economic concerns of museums, where works of art are costly to replace and repair. He underscores that it is important for him that such narratives of democratic "infiltration" are taking place within the power structure of museums, not outside of them; thus, museum visitors pick up parts of his work, candy, or embossed paper, and leave with them, while the guards watch.

The museum has the right and the responsibility to manifest the work of art, to keep it alive as opposed to owning the work. Mergel says that she experiences the relationship between the work and the museums directly: She sees the great exuberance in visitors of all ages as they pass through the curtain. At the end of the day she tends to the artwork as if it were a garden. When the strands of beads stretch as the hundreds of visitors pass through them, she trims the strands. "It is a living piece, an experience as opposed to the object. Unlike the object, it is not just placed in the room, but needs to be tended. It cannot be owned or possessed in traditional ways. It is quite democratic" (Mergel, 2013).

TOUCH AS NATURAL PHENOMENON

Patrick Dougherty creates large whimsical structures—part fairy-tale palaces, part hobbit dwellings—out of branches and sticks. These stick sculptures have been created on museum grounds all over the United States and abroad. Sometimes they look like oversized baskets, bottles, or water pitchers; sometimes they remind us of temples or huts. All of his works are site-specific, and they all begin with his learning about local materials, going through the woods, and picking out saplings. Dougherty speaks of the deeper understanding and familiarity with the materials that he gains by touching and handling sticks and branches and reflecting on their potential. The physicality of the material is important to his process and, then, to the viewers' experience. Dougherty says that he strives to recreate the visceral and tactile experience of the forest, to bring back the textures, odors, and sounds of the woods,

Figure 5.2. "Hedging Your Bets," 2009, by Patrick Dougherty. Mulvane Art Museum of Washburn University, Topeka, Kansas. Photo courtesy of Washburn University

the feeling of brushing through the branches. His structures are layered and interwoven, like baskets. By adding layers, Dougherty creates what he calls the "luxury of surface." Working with saplings is akin to drawing, except that the result is touchable. The tapered saplings, when organized in one direction, create a sense of movement almost in the same way as a drawing does.

Dougherty's early "branchworks" began as small objects and evolved to large sculptures, architectural dwellings, and walk-through spaces. They evoke memories of childhood games, children's forts and tree houses, indigenous homes, fishing shacks. The spaces are comforting rather then confined; many have the womblike cavernous quality of a bird nest. Dougherty's works are created to be reminiscent of a natural phenomena, a live mass of branches that scales walls of buildings, "grows over" architectural elements.

Touch is sometimes seen as contributing to or causing deterioration of artworks. For Dougherty's sculptures the physical handling of the works is part of creating and enjoying the work. Dougherty shares his sentiments about touch and nature with other environmental artists of his generation, such as Andy Goldsworthy, whose stone sculptures are built to blend into the natural environment and will one day become a part of that environment again (Pheby, 2010). Dougherty's branch structures are temporary and last on average about two years. The transient nature of these works contributes to the intensity of experience. Elements such as wind, rain, frost, snow, and human touch are all part of these works, which change with the seasons and with handling. A certain sadness is always felt when these sculptures are coming down.

TOUCH IS DANCE

Deborah Butterfield, renowned for her sculptures of horses, also began her career using wood, mud, sticks, and branches. Later she used scrap metal, and now many of her horses are welded together from cast-bronze pieces. Butterfield's horse sculptures—exhibited indoors and outdoors—are in the collections of major American museums, including The Metropolitan Museum of Art, San Diego Museum of Art, Yale University, The Baltimore Museum of Art, and The Hirshhorn Museum & Sculpture Garden.

Butterfield works on her sculptures wearing gloves; she thinks of touch as more than just skin contact—it is a proprioceptive sense that communicates scale, mass, flexibility, and relationship between object and self. "For me the touch is a matter of moving, lifting, piling . . . it is a matter of the whole body, not just the hand . . . it is the same with riding horses. It is almost like a dance," she says. The sculptor feels that her works should be understood in the same way they are created, through the hands as well as through the eyes. The works that are not fragile and those that do not have a lot of sharp edges should be touched. "Certainly the people who own them, touch them," says Butterfield, speaking of private collectors. Reflecting back on the source of her inspiration, Butterfield notes that "we think about horses in terms of handling, we measure horses in hands . . . my horse is six hands tall" (Butterfield 2013).

MATERIALIZATION OF EPHEMERAL PHENOMENA IN NEW MEDIA ART

Scottish artist and designer Geoffrey Mann creates objects that deal with intangible phenomena such as flight, sound, and breath, which he makes into material objects that can be explored through the senses. "Intangible is a common theme in my work. I am curious about things I cannot touch. It is perhaps a reaction to how the world has become digital . . . I want to touch everything," he says. As someone whose work involves digital technology,

Figure 5.3.   Cross-Fire teapot, Natural Occurrence series by Geoff Mann, Bone China, 30 x 22 x 23 (cm). Photo by Stuart Johnstone

3D scanning, and printing, Mann feels compelled to explain that he uses technology not for its sake but in a "humanizing way."

His "Flight" series comprises sculptures that are based on long-exposure shots of birds in flight. The movement of the bird wings is so fast that it is not accessible for sighted people, in addition to blind people. One of these artworks was a part of the BlindArt show in London and New York, where it could be touched by both blind and sighted patrons. "It is a common denominator. I cannot see flight," says Mann. The artist remembers the experience of watching visitors explore his work at the BlindArt exhibit in London: "The touch was beautiful, so sensitive and so explorative at the same time." Most of his work these days is not made for touch, but because it deals with movement and time, it often requires a whole body exploration. His "Dogfight" series are blocks of glass that have elegant traces of two flies' flight engraved and suspended in them. Mann often observes people wondering around the pieces, walking around the four sides of the rectangular glass, trying to find the right angle to see, sometimes sharing their own camping experiences and fly stories. Mann admits that the work invites touch and often comes back from being exhibited with fingerprints all over the glass, which are "a nightmare to clean."

The artist makes no secret of the fact that it is his own curiosity that drives his work: "I did not know what flight looked like. I was curious. I wanted to get a better sensory experience, to make it tangible." Mann says that his basic rule of thumb is that if he knows what the object will look like, he will not make it: "There is no excitement for me as an artist . . . I want as much excitement as the viewer." Mann says that the reason he has not mass-produced his objects is because he gets easily bored.

"What does sound look like?" is another question Mann asked himself—not the scientific representation of a sound wave, but something that carries the emotive quality of the human voice that will help us relate to the sound on a human level. Through the use of digital technology, Mann simulates how objects such as tableware can be transformed by the voices around the table. The sound waves leave an imprint on cups and pots and transform them forever. The resulting work might be a teapot that is "disfigured" by the sound of an angry human voice, but Mann says that although it might not be aesthetically pleasing to some, it is "a true representation of an intangible [a quarrel around the table]" (Mann, 2013).

Mann used a similar process of blowing on a teacup and imprinting himself in the final ceramic object that is now transformed by his breath: "It is actually me. It is as close to self-portrait as I get. It is also an honest self-portrait." Mann explains that if he worked in another medium, like paint, he would be compelled to revise his self-portrait all the time. "I like using my breath or my sound, it will embody me truthfully. The sound itself is very honest, very raw." In fact, through his app, which is available on iTunes, he made the process of creating such self-portraits accessible to anyone who has access to 3D printing. Now you, too, can create a touchable self-portrait of your breath on a cup.

THE TACTILE MUSEUM

In a culture that privileges sight and where modern Western museums emerged in the nineteenth century as "museums of sight" (Classen and Howes, 2006), it is the work of blind advocates that led to the creation of a handful of tactile art and history museums around the world, among them Museo Omero in Ancona, Italy; Museo Tiflologico in Madrid; and the Tactile Museum at the Lighthouse in Athens, Greece. These museums are parallel universes where everything on view is touchable. Most of them were originally designed by and for blind art and culture patrons, or championed by a local blindness advocacy group. Similarly, projects such as the Touch Gallery at the Louvre Museum—a touch gallery of casts in a major art museum—were also created in an effort to offer some equality of experience to museum visitors who are blind. However, although the original museum narrative might have been to offer touch experiences to visitors who are blind, the vast majority of the current visitors to these museums and touch galleries are sighted, and the educational narratives reflect this change.

Tactile museums exhibit touchable plaster, fiberglass, and bronze replicas, scale architectural models, and original works of art. Some feature regular exhibits of contemporary artists whose works can be explored through touch. Museo Omero—translated as Homer's Museum—was founded in 1993 and is one of only three art and history museums in Ancona, and thus an important destination for both local residents and tourists. Visitors and tours are not limited to those who are blind or have low vision (Trasatti, 2013). In fact, out of almost 17,000 visitors in 2012, only 390 were people with some degree of vision loss. So, if the museum was originally established to tell the Italian history of art through touch to people who could not access it otherwise, what does it offer to thousands of other visitors?

Today Museo Omero educators see their collection as "a three-dimensional art history handbook" for everyone. Museo Omero follows the extensive tradition of cast fabrication and collecting that became popular in nineteenth-century museums. Some of those cast collections are still in use or on view: The Cast courts at the Victoria and Albert Museum feature one of the most impressive cast collections. Many university museums have teaching cast collections that they acquired or inherited from art museums. The chronologically organized collection of Museo Omero includes casts of Michelangelo's Pietà and Moses as well as original works by well-known Italian twentieth-century sculptors such as Francesco Messina and Arnaldo Pomodoro.

The museum takes its role as a regional art center seriously and works closely with and promotes contemporary Italian sculptors, many of them local, asking them to create works that can be explored through touch. Educators build their tours and experiences on the strength of this encyclopedic collection, and the ability to discuss history while the visitors run their hands over the scale models of Rome's architectural monuments or replicas of artifacts. They have the luxury of juxtaposing works of art that physically will never be in the same space. Such experiences are akin to the exploration of the teaching collections used by many early universities and university museums.

Educators at the Tactile Museum in Athens, which also welcomes mostly sighted visitors, a majority of whom are school groups and tourists, begin their tours with an introduction to the five senses as well as a discussion of blindness. The educational narrative includes issues of disability awareness, disability history, the everyday lives of blind people, and the history of Braille (Karavinou, 2013).

The Touch Gallery at the Louvre Museum opened in 1995. It is a public gallery that features thematic exhibits of touchable replicas of works from the museum's collection. The exhibit typically includes about fifteen works in bronze, terracotta, and plaster, and changes every couple of years. The themes are varied and in the past have included explorations of animals as symbols of power and movement in ancient Greek and Roman art. The Louvre touch collection has become so popular that in 2005 it began traveling abroad; since then, approximately thirty exhibits based on the Louvre touch collection have taken place in Europe, Asia, and Latin America. They drew crowds in China, where 40,000 visitors viewed and touched the exhibits in just one month. The museum sees such traveling touch exhibits as an opportunity to promote the Louvre collection abroad to art lovers who have not yet traveled to France or cannot afford to do so (Gouyette, 2013).

These days the Louvre's tactile gallery is often crowded, as it has become very popular with families with young children and elementary school groups. No doubt the draw is that this is one place where children can have their hands on art without upsetting the guards, their parents, or setting off alarms. In fact, the taboo on touching has been as good as lifted at children's museums, especially in exhibits for young children. This might have something to do with the wide acceptance of the benefits of sensory learning for very young children.

Philadelphia's museum for children ages seven and younger is called Please Touch Museum, where its name communicates the behavior it encourages in younger visitors. Similar to its counterparts in Brooklyn, Boston, and India-napolis, the Please Touch Museum has a collection to draw from for exhibi-tions and programs that leverage a child's curiosity. In exhibitions, objects can be found in unexpected containers designed to complement the exhibi-tions' themes. A display case guised as a tire or low tree stump is more of an invitation to encourage the curious visitor to take a closer look, rather than a warning to keep your distance. Objects come out of storage and protective cases in the KidGlove program, where staff invite children to handle objects drawn from the collection and organized into thematic groups. Wearing white mittens to mirror the cotton gloves worn by collection staff, children develop skills in careful handling of artifacts; make comparisons between objects in a group through similarities and differences in size and weight; and participate in conversations about caring for collections. Stacey Swigart, director of collections and content/curator, explains: "KidGlove [at] PTM allows kids to really investigate and explore their own curiosity about things they like (or discover that they like) or want to know more about! Layering in standards of learning in literacy, elements of science, technology, engi-neering, math and humanities provides a rich educational experience in a really fun environment" (Swigart, 2013).

WHAT IS (AND WAS) IT LIKE? STORIES THROUGH TOUCH

The Kaunas Museum for the Blind is a newcomer, established in 2005 in the dark basement of the Kaunas Garrison Church; it features a tactile exhibit of contemporary works by Lithuanian artists. However, from the start, the mu-seum's other important narrative has been to educate their majority of sighted visitors about the life and experiences of people who do not have sight. This idea follows the strong tradition of Dialogues in the Dark, a traveling exhibit project founded in Hamburg in 1988. Dialogues in the Dark is a simple and powerful exhibition concept that involves several rooms with different en-vironments ranging from boat to stores and cafés, that visitors navigate in complete darkness with the help of a blind guide. The exhibit has little to offer to blind or low vision people, with a notable and important exception of meaningful employment opportunities for blind guides. Although the vast majority of blind people around the world have some vision and do not live in complete darkness, exhibits such as Dialogues in the Dark and the Kaunas Museum shed light on a blind person's daily life. The most profound and memorable experiences reported are those associated with the visitor's own senses, sensory challenges, and social interactions in the dark.

Dialogues in the Dark provides visitors with the spaces and sensory experiences to consider, "What is it like?" Visitors to history museums bring a similar query when beginning their exploration of past places, "What was it like?" The objects on display to an extent become the visitor's guide to exploring the unseen past. The object was actually "there"—that supposedly real place called the past. Through close interactions with objects, children can begin to populate the spaces of the past with things made, owned, or used by the characters in the stories of history.

In a student workshop titled "The Wonderful World's Fair" at the Chicago History Museum (Chicago, Illinois), children create their own narratives of "what it was like" to visit the 1893 World's Columbian Exposition. History happened somewhere and the past was a place. Working in small groups, children develop a sense of place as they locate and mark on a map of the fairgrounds their destination, such as the Agriculture Building, the Women's Building, and the Manufacturing Building—and analyze photographs of the building's interior and exterior to identify what they might have seen. The dimensionality of this past place takes form as reproductions and objects from the education department teaching collection and an unexpected exhibition experience are incorporated into the unfolding narrative. Through the narration of a skilled facilitator and grasping a reproduction of a fair ticket, children close their eyes as they are transported back to 1890s Chicago and are transformed into visitors to the fair. Students' understanding of "what it was like" is further enriched by each team receiving an actual fair souvenir ranging from a Heinz pickle pin to commemorative spoons with engraved images of fair buildings, offering hands-on analysis of three-dimensional objects and a tactile dimension to their day at the fair. The culminating experience of interacting with objects occurs when the group steps inside the centerpiece for the exhibition, Chicago: Crossroads of America—L Car no 1, one of the original fleet built to take visitors to the fair. The students' relationship with objects shifts as they are now inside an artifact. As classmates read aloud selections from two fair guide books written for children who actually visited the fair, students have a richer understanding of "what it was like" through personal connections to artifacts. Children become part of the narrative, and the past no longer seems so empty a place.

TOUCH AS DISCOVERY

Does a tactile experience always require an interaction with three-dimensional objects, or can a visitor have a tactile experience with a story? In the

Minnesota History Center (St. Paul) exhibition, Open House: If These Walls
Could Talk, design, interpretation, and experience converge in a space that
allow visitors "to make it their own" (Filene, 141). The exhibition chronicles
the stories of the residents who called 470 Hopkins Street home from 1888 to
the present. Galleries are transformed into rooms representing different eras
of the house's history. A parlor, dining room, bedroom, kitchen, and attic are
among the settings. But, unlike the visitor experience of standing on the outside and looking (or rather staring) into the traditional period rooms found in
many art and history museums, the visitor plays a more active role in making
connections to the past.

By entering the exhibition, the museum visitor becomes a guest of 470
Hopkins Street, and the museum's galleries become familiar domestic settings inviting the guest to explore, interact, and discover. Open House initiates a different exchange between the museum and the visitor. Rather than
an interpretive approach that favors the museum's voice through labels, the
visitor experience allows for the residents of Hopkins Street to come forward
and tell their own stories. Chris Husbands emphasizes that the telling of stories about the past is not a one-way exchange between the teacher and the
student, the teller and the listener. The teacher as teller must remain true to
accuracy, authenticity, and breadth of perspectives and versions for any one
story. The story in history is lost if the listener does not pose questions, offer
interpretations, examine authenticity (Husbands, 1996, 50–51).

The spaces are not literal installations of the rooms of Hopkins Street, nor
are they filled with artifacts from the History Center collections or loans from
former residents. Instead, period appropriate objects and furnishings create
immersive environments for the visitor and containers for the residents' stories. Benjamin Filene, former senior exhibit developer, explains that Open
House was never about the artifacts. The authentic evidence was in the stories
of the residents (Filene, 2013). The stories are embedded in the rooms and it
is through touch that they are revealed.

A visitor's curiosity initiates the exchange, and through interacting—sitting on a bed or a dining room chair, opening a refrigerator door or lunchbox,
cranking a meat grinder, or reaching for a coin—the visitor's actions cause
a reaction. The visitor's payoff is the surprising response that reveals another story, and the space becomes populated with another resident. Stories
are communicated through innovative techniques such as media programs
projected onto dinner plates and mirrors, and quotes appearing on sausages
and milk bottles. Filene reflects on the powerful outcome of the exchange
between visitor and resident: "Open House started as an effort to give voice
to forgotten people in history; in the end, it allowed visitors to recognize that
they themselves have something to say!" (Filene, 2011, 139).

TOUCH AS HANDS, BODY, AND MOTION

When considering the sense of touch, we tend to connect it to actions that involve the hands. But touch is associated with the largest of the sensory organs and covers the entire body (Ackerman, 1991, 64–98). The body can provide similar connections to the past through broadening the interpretation of history to include multimodal experiences.

Educational theorist Kieran Egan, professor at Simon Fraser University (Burnaby, BC, Canada) and founder of the Imaginative Education Research Group, explores the role of the imagination in teaching and learning through drawing on cognitive (or cultural) tools that effectively engage a child in meaning-making. The Theory of Imaginative Education organizes the cognitive tools into five kinds of understanding based on how a child learns to use language (from pre-linguistic to oral and written)—Somatic, Mythic, Romantic, Philosophic, and Ironic (Egan, 1997). The body emerges as a critical tool for making sense of the world and new experiences: "Somatic understanding is corporeal, physical, bodily understanding. The child's own body, the way that body moves around in space, and the way it relates to the objects and persons it encounters in the space are the primary tool, the first way of making sense of experience. Sight, hearing, touch, taste, and smell provide the child with information about her or his own body, and about her or his immediate environment" (Ruitenber, 2006). By acknowledging the function a child's body plays in exploring and meaning-making, a history museum or any museum is able to incorporate a child's affinity to movement and motion into the interpretive experience rather than label it as inappropriate museum behavior.

When creating its premier exhibition for a new children's gallery, the Chicago History Museum made several notable design choices to ensure an accessible space for children. The gallery's prime location off the main lobby makes it a bright and colorful marquee for families and children. In the exhibition Sensing Chicago, each sense has its own space. Through testing and observing children, the project team realized that whole-body experience had to be a child's introduction to the senses, that they should not hold children back with lengthy instructions. Instead, in the Touch exhibit, children intuitively know to climb onto the high-wheel bike or sit in the seats of old Comiskey Park. Whole-body challenges introduce children to other senses as they hop onto colored floor spots to activate sounds or lie down in a poppyseed bun to become a Chicago-style hot dog. "Doing" history takes on a new meaning for children as they engage their minds and bodies in experiences that incorporate the imagination and play into the interpretive process.

TOUCH AS AN INTIMATE EXCHANGE

Constance Classen describes the seventeenth- and eighteenth-century museum as a "gymnasium for the senses," lacking the velvet ropes and glass cases that dictate the visitor's proximity to the collection. Instead, a more intimate exchange was created, with the curator acting as the "gracious host" offering guests the opportunity to touch and handle the collection (Classen, 2012, 137–38). Through experimenting with new interpretative approaches and program design, the staff of Jane Addams Hull-House Museum are making the velvet ropes and cases invisible as they extend a gracious welcome to Jane Addams' west side residence and to her life and career as a settlement worker, reformer, author, and winner of the Nobel Peace Prize. Issues of social, economic, and cultural reform that Addams fought for throughout her career are made relevant to a contemporary audience through programs and exhibits that remain true to the progressive reform that defined her vision for Hull House. The Rethinking Soup monthly program brings together participants and presenters to share soup and perspectives on food-related issues, and true to the original program, the return of the Art Lending Library invites individuals to "check out" original works of contemporary art for a three-month installation in their own homes. These and other initiatives are collectively defining the museum's form of interpretation, "radical hospitality." The vision of Addams becomes timeless and a visit to the settlement house becomes as much about the present as it is about stepping back in time.

The Alternative Labeling Project pushes the boundaries of the visitor experience through questioning the traditional format and voice of exhibition labels as well as how visitors interact with a historic house. Guest artist Terri Kapsalis focuses her research and the visitor experience on a small, unobtrusive personal item, Jane Addams' travel medicine kit. Her interpretation appears not in a traditional label on the wall but instead is reproduced in a small journal. Both the medicine kit and the journal are displayed next to each other on a small shelf in Jane Addams' bedroom. While the medicine kit sits out of reach under a protective case, the journal is available for visitors to pick up and read. Mark Smith notes the shift of the sensory experience of reading a book from a solely visual experience to also one of tactile dimensions: "Books were, and are, held, carried, opened, thumbed, fingered, and stroked," (Smith, 2007, 93).

Just as Addams welcomed thousands of immigrants to Hull House, the staff also invites visitors to have a more intimate experience with the medicine kit. By appointment, a visitor can sit in a rocking chair in Addams' bedroom next to the medicine kit and leisurely read the "alternative label" from the journal. As the essay reveals the rarity of the travel medicine kit, the illnesses and ailments Addams suffered throughout her life, and her tireless career as a humanitarian, staff serves the visitor a cup of tea. Though the visitor never actually touches the kit nor meets Addams, the combined elements of this experience—the immersive environment of Addams' bedroom; the tactile engagement of rocking chair, journal, and tea cup; and the exchange between visitor and staff—create an intimate and highly personal moment that is not bound to the present or the past.

FOOD FOR THOUGHT: THINGS TO CONSIDER WHEN TELLING STORIES THROUGH TOUCH

We know that audiences desire touch experiences. When taken on touch tours, we have witnessed many a case of museum envy when museum staff observe visitors who are blind touching sculpture. Most recently, Nina Levent took part in a tour at a museum in Dallas where a docent described a marble female figure by Rodin to a visitor who was blind. It turned out that the blind visitor had been given a touch tour of the work on her previous visit. She then proceeded to explain to a stunned group of docents what the texture of marble was like in dark cavities formed by the bending figure. Parts of the sculpture are in deep shadow and thus are inaccessible through sight, but having touched it, she could testify to its curved shape and rough and unfinished surface. When another major art museum had an idea of expanding its touch tours to mixed groups of blind and sighted visitors, the tours were sold out immediately—filled by the museum's own staff from various departments. We know from the popularity of behind-the-scenes events at history museums that visitors seek the "intimate encounter" with artifacts that Classen describes in seventeenth- and eighteenth-century museums, "the thrill of coming into vicarious contact with their original creators and users" (Classen, 2012, 141).

Objects are being handled in makeshift "museums" in refugee camps, period rooms and tactile experiences bring hospital patients and elderly visitors in touch with their memories, and prison outreach museum programs allow participants to interact with objects and themes connected to artworks (O'Sullivan, 2008; Samuels, 2008; Pye, 2008). Embodied explorations of anthropology collections can prompt dynamic emotional and intellectual connections; these experiences are supported by storytelling, music, and art making (Golding, 2010).

What are the stories that can be told through touch and handling? What are the important considerations of museums, artists, and historians as storytellers? When constructing an exhibition narrative around museum objects that can be touched or handled, there are a few critical issues to keep in mind: the object's authenticity, connecting the touch experience to the meaning of the work, and understanding that the senses are a cultural as well as a natural phenomenon.

There is a valid concern among the historians of the senses that when recreating history through the senses, museums need to acknowledge that we do not possess the same sensory apparatus as the people in the past. Senses are much more than neutral perceptual instruments given to all of us by nature; they are products of cultural convention and historical contracts. Smells, sounds, tastes, and textures that were exotic a couple of centuries ago are no longer so (Smith, 2007, 117–32).

As skeptical and savvy consumers of the past, visitors, both young and old, frequently ask, "Is it real?" Objects are unique in their abilities to traverse the boundaries of time. In their timelessness, they are all that remains of an event, and to an extent, by being in their presence, the visitor is brought a little closer to that event and moment in time. In seeking verification that the object is "real," the sense of touch is a critical tool, and this is something museum conservators know only too well (Pye, 2008). Authenticity is critical in the relationship between a history museum and a visitor. Studies show that notions of objects being "true," "actual," "real" are important to visitors. Nonauthentic experiences in one study were described as commercial, fake stuff, made in China, Disneyland fictionalized. Anything that made visitors feel cheated of accuracy angered them (Wilkening and James, 2009, 138).

Museums pride themselves on their collections of authentic objects with real provenance. The practice of using reproductions is still a matter of some debate (Saunderson et al., 2010). When a replica, a scale model, a faithful reproduction, a restored part of a structure is explored, the issue of authenticity should be addressed in the narrative, as well as using alternative materials, tools, and process. In history and art museums, more often than we know, we encounter objects that were fully or partially restored, or replicas of missing originals. It does not have to take away from the richness of the story. An important issue is around creating a narrative that connects that action of touching and handling to the storyline of the exhibit, historical context, or in case of art, meaning of artwork and artists' intent.

Touch and handling is a part of our daily routine, but hands are not just the workhorse of the sensory toolkit. Touch is also a means for communicating with and connecting to other people: We wave hello to friends, shake the hands of strangers, gently pat the back of a crying child, and extend a hand to steady the gait of an older adult. It is not surprising that when visiting a history museum, we are drawn to tactile exchanges with objects. All objects, including museum objects, hold a bit of mystery in their ability to defy and traverse the boundaries of time. In their purest definition, artifacts were made, owned, or used by someone. By touching or just being in close proximity to objects, visitors feel a little closer to someone of the past. Kiersten Latham has described such highly personal exchanges or "transactions" between visitors and objects as "numinous experience," a unique, almost spiritual sensation in the presence of museum objects (Wood and Latham, 2009, 24).

When artists such as Sol LeWitt pioneered the idea of a museum owning the concept or certificate but not the object, some argued that it served to "dematerialize" art. But this movement also opened an opportunity for new art narratives, in which the works were handled, used, walked through, touched, and recreated by each visitor, and then the museum was offered the option of either recreating the work or letting it disintegrate. Dan Graham, Yoko Ono, Gonzalez-Torres, James Turrell, and Andy Goldsworthy followed this tradition (Pheby, 2010). Touch, movement, and hands-on engagement with the subject of art also allow artists to suggest narratives, stories, and questions that engage with social issues and everyday life. The art of Mel Chin, Vic Muniz, Rafael Lozano-Hammer, and Ai WeiWei is a socially engaged practice that used touch and other senses to address issues of poverty, environmental catastrophe, social inequality, value of community, and beauty.

The tactile engagement of visitors with both history and art museums is creating highly personal dialogues with museum collections. At the same time, artists and museum staff are returning to the "gracious hosts approach" as they step aside to allow space for the visitor to become part of the interpretive and creative process.

REFERENCES

Ackerman, Diane. (1991). *A Natural History of the Senses*. New York: Vintage.

Butterfield, Deborah. (2013). Interview with author.

Candlin, Fiona. (2008). Museums, modernity and the class politics of touching objects. In Chatterjee, Helen (ed.), *Touch in Museums: Policy and Practice in Object Handling*. Oxford: Berg, 9–20.

Cannon, Joanna. (2011). Duccio and devotion to the Virgin's foot in early Sienese painting. *A Wider Trecento: Studies in 13th- and 14th-Century European Art*. Leiden and Boston: Brill.

Chambers-Letson, Josh Takano. (2010). Contracting justice: the viral strategy of Felix Gonzalez-Torres. *Criticism,* (51)4, 559–87.

Chatterjee, Helen J., ed. (2008). *Touch in museums: Policy and Practice in Object Handling.* Oxford: Berg.

Classen, Constance, ed. (2005). *The Book of Touch*. Oxford and New York: Berg.

———. (2012). *The Deepest Sense: A Cultural History of Touch.* Urbana: University of Illinois Press.

———. (Summer 2007). Museum manners: the sensory life of the early museum. *Journal of Social History* (40)4, 895–914.

Classen, Constance, and Howes, David. (2006). The museum as sensescape: western sensibilities and indigenous artefacts. In *Sensible Objects: Colonialism, Museums and Material Culture,* Elizabeth Edwards, Chris Gosden and Ruth Phillips, eds. Oxford: Berg Publishers.

Egan, Kieran. (1997). *The Educated Mind: How Cognitive Tools Shape Our Understanding.* Chicago: The University of Chicago Press.

Filene, Benjamin. (2011). Make yourself at home—welcoming voices in Open House: If These Walls Could Talk. In Bill Adair, Benjamin Filene and Laura Koloski (eds.), *Letting Go? Sharing Historical Authority in a User-Centered World,* pp. 138–55. Philadelphia: The Pew Center for Arts & Heritage.

———. (2013). Director of public history/associate professor, University of North Carolina–Greensboro, conversation and personal communication with co-author.

Golding, Viv. (2010). Dreams and wishes. The multisensory museum space. In Sandra H. Dudley (ed.), *Museum Materialities. Objects, Engagements, Interpretations,* pp. 224–40. New York: Routledge.

Gonzalez-Torres, Felix. (1993). Interview with Joseph Kosuth.

Gouyette, Cyrille. (2013). Chef de l'unité education artistique, Musée du Louvre. Interview with author.

Howes, David, ed. (1991). *The Varieties of Sensory Experience: A Sourcebook in the Anthropology of the Senses.* Toronto: University of Toronto Press.

Husbands, Chris. (1996). *What Is History Teaching?: Language, Ideas and Meaning in Learning about the Past.* Buckingham, PA: Open University Press.

Johnson, Geraldine. (2002). Touch, tactility, and the reception of sculpture in early modern Italy. In P. Smith and C. Wilde (eds.), *A Companion to Art Theory,* pp. 61–74. Blackwell.

Juette, Robert. (2005). *A History of the Senses. From Antiquity to Cyberspace.* Cambridge, UK: Polity Press.

Junkins, Lisa. (2013). Interim director, Jane Addams Hull-House, Chicago, IL. Personal communication with co-author.

Kapsalis, Terri. (2012). "Jane Addams' Medicine Kit" for the Alternative Labeling Project, Jane Addams Hull-House Museum, http://www.uic.edu/jaddams/hull/_museum/_exhibits/Alternative%20Labeling/alternativelabeling.html.

Karavinou, Argyro. (2013). Tactual Museum of the Lighthouse for the Blind of Greece. Interview with author.

Mann, Geoffrey. (2013). Interview with author.

Mergel, Jen. (2013). Interview with author.

O'Sullivan, Jackie. (2008). See, touch, and enjoy: Newham University Hospital's Nostalgia Room. In Helen Chatterjee (ed.), *Touch in Museums: Policy and Practice in Object Handling.* Oxford: Berg.

Pheby, Helen. (2010). Contemporary art. An immaterial practice? In Sandra H. Dudley (ed.), *Museum Materialities. Objects, Engagements, Interpretations,* pp. 224–40. New York: Routledge.

Pye, Elizabeth, ed. (2008). *The Power of Touch: Handling Objects in Museum and Heritage Context.* Walnut Creek, CA: Left Coast Press.

Reich, Christine, Lindgren-Streicher, Anna, Beyer, Marta, Levent, Nina, Pursley, Joan and Mesiti, Leigh Ann. (2011). SPEAKING OUT ON ART AND MUSE-UMS: Study on the Needs and Preferences of Adults Who Are Blind or Have Low Vision. Report, April 2011.

Romanek, Devorah and Lynch, Bernadette. (2008). Touch and the value of object handling. In Helen Chatterjee (ed.), *Touch in Museums: Policy and Practice in Object Handling*, pp. 275–86. Oxford: Berg.

Ruitenber, Claudia. (2006). What Is Imaginative Education? http://ierg.net/about/whatis.html (last modified November 5, 2006).

Ruitenber, Claudia and Mark Fettes, ed. (2006). Imaginative education: an introductory expotition. Imaginative Education Research Group portal: What Is Imaginative Education? http://ierg.net/about/whatis.html#intro (last modified November 5, 2006).

Samuels, Jane. (2008). The British Museum in Pentonville Prison: dismantling barriers through touch and handling. In Helen Chatterjee (ed.), *Touch in Museums: Policy and Practice in Object Handling*. Oxford: Berg.

Saunderson, Helen et al. (2010). The eyes have it. Eye movements and the debatable differences between original objects and reproductions. In Sandra H. Dudley (ed.), *Museum Materialities. Objects, Engagements, Interpretations*. New York: Routledge.

Smith, Mark M. (2007). *Sensing the Past. Seeing, Hearing, Smelling, and Touching in History*. University of California Press.

Swigart, Stacey A. (2013). Director of collections and content/curator, Please Touch Museum. Personal communication with author.

Trasatti, Annalisa. (2013). Museo Omero. Interview with author.

Wilkening, Sussie and Chung, James, eds. (2009). *Life Stages of the Museum Visitor: Building Engagement over a Lifetime.* Washington DC: AAM Press.

Wood, Elizabeth and Latham, Kiersten F. (2009). Object knowledge: researching objects in the museum experience. *Reconstruction*, (9)1.

Part II

MUSEUMS AND SOUND

6

A Brain Guide to Sound Galleries

Stephen R. Arnott and Claude Alain

Imagine yourself sitting at the edge of a lake on a peaceful summer's evening. With the setting sun glinting off the water and the waves lapping at the shore, the moment is undeniably beautiful. But what if all sounds—the bird songs, the rustling tree leaves, the rhythmic surf—were removed? Would the moment be just as enjoyable? It certainly would be different, for sound not only provides salience to visual events but it informs us of objects and events outside of our field of view. Sound "colors" our world, adding a dimension to our perceptual experience that none of the other four senses ever truly capture. Precisely how this comes to be has, at its roots, everything to do with how auditory information is processed in our brains. While our conscious awareness of sound's importance is often overshadowed by the shear amount and prominence of visual information around us, we become keenly aware of it in instances of auditory illusions or in situations where our vision is rendered useless (e.g., camping on a cloudy night; walking out of a dark room and into bright sunlight, and so forth).

Perhaps some of the best insight into the world of sound comes from those who have lost their vision permanently such that their distal world is almost entirely created from sound alone. In his memoir entitled *Touching the Rock: An Experience of Blindness*, John Hull, an Australian theologian who became totally blind by his mid-forties, wrote about sound and how rainfall enabled him to "see" again.

> I opened the front door, and rain was falling. I stood for a few minutes, lost in the beauty of it. Rain has a way of bringing out the contours of everything; it throws a coloured blanket over previously invisible things; instead of an

85

intermittent and thus fragmented world, the steadily falling rain creates continuity of acoustic experience . . . I hear the rain pattering on the roof above me, dripping down the walls to my left and right, splashing from the drainpipe at ground level on my left, while further over to the left there is a lighter patch as the rain falls almost inaudibly upon a large leafy shrub. On the right, it is drumming, with a deeper, steadier sound upon the lawn. I can even make out the contours of the lawn, which rises to the right in a little hill . . . I think that this experience of opening the door on a rainy garden must be similar to that which a sighted person feels when opening the curtains and seeing the world outside . . . If only rain could fall inside a room, it would help me to understand where things are in that room, to give a sense of being in the room, instead of just sitting on a chair . . . This is an experience of great beauty. (Hull, 1990, pp. 22–24)

As astonishing as Professor Hull's ability may seem, every hearing individual possesses a similar skill that while perhaps not as well-honed, nevertheless enables him or her to become implicitly aware of and appreciate surrounding objects and the environment. One may be surprised to learn for example, that even when blindfolded we are still adept at detecting the proximity of a wall as we walk toward it (Supa, Cotzin, and Dallenbach, 1944), or that from the sound alone, we are able to know when to stop filling a container with water so as to prevent it from overflowing (Cabe and Pittenger, 2000). Indeed, in an offshoot of Edward Wilson's "biophilia" hypothesis that underscores the impact that thousands of years of evolution in natural settings has had on our hearing abilities and preferences (Wilson, 1984), the argument has been made that our very health and well-being is improved by the presence of natural sounds and detrimentally impacted by the lack of it (c.f., Depledge, Stone, and Bird, 2011; Lechtzin et al., 2010).

Over the last century and especially in the last couple of decades, significant progress has been made in our understanding of sound perception and the auditory system. While the system is best thought of as one designed under the evolutionary pressure to process behaviorally relevant sounds (Barlow, 1961), it has become increasingly recognized that brain areas devoted to audition, as well as other sensory information, are not so rigidly defined as was once thought (Pascual-Leone and Hamilton, 2001). As auditory neuroscientists, we present this chapter with the intent to highlight these principles and to do so in a manner that inspires artists and curators to celebrate this wonderful medium. To begin though, it is necessary to have at least a rudimentary understanding of the auditory system (refer to figure 6.1). The interested reader is directed to much more detailed accounts (Cohen, Popper, and Fay, 2012; Moore, 2012; Yost, 2007).

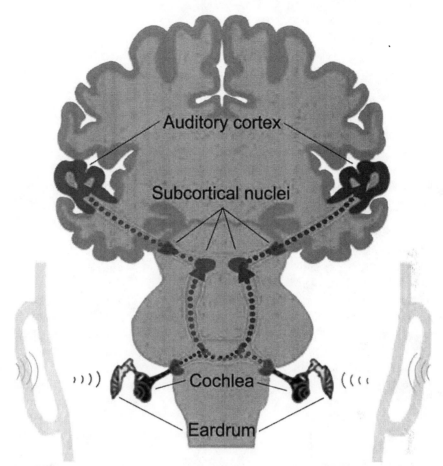

Figure 6.1. Schematic of a coronal view of the human brain that encompasses different relays in the ascending auditory system, beginning with sound input into the ear
canals and cochlea, up through various nuclei in the brainstem, and finally up into the
left and right auditory cortices in the temporal lobes of the brain.

SOUND PERCEPTION AND AUDITORY PROCESSING

What would you think if someone asked you to determine, based only on the
water ripples at the edge of an adjoining inlet, whether there are any boats out
on the ocean? Not only that, but to determine how many boats were out there,
what types of vessels they were, and where they were located? As outrageous
as this may seem, it is in many ways analogous to the task that our auditory
system faces (and successfully accomplishes) on a moment-to-moment basis
as an endless parade of overlapping sound waves travels down our ear canal.

Simply put, sound perception is the registration in our brain of distur-
bances in surrounding air pressure. Whenever molecules vibrate back and
forth, as when the diaphragm of a loudspeaker rapidly pushes forward and
moves backward, or when your heel strikes a marble floor, the air pressure
changes radiate outward from the point of collision like water ripples from
a coin tossed into water. While the speed of sound vibration is quite rapid
(hundreds of meters per second through air and even faster through water or
solid objects), it pales in comparison to the speed of light (millions of meters
per second), as is apparent from the timing delay of distant audiovisual events
like thunder and lightning. And like water ripples moving outward from a
coin thrown into water, the air pressure changes will weaken with increasing
distance from the source. If these pressure changes are sufficiently strong
when they reach a person's ear, they will travel down the ear canal and cause
the eardrum to vibrate as well. These vibrations are transferred into the fluid
of a snail shell–shaped structure inside the head called the cochlea. Inside the
cochlea, running its entire coiled length is a thin membrane that will ripple
with the vibrations. Owing to the membrane's graded stiffness, the location
of maximum ripple varies along the membrane depending on how fast (high
frequency) or slow (low frequency) the vibrations are.

In addition, sound pressure changes can be transferred into the cochlea by
other, non-eardrum means. For example, because the cochlea is encased in
bone attached to the skull, vibrations in the skull bone can also set the membrane into motion, leading to the perception of sound (plug your ears and tap
your head if you need convincing). It is also precisely for this reason that our
own voice inevitably sounds strange to us when we hear it over a speaker or
earphones: The voice that we hear from the speaker lacks the audio richness
that bone conduction provides when we are talking.

Due to the physiology of the auditory system, vibrations that are too slow
or fast (typically below 20 or beyond 20,000 times a second) will not be
registered no matter how intense (~loud) the vibrations are. Furthermore, by
age eighteen, most people have begun to show signs of age-related hearing
loss, or *presbycusis*, in which the maximum rate of vibration that we can
hear begins to fall off. For example, by age thirty most people can no longer
hear frequency rates above 15,000 times per second (i.e., 15,000 Hertz (Hz)),
and by age fifty we can no longer hear above 12,000 Hz (Davis and Silverman, 1960). The causes of this hearing loss are numerous (e.g., cumulative
effects of repeated exposure to loud noises, changes in blood supply to the
ear, conductive disorders of the outer and middle ear, and so forth) and they
may exert their effects at a number of stages along the auditory pathway.
While such frequency loss is generally not a major concern in many hearing
situations (the important frequency information contained in speech, for example, lies between 300-3,400 Hz), it does start to pose a problem when the

presbycusis is advanced and/or when the sound signal is very faint or is in competition with other background noise. Interestingly, some entrepreneurs have taken advantage of this age-related hearing change to design antisocial sound deterrents for youth like sonic alarms that blast a 17,400 Hz tone at 108 dB out front of storefronts where loitering is a problem (for information and demonstrations, see "The Mosquito" alarm at www.movingsoundtech. com). Although inaudible to older adults, people below the age of twenty-five years experience the alarm as an uncomfortably loud, high-pitched tone. Conversely, this principle has also been employed as a youth advantage (e.g., creating mobile phone ringtones that adults cannot hear). Within the context of a museum of sounds, curators should keep relevant sound information below frequencies of 8,000 Hz in order to be heard by the general population. However, exhibits specifically designed for youth could incorporate frequencies between 15,000 and 20,000 Hz.

It is important to realize that any sound in the environment is almost always registered by both ears, thus two copies of the sound will be relayed to the brain. Depending on the location of the sound source (i.e., closer to the left ear or right ear) there will be *very* slight frequency, intensity, and timing differences between these two auditory signals (on the order of fractions of a millisecond). Although we are consciously unaware of these very small interaural acoustic differences, our auditory systems use the information to localize sounds in the environment.

Returning to our account of the ascending auditory system, it is within the cochlea that the mechanical vibrations are transformed into chemical and electrical signals that the brain can understand. Specifically, whenever the membrane in the cochlea moves, tiny hairs lying immediately below it bend and send a signal through the auditory nerve up into the brain. In a deceptively simple yet elegant manner, individual frequency information contained within complex sounds is extracted in the cochlea based on the location of the ripples along its membrane, and then faithfully relayed up through the lower brain, terminating in tonotopically (i.e., ~pitch) organized brain regions on the left and right sides of the brain in an area of the temporal lobe known as the auditory cortex. By comparison, the majority of visual information input is sent to the back of the brain in the occipital lobe, while touch (somatosensory) information travels to the top sides of the brain in the parietal lobe.

CORTICAL AUDITORY PROCESSING

The primary auditory cortex is the first cortical region of the auditory pathways and its chief function is to "transform" auditory sensation into sound perception. Damage to the primary auditory cortex can impair a person's ability to hear, discriminate, localize, and/or recognize verbal as well as nonverbal sounds. In addition to being tonotopically organized, the auditory cortex shows hierarchical organization such that bands of neurons surrounding the core respond to increasingly complex sounds (i.e., from pure tones to speech sounds, Kaas and Hackett, 2000). Research has also established that, as one moves outward from the auditory cortex, sound object recognition (what it is) and localization (where it is) are preferentially processed along two parallel processing streams in ventral and dorsal brain regions, respectively (Alain, Arnott, Hevenor, Graham, and Grady, 2001; Rauschecker, Tian, and Hauser, 1995; Romanski et al., 1999). For instance, brain damage to the temporal lobe (ventral) often yields deficits in identifying sounds but has little impact on a listener's ability to localize the sound source (Clarke et al., 2002). Conversely, damage to parietal (dorsal) cortices impairs sound localization but leaves sound identification abilities intact (Clarke et al., 2002). Lesions to the right parietal cortex may also cause auditory neglect, which is a deficit in noticing sounds that occur in the left hemispace (Bellmann, Meuli, and Clarke, 2001; Heilman and Valenstein, 1972).

More recently, accumulating evidence also hints to an "action" pathway that responds preferentially to sounds associated with body movements, such as the sound of paper being crumpled in someone's hands (Arnott, Cant, Dutton, and Goodale, 2008), hand tools being operated (e.g., drill, hammer, etc. Lewis, Brefczynski, Phinney, Janik, and DeYoe, 2005; Lewis, Phinney, Brefczynski-Lewis, and DeYoe, 2006), or in the case of vocal production, spoken words (Rauschecker and Scott, 2009). In addition, nonverbal sounds such as yawning (Arnott, Singhal, and Goodale, 2009) or laughing and crying (Sander and Scheich, 2001) generate enhanced cortical activity in brain areas thought to be related to action understanding. Whether the neural activity triggered by action sounds is a byproduct of associative learning or in fact indexes higher order functions, like learning new skills or understanding the goals and intentions of others, is currently the topic of much controversy (Gazzola, Aziz-Zadeh, and Keysers, 2006; Hickok, 2009).

Apart from helping the listener understand the "what" and "where" of sounds, the way in which our brains analyze auditory input can also directly affect our emotions. Music is a wonderful example of this, with fast tempo and major chords being categorized as "happy," whereas those of slow tempo and minor chords are more likely to be rated "sad" (Dalla Bella, Peretz, Rousseau, and Gosselin, 2001; Pallesen et al., 2005; Peretz, Gagnon, and Bouchard, 1998). Underscoring the importance of such auditory features, brain imaging research has found that when people listen to "emotional" relative to "neutral" music, there is not only increased activity in the areas of the auditory cortex responsible for processing these sound features (Brattico et al., 2011) but evolutionarily older brain areas known as the limbic and paralimbic systems located deep in the temporal lobes are also consistently modulated (Koelsch, 2010). These brain regions are thought to play a central role in determining a person's emotional state, given the profound emotional dysfunction that individuals exhibit following damage to these brain regions (Dalgleish, 2004). Within the limbic system is an almond-shaped structure known as the amygdala, which plays a key role in the detection, generation, initiation, and maintenance of emotion as it relates to survival (Price, 2005) and memory for events (Markowitsch and Staniloiu, 2011). When the amygdala is damaged or removed, as can happen with complications from epilepsy or encephalitis, one of the behavioral deficits often observed is an inability to recognize fear from music (Gosselin, Peretz, Johnsen, and Adolphs, 2007). Some researchers have described the structure as being important for tagging particular memory events with an emotional valence (e.g., the assassination of JFK or the September 11 attacks). While happy music can decrease amygdala activity, sad music is particularly effective at increasing the activation (Adolphs and Tranel, 2004; Mitterschiffthaler, Fu, Dalton, Andrew, and Williams, 2007), possibly because it conjures up distressing memories.

Nonmusical sounds also elicit emotional responses. Listening to aversive sounds such as fingernails being raked across a blackboard, or a knife scraped across a bottle, activates the amygdala (Kumar, von Kriegstein, Friston, and Griffiths, 2012), as does the sound of crying (Sander and Scheich, 2001). Differential brain responses have even been found within sound types. For example, human laughter can be considered emotional in some contexts (e.g., joyful laughter, taunting laughter), whereas it has been considered to play more of a nonemotional role in other situations (e.g., tickling laughter). Compared to tickling laughter, emotional laughter evokes more activity in frontal brain regions (Szameitat et al., 2010), presumably reflecting the increased demands on social awareness. In a similar manner, audio recordings of people yawning have been found to activate inferior frontal cortical regions of listeners (Arnott et al., 2009), with this activity level increasing as the yawns become more "contagious" (i.e., more likely to elicit a yawn from the observers).

To summarize then, the way in which we decipher complex auditory scenes is dependent on the successful transfer and decoding of sound pressure waves from the auditory nerve up to the primary auditory cortex, as well as a widely distributed set of brain regions that work in concert during identification (what) and localization (where) of sound objects. Moreover, the involvement of additional brain areas is determined by the particular nature of each complex sound, with some action sounds stimulating motor regions responsible for carrying out motor actions, while other areas tap into emotion states, memories, and social and communicative brain processing regions. As will be evident in the next section, nonauditory inputs can also substantially influence how sounds are processed and, when faced with the loss of sensory input (e.g., the loss of visual input to the occipital lobe in blind individuals), these sensory regions can also begin to respond to auditory input. For now, we will turn to a discussion of sound illusions.

AUDITORY ILLUSIONS

With a basic understanding of auditory processing in hand, we are now in a position to discuss some auditory illusions that could easily be implemented as museum exhibits. These illusions can be thought of as "mistakes" from which we can learn how the brain organizes and interprets auditory scenes. They can be divided into two major categories. The first type arise because of limits or constraints within the auditory system, such as hearing a pure tone "passing" through a broadband noise, even when the tone is not playing (i.e., continuity illusion). Illusions may also occur because visual stimuli "capture" the sound, such as in the ventriloquist effect described below. By no means is the list exhaustive, but it provides a glimpse of phenomena that could provide the foundation for a sound gallery. Audio examples of these illusions are readily available online.

Scale Illusion

The scale illusion, one of many auditory illusions discovered by cognitive psychologist Diana Deutsch (1975), is a compelling example of how the brain groups similar notes together using tone frequency (~ pitch). Listeners are presented with the notes of two major scales (one ascending in frequency, the other descending), which alternate from ear to ear such that the right ear hears the first note of one scale, and then the second note of the other. The stimuli are usually presented through stereo headphones, but the effect can also be achieved with loudspeakers placed some distance apart on the left and right side of the listener.

People listening to such stimuli often report hearing a descending and re-ascending melody in one ear, and an ascending and descending melody in the other ear. Put another way, the brain reorganizes some of the notes to a different ear in order to make a coherent melody. There is some indication that right-handed people tend to hear the high melody in the right ear and the low one in the left, while left-handers show a more diverse response (Deutsch, 1975).

Continuity Illusion

Just as we tend to interpret a line as continuous even when a portion of it is obscured by another object (e.g., perceiving a roadway or power line as intact even when it is partially obscured by a high-rise building), sound events are also perceived as continuous even when momentarily obscured by another, louder sound event (e.g., the sound of a distant train whistle that is momentarily masked by the "caw" of a nearby crow). An interesting illusory example of this continuity effect occurs when a brief pure tone is played at regular intervals (e.g., "beep, beep, beep") and then a noiseburst sound is added to the silent intervals between tone beeps. When the noiseburst is made sufficiently loud, the tones no longer sound separate, but are perceived as one entire (i.e., continuous) tone with a pulsing noiseburst being played at the same time. Recent research indicates that such illusions are associated with the reduction of a particular brain rhythm within the auditory cortex (Riecke et al., 2012), which in the future could serve as a way to alter the resistance of the auditory system to extraneous noise or sudden pitch changes.

Stereo Effects

Stereo sound files created from audio recordings using in-ear microphones, or by manipulating stereo sound files with head-related transfer functions (i.e., audio filters that replicate how an ear receives a sound from a particular point in space), can also be used to create amazingly realistic illusions of an external auditory environment when played back over stereo headphones. Among many, two of the more convincing head-related transfer function stereo effect illusions available online are the "Matchbox Rattle" and the "Virtual Barbershop" (QSounds Labs, Inc.). While the former provides a very vivid experience of a shaking matchbox being moved around one's head, the latter creates the uncannily realistic experience of sitting in a barber's chair while the barber operates his scissors around your head. So convincing is this illusion, that listeners may experience goose bumps as the illusory hair clipping shears are brought close to the ear!

Pseudophone

Another interesting illusion occurs when left and right ear sound inputs are artificially reversed. This can be achieved using a pseudophone (figure 6.2a) such that the left ear hears what the right ear normally hears and vice versa. For instance, listeners may be presented with speech from two different talkers: one male on the left and one female on the right. With their eyes closed, the listener will perceive the male as if he was standing to the right and the female as if she was positioned to the left. However, when that same person wearing the pseudophone opens their eyes and sees the talkers, the positions of the talkers will no longer be heard as reversed (Young, 1928). In other words, sight overrules what the ears are hearing in this case.

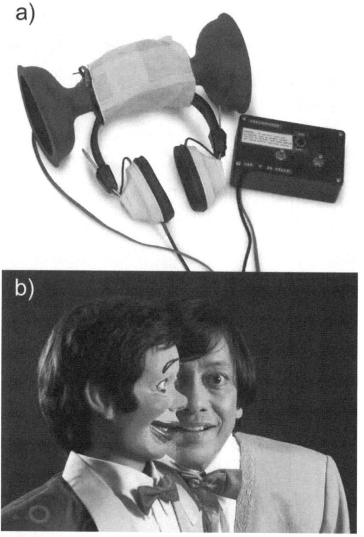

Figure 6.2. a) The Pseudophone. A home-made device created by Professor Raymond C. Bice Jr. comprised of headphones combined with two "ears" from which sound is redirected to the opposite headphone. b) Ventriloquist Ramadas Padhye with his puppet, Ardhavatrao. Courtesy of a) *University of Virginia Magazine;* b) Indiapuppet

The pseudophone example reminds us that our perception of the auditory environment is highly influenced by what we see. A more well-known example of this is the ventriloquist effect where a sound is perceived to emanate from one location (e.g., a puppet's mouth), when in fact it is being generated at a different location (e.g., the puppeteer's mouth; figure 6.2b). The illusion results from the overriding spatial influence of a simultaneously occurring visual event and is another example where vision appears to "capture" sounds, thereby causing a mislocation of sound source. Interestingly, in ventriloquist lab experiments where participants have been subjected to a consistent audiovisual spatial disparity for an interval of ten minutes or more, a ventriloquist aftereffect is observed such that sounds presented in a dark room are subsequently mislocalized for a period of time in a direction that coincides with the disparity of the previously trained visual stimulus (Lewald, 2002; Recanzone, 1998). Moreover, the aftereffect is frequency-specific. That is, if the ventriloquism illusion had been experienced with a 1,000 Hz tone, a 4,000 Hz tone subsequently localized in the dark would *not* be mislocalized like the 1,000 Hz tone would be. Though the aftereffect is not long lasting, it suggests that the representation of acoustic space in the brain can be (temporarily) recalibrated by a disparate visual experience.

McGurk Effect

Another example of visual capture occurs when the lip movements of a person speaking a particular word are paired/dubbed with the voice of that person speaking a different word, a phenomenon known as the McGurk effect (McGurk and MacDonald, 1976). For example, when a /ga/ sound is played at the same time that a silent video of a person speaking the syllable /ba/ is observed, a good portion of people will report hearing the entirely new sound of /da/. Similarly, the sound of the word "tough" presented with the lip movements for "hole" will sometimes result in the perception of hearing "towel" (Dodd, 1977). Interestingly, not all people are susceptible to McGurk illusions, and researchers have recently found that activity in a brain region just behind and below the left auditory cortex predicts whether or not they will experience the McGurk effect (Nath and Beauchamp, 2012).

This is not to say that vision always dominates auditory perception. For example, when two identical animated balls move toward each other, they are perceived to bounce back off one another if a sound (e.g., a click) occurs at the time of contact. Without the sound, the balls appear to "pass over" one another (Sekuler, Sekuler, and Lau, 1997). Another example of sound influencing vision is the "sound-induced flash illusion," where a single flash of light is perceived as multiple flashes when it is presented at the same time as multiple auditory beeps (Shams, Kamitani, and Shimojo, 2000).

In general, auditory processing trumps visual input when it comes to rapid temporal processing, whereas vision tends to influence audition when it comes to spatial mapping. The reason for these effects lies largely within the neural architecture of the visual and auditory systems. Unlike the auditory system, which as we have reviewed earlier, creates spatial perception and sound source locations through a comparison of the interaural timing, frequency, and amplitude differences, the visual system has a direct mapping of two-dimensional visual space based on where the light falls on the back of the eye. What is more, this spatial organization of visual information (i.e., retinotopic organization) is maintained as the neural information travels to the back of the brain, such that objects in the left visual field will preferentially activate the right visual cortex and objects in the right visual field will stimulate the left visual cortex. No such topographic map of auditory space has been found in the human brain, and hence the more reliable map of space often lies within the visual system. On the other hand, when one considers our ability to process and understand speech and music, it is apparent that our auditory system is exquisitely good at temporal processing, which is critical for separating rapidly occurring events. This auditory temporal advantage may stem in part from having a greater number of subcortical nuclei compared to those devoted to the visual or somatosensory pathways, because having more subcortical nuclei increases the opportunity for establishing early simultaneous, parallel processing of the incoming information (Camalier and Kaas, 2011). As a general rule, the perception of multimodal events is thought to be more heavily influenced by the modality that contains the most reliable information (Alais and Burr, 2004). In an offshoot of this, our perception of very weak, sub-threshold visual stimuli such as the appearance of a light gray object on a light gray background, can often be enhanced by yoking its appearance to an auditory event (Bolognini, Frassinetti, Serino, and Ladavas, 2005).

SOUND AND THE ENVIRONMENT

To this point, we have discussed sound perception in terms of just the sound itself. However, some mention should be given to the fact that the environment and objects within it can substantially shape or alter the sounds that we hear. A good example of this is Eusebio Sempere's sculpture *Órgano*, in which metal tubes of different lengths are vertically mounted on a rotating base (see figure 6.3a). Designed to dynamically filter and reflect sunlight, it was later realized that the periodic arrangement of the tubes formed a phonic crystal structure such that impinging sound waves of a particular frequency (i.e., around 1,600 Hz) underwent a destructive interference that greatly attenuated their transmission through the sculpture (Martínez-Sala et al., 1995;

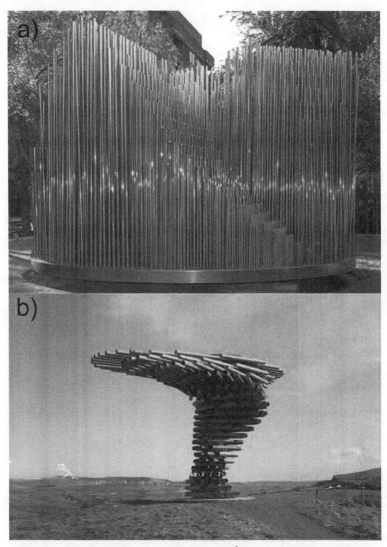

Figure 6.3. a) Eusebio Sempere's sculpture, *Órgano*. In addition to filtering light waves, the arrangement of the steel tubes serves to selectively filter particular sound frequencies, thereby altering what a listener hears. b) *The Singing Ringing Tree* in the Pennine mountain range overlooking Burnley, in Lancashire, England. Designed by architects Mike Tonkin and Anna Liu, the piece consists of galvanized steel pipes of various lengths stacked horizontally on top of one another such that it resembles a life-size windblown tree. Owing to the fact that the pipes are oriented in different directions, multiple notes will be heard onsetting/offsetting at different moments in time and fluctuating in volume depending on the prevailing wind that constantly changes strength and direction. a) Reprinted by permission from Macmillan Publishers Ltd., *Nature*, 378, p. 241, copyright 1995. b) Photo by Daniel Childs

Thomas, 2009). As a result, complex sounds occurring on the other side of the sculpture (e.g., a person's voice) are heard as dramatically different from what they otherwise would be if the structure were absent.

Interestingly, the field of archaeoacoustics suggests that the design of sound-shaping sculptures by humans may have a much longer history than previously thought. For example, some researchers maintain that the unusually high risers in the stairs of the ancient Mayan pyramid of Kukulkan were designed so that the echoes from handclaps would sound like the chirp of the sacred Quetzal bird. Similarly, others claim that the locations of prehistoric rock paintings made in the caves of Font-de-Gaume and Lascaux in in France may have been chosen because the echoes of handclaps made at those particular locations mimicked the sounds that the animals in the paintings made (e.g., the galloping sound of horses). Whether such occurrences are the result of intentional design or mere happenstance is certainly debatable. On the other hand, both examples demonstrate the potential that sound echo information has for communicating information. Importantly, the echo information need not be so obvious in order to be of use to a listener. As it turns out, our auditory system is very good at extracting information from subtle echoes that we may not even be aware of.

ECHOES: "SEEING" WITH SOUND

With the exception of highly reverberant environments like stairwells, cathedrals, or canyons where the timing delays between a given sound and its reflected echo are quite apparent, echo information often goes unnoticed and is in fact actively suppressed by our brains (Cremer, 1948; Wallach, Newman, and Rosenzweig, 1949). This is desirable in many instances because not only is the echo information largely redundant, but it could lead to errors in sound source localization if misinterpreted as another sound source. However, as subtle as they may be, echoes—especially those that are purposely elicited by a listener—contain a rich array of information that the brain can use to glean information about the environment and the location and identity of objects present within it. In the next section, we will describe these echo abilities in greater detail.

ECHOLOCATION AND HUMANS

The ability to echolocate is well known in the animal kingdom, especially for those that inhabit low-light environments. Many types of bats and cave-dwelling birds, for instance, use echolocation in low-light conditions to avoid obstacles and hunt flying insects. Similarly, dolphins and other small-toothed whales are known to navigate their waterways with echolocation. While bats and birds produce sounds using vocal chords and then detect the echoes through their ears, dolphins produce a series of rapid click sounds through a structure in their forehead (the melon), detecting returning echoes in their jaw bone and in their head. But what about humans? Can we use echoes to perceive objects? As should be apparent from the opening paragraphs of this chapter, the answer to this question is an emphatic "yes." Nowhere is this more evident than in the extraordinary echolocation skills exhibited by some visually impaired individuals.

The notion of humans being able to echolocate was first discussed centuries ago, having its roots in the term "facial vision." The French philosopher Denis Diderot, for example, in his "Letter on the Blind" of 1749, documented the amazing ability of "the blind man of Puisaux" who was "so sensitive to the least atmospheric change, that he could distinguish between a street and a closed alley" (Jourdaine, 1916, 78). At the time, Diderot thought that such feats were accomplished by the person's ability to sense an object's presence through the effect of the air on heightened nerves in the face and end-organs. This ability became known as "facial vision" and the belief persisted well into the twentieth century, when a series of experiments by Karl Dallenbach made it evident that it was actually sound perception that was responsible for much of what had been termed facial vision. In Dallenbach's experiments, blind and sighted blindfolded individuals were asked to walk toward walls, stopping as close as they could without colliding. Interestingly, both groups were able to execute this successfully, albeit with superior performance being exhibited by the blind. Next, in an attempt to "defeat" this facial vision, a number of manipulations were carried out, including the unsuccessful attempt of placing a hood over the person's head and covering all exposed skin so as to block the skin receptors from detecting any "air-waves." Participants were still able to detect the presence of the wall. The clearest impedance to performance occurred, however, when the person's hearing was occluded with ear muffs, eliminating the sound of footsteps and ambient noise. So impressive was this ability to detect the presence of the wall through sound alone, that when one of the experimenters held a microphone and walked toward the wall, one of the blind individuals listening to the audio recording through headphones in another room was able to tell the experimenter when to stop before he collided with the wall.

Today, thanks in large part to media coverage and scientific interest, awareness that a segment of the blind/low vision population consciously use echolocation to sense their surroundings has increased dramatically. While many intentional sounds can be used for the purpose of eliciting echoes from the environment (e.g., the tapping of a cane, footsteps, hand claps, finger snaps, vocalizations, and so forth), the most versatile, resilient, and informative stimulus seems to be mouth clicks produced by placing one's tongue against the back of the teeth or the roof of the mouth and then rapidly pulling it away so that the rush of air into the low-pressurized pocket creates a popping sound (Rojas, Hermosilla, Montero, and Espi, 2009). One of the more celebrated cases of human echolocation was that of Ben Underwood, an American teenager who would use the mouth-click sound not just to identify objects but to run, skateboard, ride a bike, and play basketball and table football. Other notable echolocaters include Tom De Witte, Dr. Lawrence Scadden, Lucas Muray, Kevin Warwick, Brian Bushway, and Juan Ruiz. But perhaps the most well-known ambassador for echolocation is American Daniel Kish. Kish has been echolocating since he was a toddler, after having his eyes removed at age one due to retinoblastoma. Like Underwood, Kish incorporated echolocation in his everyday activities to augment his awareness of his immediate and distal environment. So helpful and adaptable is this skill to the visually impaired that Kish and other orienting and mobility instructors within Kish's not-for-profit organization, World Access for the Blind, enthusiastically promote and instruct active echolocation (i.e., flash sonar) to others.

But what are the neural factors that underlie such abilities? Given the auditory nature of these stimuli, a good guess would be that the auditory cortex of these echolocaters has become more highly tuned to echo information. After all, the auditory cortex has been shown to be important for separating sounds that overlap in time, generating the same characteristic electrical waveforms that have also been found during echo processing (Alain, Arnott, and Picton, 2001; McDonald and Alain, 2005; Sanders, Zobel, Freyman, and Keen, 2011). To answer this question, we placed microphones into the ears of blind expert echolocaters and recorded what their ears heard when they made mouth clicks at various silent objects in the environment (e.g., a lamp post, a car, a tree). Those audio recordings not only captured the sound of the mouth click itself but also the subtle echoes that bounced back to the ears off of surrounding objects. When such recordings were played back into the blind expert's ears, they were accurately able to identify the silent object that was present when the recording was made, even as they lay on their backs inside a functional magnetic resonance imaging (fMRI) machine. Surprisingly, functional brain activity recorded as they carried out these tasks showed, in addition to auditory cortical activity, activation in brain areas normally reserved for visual processing in sighted people (i.e., occipital cortex; Arnott, Thaler, Milne, Kish, and Goodale, 2013; Thaler, Arnott, and Goodale, 2011). The most interesting finding, however, occurred when this activity was compared to that associated with listening to the same recordings but with the very faint echoes artificially removed. While the activity in auditory cortices was the same in both instances, the activity in occipital cortex was much greater in the intact recordings. The gist of these neuroimaging results then is that brain areas typically reserved for the processing of visual information in sighted people have actually been adapted to process echo information in blind echolocation experts.

Not only that, but we have further shown that the type of occipital activation depends in part on the particular type of object feature that is being extracted from the echo recordings (Arnott et al., 2013). In effect, the echo information is being processed in a feature-specific rather than a general manner. For example, when the listener was either asked to report the shape of the object or the object's surface covering (e.g., aluminum foil or a soft towel), the shape task resulted in greater activity in areas of the occipital cortex typically associated with visual shape processing. In fact, much of the way in which this auditory echo information was processed appeared consistent with the way that visual information is processed in sighted individuals. These results suggest that the auditory system (and the human brain in general) is highly plastic (i.e., able to modify according to experience) and is not nearly as functionally rigid as was once thought. It also suggests that brain areas originally dedicated to a particular modality can be recruited by another sensory modality to enrich the perceptual experience.

Interestingly, echolocaters listening to mouth-click echolocation recordings from other echolocaters are not only able to "see" silent objects but are able to physically experience particular perspectives of the other person. For example, when we presented outdoor echolocation recordings from one blind echolocating expert to another blind echolocating expert who was several inches shorter, the latter could not only detect and identify the silent object that had been present during the recording, he remarked that he felt closer to the tree canopy than he had when he listened to the same recordings made from his own ears. This suggests that it may be possible to share remote echo experiences with other people who are adept at echolocation, simply by playing back in-ear click-echo recordings.

What about sighted individuals? Can those people echolocate too? In fact, it has been shown that after only one or two hours of practice, novice sighted listeners can acquire echolocation skills (that is, determining a silent object's size and position from mouth click echo information; Teng and Whitney, 2011). Although the sighted individuals did not reach the same level of performance as did the blind experts, in the particular tests that the researchers carried out the sighted individuals attained a level of echolocation proficiency that certainly rivaled that of the blind echolocation experts (Teng and Whitney, 2011). While these results may seem surprising, recall that blindfolded humans asked to approach a wall are actually quite good at stopping just prior to collision when relying only on auditory input (i.e., echo information; Supa et al., 1944). In this regard, the subject of echoes and silent object perception offers interesting and fruitful possibilities as a museum exhibit.

SENSORY SUBSTITUTION DEVICES

An alternative way of seeing with sound is through the use of electronic devices that convert visual information into sound (Ciselet, Pequet, Richard, Veraart, and Meulders, 1982; Heyes, 1984; Hughes, 2001; Kay, 1964) One of the better known devices designed for the blind (the vOICe; Meijer, 1992) consists of a pair of a cameras mounted on a pair of glasses, a transducer device, and a pair of earphones. Every second, the device converts the camera's image (i.e., the visual scene immediately in front of the user) into a stereo soundscape that is played through the earphones. The sound of the converted image is one that sweeps from the left ear to the right ear over a one-second duration, corresponding to the left-to-right axis of each visual image. The loudness of the sound corresponds to the brightness of the visual scene (e.g., black color is associated with no sound, whereas bright contrasts like white correspond to the maximum amplitude), and elevation in the visual image is represented by pitch (low pitch represents the bottom of the visual image, high pitch represents the top of the visual image). Consequently, one can imagine that a museum patron wearing such a sensory substitution device and standing, for example, in a dark room in front of an illuminated yellow bar running diagonally from the bottom left of her visual field to the upper right, would hear a left-to-right tone that steadily increased in pitch. A similar bar positioned from the top left to bottom right would have a steadily decreasing pitch, and a bar that had a left-to-right brightness increase (e.g., from black to vivid yellow) would also have a steady rise in loudness over each one-second sweep. Like the echolocation work, functional imaging research examining brain activity associated with this type of auditory processing implicates brain areas normally associated with *visual* processing (Amedi et al., 2007). Further information and examples, including a free download of the software, are available at http://www.seeingwithsound.com.

CONCLUSION

In the preceding sections, we have discussed certain facets of hearing research. Our aim was not to be exhaustive but rather to explore how auditory neuroscience may inform and guide us in developing a sound gallery. The way neuroscientists think about sounds has changed tremendously in the past two decades. Research has grown from the study of individual acoustic features toward a focus on understanding how the brain processes entire soundscapes, and how it is able to separate and identify the various sounds in the environment by allocating attention to auditory objects of interest. Without in any way minimizing the more obvious notions of aural art such as notes played by an orchestra or even a visual sculpture (see figure 6.3b), we hope that our discussion of auditory processing in the brain has prompted the reader to consider other aspects of sound and sound perception that they may not have before.

ACKNOWLEDGMENTS

This research was supported by grant MOP106619 from the Canadian Institutes of Health Research (CIHR) and a grant from the Natural Sciences and Engineering Research Council of Canada (NSERC) to Claude Alain.

REFERENCES

Adolphs, R., and Tranel, D. (2004). Impaired judgments of sadness but not happiness following bilateral amygdala damage. *Journal of Cognitive Neuroscience,* 16(3), 453–62.

Alain, C., Arnott, S. R., Hevenor, S. J., Graham, S., and Grady, C. L. (2001). "What" and "where" in the human auditory system. *Proceedings of the National Academy of Sciences of the United States of America,* 98(21), 12301–306.

Alain, C., Arnott, S. R., and Picton, T. W. (2001). Bottom-up and top-down influences on auditory scene analysis: evidence from event-related brain potentials. *Journal of Experimental Psychology: Human Perception and Performance,* 27(5), 1072–89.

Alais, D., and Burr, D. (2004). The ventriloquist effect results from near-optimal bimodal integration. *Current Biology,* 14(3), 257–62.

Amedi, A., Stern, W. M., Camprodon, J. A., Bermpohl, F., Merabet, L., Rotman, S., . . . Pascual-Leone, A. (2007). Shape conveyed by visual-to-auditory sensory substitution activates the lateral occipital complex. [Research Support, N.I.H., Extramural Research Support, Non-U.S. Gov't]. *Nature Neuroscience,* 10(6), 687–89. doi: 10.1038/nn1912.

Arnott, S. R., Cant, J. S., Dutton, G. N., and Goodale, M. A. (2008). Crinkling and crumpling: an auditory fMRI study of material properties. *Neuroimage,* 43(2), 368–78.

Arnott, S. R., Singhal, A., and Goodale, M. A. (2009). An investigation of auditory con-tagious yawning. *Cognitive, Affective and Behavioral Neuroscience,* 9(3), 335–42.

Arnott, S. R., Thaler, L., Milne, J. L., Kish, D., and Goodale, M. A. (2013). Shape-specific activation of occipital cortex in an early blind echolocation expert. *Neuro-psychologia,* 51(5), 938–49.

Barlow, H. (1961). Possible principles underlying the transformation of sensory mes-sages. In W. Rosenblith (Ed.), *Sensory Communication,* pp. 217–34. Cambridge: MIT Press.

Bellmann, A., Meuli, R., and Clarke, S. (2001). Two types of auditory neglect. *Brain,* 124(Pt 4), 676–87.

Bolognini, N., Frassinetti, F., Serino, A., and Ladavas, E. (2005). "Acoustical vision" of below threshold stimuli: interaction among spatially converging audiovisual inputs. *Experimental Brain Research,* 160(3), 273–82.

Brattico, E., Alluri, V., Bogert, B., Jacobsen, T., Vartiainen, N., Nieminen, S., and Tervaniemi, M. (2011). A functional MRI study of happy and sad emotions in music with and without lyrics. *Frontiers in Psychology,* 2, 308.

Cabe, P. A., and Pittenger, J. B. (2000). Human sensitivity to acoustic information from vessel filling. *Journal of Experiment Psychology: Human Perception and Performance,* 26(1), 313–24.

Camalier, C. R., and Kaas, J. H. (2011). Sound. In J. A. Gottfried (Ed.), *Neurbiology of Sensation and Reward.* Boca Raton: CRC Press.

Ciselet, V., Pequet, E., Richard, I., Veraart, C., and Meulders, M. (1982). Substitution sensorielle de la vision par l'audition au moyen de capteurs d'information spatial. *Archives Internationales de Physiologie et de Biochimie,* 90, 47.

Clarke, S., Bellmann Thiran, A., Maeder, P., Adriani, M., Vernet, O., Regli, L., . . . Thiran, J. P. (2002). What and where in human audition: selective deficits follow-ing focal hemispheric lesions. *Experimental Brain Research,* 147(1), 8–15.

Cohen, Y. E., Popper, A. N., and Fay, R. R., eds. (2012). *Neural Correlates of Audi-tory Cognition.* New York: Springer.

Cremer, L. (1948). *Die wissenschaftlichen Grundlagen der Raumakustik* (1 ed.). Stuttgart: Hirzel-Verlag.

Dalgleish, T. (2004). The emotional brain. *Nature Reviews Neuroscience,* 5(7), 583–89.

Dalla Bella, S., Peretz, I., Rousseau, L., and Gosselin, N. (2001). A developmental study of the affective value of tempo and mode in music. *Cognition,* 80(3), B1–10.

Davis, H., and Silverman, S. R. (1960). *Hearing and Deafness.* New York: Hold, Rinehart & Winston.

Depledge, M. H., Stone, R. J., and Bird, W. J. (2011). Can natural and virtual environ-ments be used to promote improved human health and wellbeing? *Environmental Science & Technology,* 45(11), 4660–65.

Deutsch, D. (1975). Two-channel listening to musical scales. *The Journal of the Acoustical Society of America,* 57(5), 1156–60.

Dodd, B. (1977). The role of vision in the perception of speech. *Perception,* 6(1), 31–40.

Gazzola, V., Aziz-Zadeh, L., and Keysers, C. (2006). Empathy and the somatotopic auditory mirror system in humans. *Current Biology,* 16(18), 1824–29.

Gosselin, N., Peretz, I., Johnsen, E., and Adolphs, R. (2007). Amygdala damage impairs emotion recognition from music. *Neuropsychologia,* 45(2), 236–44.

Heilman, K. M., and Valenstein, E. (1972). Auditory neglect in man. *Archives of Neurology,* 26(1), 32–35.

Heyes, A. D. (1984). Sonic Pathfinder: A programmable guidance aid for the blind. *Electronics and Wireless World,* 90, 26–29.

Hickok, G. (2009). Eight problems for the mirror neuron theory of action understanding in monkeys and humans. *Journal of Cognitive Neuroscience,* 21(7), 1229–43.

Hughes, B. (2001). Active artificial echolocation and the nonvisual perception of aperture passability. *Human Movement Science,* 20(4-5), 371–400.

Hull, J. M. (1990). *Touching the Rock: An Experience of Blindness*. New York: Pantheon Books.

Jourdaine, M. (1916). *Diderot's Early Philisophical Works* (M. Jourdaine, Trans.). Chicago: The Open Court Publishing Company.

Kaas, J. H., and Hackett, T. A. (2000). Subdivisions of auditory cortex and processing streams in primates. *Proceedings of the National Academy of Sciences of the United States of America,* 97(22), 11793–799.

Kay, L. (1964). An ultrasonic sensing probe as a mobility aid for the blind. *Ultrasonics,* 2, 53.

Koelsch, S. (2010). Towards a neural basis of music-evoked emotions. *Trends in Cognitive Sciences,* 14(3), 131–37.

Kumar, S., von Kriegstein, K., Friston, K., and Griffiths, T. D. (2012). Features versus feelings: dissociable representations of the acoustic features and valence of aversive sounds. *The Journal of Neuroscience,* 32(41), 14184–192.

Lechtzin, N., Busse, A. M., Smith, M. T., Grossman, S., Nesbit, S., and Diette, G. B. (2010). A randomized trial of nature scenery and sounds versus urban scenery and sounds to reduce pain in adults undergoing bone marrow aspirate and biopsy. *Journal of Alternative and Complementary Medicine,* 16(9), 965–72.

Lewald, J. (2002). Rapid adaptation to auditory-visual spatial disparity. *Learning and Memory,* 9(5), 268–78.

Lewis, J. W., Brefczynski, J. A., Phinney, R. E., Janik, J. J., and DeYoe, E. A. (2005). Distinct cortical pathways for processing tool versus animal sounds. *Journal of Neuroscience,* 25(21), 5148–58.

Lewis, J. W., Phinney, R. E., Brefczynski-Lewis, J. A., and DeYoe, E. A. (2006). Lefties get it "right" when hearing tool sounds. *Journal of Cognitive Neuroscience,* 18(8), 1314–30.

Markowitsch, H. J., and Staniloiu, A. (2011). Amygdala in action: relaying biological and social significance to autobiographical memory. *Neuropsychologia,* 49(4), 718–33.

Martínez-Sala, R., Sancho, J., Sanchez, J. V., Gomez, V., Llinares, J., and Meseguer, F. (Writers). (1995). Sound attentuation by sculpture, *Nature.*

McDonald, K. L., and Alain, C. (2005). Contribution of harmonicity and location to auditory object formation in free field: evidence from event-related brain potentials. *The Journal of the Acoustical Society of America,* 118(3 Pt 1), 1593–1604.

McGurk, H., and MacDonald, J. (1976). Hearing lips and seeing voices. *Nature,* 264(5588), 746–48.

Meijer, P. B. (1992). An experimental system for auditory image representations. *IEEE Transactions on Biomedical Engineering,* 39(2), 112–21.

Mitterschiffthaler, M. T., Fu, C. H., Dalton, J. A., Andrew, C. M., and Williams, S. C. (2007). A functional MRI study of happy and sad affective states induced by classical music. *Human Brain Mapping,* 28(11), 1150–62.

Moore, B. C. J. (2012). *An Introduction to the Psychology of Hearing.* Bingley: Emerald Group Publishing Limited.

Nath, A. R., and Beauchamp, M. S. (2012). A neural basis for interindividual differences in the McGurk effect, a multisensory speech illusion. *NeuroImage,* 59(1), 781–87.

Pallesen, K. J., Brattico, E., Bailey, C., Korvenoja, A., Koivisto, J., Gjedde, A., and Carlson, S. (2005). Emotion processing of major, minor, and dissonant chords: a functional magnetic resonance imaging study. *Annals of the New York Academy of Sciences,* 1060, 450–53.

Pascual-Leone, A., and Hamilton, R. (2001). The metamodal organization of the brain. *Progress in Brain Research,* 134, 427–45.

Peretz, I., Gagnon, L., and Bouchard, B. (1998). Music and emotion: perceptual determinants, immediacy, and isolation after brain damage. *Cognition,* 68(2), 111–41.

Price, J. L. (2005). Free will versus survival: brain systems that underlie intrinsic constraints on behavior. *The Journal of Comparative Neurology,* 493(1), 132–39.

Rauschecker, J. P., and Scott, S. K. (2009). Maps and streams in the auditory cortex: nonhuman primates illuminate human speech processing. *Nature Neuroscience,* 12(6), 718–24.

Rauschecker, J. P., Tian, B., and Hauser, M. (1995). Processing of complex sounds in the macaque nonprimary auditory cortex. *Science,* 268(5207), 111–14.

Recanzone, G. H. (1998). Rapidly induced auditory plasticity: the ventriloquism aftereffect. *Proceedings of the National Academy of Science: USA,* 95(3), 869–75.

Riecke, L., Vanbussel, M., Hausfeld, L., Baskent, D., Formisano, E., and Esposito, F. (2012). Hearing an illusory vowel in noise: suppression of auditory cortical activity. *The Journal of Neuroscience,* 32(23), 8024–34.

Rojas, J. A. M., Hermosilla, J. A., Montero, R. S., and Espi, P. L. L. (2009). Physical analysis of several organic signals for human echolocation: Oral vacuum pulses. *Acta Acustica United with Acustica,* 95(2), 325–30. doi: 10.3813/aaa.918155.

Romanski, L. M., Tian, B., Fritz, J., Mishkin, M., Goldman-Rakic, P. S., and Rauschecker, J. P. (1999). Dual streams of auditory afferents target multiple domains in the primate prefrontal cortex. *Nature Neuroscience,* 2(12), 1131–36.

Sander, K., and Scheich, H. (2001). Auditory perception of laughing and crying activates human amygdala regardless of attentional state. *Cognitive Brain Research,* 12(2), 181–98.

Sanders, L. D., Zobel, B. H., Freyman, R. L., and Keen, R. (2011). Manipulations of listeners' echo perception are reflected in event-related potentials. *The Journal of the Acoustical Society of America,* 129(1), 301–9.

Sekuler, R., Sekuler, A. B., and Lau, R. (1997). Sound alters visual motion perception. *Nature,* 385(6614), 308. doi: 10.1038/385308a0.

Shams, L., Kamitani, Y., and Shimojo, S. (2000). Illusions. What you see is what you hear. *Nature,* 408(6814), 788. doi: 10.1038/35048669.

Supa, M., Cotzin, M., and Dallenbach, K. M. (1944). "Facial vision": The perception of obstacles by the blind. *The American Journal of Psychology,* 57(2), 133–83.

Szameitat, D. P., Kreifelts, B., Alter, K., Szameitat, A. J., Sterr, A., Grodd, W., and Wildgruber, D. (2010). It is not always tickling: distinct cerebral responses during perception of different laughter types. *NeuroImage,* 53(4), 1264–71.

Teng, S., and Whitney, D. (2011). The acuity of echolocation: Spatial resolution in the sighted compared to expert performance. *Journal of Visual Impairment and Blindness,* 105(1), 20–32.

Thaler, L., Arnott, S. R., and Goodale, M. A. (2011). Neural correlates of natural human echolocation in early and late blind echolocation experts. *PLoS One,* 6(5), e20162. doi: 10.1371/journal.pone.0020162PONE-D-11-04391 [pii].

Thomas, E. L. (2009). Applied physics: bubbly but quiet. *Nature,* 462(7276), 990–91.

Wallach, H., Newman, E. B., and Rosenzweig, M. R. (1949). The precedence effect in sound localization. *The American Journal of Psychology,* 62(3), 315–36.

Wilson, E. O. (1984). *Biophilia.* Cambridge: Harvard University Press.

Yost, W. A. (2007). *Fundamentals of Hearing* (5th ed.). San Diego: Academic Press.

Young, P. T. (1928). Auditory localization with acoustical transposition of the ears. *Journal of Experiment Psychology,* 11, 399–429.

7

Ephemeral, Immersive, Invasive

Sound as Curatorial Theme, 1966–2013

Seth Cluett

BACKGROUND

From the silence encouraged by the museum to the environmental immersion of earthworks and other site-specific interventions, sound—or its absence—often marks both the means of production and the condition of reception of the work of art. More than a mere thematic concern, sound occupies a component position in the curation and production of works from painting and drawing to installation and web-based work. Regardless of medium or intent, the works need not be about sound directly but might make or engage sound as part of a multimodal whole. Most often, though, works produce sound as a consequence of the use of other materials and at the service of larger ideas. Whether highlighting the coded acoustics of the place of reception, the figuring of listening in representational practices, or the evocation of the acoustic-imaginary in conceptual art and music, sound can be worked as material, developed as medium, and can also function as support. By exploring this breadth of concerns, curatorial practices addressing the multimodal features of art open up a rich body of work to analysis, constantly expanding the discursive field surrounding the artistic deployment of sound.

The myriad complexities introduced to art practices by attending to the role of sound in art has led to generalizations, formalizations, and philosophical declarations that muffle the historical placement, artistic intent, or physical experience of the works themselves. Curators and theorists who champion sound as a defined artistic medium have problematically searched for precedents to legitimate the emergence of what is better understood as a constellation of diverse practices (Bosseur, 1993; Kahn, 2001; Kim-Cohen, 2009; Licht, 2007). Claiming the roots of a unified discourse of sound in the work of the historical avant-gardes—such as Futurism, Dada, and Surrealism, the iconoclastic praxis of the composer John Cage, as well as (mis)readings of the philosophy and techniques of the French Musique Concrète composers Pierre Schaeffer and Pierre Henry—has had the unintended consequence of reducing an open genealogy to a linear, positivist parentage. In searching for an originary moment for the emergence of a "sound art" as such, critics have stopped listening to the sound that art has been making for decades. Likewise, the indexing of works into categories such as sound-art, sonic art, *lydkunst*, *arte sonoro*, and *klangkunst*, while productively raising awareness and aiding research, has at the same time ghettoized practitioners and exposed a critical gap in the methodological tools available to the history and theory of art. Attending to soundworks as a crucial part with an irreducible whole will help avoid a counterproductive medium-specific myopia, while at the same time developing an inclusive vocabulary for reading each piece as a whole.

As sound is folded into the overall experience of artworks, the clarity with which its subjects, concerns, and expressions can be addressed in contemporary curatorial practice hinges on the ability of our theoretical models to account for information beyond the optical and haptic modes. An acknowledgment of the role of space and place in the production of works of art and music began in the 1990s, providing a vocabulary and critical tools to reassess practices back to the mid-nineteenth century. Histories and theories of both art and music have, in large part, focused on the other senses rather than incorporating them into existing discourse. This focus has left a deaf spot that, with the right reattention, might simultaneously integrate and counterpoint sound while recontextualizing the aesthetic sensorium.

There have been at least 350 sound-themed group exhibitions since 1966 (Cluett, 2013). This number can be broken down further into an initial constellation of about ten exhibitions between 1966 and 1972, followed by about three to five exhibitions per year until 1979, when another constellation of twenty or so exhibitions appears that lasts until roughly 1982. From 1982 on, the yearly count increases to ten to fifteen per year until a steady twenty exhibitions per year over the last fifteen years. These three stages—the initial flourish at the cusp of the late 1960s, then the build-up of exhibitions from 1979-1982, and lastly the last fifteen years of sustained practice—will inform the bulk of this chapter. While the present text is centered on the curation of group exhibitions, it should be noted that dozens of pieces, practices, and practitioners, and a substantial number of solo sound exhibitions, exist well before 1966. While the number of group-themed exhibitions may be small through the late 1960s and early 1970s, it is crucial to realize that the exhibition of work and the development of a vocabulary of sound in artistic practice is well underway during this time.

The identification of ephemeral, immersive, and invasive here refers to common ways of theorizing modes of acoustic reception: the fleeting temporality of the ephemeral nature of sound, the immersive saturation and envelopment of the body while listening, or the invasive inescapability of technologies and techniques of audition. And while these modes of reception have served regally as the topic of sound-themed group exhibitions, it has not been until recently that a critical lexicon has settled into place, allowing a shared discourse encouraging competing theories to emerge. As space doesn't allow for a thoroughgoing analysis of the subtleties of each exhibition and the curators' specific intent, and the written format prevents the handling of the objects themselves, a blurring of our historical eyes and an opening of our contemporary ears reveals a dynamic condensation of sensibilities where sound can be observed, engaged with, and in some cases lends the curatorial interests of the last fifty years.

This chapter will attempt to define three distinct states in the development of curatorial themes and sensibility related to sound primarily (and only pragmatically) in American curatorial practice. The initial stage represents an acknowledgment by curators around 1965/1966 that the art world is becoming increasingly soundful and that composers and choreographers are becoming consciously aware of the visual and performative potential of their work and ideas. The second stage is the emergence of a curatorial focus on the growing number of practitioners whose primary mode of expression involves sound in some way, a moment around 1980 that is very medium-conscious and aware of a somewhat shared vocabulary among artists. Lastly, and perhaps most difficult to articulate, begins a self-conscious awareness of something that might be described as a sound art (and a community of practitioners that describes themselves in that way)—a moment that happens in parallel with an increasing exploration of what sound affords practitioners, and goes on, in many ways as it began, with an excitement about the sound that things make, regardless of medium or stylistic affiliation.

EPHEMERAL: APPROACHING SOUND
AS CONCEPT AND PHENOMENON

In 1966, Ralph T. Coe, then curator of the Nelson Gallery of Art in Kansas City, Missouri, identified "Sound, Light, and Silence as the polarities of the late 1960s in art." In the exhibition catalog for the show of the same name, Coe identified the stylistic hallmarks of the decade leading up to 1966—Pop Art, Op Art, Kinetic, Minimal, Primary Structures, System or Process Art, Experiments in Art and Technology—and set out an agenda for an exhibition meant to "probe beneath themes to expose polarities of artistic production from which the art of the next decade may develop" (Coe, 1966).

This exhibition is remarkable neither for its notoriety nor for its having traveled widely and exposing the art world to sound as a medium, but rather for the timeliness with which a conscientious curator was able to assess and assemble the work of the era for consumption by the public. Citing Robert Rauschenberg's "Broadcast"—a combine construction that included three working radios and presented the viewer with knobs to tune the dial—as a pivot-point between the painting practices of abstract expressionism and pop art and the developing multimedia works that would initiate what Lucy Lippard would term the "dematerialization" of the art object in the years to follow (Lippard, 1997), Coe realized, like Rauschenberg had said, "that, listening happens in time, and looking happens in time" (Coe, 1966). It is this notion that art begins to embrace time and must be experienced that draws artists like Nauman, Morris, and Darboven to investigate the sound.

The Sound, Light, and Silence exhibition juxtaposed works by Rauschenberg, Stella, and Judd, with kinetic sculptures and films by Len Lye, a film by Andy Warhol, and a light and sound installation by Howard Jones. Coe understood sound not as a thematic unifying principle but as one of a number of common denominators for the ever-so-ephemeral experience of the art world of his time. Sound, like light, was for the 1960s gallery public the fleeting trace of the work that could not be captured by the catalog, work that had to be experienced—work that Coe would feel obligated to bring to the geographic center of the United States for Kansas City to experience firsthand.

The 1969/1970 season saw at least three exhibitions across the United States that treated the intersection of sound, system, or concept: Art by Telephone at the Museum of Contemporary Art in Chicago, the first exhibition at the San Francisco–based Museum of Conceptual Art started by the artist Tom Marioni, called Sound Sculpture As . . . , and The Sound Show exhibition at the American Museum of Contemporary Crafts in New York. Issues of documentation and distance, of real-time experience, and documents of action are themes that would continue to develop through the conceptual art practices of the late 1960s and early 1970s in the United States.

An illustration of this can be heard when Sol LeWitt picked up the telephone and dialed the number for the Museum of Contemporary Art in Chicago in 1968, and said:

Using a hard pencil draw a sixty-by-sixty-inch square on a wall. Draw the square into a grid of one-inch squares. Draw horizontal lines in some of the one-inch squares; draw vertical lines in some of the one-inch squares; draw diagonal lines from upper left to lower right in some of the one-inch squares; draw diagonal lines from lower left to upper right in some of the one-inch squares. The lines may be superimposed and some of the one-inch squares may be left blank. (LeWitt, 1969)

This telephone call is how LeWitt delivered "Variation on Wall Drawing #26" to the large-scale group exhibition titled Art by Telephone. Like contemporaneous explorations by Max Neuhaus, Keith Sonnier, and Maryann Amacher that exploited the technological potential of telephony, the exhibition took up themes at the heart of conceptual art as it was forming during the 1960s across the United States, and later in the decade in both Europe and Asia.

Art by Telephone presented work by thirty-seven artists whose instructions were received by the curator over the telephone and recorded; the preparators were then to construct the works in the space of the museum, following the directions explicitly. The museum produced a gatefold vinyl record accompanied by printed statements by the artists and an essay by the curator Jan van der Marck. This catalog was produced in a small edition that presented the unedited telephone calls from each of the artists to the museum. The record could then be used by anyone in possession of a turntable and a loudspeaker to execute the works on their own.

The distribution of the catalog as a long-playing record was a natural extension of the agenda of conceptual practices at the time. Referring to the role of the exhibition catalogue in the "communication (and dissemination) of conceptual art," curator Seth Seiglaub suggests that, "when art concerns itself with things not germane to physical presence, its intrinsic communication value is not altered by its presentation in [printed] media. The catalogue can now act as the primary information for the exhibition" (Buchloh, 1990). While the telephone enables two-way communication, and radio, broadcast distribution, the record offers repeatability. The work presented by Sol LeWitt loses nothing in the translation from transcription of a recorded phone call to the distributed record as catalogue; in both cases the loudspeaker enables the (re)presentation of his voice, allowing the transmission of his work.

Record-based artworks would continue through the 1970s—as evinced by Germano Celant's landmark exhibition the Record as Artwork at the Royal College of London in 1973 that traveled across North America in 1978. The record became a tangible object, alongside video and the compact cassette, that could capture the work of the artist in yet another modality, and in some cases would become a curatorial venue unto itself.

In a way, the urgency Ralph T. Coe felt as he presented the poles of Sound, Light, and Silence is set to rest by the catalogue for Art by Telephone. The experience of immediacy of a mass-producible media for artistic expression at the very least enabled repeatability for what would in the gallery be ephemeral.

IMMERSIVE: SOUND AS ARTISTIC MEDIUM

For many curators, the now-iconic exhibition Für Augen und Ohren, curated by Rene Block in 1980 at the Akademie der Künste in Berlin, stands as a milestone in the curation of soundworks. What is less well known is that this exhibition would ripple throughout the continent, either traveling in smaller form to the Museé Nationale d'Art Moderne in Paris as Ecouter par les Yeux, or as inspiration for the Sound Re:Visited exhibition at Time Based Arts in Amsterdam. Less familiar still are a series of events in the years leading up to 1980 in the United States that serve as the first survey of sound practices up to that point in North America. These exhibitions are an explicit acknowledgment of the increasing volume of sound in the growing multimodal, mixed media, and burgeoning installation practice of what had traditionally been understood as the visual arts.

This story begins at Artist Space in New York City, which has been one of the most consistently influential gallery spaces in the United States since its opening in 1973. The mission of Artists Space began from the premise that artists would curate the work of other artists—a common practice now, but novel for its time and place. This open, immediate curatorial practice would, in the years leading up to 1980, start a dialogue about the role of sound in the arts that would travel back and forth three thousand miles between New York City and Los Angeles.

Artist Space opened its doors for only three exhibitions in 1973. During its first full season in 1974, however, they produced Liz Philips' "Sound Structures" installation, as well as Laurie Anderson's first solo exhibition, curated by the video and performance artist Vito Acconci. Later, they went on to present the California-based artist Michael Brewster's first New York solo exhibition, Acoustic Sculpture and a Clicker Drawing, in 1977. At the time of the Brewster exhibition, the director, Helen Winer, was planning a large exhibition of sound work called A Sound Selection: Audio Works by Artists (Rosen, 1980).

The exhibition consisted of a number of listening stations that allowed for the playback of edited reels of tape as well as vinyl-based pieces. Four installations were also presented—two by Rhys Chatham and Scott Johnson, as well as a telephone installation by Beth B and a silent work by Bill Beirne— and a series of performances, including one by John Zorn, paralleled the exhibition. In the same year, art critic Douglas Crimp mounted the groundbreaking Pictures exhibition at Artists Space, an exhibition that would identify the growing plurality of practices that were dissolving traditional conceptions of medium in the wake of conceptual art practices and minimalism. This exhibition toured the country and ended at the Los Angeles Institute of Contemporary Art in 1978. While installing Pictures in New York and preparing for the opening of A Sound Selection, the curatorial staff was made aware of an exhibition at the Los Angeles Institute of Contemporary Art (LAICA) opening at the same time as Pictures in New York, entitled Narrative Themes/ Audio Works, An Exhibition of Artists Cassettes. An audio reel of the pieces from this exhibition was quickly edited together and included in the listening stations at Artists Space for A Sound Selection.

After the success of LAICA's Narrative Themes/Audio Works, which included pieces by John Baldessari, Barbara Kruger, and Laurie Anderson, LAICA curator Robert Smith invited the artist Bob Wilhite (who had exhibited in the Narrative Themes/Audio Works exhibition) to assist in the curation of an ambitious survey of contemporary sound practices called, creatively, Sound. Where the A Sound Selection exhibition focused on fixed works for audio media by artists, Sound would present the most substantial exhibition to date, chronicling both artists and musicians working with "sound sculpture, instrument building, and acoustically tuned spaces" (Smith, 1979). While the curatorial approach at Artists Space was to present fixed works on record and tape while supporting the exhibition by performances and only a few installations, the LAICA exhibition would develop a system whereby the works would be turned on and off in succession, such that in any given room only one work was on at a time.

Both of these strategies are now common among curators dealing with soundworks—the sequential turning on and off of works was used in the 2011 Thing/Thought: Fluxus Editions 1962-1968 exhibition at the Museum of Modern Art in New York, as well as the 2009 23'17" exhibition at Mains D'oeuvre in Paris. The installation strategy of limiting the scope of audible work was used at the re(sound) exhibition at the Webster College Art Galleries as well as the Ear to the Page exhibition at the Center for Book Arts in Manhattan, both of which featured headphone-based listening stations.

The LAICA show went on to travel back to New York to be exhibited at PS1 during February of 1980, following shortly after the seminal New Music/New York events earlier that season. This story paints a clear picture of a vibrant art community sharing ideas and young, interesting venues doing aggressive work to stay current with practices. The nested overlap of the pictures exhibition, the narrative themes show, a sound selection, and finally the sound exhibition demonstrates the immediacy and awareness of sound during a period where artists were moving away from traditional medium-specific categories and being exhibited in institutions eager to question the nature of accepted disciplines and specific aesthetic practices.

Just as Douglas Crimp had identified works that were "constituted in a situation and for a duration by the artist or the spectator, or both together," A Sound

Selection and Sound would, through two very different curatorial strategies, assemble practices that complicated the boundaries between music, architecture, art, and theatre—works that mobilized sound as a critical tool and also as a means to an end that is very individual to each artist and piece (Crimp, 1979).

INVASIVE: SOUND AS PERVASIVE TOPIC

Where Art by Telephone used recorded telephone calls as a prompt for the materialization of conceptual works, and both A Sound Selection and the Sound exhibitions attempted to immerse visitors in a plurality of sound practice, sound invades the concept of the 2007 exhibition Voice and Void at the Aldrich Museum in Ridgefield, Connecticut. Since the late 1960s, the voice has been a recurring theme throughout many group exhibitions dealing with text, speech, or technology; exhibitions thematically concerned with the voice, however, begin in earnest in the late 1980s and have continued with frequency since.

In the din of listening for the content of words, it is easy to forget that the voice is also physical sound. The same voice that whispers can also sing, shout, and scream, as it emanates externally from the body or suggests itself within the mind as a memory or thought. The Austrian-born curator of the Voice and Void exhibition, Thomas Trummer, describes the voice as a "fundamental component of corporeal manifestation and a bearer of verbalism, it is the trace of the human body in language, and therefore information, gesture, and statement in equal measure" (Trummer, 2008). By acknowledging the complicated dualism of public and private speaking, as well as the role of the voice as both metaphor and material in contemporary art practice, Voice and Void follows a thread of sound as it runs through a body of work engaged much more broadly in the din of communication technologies, the silence of speechlessness, and the charged balance between interior and exterior manifestations of the self.

The fifteen artists exhibited in Voice and Void don't provide a survey; through the carefully crafted intersection of the "undefinable, indeterminable space between manifestation and internalization, between the innate—that pushes to the outside—and the other, that turns itself inward," these works are not about sound, but rather interrogate the potential of sound as both outward and inward manifestations of voice (Trummer, 2008).

AFTERWARD: CONTEMPORARY
CURATORIAL ENGAGEMENT WITH SOUND

Contemporary practice is beginning to acknowledge the ways in which the ephemeral phenomenon of sound was used as a component in the art of the late 1960s, as well its use in the medium-specific practices of the seventies and eighties. Curators are approaching the twenty-first century with an openness that aims not to merely justify the presence of sound in the art world as such but, rather, critiques the constantly and consistently expanding critical vocabulary of sound studies toward exhibitions that elucidate the auditory complexity of our culture and history. These practices are initiating a reassessment, a reevaluation of the growth of the multivalent potential of sound to work both through and against its establishment as a medium, and acknowledgment as a phenomenon.

Curatorial engagement with sound between 2003 and 2013 has been markedly—though not ideologically or rigidly—polarized. The first extreme represents a trend toward museum retrospectives surveying iconic works; these exhibitions are largely concerned with applying the stamp of canonization to sound as a practice and sound artists as an independent community. The most iconic example of this recent trend toward overarching survey is the 2012 Sound Art: Sound as a Media of Art exhibition at the Zentrum für Kunst und Medientechnologie in Karlsruhe, Germany. It included works from over ninety artists, and two-thirds of the works were produced during the twentieth century. An alternative example of this trend is shown by the 2013 Soundings: A Contemporary Score, curated by Barbara London at the Museum of Modern Art. Exhibiting only sixteen artists, the works in Soundings were by young artists representing diverse, almost iconoclastically individual, approaches to sound as an artistic medium.

The opposite pole suggests a move toward increasingly creative approaches to topics, idea, concepts, and resonances that cut across works where sound is manifested as a vehicle, carrying content that alternately transcends and subsumes the affordances of the medium. Sonel Breslav's 2012 exhibition Render Visible at Present Company Gallery in Brooklyn, New York, Seth Kim-Cohen's 2010 Non-Cochlear Sound exhibition at Diapason Gallery, and the 2009 Several Silences show at the Renaissance Society at the University of Chicago are representative of this move toward topic and idea in sound curatorial practice. Similar to the development of curatorial approaches to video in the late 1980s and early 1990s, sound is beginning to shed the stigma of curatorial novelty.

Even more important has been the gradual inclusion of soundworks into group exhibitions where sound is not the exhibition theme. As curators have become more comfortable with the implications and affordances of sound in art, nonsound-themed group exhibitions centered around topics, concepts, and ideas that span medium, discipline, and generation become richer and more varied. This broad inclusion would be impossible without the current availability of historical materials and critical texts providing curators with the resources to make informed decisions (Kelly, 2011).

Another factor whose importance should not be underestimated is the widespread, cost-effective availability of reproduction, amplification, and distribution technologies for audio, as well as improvements in low-cost architectural acoustic treatments. Many exhibitions have suffered from ill-considered installation practices that did little to discourage sound-bleed between works; however, recent advancements in acoustically-rated sound isolating, diffusing, and absorbing building materials as well as surface treatments have made contemporary exhibitions much more legible for museum- and gallery-goers.

Where the shows of the 1960s were novel experiments, and the 1980s saw the first surveys, the curation of soundworks is returning in a way to an awareness of the noisiness of the art world, but it is doing so now with a greater focus on the intent of the work and less attention to the identification of practitioners as sound artists per se. This post-medium stage shows—much like the late 1990s for artworks involving video—that artists, curators, and the public are less concerned that pieces are soundful and more interested in reevaluating the soundful for meaning, intent, idea, and relevance.

REFERENCES

Bosseur, J.-Y. (1993). *Sound and the Visual Arts*. Paris: Dis Voir.

Buchloh, B. (1990). Conceptual Art 1962–1969: From the Aesthetic of Administration to the Critique of Institutions. *October*, 55, 105–43.

Cluett, S. (2013). *Loud Speaker: Towards a Component Theory of Media Sound*. Dissertation. Princeton: Princeton University. http://arks.princeton.edu/ark:/88435/dsp01bc386j27h.

Coe, R. (1966). *Sound Light Silence: Art That Performs*. Kansas City: Nelson-Atkins Gallery.

Crimp, D. (1979). Pictures. *October*, 8, 75–88.

Kahn, D. (2001). *Noise, Water, Meat: A History of Sound in the Arts*. Cambridge: MIT Press.

Kelly, C., ed. (2011). *Sound*. Cambridge: MIT Press.

Kim-Cohen, S. (2009). *In the Blink of an Ear: Toward a Non-Cochlear Sonic Art*. New York: Continuum.

LeWitt, S. (1969). "Variation on Wall Drawing #26," in *Art by Telephone*. Museum of Contemporary Art, Chicago.

Licht, A. (2007). *Sound Art: Beyond Music, Between Categories*. New York: Rizzoli.

Lippard, L. (1997). *Six Years: The Dematerialization of the Art Object from 1966 to 1972*. Berkeley: University of California Press.

Rosen, B. (1980). *A Sound Selection, Audio Works by Artists*. New York: Committee for the Visual Arts.

Smith, R. (1979). *Sound: An Exhibition of Sound Sculpture, Instrument Building, and Acoustically Tuned Spaces*. Los Angeles: Los Angeles Institute of Contemporary Art.

Trummer, T., ed. (2008). *Voice & Void*. Ridgefield: The Aldrich Museum.

8

Soundwalking the Museum

A Sonic Journey through the Visual Display

Salomé Voegelin

PROLOGUE

Vienna is a filthy, noisy, city. Is this what happens when the public turns
its attention to the concert hall and museum, but forgets about the soundscape and the landscape of everyday life?

—Broomfield in R. Murray Schafer, ed., 1977, p. 31

This opinion, voiced by Howard Broomfield, one of the original members of
the World Soundscape Project, bemoans the separation between viewing and
listening in the museum, the concert hall, and the perception of the everyday.
His statement suggests that building a rarefied space for art and performance
causes us to abandon the aesthetics of the everyday and opens a chasm between the ideology of art and the reality of life. While this might lead to a
filthy, noisy urban environment, the consequence of this separation must also
be a lack of relevance of what is on display inside the museum or performed
in the concert hall. The disconnection of inside and outside, actually and
metaphorically, takes away the power of reciprocity, and thus it must dimin-
ish the works' capacity to illuminate and reconsider the world beyond their
walls. It is a question of inside and outside, of architecture, urban planning,
education, social relations, and political determination, all rolled into the idea
of curation: "showing art."

Broomfield made his forceful observations in 1975; much has changed since,
and other things have stayed just the same. The Viennese museums will look
more or less the same, from the outside at least; the traffic noise if anything has
probably increased, but the people who visit the museums have changed dramatically. It is with less awe and wonder, and with a more equivalent enquiry

that most of us now step into the grand halls of the museum's display. We are more critically aware—touched by discourse, we know to put our own words to what we see and merge art into colloquial discussions.

Crucially, too, computer interfaces have developed our consciousness away from fixed architectural boundaries that create the inside-outside dichotomy, toward more fragile, fluid, and lucent barriers. Digital walls are permeable and connect rather than separate spaces, building a virtual place through association rather than opposition.

INTRODUCTION

This chapter brings the practice of soundwalking—walking the landscape with a focus on listening to one's environment—to the museum, expanding the roaming pursuit of walking into the locale of its galleries, to use the boundless ephemerality of sound to illuminate museological conventions and traditions and the way we interact with these.

The invisible materiality of sound connects inside and outside, and illuminates unseen relationships between reality, possibility, materiality, and immateriality, inviting a different appreciation of architecture and artifacts as well as encouraging different curatorial concepts and strategies—to build and rebuild the museum from the contingent experience of its soundscape; to ignore and play with actual and ideological confines in the lucent fluidity of sonic possibilities that resemble and predate digital boundlessness.

The museum is not a visual place but an audiovisual environment, unfolding its space in the time of ricocheting footsteps, sincere whispers, loud echoes of children's laughter, security guards' fuzzy walkie-talkies, tour guides' hushed lectures, and a few audiovisual works that remind us that even the work is not as quiet as we might expect. Exploring this environment through listening allows us to experience not what it appears to be in its visual immediacy but hear all it could possibly be in the temporal and ever-changing invisibility of its sound.

Soundwalks stage a journey of exploration, a phonographic expedition, whose aim is to re-experience, question, and expand staid assumptions about the museum, about curatorial practice, and the contemplation of art. The intention of this chapter is part documentation and part debate on the process of soundwalking the museum for the purpose of exploring the way the museum is, and imagining the way it could be. This topic and methodology is born out of a concern about the visual focus of museums' architecture and design, signposting and curatorial approach, and the consequent lack of a more complete sensorial engagement with the museum as an environment for visual, sonic, and multimodal work. The chapter extends an invitation to curators and visitors to soundwalk the museum, and produces some reflections on the heard that propose other possibilities, other environments and other curatorial strategies, that start not from historical traditions and conventions but from the experience and demands of the place and the work itself.

For the purpose of this exploration I designed ten soundwalks, five to take place at Tate Britain and five at Tate Modern in London. These phonographic expeditions served as the case studies for a discussion of the museum as a sensorial environment. The suggestion is that before any future of the museum that can accommodate multisensory and multimodal work can be proposed, the status quo needs to be explored beyond its visual sphere of influence.

These phonographic expeditions were determined by written instructions and were undertaken by the MA Sound Arts students from the London College of Communication, University of the Arts London, 2012 cohort. They went on their own, or in groups of two, to soundwalk the museum, and were then invited to discuss their experience and ideas through prepared listening questions.

LISTENING QUESTIONS

How do you listen to the museum?

Does the gallery space invite listening?

Does that listening, or not listening, have an influence on how you perceived the work displayed?

Do you, when looking at artworks in the space, also hear the space?

Was there any sound work?

How does your walking, your footsteps, your talking, your breathing, your own sounds influence what you see?

How do other people's sounds, those with you deliberately or just coincidentally in the gallery at the same time, influence how you view the work?

Where would you have installed a sound work?

How would you work with sound in this museum?

What would the ideal sound museum look and sound like?

SOUNDWALKS

I include two of the ten soundwalks here for your information and as an invitation to go to your nearest museum and try them yourself.

Sound Walk 1: Tate Britain

Start here (on Millbank):

> Stand at the bottom of the steps and listen for approximately two minutes* to yourself, then listen for another three minutes to yourself in the environment.
> Walk up the stairs, listening to the people who come toward you.

Figure 8.1.

Enter the museum.

Go through to the second entrance hall, round space.

Close your eyes in the middle of this space and listen for five minutes.

Open your eyes.

Walk all the way in a straight line to the very back of the gallery, all the
while listening to yourself and other visitors inside the space.

Go to the first piece of work you find; listen to it.

Go to the next piece of work you find; look at it.

Roam the gallery on any floor, in any room for twenty minutes.

Go to the bookshop on the ground floor (where you entered); stay there listening and looking at things and people until it's time to meet in the little
garden to the left of the museum when you come down the long stairs.

Sound Walk 2: Tate Modern

Start here (ramp entrance on the west side of museum):

From the top of the external ramp, slowly walk all the way down, through
the doors and all the way to the other end of the gallery, listening to
yourself in your changing space.

Figure 8.2.

Go to the staircase, walk up one floor.
Stand at the balcony for five minutes* listening to the space.
Look at artworks for five minutes.
Walk up another floor.
Stand at the balcony for five minutes listening to the space.
Look at artworks for five minutes.
Walk up one floor.
Stand at the balcony for five minutes listening to the space.
Look at artworks for five minutes.
Walk up one floor.
Stand at the balcony for five minutes listening to the space.
Look at artworks for five minutes
Take lift down to exit level, listen to the lift journey.
Go to meeting point: lawn at side entrance of museum.

*All the time indications are approximate; do not distract yourself by looking at a watch—try to feel the time.

MEASURING THE MUSEUM IN MY EARS

When R. Murray Schafer and his colleagues from the World Soundscape Project in Vancouver (of which Broomfield, quoted above, was one) took a VW camper van trip around Europe in 1975, they also visited the Louvre. The aim of their trip was to write a European Sound Diary, to document, comment upon, and record the soundscape of Europe at the time. Their visit to the Louvre was documented in five columns noting time, location, sound intensity levels, sound descriptions, and materiality. This neat handwritten table offers an interesting insight not so much into the sound profile of the Louvre in the mid-seventies, but rather into the aims and reasons for noting and recording sounds in a big visual arts gallery at the time. The focus of their documentation is on sound pollution, noise, activity levels, decibels, materialities, and sound sources. It is a measuring of the space by its sound, trying to express the sonic scale and volume of its place. It offers the museum not as a place in space but as a place in time—the swelling and abating of noise, the character of sound depending on surfaces and materials—and hints at rather than articulates the impact this sound might have on our experience of the work and the museum.

I would like to add two more columns to their survey—experience and consequence: the aesthetic knowledge gained from such a detailed sonic scrutiny, and the subsequent discussion of what it might mean for the appreciation and curation of sound within the museum. My added columns would be different, however; they would not be neat columns drawn with a ruler, juxtaposing in clear corresponding lines material observations with decibels, decibels with time and location, time and location with activity, and so on, relying on the juxtapositions of data to construct a sonic insight into the place. Instead, my columns would be the wriggly lines of personal experience that develops from a contingent listening and produces personal narrations about an equally contingent aesthetic knowledge of the museum that might not co-incide with yours at all but finds its authority in the doing, the soundwalking, walking the museum with my ears, and hearing what it looks like.

Such an exploration of the museum is much less obvious. It is not a quan-titative gathering of data. Instead, it is through listening and looking and looking and listening that the gallery gets to be known temporarily. This is knowing as a contingent aesthetic impression that has a direct consequence on how I understand the work displayed and how I understand its relationship to space and time, producing the place of the museum as a contingent place for me.

In its lack of an obvious description, such a personal narration uncovers that which is left out of a seemingly transparent and quantitative scheme, and instead points at hidden interpretations: "What comes together through sound is emergent and passing time—a sense of duration, the field of memory, a fullness of space that lies beyond touch and out of sight, hidden from vision" (Toop, 2010, p. xv).

Sound can go into the actual and metaphorical nooks and crannies of a space and explore them aside from the main purpose and signification of the place that hides them. A personal listening journey does not gather data of the museum but produces personal measurements from the niches of the possible museum that I walk through and that holds its own meaning.

It is the invisible sound that generates the space in the time of my pass-ing through it, leaving no residue in the place but only in my memory as an imprint of its experience. The only proof I have of it sounding is on my body, the body that walks on into the next gallery to hear in space that which in time will become the next imprint and currently triggers what I see. This is the body of the curator and of the visitor exploring the apparent visual work in the invisible temporality of its sound.

This temporal particularity is central to soundwalking since, although the instructions given are universal, the moment of their application is specific and contingent. They are not a map, but an invitation to map, build, trash, and rebuild the museum from its sound. In my ears the museum is built temporarily, again and again, out of the rickety shapes of all that sounds as a formless form, invisible and ephemeral, fragmented and fragmenting, and it is the complexity of this impression into which and out of which the work comes. The sonic museum is not one stable whole holding inside itself artifacts for our perusal. Rather, the sonic museum holds nothing but is the conglomeration of things building each other reciprocally in complex equivalence: walls and paintings, floors and sculptures, inside and outside, are not separated but merge and produce the complex materiality that is the museum in my ears. The walls are not more stable than the paintings, the staircase not more permanent than the video piece, the floors not separated from the sculptural work.

Sounds have no outline, no visual boundary and distinction, but inexhaustibly diffuse associations. Rather than categorizing works and separating them from the infrastructure and architecture of the museum, sound makes relationships apparent: the relationship between moments—handing in our coat to the clerk and the moment we look at a painting; between people—the people I heard chatting in the lift and that are now looking at the same sculpture as me; and between spaces—the sounds of the footsteps echoing through the entrance hall meet those on the carpets in smaller gallery rooms upstairs. Sound unpacks the visual unity and dissolves it to build a place of invisible connections, experienced differences, real relationships, and imagined associations that is contingent and personal and in which the work is not shown but shows itself and produces the timespace of its encounter.[1] Sonically I become aware of the complexity of the curated space, which is visually (at least seemingly) one unified place but fragments in sound. Listening I dissolve the separation of galleries, works, inside and outside, and produce sonic connections that make the work relevant not only to discourse but to the reality and aesthetics of the everyday. I hear the relationship between the "filthy, noisy" Viennese streets and the museum's display, and make that connection relevant.

READYING THE MUSEUM FOR MULTIMODAL WORK

Juliane Rebentisch, writing toward an aesthetic of installation art—an art that includes multimodality and multimateriality, fragmented in space and demanding time—bemoans the installation shot that seeks to arrest the timespace complexity of the work into the fixity of material categorization, which is purely visual and of no time (Rebentisch, 2003, p. 18). The catalogue demands the photograph and a generic description, which in turn informs the engagement of the visitor: to see the work as it is represented and described, to understand it through the authority of its reproduction.

Rebentisch associates this problem with the lack of sensorial engagement in contemporary art, a lack which I recognize in the meta-discursive stance of criticism and curatorial practice, and which results in the distance the audience takes to the work: to try to understand the work in its totality rather than sense it as process.

"This fascination with totalization and transparency, the production of seamless narrative of local, national, or universal history, whether through the display of history and antiquities themselves, or ethnography, art, or nature, continues to remain at the heart of most national and large regional museums" (Shelton, 2006, p. 481).

Sound cannot totalize and cannot be totalized.[2] In listening to the museum I cannot take a meta-position, and I do not synthesize nor sum up different meta-positions in an attempt to achieve one representation, one transparent knowledge about the work. Instead, I practice the fragments and different materials, times, and spaces that produce the work contingently without necessarily reaching one understanding, but rather a serendipitous aesthetic knowing as a sensate sense of the work.

This sensate sense is generated in my engagement with the work in the practice of an actual and a conceptual listening. Listening not only as an activity of hearing sound, but as a conceptual strategy of engaging with any sensorial material, allows me to connect, to network, and to experience the fragmented spatiality and temporality of multimodal work. The fragmented complexity and complex temporality of any work can be accessed via a "conceptual sonic" that practices its material and immaterial relationships through a sonic sensibility—focused on the invisible and fluid relationships that are generated contingently and reciprocally, rather than closing them off into the shape of their immediate appearance.

Sound, conceptual and actual, in the sense of its absence, "hidden from vision," its invisible ability to conjure things up and broker relationships, intervenes in the desire for totality and transparency. Instead, it opens a multiplicity of pathways and possibilities; a dense heterogeneity that the curator must embrace to be able to deal with the multimodality of contemporary work and also to revisit the complexity of monomodal work in the understanding of the museum as a multimodal environment rather than a monomode display case—a neutral vessel for artifacts.

The soundwalk belies the certainty of the gallery floorplan and the artifact. Sound as material, as metaphor and as concept, invites an engagement that impedes the total vision of the museum as well as the totalization of the work. This sonic sensibility is not antivisual but revives the multidimensionality, temporality, and complexity of the visual, making it ready to receive multimodal work.

A SONIC SENSIBILITY FOR CURATION

The museum is a timespace, an environment configured in my walking through it, built in my imagination from all that is there and all that is hinted at through what sounds invisibly and looks inconspicuously. What is needed is the sensibility to reach beyond the obvious to those layers of discreet visibility and invisibility that are the museum with the work, not the work in the museum; to expand and challenge its knowledge and totality of what appears to be there as expected, and instead propose the aesthetic production of what might be there and insist on the generative engagement of the viewer as listener.

Whatever the architectural shape of the museum, it is the task of the curator to make the visible and the invisible accessible; to offer the visitors not the detached contemplation of a display but to seduce them into the environment of the work. When the museum ceases to be a hall of reverence and quiet contemplation of what is, by sheer dint of being inside it, granted authority and transparency, and becomes another landscape, another place, just like the street outside, then our experience of the work becomes one of active exploration, finding paths rather than following them, and hearing relationships rather than muting them to distill the art.

The building of the museum might be there, but the experience of this building is produced in the activity of walking around it and through it. My soundwalk is generative: I invent and build the place through the invisible connections my listening makes. It is the curator's responsibility to do soundwalks as part of his/her curatorial practice, and it is his/her task to produce an environment of work that I can walk through with the same sonic sensibility—invited to explore the multidimensionality, temporality, and complexity of the place, enabling my engagement and generative interaction with the multimodality of the work.

It is through walking the galleries with her/his ears, from the midst of things, that the curator can revisit the museum and subsequently the visitor can join in to produce spaces that do not hold and represent multimodal and sonic works but that encourage and facilitate a multimodal engagement that is mobile and fluid, all-encompassing, whose criticality comes from this engagement rather than from "totalization transparency," and whose exchange produces the wiggly lines of a personal narration rather than "the production of seamless narrative of local, national or universal history . . ." (Shelton, 2006, p. 481).

The curator has to remember that he/she curates time as well as space, the time of walking through—curating environments and zones that are activated by my walking through and whose boundaries are less certain than its architecture might have us believe. They are more like those of a computer game: membranes made up of hidden code; invisible and permeable, swiftly crossed, moving with ease into real spaces adjacent as well as into imaginary spaces that exist in "the field of memory" that forms our present perception.

It is, then, not about the actual modulation of a place but the modality of what is possible in our engagement with work, with the space and the time it takes. The actual walls do not have to be mobile to produce a space that in its own fragmentation and multimodality can embrace and facilitate the unfolding complexity of multimodal work, but the ideological, curatorial, and discursive walls have to be moveable.

Any architectural space can offer the platform for such curation. It is a matter of listening and understanding that the impact of the heard on our experience of the museum as an environment is important. This redeems the conventional museum, as it can prevail in its current architectural shape so long as it listens to the shapes its sounds make. At the same time, it also liberates new museums, not yet built, in that they do not have to follow conventions and traditions, as it is the invisible sphere of sound that will produce a contingent narration out of conspicuous and inconspicuous visuals that are things rather than objects, aesthetic sensations rather than artifacts.

This brings curation close to the political and the social, but also embraces pedagogy on its way. We need to learn to do soundwalks to listen in order to expand the way we look at work. Maybe we need soundwalks for every museum, to let the invisible ghost of sound into the gallery, celebrating its impact on the work and ourselves, and letting it unfold the material relationships between works, spaces, times, and viewers, rather than allowing the work to distill itself into an installation shot. Taking off doors, laying down heavy carpets, asking visitors to wear big woolly socks, or heavy wooden shoes, to sing, to talk loud, to whisper . . . and to hear themselves in the environment built of invisible connections and visible material, fragmenting each other to produce the museum as a multisensorial environment with work unfolding and refolding its space in the time of our engagement.

EPILOGUE

Tate Britain

sounds voices reverberating deferential halls. The whirr of humankind staring at reflections of their own making. Every hush escalates and spreads out into its space, confirming its authority and rendering it a hallowed hall. My sonic body shrinks into itself, self-consciously aware of the space I take; children's voices confidently fire up the echo, expanding themselves happily into the architecture, practicing loud footsteps, squeals and laughter.

NOTES

1. The relationship between time and space in sound challenges the possibility of a dialectic definition that purports their autonomous discussion and pretends them as stable absolutes: time exclusive of space, and space exclusive of time. The notion of time in sound is neither time as opposed to space nor is it time plus space. At the same time, the sonic idea of space is not opposed to that time nor is it space plus time. Time and space extend each other and produce each other without dialectical conflict, creating place from the critical equivalence between temporal and spatial processes: timespace.

2. Sound can be totalized only in its visual or linguistic guise: as the score, or the description of its source. Only when we take on the meta-position of musical discourse, or semiotic readings, do we encounter a total sound. When listening, however, we are faced with the fragmented complexity and infinite possibilities of sound that are realized as contingent actualities in my temporal engagement and which are never exhausted and finalized but perpetually take on new shapes—formless and invisible.

REFERENCES

Blesser, B., and Salter, L. R. (2007). *Spaces Speak, Are You Listening? Experiencing Aural Architecture*. Cambridge, MA: MIT Press.

Drever, J. Levack. (2009). Soundwalking: aural excursions into the everyday. In James Saunders, ed., *Ashgate Research Companion to Experimental Music*. Farnham: Ashgate.

LaBelle, Brandon. (2010). *Acoustic Territories*. London and New York: Continuum Press.

Oliveros, P. (2005). *Deep Listening; A Composer's Sound Practice*. New York: iUniverse.

Rebentisch, J. (2003). *Aesthetik der Installation*. Frankfurt am Main: Suhrkamp Verlag.

Schafer, R. Murray. (1977). *European Sound Diary*. World Soundscape Project, Simon Fraser University, Canada

Schaub, M. (2005). *Janet Cardiff: The Walk Book*, edited by Thyssen-Bornemisza. Art Contemporary, Vienna, in collaboration with Public Art Fund, New York, Walther König Cologne.

Shelton, Anthony A. (2006) Museum and museum's displays. In C. Tilley, W. Kean, S. Küchler, M. Roowlands, P. Spyer, eds, *Handbook of Material Culture*. London: Sage Publication.

Toop, D. (2010). *Sinister Resonances*. London and New York: Continuum Press.

9

The Role of Sensory and Motor Systems in Art Appreciation and Implications for Exhibit Design

A. Casile and L. F. Ticini

Every day, millions of people travel long distances, queue for extended periods, and pay occasionally large entrance fees in order to visit museums and opera halls all over the world. Humans are constantly attracted to art and, even in periods of depression, we are willing to pay to enjoy exhibitions, dance performances, and concerts. Why do we seek art and value it so much? Where does such desire come from? Although these questions are deceitfully simple, scientifically grounded answers are terribly difficult as, for instance, there is no objective or quantitative measure of "artistic content." The value of a piece of art (assuming that we can even define artistic value) can vary, sometimes by a very large amount, across individuals, cultures, and time. Artworks considered important in the past may no longer be considered so today, and vice versa. In a bid to explore these issues, several modern neuroscientists are engaged in the difficult enterprise of deepening our understanding of the neuronal and cognitive processes that underlay aesthetic appraisal.

ART AND THE BRAIN: EARLY PROPOSALS

Despite apparently insurmountable problems related to the definition of art and aesthetics, heroic efforts have been made in the last several decades to investigate the biological basis of aesthetic experiences. Interest in understanding the neuronal correlates of aesthetic appreciation began with the neurophysiological investigation of the primate visual system. Although we do not often realize it, making sense of a visual scene is a tremendously difficult endeavor. It is, therefore, remarkable to observe how efficient the brain is at accomplishing this task. As an example, when we observe a tree on a nice spring day, the stimulus striking our eyes—from a physical point of view—is simply a jumble of colored, moving blobs. It is only after a considerable amount of processing that our brain organizes these blobs into a structured, coherent percept consisting of a trunk and branches with leaves slowly oscillating in the wind.

Clarifying the processing steps in our visual system is one of the biggest achievements in modern neuroscience, and the scientists that have contributed to this achievement are too many to list (for a comprehensive review, see Chalupa and Werner, 2003). In many popular explanations, the process of visual perception is often compared to that of a camera that recreates a faithful picture of what we are seeing. Several decades of neuroscience studies have provided compelling evidence that this is a mistaken analogy. Indeed, the goal of our visual system is not to "take a picture" of the external world but, rather, to interpret and identify what we see by capturing only "essential" components. This is achieved through a complex sequence of steps that starts with the extraction of low-level features (edges, blobs of color, local motion, and so forth) and concludes with the "reassembling" of these features into higher-level representations (complex shapes, moving objects, faces, etc.).

One striking characteristic of our visual system is that it processes the different features of a visual stimulus (form, color, and spatial information) in different channels (Livingstone and Hubel, 1987). This segregation starts at the level of the retina and remains present at the primary cortical level. There exist multiple areas within the visual cortex, each of which processes a different aspect of the retinal input. For example, area V4 is involved in the processing of color information (Zeki, 1980) whereas area MT+ processes mainly information related to motion and stereopsis (Born and Bradley, 2005). Notably, these different processing channels have different characteristics. For example, color information is elaborated at lower spatial resolution with respect to shape information, whereas the motion channel is largely color-blind; that is, the perception of movement is greatly reduced when the moving stimuli have the same luminance but different colors (Cavanagh, Tyler, and Favreau, 1984).

Do the characteristics of our visual system have implications for art? The answer to this question can only be *yes*. By definition, visual art is perceived through the visual system. Furthermore, artists, similar to our brains, do not faithfully reproduce the external world but, rather, they represent it through a set of features that are tuned to excite our brain in a particular fashion. Thus, it is conceivable that there is a connection between how our brain processes visual information and the characteristics of a work of art. One of the first scientists to explore this connection was Margaret Livingstone, who suggested that artists seem to be empirically aware of the principles underlying the processing of visual information in the brain (Livingstone, 1988, 2008). An example is that of Pointillism, which "is a technique of painting in which small, distinct dots of pure color are applied in patterns to form an image" ("Pointillism," 2013). When seen from an appropriate distance, nearby dots in Pointillist paintings blend and an overall pattern (e.g., a human figure) emerges. When the same painting is observed from a short distance, however, the perception of individual dots obscures the overall pattern. This phenomenon can be explained by the characteristics of our visual system. As mentioned above, color information is processed at lower spatial resolutions than form information. Thus, at large distances, it cannot resolve the individual dots in a Pointillist painting. As we approach the same painting, the resolution of our color system will eventually match that of the dots and we will be able to see them individually (Livingstone, 1988).

The investigation of the connection between art and the brain was further advanced by Semir Zeki, who coined the word *neuroaesthetics*. Similar to Livingstone, Zeki investigated visual art in relation to the functional organization of our visual system. His point of view can be synthesized in his bold statement: "All visual art must obey the laws of the visual system" (Zeki and Lamb, 1994; Zeki, 1999a). In particular, he suggested that since color, form, and motion appear to have primacy in vision, they should have primacy in the visual arts. One example of this connection between art and the organization of the brain is that of kinetic art: "art from any medium that contains movement perceivable by the viewer or depends on motion for its effect" ("Kinetic Art," 2013.) Zeki suggested that the appeal of pieces of kinetic art is related to the fact that motion is processed separately from other features of a visual stimulus (Zeki and Lamb, 1994). The perceptual effects and the aesthetic appeal of kinetic arts are, thus, potentially a consequence of the organization principles of our visual system. A further example of the connection between art and the visual brain is that of artists, such as Malevich or Mondrian, using lines as the predominant or sometimes *only* feature in their works. In Mondrian's words, "(the line) is a stronger and more profound expression than the curve" (Mondrian, 1986, cited in Zeki, 1999b). Interestingly, there are specific neurons in the first stage of the visual system (area V1) that preferentially respond to straight lines of particular orientation (Hubel and Wiesel, 1959, 1968). Thus, lines could be considered "building blocks" used by our visual system to construct complex objects. This suggests that the aesthetic appeal of a masterpiece by Mondrian can be potentially due to the fact that, similar to kinetic art, the work taps onto the basic structure of our visual perception. From these specific examples, Zeki made the more general point that "artists are unknowingly exploring the organization of the visual brain though with techniques unique to them" (Zeki and Lamb, 1994; Zeki, 1999b:

for critique, see Hyman, 2010). In other words, the appeal of many pieces of visual art might be due to the fact that they are built in terms of "basic blocks" (motion in case of kinetic art or lines in the case of Mondrian's art) that are similar to the "basic blocks" of our visual perception.

ART AND THE BRAIN: VISUAL AND REWARD PROCESSES

Starting from the anecdotal observations and suggestions of Zeki's earlier work, several investigators sought to more quantitatively investigate the neuronal correlates of aesthetic preference. The specific question addressed is whether there was a particular area or a set of areas that were specifically activated during the perception of beauty.

To address this issue, Vartanian and Goel (2004) measured brain activation by means of functional magnetic resonance imaging (fMRI) while subjects observed representational and abstract paintings. The results showed that the subjects' early visual areas were consistently more active while they observed paintings that they reported as pleasant, and that this activation was highly correlated with their subjective ratings of each piece (Vartanian and Goel, 2004). In a similar vein, Kawabata and Zeki (2004) presented subjects with a set of paintings belonging to four different categories (portraits, landscapes, still lives, and abstract art) that had previously been classified into three categories: ugly, neutral, or beautiful. Each category of painting activated different areas of the visual cortex, potentially indicating category-specific processing of the visual details of the paintings. When the subjects' aesthetic scores were taken into account, the authors found that an area in the medial orbito-frontal cortex (mOFC) was consistently more active during the observation of paintings that were rated as beautiful. Interestingly, the OFC is also engaged by the perception of pleasant stimuli in different sensory modalities (i.e., touch, taste, and hearing). Thus, overall, it seems the OFC may encode the reward value of any given stimulus (Francis et al., 1999; Ishizu and Zeki, 2011; Small, Zatorre, Dagher, Evans, and Jones-Gotman, 2001). Kawabata and Zeki found that there was no specific brain area coding for the "sense of ugly," as no single area was more active during the perception of ugly painting with respect to beautiful paintings. Rather, the perception of ugly paintings resulted in less activation of the mOFC. This result might indicate that our brain rates stimuli along only one continuum, with stimuli at one end being perceived as ugly and stimuli at the other hand being perceived as beautiful (Kawabata and Zeki, 2004). In a further study, Cela-Conde and colleagues (2004) assessed brain activation by means of magnetoencephalography while subjects observed and rated the beauty of visual stimuli belonging to five categories: abstract art, classic art, Impressionist art, Postimpressionist art, and landscapes. Results of this experiment showed that pictures rated as beautiful produced a stronger activation of the left dorso-lateral prefrontal cortex (lDLPFC).

Taken together, the studies discussed in this section suggest that aesthetic appraisal and judgments are complex phenomena in which perceptual, cognitive, and affective processes are integrated to reach a decision regarding the beauty of a stimulus (Chatterjee, 2003; Jacobsen, Schubotz, Höfel, and Cramon, 2006; Nadal, Munar, Capó, Rosselló, and Cela-Conde, 2008; Zeki and Stutters, 2012).

ART AND THE BRAIN: EMBODIED PERCEPTION

Aesthetic experience is not merely based on visual processing. Emotions conveyed by artistic content are capable of triggering physiological responses in the whole of our body. According to some scholars, our knowledge of the neurobiology of aesthetics would be incomplete if we did not consider "bodily resonance" with art (Freedberg and Gallese, 2007). By this, scholars mean to emphasize the role of covert (imagined) simulation of actions, emotions, and corporeal sensations represented in artworks. Experimental evidence consistently suggests that resonance mechanisms might subserve the perception of actions. Indeed, motor and pre-motor areas are active during observation of other's motor acts, even when the observer is not overtly moving or preparing to move (Molenberghs, Cunnington, and Mattingley, 2012; Rizzolatti and Craighero, 2004; Rizzolatti and Fabbri-Destro, 2010). Clear evidence for this tight functional link between the visual and the motor systems in the service of action observation was obtained with the discovery of mirror neurons in monkeys. Mirror neurons are a class of neurons in the monkey brain that respond *both* during the execution and observation of goal-directed motor acts (see figure 9.1: Casile, 2013; di Pellegrino, Fadiga, Fogassi, Gallese, and Rizzolatti, 1992; Fogassi et al., 2005; Gallese, Fadiga, Fogassi, and Rizzolatti, 1996). It has been proposed that mirror neurons are the neuronal substrate subserving the embodied perception of actions, possibly by mapping visual representations of motor acts onto their internal motor representations (Rizzolatti, Fadiga, Gallese, and Fogassi, 1996; Rizzolatti, Fogassi, and Gallese, 2001; Rizzolatti and Sinigaglia, 2010). There is evidence supporting the existence of a mirror neuron system in humans that might be involved not only in action perception but also in emotional perception and empathy (Dapretto et al., 2006; Iacoboni and Dapretto, 2006; Iacoboni, 2009).

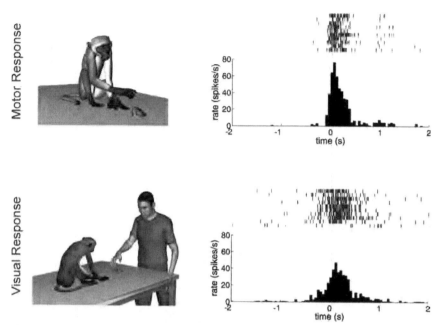

Figure 9.1. Typical response of a mirror neuron (Di Pellegrino et al., 1992; Gallese et al., 1996). The panels in the left column represent the experimental conditions and the panels in the right column the corresponding neuronal responses in the form of a raster plot (upper part) and peristimulus histogram (bottom part). (Upper row, right panel) Responses of a mirror neuron during grasping of an object. (Bottom row, right panel) Response of the same mirror neuron during the observation of goal-directed motor acts performed by the experimenter. In both figures time t = 0 represents the contact between the monkey's (upper row) or the experimenter's (lower row) hand and the object.

An influential proposal by Gallese and Freedberg (2007) holds that, given its role in empathy, the mirror neuron system might play a role in aesthetic appraisal. Proponents of this interpretation have used the celebrated Caravaggio canvas "Boy with a Lizard" to exemplify their point, suggesting the passive observation of a work of art may elicit the experience of a peculiar physical correspondence with the subject of the canvas (who, in this instance, is retracting his hand after a bite from the lizard: Freedberg and Gallese, 2007). Although speculative, this hypothesis has inspired numerous experiments aimed at clarifying the involvement of sensorimotor areas in dance (Calvo-Merino, Jola, Glaser, and Haggard, 2008; Cross, Kirsch, Ticini, and Schütz-Bosbach, 2011), music (D'Ausilio, Altenmüller, Olivetti Belardinelli, and Lotze, 2006), and pictorial art (Leder, Bär, and Topolinski, 2012; Umiltà, Berchio, Sestito, Freedberg, and Gallese, 2012). Consistent with Freedberg and Gallese's proposal, various researchers have shown aesthetic-related activity in brain regions usually associated with the execution of one's own actions. For instance, two fMRI studies measured brain activity while participants observed dance movements (Calvo-Merino et al., 2008; Cross et al., 2011). Both groups found that, beyond early visual cortices, premotor regions were activated for preferred dance movements, suggesting that—at least to a certain degree—a covert simulation of the observed movements is correlated to the level of liking. Further evidence of the association between aesthetic experience and motor activation came from two experiments on rhythm perception by Kornyscheva and colleagues (2010; 2011). In the first, the authors reported that activation of ventral premotor cortex correlated with appreciation of musical rhythms. In the second, they showed that transient interference (by means of repetitive transcranial magnetic stimulation) with ventral premotor cortex activity affected the preference to rhythm (Kornysheva, Von Anshelm-Schiffer, and Schubotz, 2011). Overall, one might argue that dance and music are but special forms of art that involve the perception of bodily movements that are likely to be internally simulated. However, these studies cannot ascertain whether in *all* forms of art the simulation of observed movements contributes to the aesthetic experience. Indeed, most known art, including prehistoric art, is captured in a static medium such as stone or canvas. The question is whether simulation takes place when the art-piece is static and whether a process of stimulation of the artist's actions discernible from the static medium are somehow related to the hedonistic aspect of artistic appreciation.

Some evidence suggests that this may indeed be the case. Sensorimotor activation can be triggered by passive observation of static artistic creations, such as paintings on canvas and sculptures. In a pioneering study, Di Dio and colleagues (2007) reported larger activation in sensorimotor brain regions (ventral premotor and posterior parietal cortices) when observing Classical and Renaissance human body sculptures respecting—in their proportions—the golden ratio (an accepted index of beauty in Western cultures). Further experiments by Battaglia and colleagues (2011) presented participants with a reproduction of Michelangelo's fresco "Expulsion from Paradise" while measuring changes in corticospinal excitability, an index of sensorimotor activation. They found that viewing Michelangelo's work elicited higher activity in the motor system compared to viewing a real hand photographed in the same pose. In a similar vein, the authors of a recent electroencephalographic experiment showed that Lucio Fontana's true slashed canvas, when compared to graphically modified versions of the canvas, increase brain activity associated to sensorimotor experience (Umiltà et al., 2012).

On the one hand, these results point toward a tight relationship between the aesthetic quality of a work and the perception of implied movement within it.

It is still unclear, though, whether the traces left by the artist on canvas can be accurately interpreted by the motor system of the observer's brain and, more importantly, whether this process of embodiment is efficient enough to contribute to the affective appreciation of artworks. A psychophysical investigation by Leder and colleagues (2012) contributed to clarifying this issue. The authors tested covert simulation of static brushstrokes on canvas left by the painter's hand gestures by interfering with motor simulation itself. In particular, participants were asked to execute with their dominant hand (hidden from view) either stroking or stippling movements while observing images of Pointillism-style (e.g., Seurat) or stroke-style paintings (e.g., van Gogh). Interestingly, when the participants executed the movements that were congruent with the gestures that the artist is likely to have performed to produce the observed painting, aesthetic appreciation increased. When the participants executed incongruent movements—which interfered with the process of action simulation—the very same paintings were liked less. This study suggests that might be able to extract information regarding the gestures performed by the artist. As exemplified in figure 9.2, this result is potentially achieved through a process of internal motor simulation that, as their results suggest, may systematically accompany the aesthetic appraisal.

Overall, the studies reviewed in this section strongly suggest that there is an activation of motor areas in the human brain while observing artistic stimuli (see also: Di Dio and Gallese, 2009). Does this activation play a causal role in producing aesthetic states? On the one hand, it might be that sensorimotor activation is purely due to the emotional state obtained during art appreciation. As a matter of fact, viewing emotional stimuli produces a general arousal state in the observer, which is known to facilitate motor activity (Hajcak et al., 2007). On the other hand, experimental evidence supports a more bidirectional association between emotion and motor behavior. For instance, injecting botox in facial muscles decreases the strength of emotional experience (Davis, Senghas, Brandt, and Ochsner, 2010) and of activity within emotional centers of the brain (Hennenlotter et al., 2009). Conversely, in the monkey, stimulating the insula—part of the affective system—evokes emotional behaviors (Caruana, Jezzini, Sbriscia-Fioretti, Rizzolatti, and Gallese, 2011). Ishizu and Zeki (2013) investigated this issue in an experiment in which they measured brain activation whilst participants observed paintings and gave a subjective rating of beauty or brightness. They found that, similar to a previous study (Kawabata and Zeki, 2004), the mOFC was engaged by paintings judged as beautiful. Interestingly, motor areas (more specifically premotor cortex and DLPFC) were activated during both aesthetic and brightness judgments. From these results, they concluded that the motor cortex

Figure 9.2.   Esthetic appraisal and motor simulation. Experimental results show that motorrelated processes are activated when observing pieces of art even when they are not related to the representation of the human body or bodily movements (Leder et al., 2012; Umiltà et al., 2012). It has been hypothesized that, in this case, what activates the observer's motor system is a covert motor simulation process whose goal is to extract information regarding the gestures performed by the artist (Freedberg and Gallese, 2007).

likely serves as an intermediate step for both perceptual and affective judgments, whereas the mOFC is specifically engaged by affective judgments. This result is in line with Gallese and Freedberg's proposal. Indeed, in a 2007 letter they stressed that their proposal does not hold that activation of the motor cortex is sufficient for aesthetic appraisal or for judgments about artworks. Rather, motor processes play a crucial role in aesthetic response because of their involvement in simulated embodiment, which appears to be critical to produce empathetic reactions to works of art (Casati and Pignocchi, 2007; Gallese and Freedberg, 2007).

Taken together, the papers discussed in this section clearly suggest that the embodied aesthetic hypothesis seems to be one critical element for the affective response to art (Chatterjee, 2003; Nadal et al., 2008).

FACTORS POTENTIALLY MODULATING AESTHETIC APPRAISAL

In the previous sections, we described several studies showing that aesthetic appraisal engages a widespread network of areas in the brain related to perceiving the work or art and judging its aesthetic and reward value. Potentially critical to these steps is a process of simulated embodiment that engages the motor cortex and allows one to empathize with a work of art (Freedberg and Gallese, 2007). In this section, we will discuss factors that modulate both artistic perception and embodiment. These modulating factors need to be taken in consideration when designing an art museum or artistic exhibition (e.g., music or dance).

A first important factor to consider is social context. When we make choices, we often rely on others' advice. In this context, an experiment by Huang and colleagues (2011) showed that artistic judgments are no exception. In this experiment, the authors presented participants with Rembrandt paintings that were described either as "originals" or "copies" (regardless of their true authenticity). They found an increased activation, albeit modest, in the mOFC when participants observed paintings labeled as "original" versus those labeled "copy." Interestingly, this area was previously reported by Zeki and colleagues (2011) as active during perception of beauty independent of the sensory modality of perception (i.e., vision or hearing). This result suggests that knowledge about authenticity of artwork can bias subjective appraisal, independent of true authenticity. In addition, greater activation was reported in various regions of the frontal cortex when the subjects observed "copy" paintings. Activation in these areas has previously been associated with the evaluation of multiple hypotheses (Koechlin and Hyafil, 2007). Taken together, these results suggest that information about artworks can bias the observer's perception, producing a lesser degree of appraisal and a closer scrutiny for artworks that are considered to be "fake," independent of their true authenticity.

In the case of visual art, one additional potential modulating factor is that of the viewing quality. For example, it has been shown that presentation of median noise–filtered paintings (a manipulation that significantly degrades the quality of the image) produced significantly less activation of low-level visual areas with respect to observation of unaltered versions of the same paintings. This result may be due to an increase in emotional or reward properties of original paintings, which is reflected in a top-down increase in the activation of low-level visual areas (Vartanian and Goel, 2004). Whatever the reason, it clearly suggests that degraded viewing conditions alter the overall pattern of brain activity usually produced by aesthetic appraisal.

In addition to factors that directly modulate the responses of brain areas engaged by aesthetic appraisal, there are a number of factors that modulate embodied perception and can have an indirect effect on aesthetic appraisal. The distance between the observer and the observed action is one. By means of neurophysiological recordings, Caggiano and colleagues (2009) found that approximately half out of a set of 105 investigated mirror neurons were modulated by the distance at which the action was executed from the monkey's body. Forty-nine percent of these neurons responded more strongly when the action was executed inside the monkey;s peri-personal space (the space immediately surrounding the body), while 51 percent responded more strongly when the action was executed outside of the monkey's peri-personal space. The importance of the peri-personal space is further highlighted by results in humans showing that objects close to the body can automatically trigger the representations of potential actions (Costantini, Ambrosini, Tieri, Sinigaglia, and Committeri, 2010). Furthermore, the responses of mirror neurons are also modulated by point of view. In a neurophysiological study, Caggiano and colleagues (2011) presented monkeys with the same action observed from three different points of view: the monkey's own perspective (first-person point of view), a side view (third-person side view), and a frontal point of view (third-person frontal view). They found that the majority of the visually responsive neurons (74%) exhibited view-dependent responses and only a minority exhibited view-independent responses (26%). A further analysis showed that the most represented point of view was the first-person perspective. These results suggest that the majority of mirror neurons encode actions in a view-dependent manner. Finally, the subjective reward value of an observed action can influence the responses of mirror neurons (Caggiano et al., 2012).

POTENTIAL IMPLICATIONS FOR THE DESIGN OF ART EXHIBITS

Taken together, the results discussed in the previous section suggest that embodied perception, one of the putative mechanisms of aesthetic appraisal, can be modulated by contextual information. This has potentially important implications for the appreciation of art, as it suggests that both the piece of art and the context in which it is embedded contribute to the observer's experience. In this section, we will discuss how neuroscience might help improve artistic appreciation. Our discussion will be necessarily speculative, as most of the results discussed above were obtained in the laboratory setting and their extrapolation to more complex environments, such as art exhibitions, might not be so straightforward.

The first potentially important factor in designing art exhibits is spatial lay-out. To be fair, the spatial arrangement of art pieces already receives a great deal of attention during the design of any art exhibition—though results from neuroscience may inform portions of this process. In the previous section, we reviewed evidence that embodiment processes are modulated by the location of an observed object (Costantini et al., 2010) or action (Caggiano et al., 2009) with respect to the observer. In order to better understand how to use this in-formation, it would be helpful to briefly look at how the brain represents the positions of objects in space. One counterintuitive result of modern neurosci-ence is that our brain does not appear to contain a single "map" of the external world that is used for different purposes. Rather, there are a multitude of maps, each used in the service of different behaviors. There is extensive evidence that the brain contains not only several egocentric representations of space that are linked to eye, head, and hand actions (Andersen, Snyder, Bradley, and Xing, 1997; Colby and Goldberg, 1999) but also an "absolute" (or allocentric) map of the external world (Bird, Bisby, and Burgess, 2012; Burgess, 2006; Moser, Kropff, and Moser, 2008). Notably, among the different regions of space, the peri-personal space is also encoded in motor areas (Fogassi et al., 1996; Graziano, Yap, and Gross, 1994). Taken together, these results suggest that the representation of space in our brain is linked to the effector (e.g., hand, foot, or eye) that could be potentially used to interact with external objects. Hence, the spatial layout of art pieces might depend on the effect that the designer of the exhibition wants to achieve. For example, a work of art close to our body will activate, in addition to visual representations, action repre-sentations related to the hand or foot and, thus, produce a higher degree of embodiment. On the other hand, a work of art displayed far away will likely activate action representations that are related to eye and head movements and, potentially, more abstract allocentric spatial representations. This will likely induce a lower degree of embodiment and a potentially higher degree of more abstract representations. These observations, albeit speculative, might give an additional degree of freedom to the designer of an art exhibition in targeting different processes of aesthetic appraisal.

A second potentially relevant factor to be taken into account in designing museums and art exhibits is perspective. As reviewed above, point of view strongly modulates the responses of mirror neurons, the putative neuronal substrate for embodied perception (Caggiano et al., 2011). The importance of the point of view in embodiment is, thus, similar to the role of the peri-personal space in spatial perception. Indeed, both are associated with be-haviorally relevant situations. The peri-personal space is directly linked to acting upon the external world, while the first-person point of view is how we usually perceive the world (in contrast, for example, to a TV show in which persons and objects are seen from the perspective of the camera). Given its high behavioral relevance, it is not surprising that the first-person perspective seems to produce a higher activation of embodiment processes. For example, observing actions from a first-person point of view produces a stronger activation of sensory-motor cortex (Jackson, Meltzoff, and Decety, 2006; Maeda, Kleiner-Fisman, and Pascual-Leone, 2002) and allows the observer to extract more precise information about the goal object (Campanella, Sandini, and Morrone, 2011). These results suggest that not only the distance from the observer but also the point of view under which a painting or a statue is observed can modulate aesthetic appraisal. In particular, it is conceivable that points of view that are closer to our direct everyday experience of the represented object (such as displaying a Hollywood costume on an even plane with the viewer) are more likely to activate embodiment processes. On the contrary, views of the represented object that are seldom or never experienced (such as displaying the same costume elevated on a wall) are likely to activate more abstract processes. Similar to spatial layout, it is ultimately a choice of the designer of the exhibition which processes in the observer's brain to target.

The third, and perhaps most important, factor that appears to modulate aesthetic appraisal is reward. That is, the more a work of art matches our personal taste, the more it will activate processes of aesthetic appraisal. Differently from the factors discussed above, reward cannot be manipulated by a designer of an art exhibition. It is something deeply rooted in the personality of the end-user and tightly connected to his/her past experiences. This reminds us that art is first and foremost a personal experience that "rewards" our sensory system, be it sight, hearing, taste, smell, or touch. This "sense of reward" is purely abstract, as it is not directly related to any materialistic compensation or "value" of the experienced piece of art. More than our intelligence, it is this disinterested sense of reward inherent in aesthetic appraisal that makes us human and separates us from any other species on the planet.

ACKNOWLEDGMENTS

LFT acknowledges the support of the French Agence Nationale de la Recherche (ANR) under reference ANR-10-CREA-005 (AVE project).

REFERENCES

Andersen, R. A., Snyder, L. H., Bradley, D. C., and Xing, J. (1997). Multimodal representation of space in the posterior parietal cortex and its use in planning movements. *Annual Review of Neuroscience*, 20, 303–30.

Battaglia, F., Lisanby, S. H., and Freedberg, D. (2011). Corticomotor excitability during observation and imagination of a work of art. *Frontiers in Human Neuroscience*, 5, 79. doi:10.3389/fnhum.2011.00079.

Bird, C. M., Bisby, J., and Burgess, N. (2012). The hippocampus and spatial constraints on mental imagery. *Frontiers in Human Neuroscience*, 6(May), 142. doi:10.3389/fnhum.2012.00142.

Born, R. T., and Bradley, D. C. (2005). Structure and function of visual area MT. *Annual Review of Neuroscience*, 28, 157–89. doi:10.1146/annurev.neuro.26.041002.131052.

Burgess, N. (2006). Spatial memory: how egocentric and allocentric combine. *Trends in Cognitive Sciences*, 10(12), 551–57. doi:10.1016/j.tics.2006.10.005.

Caggiano, V., Fogassi, L., Rizzolatti, G., Casile, A., Giese, M. A., and Thier, P. (2012). Mirror neurons encode the subjective value of an observed action. *Proceedings of the National Academy of Sciences of the United States of America*, in press. doi:10.1073/pnas.1205553109.

Caggiano, V., Fogassi, L., Rizzolatti, G., Pomper, J. K., Thier, P., Giese, M. A., and Casile, A. (2011). View-based encoding of actions in mirror neurons of area F5 in macaque premotor cortex. *Current Biology*, 21(2), 144–48. doi:10.1016/j.cub.2010.12.022.

Caggiano, V., Fogassi, L., Rizzolatti, G., Thier, P., and Casile, A. (2009). Mirror neurons differentially encode the peripersonal and extrapersonal space of monkeys. *Science*, 324(5925), 403–6. doi:10.1126/science.1166818.

Calvo-Merino, B., Jola, C., Glaser, D. E., and Haggard, P. (2008). Towards a sensorimotor aesthetics of performing art. *Consciousness and Cognition*, 17(3), 911–22. doi:10.1016/j.concog.2007.11.003.

Campanella, F., Sandini, G., and Morrone, M. C. (2011). Visual information gleaned by observing grasping movement in allocentric and egocentric perspectives. *Proceedings of the Royal Society of London. Part B*, 278(1715), 2142–49. doi:10.1098/rspb.2010.2270.

Caruana, F., Jezzini, A., Sbriscia-Fioretti, B., Rizzolatti, G., and Gallese, V. (2011). Emotional and social behaviors elicited by electrical stimulation of the insula in the macaque monkey. *Current Biology*, 21(3), 195–99. doi:10.1016/j.cub.2010.12.042.

Casati, R., and Pignocchi, A. (2007). Mirror and canonical neurons are not constitutive of aesthetic response. *Trends in Cognitive Sciences*, 11(10), 410; author reply 411. doi:10.1016/j.tics.2007.07.007.

Casile, A. (2013). Mirror neurons (and beyond) in the macaque brain: An overview of 20 years of research. *Neuroscience Letters*, 540, 3–14. doi:10.1016/j.neulet.2012.11.003.

Cavanagh, P., Tyler, C. W., and Favreau, O. E. (1984). Perceived velocity of moving chromatic gratings. *Journal of the Optical Society of America. A, Optics and image science*, 1(8), 893–99. Retrieved from http://www.ncbi.nlm.nih.gov/pubmed/647084.

Cela-Conde, C. J., Ayala, F. J., Munar, E., Maestú, F., Nadal, M., Capó, M. A., Del Río, D., et al. (2009). Sex-related similarities and differences in the neural correlates of beauty. *Proceedings of the National Academy of Sciences of the United States of America*, 106(10), 3847–52. doi:10.1073/pnas.0900304106.

Cela-Conde, C. J., Marty, G., Maestú, F., Ortiz, T., Munar, E., Fernández, A., Roca, M., et al. (2004). Activation of the prefrontal cortex in the human visual aesthetic perception. *Proceedings of the National Academy of Sciences of the United States of America*, 101(16), 6321–25. doi:10.1073/pnas.0401427101.

Chalupa, L. M., and Werner, J. S. (2003). *The Visual Neurosciences*. Bradford.

Chatterjee, A. (2003). Prospects for a cognitive neuroscience of visual aesthetics. *Bulletin of Psychology and the Arts*, 4, 55–60.

Colby, C. L., and Goldberg, M. E. (1999). Space and attention in parietal cortex. *Annual Review of Neuroscience*, 22, 319–49. doi:10.1146/annurev.neuro.22.1.319.

Costantini, M., Ambrosini, E., Tieri, G., Sinigaglia, C., & Committeri, G. (2010). Where does an object trigger an action? An investigation about affordances in space. *Experimental Brain Research*. doi:10.1007/s00221-010-2435-8.

Cross, E. S., Kirsch, L., Ticini, L. F., and Schütz-Bosbach, S. (2011). The impact of aesthetic evaluation and physical ability on dance perception. *Frontiers in Human Neuroscience*, 5, 102. doi:10.3389/fnhum.2011.00102.

Dapretto, M., Davies, M. S., Pfeifer, J. H., Scott, A. A., Sigman, M., Bookheimer, S. Y., and Iacoboni, M. (2006). Understanding emotions in others: mirror neuron dysfunction in children with autism spectrum disorders. *Nature Neuroscience*, 9(1), 28–30. doi:10.1038/nn1611.

D'Ausilio, A., Altenmüller, E., Olivetti Belardinelli, M., and Lotze, M. (2006). Cross-modal plasticity of the motor cortex while listening to a rehearsed musical piece. *European Journal of Neuroscience*, 24(3), 955–58. doi:10.1111/j.1460-9568.2006.04960.x.

Davis, J. I., Senghas, A., Brandt, F., and Ochsner, K. N. (2010). The effects of BOTOX injections on emotional experience. *Emotion*, 10(3), 433–40. doi:10.1037/a0018690.

Di Dio, C., and Gallese, V. (2009). Neuroaesthetics: a review. *Current Opinion in Neurobiology*, 19(6), 682–87. doi:10.1016/j.conb.2009.09.001.

Di Dio, C., Macaluso, E., and Rizzolatti, G. (2007). The golden beauty: brain response to classical and renaissance sculptures. *PloS ONE*, 2(11), e1201. doi:10.1371/journal.pone.0001201.

Di Pellegrino, G., Fadiga, L., Fogassi, L., Gallese, V., and Rizzolatti, G. (1992). Understanding motor events: A neurophysiological study. *Experimental Brain Research*, 91(1), 176–80. doi:10.1007/BF00230027.

Fogassi, L., Ferrari, P. F., Gesierich, B., Rozzi, S., Chersi, F., and Rizzolatti, G. (2005). Parietal lobe: from action organization to intention understanding. *Science*, 308, 662–67.

Fogassi, L., Gallese, V., Fadiga, L., Luppino, G., Matelli, M., and Rizzolatti, G. (1996). Coding of peripersonal space in inferior premotor cortex (area F4). *Journal of Neurophysiology*, 76(1), 141–57. Retrieved from http://www.ncbi.nlm.nih.gov/pubmed/8836215.

Francis, S., Rolls, E. T., Bowtell, R., McGlone, F., O'Doherty, J., Browning, A., Clare, S., et al. (1999). The representation of pleasant touch in the brain and its relationship with taste and olfactory areas. *Neuroreport*, 10(3), 453–59. Retrieved from http://www.ncbi.nlm.nih.gov/pubmed/10208571.

Freedberg, D., and Gallese, V. (2007). Motion, emotion and empathy in esthetic experience. *Trends in Cognitive Sciences*, 11(5), 197–203. doi:10.1016/j.tics.2007.02.003.

Gallese, V., Fadiga, L., Fogassi, L., and Rizzolatti, G. (1996). Action recognition in the premotor cortex. *Brain*, 119(2), 593.

Gallese, V., and Freedberg, D. (2007). Mirror and canonical neurons are crucial elements in esthetic response. *Trends in Cognitive Sciences*, 11(10), 411.

Graziano, M. S., Yap, G. S., and Gross, C. G. (1994). Coding of visual space by premotor neurons. *Science*, 266(5187), 1054–57. Retrieved from http://www.ncbi.nlm.nih.gov/pubmed/7973661.

Hajcak, G., Dunning, J. P., and Foti, D. (2007) Neural response to emotional pictures is unaffected by concurrent task difficulty: An event-related potential study. *Journal of Experimental Psychology: Human Perception and Performance*, 34, 1078–91.

Hennenlotter, A., Dresel, C., Castrop, F., Ceballos-Baumann, A. O., Baumann, A. O. C., Wohlschläger, A. M., and Haslinger, B. (2009). The link between facial feedback and neural activity within central circuitries of emotion—new insights from botulinum toxin-induced denervation of frown muscles. *Cerebral Cortex*, 19(3), 537–42. doi:10.1093/cercor/bhn104.

Huang, M., Bridge, H., Kemp, M. J., and Parker, A. J. (2011). Human cortical activity evoked by the assignment of authenticity when viewing works of art. *Frontiers in Human Neuroscience*, 5, 134. doi:10.3389/fnhum.2011.00134.

Hubel, D. H., and Wiesel, T. N. (1959). Receptive fields of single neurones in the cat's striate cortex. *Journal of Physiology*, 148, 574–591. Retrieved from http://jp.physoc.org/content/148/3/574.full.pdf.

———. (1968). Receptive fields and functional architecture of monkey striate cortex. *Journal of Physiology*, 195(1), 215–43. Retrieved from http://www.pubmedcentral.nih.gov/articlerender.fcgi?artid=1557912&tool=pmcentrez&rendertype=abstract.

Hyman, J. (2010). Art and neuroscience. In R. Frigg and M. Hunter (eds.), *Beyond Mimesis and Convention,* pp. 245–61. Dordrecht: Springer Netherlands. doi:10.1007/978-90-481-3851-7.

Iacoboni, M. (2009). Imitation, empathy, and mirror neurons. *Annual Review of Psychology*, 60, 653–70. doi:10.1146/annurev.psych.60.110707.163604.

Iacoboni, M., and Dapretto, M. (2006). The mirror neuron system and the consequences of its dysfunction. *Nature Reviews Neuroscience*, 7(12), 942–51. doi:10.1038/nrn2024.

Ishizu, T., and Zeki, S. (2011). Toward a brain-based theory of beauty. *PloS ONE*, 6(7), e21852. doi:10.1371/journal.pone.0021852.

———. (2013). The brain's specialized systems for aesthetic and perceptual judgment. *European Journal of Neuroscience*, in press, 1–8. doi:10.1111/ejn.12135.

Jackson, P. L., Meltzoff, A. N., and Decety, J. (2006). Neural circuits involved in imitation and perspective-taking. *NeuroImage*, 31(1), 429–39. doi:10.1016/j.neuroimage.2005.11.026.

Jacobsen, T., Schubotz, R. I., Höfel, L., and Cramon, D. Y. V. (2006). Brain correlates of aesthetic judgment of beauty. *NeuroImage*, 29(1), 276–85. doi:10.1016/j.neuroimage.2005.07.010.

Kawabata, H., and Zeki, S. (2004). Neural correlates of beauty. *Journal of Neurophysiology*, 91(4), 1699–705. doi:10.1152/jn.00696.2003.

Kinetic Art. (2013). Retrieved May 3, 2013, from http://en.wikipedia.org/wiki/Kinetic_art.

Koechlin, E., and Hyafil, A. (2007). Anterior prefrontal function and the limits of human decision-making. *Science*, 318(5850), 594–98. doi:10.1126/science.1142995.

Kornysheva, K., Von Anshelm-Schiffer, A.-M., and Schubotz, R. I. (2011). Inhibitory stimulation of the ventral premotor cortex temporarily interferes with musical beat rate preference. *Human Brain Mapping*, 32(8), 1300–10. doi:10.1002/hbm.21109.

Kornysheva, K., Von Cramon, D. Y., Jacobsen, T., and Schubotz, R. I. (2010). Tuning-in to the beat: aesthetic appreciation of musical rhythms correlates with a premotor activity boost. *Human Brain Mapping*, 31(1), 48–64. doi:10.1002/hbm.20844.

Leder, H., Bär, S., and Topolinski, S. (2012). Covert painting simulations influence aesthetic appreciation of artworks. *Psychological Science*, 23(12), 1479–81. doi:10.1177/0956797612452866.

Livingstone, M. S. (1988). Art, illusion and the visual system. *Scientific American*, 258, 78–85.

———. (2008). *Vision and Art: The Biology of Seeing*. Abrams.

Livingstone, M. S., and Hubel, D. H. (1987). Psychophysical evidence for separate channels for the perception of form, color, movement, and depth. *Journal of Neuroscience*, 7(11), 3416–68. Retrieved from http://www.ncbi.nlm.nih.gov/pubmed/3316524.

Maeda, F., Kleiner-Fisman, G., and Pascual-Leone, A. (2002). Motor facilitation while observing hand actions : specificity of the effect and role of observer's orientation. *Journal of Neurophysiology*, 87, 1329–35.

Molenberghs, P., Cunnington, R., and Mattingley, J. B. (2012). Brain regions with mirror properties: a meta-analysis of 125 human fMRI studies. *Neuroscience and Biobehavioral Reviews*, 36(1), 341–49. doi:10.1016/j.neubiorev.2011.07.004.

Mondrian, P. (1986). *The New Art-The New Life : The Collected Writings of Piet Mondrian*. Boston: J.K. Hall.

Moser, E. I., Kropff, E., and Moser, M.-B. (2008). Place cells, grid cells, and the brain's spatial representation system. *Annual Review of Neuroscience*, 31, 69–89. doi:10.1146/annurev.neuro.31.061307.090723.

Nadal, M., Munar, E., Capó, M. A., Rosselló, J., and Cela-Conde, C. J. (2008). Towards a framework for the study of the neural correlates of aesthetic preference. *Spatial Vision*, 21(3-5), 379–96. doi:10.1163/156856808784532653.

Pointillism. (2013). Retrieved May 8, 2013, from http://en.wikipedia.org/wiki/Pointillism.

Rizzolatti, G., and Craighero, L. (2004). The mirror-neuron system. *Annual Review of Neuroscience Neurosci*, 27, 169–92.

Rizzolatti, G., and Fabbri-Destro, M. (2010). Mirror neurons: from discovery to autism. *Experimental Brain Research*, 200(3-4), 223–37. doi:10.1007/s00221-009-2002-3.

Rizzolatti, G., Fadiga, L., Gallese, V., and Fogassi, L. (1996). Premotor cortex and the recognition of motor actions. *Brain Research. Cognitive Brain Research*, 3(2), 131–41. Retrieved from http://www.ncbi.nlm.nih.gov/pubmed/8713554.

Rizzolatti, G., Fogassi, L., and Gallese, V. (2001). Neurophysiological mechanisms underlying the understanding and imitation of action. *Nature Reviews Neuroscience*, 2(9), 661–70. doi:10.1038/35090060.

Rizzolatti, G., and Sinigaglia, C. (2010). The functional role of the parieto-frontal mirror circuit: interpretations and misinterpretations. *Nature Reviews Neuroscience*, 11(4), 264–74. doi:10.1038/nrn2805.

Small, D. M., Zatorre, R. J., Dagher, A., Evans, A. C., and Jones-Gotman, M. (2001). Changes in brain activity related to eating chocolate: from pleasure to aversion. *Brain*, 124(Pt 9), 1720–33. Retrieved from http://www.ncbi.nlm.nih.gov/pubmed/11522575.

Umiltà, M. A., Berchio, C., Sestito, M., Freedberg, D., and Gallese, V. (2012). Abstract art and cortical motor activation: an EEG study. *Frontiers in Human Neuroscience*, 6, 311. doi:10.3389/fnhum.2012.00311.

Vartanian, O., and Goel, V. (2004). Neuroanatomical correlates of aesthetic preference for paintings. *NeuroReport*, 15(5), 893–97. doi:10.1097/01.wnr.00001.

Zeki, S. (1980). The representation of colours in the cerebral cortex. *Nature*, 284(5755), 412–18. Retrieved from http://www.ncbi.nlm.nih.gov/pubmed/6767195.

———. (1999a). *Inner Vision: An Exploration of Art and the Brain*. Oxford: Oxford University Press.

———. (1999b). Art and the Brain. *Journal of Consciousness Studies*, 6(6-7), 76–96.

Zeki, S., and Lamb, M. (1994). The neurology of kinetic art. *Brain*, 117, 607–36. Retrieved from http://www.ncbi.nlm.nih.gov/pubmed/8032869.

Zeki, S., and Stutters, J. (2012). A brain-derived metric for preferred kinetic stimuli. *Open Biology*, 2(2), 120001. doi:10.1098/rsob.120001.

Part III

SMELL AND TASTE IN MUSEUMS

10

The Forgotten Sense

Using Olfaction in a Museum Context: A Neuroscience Perspective

Richard J. Stevenson

INTRODUCTION

While smell may be the forgotten sense, many museums are now starting to make use of its unusual psychological properties. In this chapter I want to start by giving some sense of how smell is currently being deployed, before turning to explore the unusual—and exploitable—psychological characteristics of this sense. The second part of the chapter focuses on smell and the vision impaired, who because museums are highly visuocentric, are most deprived in terms of access (Hetherington, 2000). The final part of the chapter examines how the unusual characteristics of smell can be used to enhance the museum experience for all patrons and how this can be practically achieved. Ironically, this developing trend for more direct contact with artifacts— smelling, touching, and even tasting—represents a return to the pre-Victorian museum experience, where multisensory engagement was the norm (Classen, 2007; Classen and Howes, 2006).

The deliberative use of smell in museums can be divided into two major types. The first concerns activities that routinely and directly engage the nose. There are to my knowledge at least ten museums that are wholly devoted to smell. These museums are all focused on the perfume industry— hence three being in France (Museum of Perfume in Paris; Osmotheque in Versailles; and the International Museum of Perfume in Grasse)—with exhibits including perfumery ingredients and famous perfumes (past and present), with many available for smelling. Also within this category would fall museums primarily devoted to food and drink. These are included here because a significant component of flavor perception comes from retronasal olfaction, the process by which volatile chemicals from food or drink pass up the back of the throat to stimulate the nose (Rozin, 1982). According to the food history society (see foodhistorynews.com), worldwide, there are over 1,400 museums devoted to different aspects of eating and drinking. Many of these involve sampling (i.e., retronasal olfaction) or sniffing foods or ingredients—be it noodles in Japan or condiments at the National Mustard Museum in Wisconsin. Also subsumed under this category are the twenty or so museums devoted solely to wine (see oenologist.com for listings), again with a focus on history, manufacturing techniques, and, of course, appreciation of this product. A final grouping, which I have also subsumed under this class, is special exhibitions that draw attention to the olfactory sensorium. Recent examples include Adventures in Scent at the British Museum in London (2011), Sensorium in New York (2011), and the Center for Olfactory Art, which has yet to debut at the New York Museum of Art and Design (see *New York Times*, March 16, 2011).

The second category, and the one closest to the focus of this chapter, concerns the use of smell as one part of a wider multimodal exhibit. There are probably many other examples than the ones I have been able to find, but Table 10.1 provides a sense of the sort of situations in which odors are currently being used. In the majority of the examples listed here, the idea seems to be to create a more realistic and engaging sense impression. One interesting caveat to this idea concerns odors from societies that have long since ceased to exist (e.g., what *did* the ancient Romans smell like?). Odors are rarely ever preserved in the way that artifacts from the other sense modalities are (e.g., paintings [visual], musical instruments [sound], clothes [touch]), so many of the more ancient historical examples are often little more than well-educated guesses at what things *may* have smelled like (Jenner, 2011). Notwithstanding this accuracy caveat, odorizing particular exhibits clearly has benefits. Odors can serve as powerful retrieval cues, bringing to mind evocative memories from a person's childhood. More generally, they can make one feel a *part* of what is being smelled and can create powerful, and often negative emotions—emotions that may be quite appropriate and add significantly to the impact of particular exhibits (e.g., fear/disgust in the context of a World War I trench—see Table 10.1). Finally, at a subtler level, they can affect mood and arousal, without a person realizing that these effects are being driven by olfaction. Before turning to look in more detail at these three properties of the olfactory sense, I have provided a brief overview of how olfaction works and its inherent limitations. There are two reasons for including this. First, many readers of this book, while familiar with the basics of the major senses, are probably less familiar with the mechanisms underpinning olfactory perception. Second, for anyone contemplating using this sense, it is obviously useful to know its capacities—and limitations.

Table 10.1.   Some examples of odors used to create multimodal museum exhibits

Museum name
  Odors and exhibits

American Museum of Natural History, New York
  Gunpowder smell of moonrock in "Beyond Planet Earth"
  Tropical rain forest smells in "Dzanga-Sangha" rain forest exhibit
Boston Museum of Science
  "What's the Message Exhibit"—siren, flashing lights, and the smell of smoke
Chicago History Museum
  Steel, livestock production, etc., reflecting odors associated with local industry
Children's Museum of Indianapolis
  Scented dinosaur breath (T-rex)
Creation Museum, Petersburg, Kentucky
  Scent of freshly cut timber on the "Noah's ark construction site"
Dewa Roman Experience, Chester, UK
  Roman-related scents, associated with each exhibit (e.g., latrines)
Dresden Military History Museum
  Smell of decaying flesh, dirt, sweat, and gunpowder in a World War I trench
Fort Worth Museum of Science and History
  "Grossology" traveling show—match body odor smells to body parts
Jorvik Viking Museum, York, UK
  Viking-related scents, associated with each exhibit (e.g., blacksmith)
Natural History Museum, London
  Scented dinosaur breath (T-rex)
Tower of London
  Royal bedchamber, with exhibits imbued with appropriate "medieval" odors
Winston Churchill's Britain at War Experience, London
  Smoke, musty tube smell, etc.—recreating the "blitz" experience

THE SENSE OF SMELL

People use their nose for smelling and, as noted above, for perceiving flavor, and this dual mode of stimulation—sniffing and smelling (technically orthonasal perception) and flavor (technically retronasal smelling)—is unique among the senses (Rozin, 1982). The flavor mode, which passes largely unrecognized, involves the passage of food smells from the mouth up the back of the throat (via the nasopharynx), to the same set of receptors that are stimulated by orthonasal olfaction.

Things that smell—odors—are usually composed of tens or hundreds of individual chemicals that readily evaporate at room temperature. Coffee, for example, has several hundred constituent chemicals, and the brain's task in perceiving coffee odor is to recognize this *combination* of chemicals (Stevenson and Wilson, 2007). This task is made harder because the air we breathe is full of odorous molecules. To get around this, and so we can notice the "appearance" of new odors, we adapt fairly rapidly to smells present within our environment. For example, recall when you enter someone's house—the odor of the house is noticeable, but after a while it slips out of consciousness and is no longer available for perception. When a new combination of chemicals is detected by the receptors on the olfactory epithelium, which is located a few centimeters back from the bridge of your nose, the brain starts the process of recognizing this chemical blend. Crucially, it does this using a recognition-based process that is heavily dependent upon memory. The brain attempts to match the incoming neural pattern, which represents the blend of chemicals in the nervous system, with previous stored patterns. The closer the match, the more likely you are to perceive what you smell as *that* particular odor. This raises an important point. My history of smelling may be different from yours, and this means that to varying degrees, what you perceive is probably somewhat different to what I perceive, when we both sniff the same odorant. This difference may become more marked between different cultures where each has been exposed to different types of environmental odorants (foods, perfumes, plants, etc.). This is further compounded by genetic variability. Humans have over 300 different olfactory receptors, and many of us have subtle and not so subtle differences in this receptor set that may further individualize our sense of smell (Hudson and Distel, 2002). The upshot of all this is that there may be considerable individual differences in what we perceive when we smell the same odorant. These individual differences are likely to be most pronounced when an odor is smelled out of context, as contextual cues seem to be a very powerful influence in shaping what we smell. For example, participants appear to *smell* red wine when they sniff white wine that has been colored red (Morrot, Brochet and Dubourdieu, 2001).

The neuroanatomy of olfaction is also unusual, and this contributes in no small measure to its psychological qualities (Stevenson, 2009). The olfactory system is closely connected to the brain systems responsible for personal memory (i.e., episodic memory), and indeed one of the first signs of Alzheimer's disease—before it is in any other way apparent—is an impaired sense of smell (Hawkes and Doty, 2009). More broadly, age itself takes a significant toll on olfactory perception, as it does on memory, and this may impair older adults' ability to enjoy their sense of smell (Hawkes and Doty, 2009). It has been suggested that the anatomical overlap between memory and smell contributes to olfaction's ability to tap and retrieve far older memories than other sensory systems. Relatedly, the close anatomical proximity to memory structures may also be responsible for strongly imbuing olfactory experiences with affect. Limbic structures such as the amygdala—also involved in emotional memory—are closely connected to the olfactory system (Herz, Eliassen, Beland and Souza, 2004). In addition, considerable olfactory processing takes place in the orbitofrontal cortex of the brain, which is also important in the regulation of emotion and motivation (Hawkes and Doty, 2009). It may be these close anatomical relationships that lend olfaction the capacity to evoke strong emotions such as fear and disgust, to stimulate our appetites for food or bodily contact (i.e., perfume), and to make us feel as if we are in actual contact with the odorous object. Finally, unlike all of the other senses, olfactory information can reach the highest centers of the brain—cortical structures—without passing through the "gatekeeper," the thalamus (Tham, Stevenson and Miller, 2009). This may be why odors can affect conscious experience (i.e., mood, arousal) without us being aware of the cause. These olfactory capacities—retrieval of early memories, the sense of being part of the odor, powerful affective states, and behavior change without awareness of its cause—are the focus of the next section of the chapter.

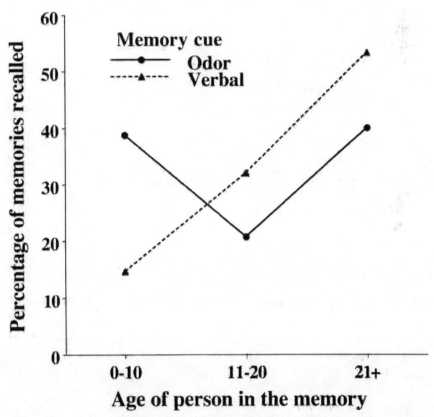

Figure 10.1. Percentage of memories recalled plotted against the age of the person in the memory (i.e., broadly memories of childhood [0-10], of teenage years [11–20], and of adulthood [21+]), when an odor cue is used and when an equivalent verbal cue is used, with elderly adult participants (data, averaged across studies, drawn from Chu & Downes, 2000; Willander & Larsson, 2006; Willander & Larsson, 2007).

MEMORY, AFFECT, AND MOOD

As can be seen in figure 10.1, ordinary household odors such as paint, coffee, or wine, are better able to evoke memories from childhood in older people, relative to verbal and other types of nonolfactory cues (Chu and Downes, 2000; Goddard, Pring and Felmingham, 2005; Willander and Larsson, 2006; Willander and Larsson, 2007). Indeed, in all of the studies that have examined the age of memories retrieved following an olfactory cue (i.e., sniff the odor and describe any memory it may bring to mind), all have found that odors lead to the retrieval of more memories drawn from the first decade of that person's life than other sensory cues. Some good examples of odor-cued memories are presented by Laird (1935), and although he did not quantify his participants' responses, the descriptions nicely illustrate some of the qualities of these odor-cued memories—their age, evocativeness, and notable emotional content. One participant described how

> The smell of fresh sawdust invariably takes me back to the sawmill where my father worked when I was a small boy. The sight of sawdust does not call up these boyhood memories, but the odor of fresh sawdust never fails to reconstruct a series of vivid pictures so graphic that for the moment I live the scenes again. (Laird, 1935, p. 126)

And another

> When 10–13 years of age I had much to do with horses and stables. Then nothing. At 20 years of age I one day was walking down a country road and a cart laden with stable manure was some 100 yards ahead of me. The odor caused a sudden shock of memory of the years of my childhood, which thrilled me into immobility. (Laird, 1935, p. 129)

These types of responses, perhaps most poignantly captured in Proust's *Swanns Way* (see p. 58 in the Chatto-Windus, 1960 edition), seem to be experienced by many people (Chu and Downes, 2000). While these odor-cued experiences may be personally unique, it is highly likely that odors common to a particular age cohort——especially relating to school and childhood—would be effective at cueing old and evocative memories in people from that group.

Two further unique characteristics of odor-cued memories, evident in the descriptions above, have also been formally demonstrated. First, odor-cued memories tend to be especially vivid and may make a person feel as if they have been transported back to the actual time and place where the memory took place. This capacity is enhanced by the olfactory system's ability to generate more emotive memories. For example, Herz (2004) conducted a study at the Smithsonian Institution in Washington, D.C., having participants first retrieve a memory to a verbal cue (e.g., popcorn), and then seeing whether odor (e.g., popcorn odor), vision (e.g., picture of popcorn) or sound (e.g., sound of popcorn popping) could affect the quality of the recalled memory. Odor cues were significantly more likely to generate both a more emotive memory and to make that memory especially evocative—feeling as if one were there. These effects were evident in both men and women, and were present irrespective of age.

Just as the memories that odors evoke seem to be more affectively laden than the memories evoked by other sensory modalities, it has also been argued that olfaction per se is the most emotionally evocative sense. This idea was most aptly captured by Engen (1982), an influential olfactory researcher, who noted that "Functionally, smell may be to emotion what sight or hearing are to cognition" (Engen, 1982, p. 3). Certainly, from a linguistic perspective, this would seem to be the case, as several researchers, examining many different languages, find that words used to refer to smell are frequently affect-laden, with unpleasant terms outnumbering the pleasant (see Ehrlichman and Bastone, 1992). The dominance of affect when experiencing odors has also been documented empirically. Here, participants are asked to make similarity ratings between a large set of odors so that a map of perceptual space can be built up (i.e., which odors cluster together or apart). Another set of participants then evaluates each odor on a whole range of rating scales (e.g., how sweet does this smell?), and then various statistical techniques are used to determine the dimensions that underlie odor's psychological space. A consistent finding from such research has been that hedonic judgments are of primary importance (e.g., Schiffman, 1974). That is, odors we like tend to cluster together, as do odors we dislike, with both clusters separated in psychological space.

While there would seem to be a fairly good case that olfaction is the emotive sense, this may be an oversimplification. For example, if you ask participants to list the first five items that come to mind for each of the sense modalities and then ask them to rate the emotion and pleasantness associated with each of these items, you find that vision either equals or exceeds olfaction on both of these measures, seemingly contradicting the findings outlined above (Ehrlichman and Bastone, 1992). However, as these authors and others note, there is a further aspect to olfactory emotional experience. Olfaction seems to be phenomenologically more proximal than vision (Ehrlichman and Bastone, 1992; Rouby and Bensafi, 2002). That is, we feel as if an odor is *actually* in contact with us, *directly* acting upon us, making us *feel* ill, disgusted, fearful (or perhaps happy), in a way that we do not feel with most forms of visual or auditory sensation. Two "thought experiments" may help illustrate this distinction. First, imagine just smelling an imitation fecal odor (and one you *know* to be an imitation) versus its visual equivalent, looking at a picture of a piece of feces. Both experiences would be unpleasant, but I suspect that the visceral nature of your response to the smell would more rapidly impel you to move away from it than from the picture. Second, imagine having a bright light shone into your eyes or a loud sound directed at your ears—what would you do? Move away, I suspect, because both of these experiences produce something more akin to what we routinely experience with smell. That is, bright lights and loud noises are often viscerally unpleasant—they drive us away—and it is this visceral response that seems to make olfaction appear especially emotive. It is probably for this reason that olfaction has such power in exhibits like the World War I trench in the Dresden Military History museum.

A key question when considering how to deploy olfaction to generate a visceral response is whether the odorant is likely to engender this effect in most people. While learning is important in shaping a particular affective response to an odor (e.g, Engen, 1982), this may be less important for unpleasant smells. This is because there may be a significant innate component to what makes a smell foul (Khan et al., 2007). A further factor, as noted earlier, is the context in which the odor is experienced. Context, and the beliefs they may generate about what odor is being smelled, have a powerful effect on one's affective reaction. This is nicely illustrated in Mark Twain's "The Invalid's Story" (Clemens, 1882), where a man is driven to spend the night outdoors in a bad storm by a smell he *believes* to be that of a rotting corpse. It turns out to be the odor from some cheese. Not only have the effects of belief on smell been demonstrated empirically (e.g., Morrot, Brochet and Dubourdieu, 2001), the important point here is that embedding a foul smell within an appropriate context will likely produce the desired effect—leading to a particularly memorable experience (see Aggleton and Waskett, 1999).

So far, the olfactory effects that I have been considering are all liminal—that is, the perceiver knows an odor to be present. However, it has long been recognized by the business world (e.g., Baron and Thomley, 1994) that odors can be used subliminally to manipulate mood and behavior to commercial advantage (e.g., piping bakery aroma to the entrance of a supermarket to entice customers in). The term subliminal is used here with some caution, because it may be that if a person had their attention directed to their olfactory sensorium, they would indeed be able to report that a smell was present—but normally the smell may be unobtrusive enough not to draw attention. Using olfactory stimuli in this way does appear to affect people's mood and behavior (e.g., Ehrlichman and Bastone, 1992; Lawless, 1991). Such effects can be classified into two types—generic effects, whereby pleasant odors induce pleasant mood, and unpleasant ones an unpleasant mood; and specific effects, where it is claimed that certain odors can produce selective impacts upon a person's mood and behavior.

Several studies have now demonstrated that placing pleasant odors in the environment can uplift and improve (or depress if using unpleasant smells) people's mood. What is especially interesting is that these effects do not seem to differ between incidental studies where participants' attention is never drawn to the odor, and nonincidental studies, which ask, for example, the participant to wear a clearly odorized mask (Lawless, 1991). This would seem to suggest that generic effects of odor on mood work irrespective of whether the odor is noticed or not. Although there is considerable disagreement about whether certain odors have specific effects—the sort of claims made by aromatherapy (e.g., sedative effects of lavender and the stimulating effects of jasmine) —there is little doubt that certain steroidal odors produced by the human body can subtly affect mood and behavior. Moreover, these effects are demonstrable at concentrations well below that required to produce conscious awareness. These include the calmative effects of female tears and human sweat (e.g., Gelstein et al., 2011; Sobel et al., 1999).

Odors, then, are adept at bringing to mind long-forgotten memories, and when these memories are recalled they may be vivid and emotional. Odors are also characterized by their capacity to induce strong affective responses, and while this may also be a characteristic of the other senses, the visceral nature of the response *combined* with this emotiveness can generate powerful feelings of reality and presence (i.e., as if one were there). In addition, odors can serve to manipulate mood, elevating it or depressing it depending upon the affective tone of the smell (i.e., pleasant or unpleasant), and these effects may occur independent of awareness. In the next section, I examine how odors can be used to augment the experience of people who lack one or more of the major senses, before turning more generally to the question of how these olfactory characteristics can be used and implemented in a museum context.

SENSORY IMPAIRMENT AND SMELL

Since the nineteenth century, museums have been highly visuocentric, with only a limited capacity to allow visitors to directly interact with exhibits (Classen, 2007; Classen and Howes, 2006; Hetherington, 2000). Although this has started to change over the last thirty years, it is arguably the vision impaired who stand most to benefit from a more interactive, experiential, and multisensory museum. For this reason, the focus here is on visual impairment.

The capacity of visually impaired people to experience the full range of artifacts held by museums, art galleries, and other cultural archives has mainly focused on touch, and not surprisingly so given that this medium can be used to represent visible objects. Notwithstanding this, smell too has been invoked as another medium with which to augment a vision-impaired patron's sensory experience (Handa, Dairoku and Toriyama, 2010). Several museums already incorporate an olfactory component in tours specifically designed for vision-impaired patrons (e.g., the Vatican Museum, with linen shrouds smelling of myrrh and aloe; sensory tours at Brooklyn Museum of Art that include smelling components of particular pictures, and so on). This movement to include smell is also reflected in an olfactory guidebook to architectural spaces (Barbara and Perliss, 2006), enabling both sighted and the vision impaired the opportunity to enjoy unique "smellscapes."

While these efforts (and many others not documented here) are an important advance, I would suggest that moving a museum to a more experiential framework, in which all of the senses are engaged, would serve to break down barriers between vision-impaired and sighted patrons, making a more inclusive space. Moreover, by moving toward multisensory access to exhibits, this returns the museum experience to its beginnings. As several academic historians have noted (Classen, 2007; Classen and Howes, 2006; Hetherington, 2000), visitors to exhibitions in the pre-Victorian era expected to be able to touch, smell, and even taste exhibits. They wanted to actively manipulate and engage with artifacts, not just look at them and hear about them. Part of the reason for this is the visceral satisfaction that comes from touching and smelling, as discussed above. There is also the visceral thrill of sampling something that is precious or old, something that may have been in contact with famous people or an event of great historical significance. Part of this derives from the magical act of transfer that occurs with the contact senses—taste, touch, and smell—that allows some essence of the object to transfer to the person doing the contacting (see Rozin and Nemeroff, 1990). This magical transfer—positive contamination—is not available from the distance senses of looking or hearing; it is a property of senses that induce a visceral sense of contact—smell, taste, and touch.

People with a visual impairment are well placed to enjoy their sense of smell. It has long been argued that losses in one sensory domain may be compensated by gains in the others, and there is certainly evidence to support this contention (e.g., Cuevas et al., 2009; Cuevas et al., 2010; Rosenbluth, Grossman and Kaitz, 2000). In the olfactory domain, until recently, anecdotes of such sensory compensation were abundant, with perhaps the best example being Julia Brace, who could seemingly sort the *washed* clothes of the inmates of Hartford Asylum using her exquisite sense of smell (Gibson, 1953). Empirical investigations have tended to confirm that olfactory abilities in vision-impaired people (blind since birth) exceed that of non-vision impaired controls. Several studies have documented a better ability to name odors, which seems to result from greater attention to this sense modality combined with a better ability to link the sense experience with a verbal label (e.g., Rosenbluth, Grossman and Kaitz, 2000). More recent investigations also suggest that vision-impaired people have enhanced perceptual abilities too. Compared to non-vision impaired blindfolded controls, vision impaired people outperform the latter group on odor discrimination and odor detection, tasks that are presumed to reflect more basic sensory processes (Cuevas et al., 2009; Cuevas et al., 2010). While vision-impaired people may not all have a nose like Julia Brace, they significantly exceed most sighted people in ability, making olfaction a great medium to augment their enjoyment of museums.

FOOD FOR THOUGHT

This section deals with two pragmatic issues—how one might utilize smell in a museum setting, and how one might actually implement it. As described above, smell has some unique characteristics that should not be disregarded. It can act as a powerful retrieval cue to childhood memories, it can induce strong negative emotions, it can subtly change one's mood, and it can induce a sense of *being* part of the thing in question. Drawing upon these special properties, it is possible to suggest at least five ways (and there are probably many more) in which olfaction could be used in a museum context. Each of these is discussed below, as well as identifying the sort of patron who may benefit from each type of use.

The first use, and one that most dominates the examples listed in Table 10.1, is to use olfaction to generate a sense of being there or phenomenological proximity. This type of odor manipulation is suitable for all age groups, assuming of course that the odor is widely recognizable (this is not a problem if it is common and presented in context). The benefits of using olfaction in this way are to make a person feel immersed in the exhibit, leaving them with a more complete impression of what it was like—and possibly, more potent and emotive memories of their museum visit (Aggleton and Waskett, 1999). A second possible use for olfaction is as a tool to "throw" an adult back to their childhood, thus engaging smells' capacity to retrieve older memories and the unique feelings associated with them. This approach may need careful focusing at particular age groups, with the type of smell being dated to that cohort's childhood or the use of generic childhood smells (e.g., crayons). This method could be used to manipulate emotion in much the same way that period music can in a movie soundtrack. A third potential use is for the induction of negative emotions such as disgust and fear. This may be particularly effective when there is a need to enhance the emotional pungency of an exhibit. Smell may render it a truly visceral experience. This approach has also been used as means of appealing to child and teenage audiences, such as with the "Grossology" traveling show (see Table 10.1). A fourth use is to engage smell for subtler forms of emotional manipulation, with the aim being to induce mild positive or negative mood states, which can then serve to augment the appreciation of a set of exhibits (e.g., scenting a larger space). The final possibility concerns the use of scent more generally within a building. Vision-impaired people use olfactory cues for wayfinding (e.g., Koutsokle-nis and Papadopoulos, 2011), and one of their complaints about museums is the difficulty they have in finding their way about (Handa, Dairoku and Toriyama, 2010). To this end it might be possible to scent certain landmarks or spaces to assist wayfinding, as vision-impaired patrons are likely to notice such olfactory cues.

How then might one go about actually utilizing olfaction? As the intro-duction above and Table 10.1 attest, many museums have successfully done so—so it is eminently achievable. In most cases commercial organizations have been tasked with both creating the odorants used in the exhibit(s) and more crucially, with developing the technology to deliver the odorants. In-deed delivery can be problematic, with a need to keep odorant levels suffi-ciently localized so as not to contaminate a larger space, while on the other hand ensuring sufficient strength at the targeted location. A brief search of the Internet reveals several commercial entities both in the United States and Europe that specialize in odor development and delivery, including for museum and exhibition spaces (please note that the author has no commer-cial affiliations and suggests commercial assistance as the task requires a certain level of expertise). In addition, it is also possible to obtain odorants from specialist suppliers. These can be found by searching the Internet for "flavor [flavour] houses" or for "perfumists and flavorists [flavourists]." Pretty much any odor can be safely imitated and obtained, but I stress again that successful delivery is likely to be the more significant obstacle and this requires specialist support.

CONCLUSION

Museums seem to be moving toward an appreciation that people have more than one sense—vision—and that the other senses can be productively em-ployed to enhance patrons' experience of exhibits. This movement returns museums to something like their original form, in which patrons could explore objects with all of their senses, allowing them to experience the sense of being there, the visceral thrill of contact, generated by the senses of smell, touch, and taste. While smell may be potent at retrieving particularly personal memories from early childhood and able to generate strong emotions and moods, good or bad, with minimal conscious awareness, it is perhaps its capacity to make the person feel *as if they were there* that may be its most potent contribution. This sense of "being there" can clearly be used to make exhibits thrill and engage in a way that many museums seem now to be embracing. While museums have, so to speak, started to come out of their glass cases, thus allowing the scent of their exhibits to enhance visitor experience, there is still a long way to go before we can truly enjoy the multisensory museum of yore.

ACKNOWLEDGMENTS

The author thanks the Australian Research Council for their continued support.

REFERENCES

Aggleton, J. P. and Waskett, L. (1999). The ability of odours to serve as state-dependent cues for real-world memories: can Viking smells aid the recall of Viking experiences? *British Journal of Psychology*, 90, 1–7.

Barbara, A. and Perliss, A. (2006). Invisible Architecture: Experiencing Places through the Sense of Smell. New York: Skira.

Baron, R. A. and Thomley, J. (1994). A whiff of reality. *Environment and Behavior*, 25, 766–84.

Chu, S. and Downes, J. (2000). Long live Proust: The odour-cued autobiographical memory bump. *Cognition*, 75, B41–50.

Classen, C. (2007). Museum manners: the sensory life of the early museum. *Journal of Social History*, 40, 895–914.

Classen, C. and Howes, D. (2006). The museum as sensescape: Western sensibilities and indigenous artifacts. In E. Edwards, C. Gosden and R. Phillips (eds.), *Sensible Objects: Colonialism, Museum and Material Culture.* Oxford: Berg.

Clemens, S. L. (1882, 1957). "The Invalid's Story." In C. Neider (ed.), *The Complete Short Stories of Mark Twain.* Garden City, NY: International Collectors Library.

Cuevas, I., Plaza, P., Rombaux, P., Collignon, O., De Volder, A. and Renier, L. (2010). Do people who became blind early in life develop a better sense of smell? A psychophysical study. *Journal of Visual Impairment and Blindness,* 104, 369–79.

Cuevas, I., Plaza, P., Rombaux, P., De Volder, A. and Renier, L. (2009). Odour discrimination and identification are improved in early blindness. *Neuropsychologia*, 47, 3079–83.

Ehrlichman, H. and Bastone, L. (1992). Olfaction and emotion. In M. Serby and K. Chobor (eds.), *Science of Olfaction*, pp. 410–38. New York: Springer-Verlag.

Engen, T. (1982). *The Perception of Odors*. New York: Academic Press.

Gelstein, S., Yeshurun, Y., Rozenkrantz, L., Shushan, S., Frumin, I., Roth, Y. and Sobel, N. (2011). Human tears contain a chemosignal. *Science*, 331, 226–30.

Gibson, E. J. (1953). Improvement in perceptual judgments as a function of controlled practice or training. *Psychological Bulletin,* 50, 401–31.

Goddard, L., Pring, L. and Felmingham, N. (2005). The effects of cue modality on the quality of personal memories retrieved. *Memory*, 13, 79–86.

Handa, K., Dairoku, H. and Toriyama, Y. (2010). Investigation of priority needs in terms of museum service accessibility for visually impaired visitors. *The British Journal of Visual Impairment*, 28, 221–34.

Hawkes, C. and Doty, R. (2009). *The Neurology of Olfaction*. Cambridge: Cambridge University Press.

Herz, R. S. (2004). A naturalistic analysis of autobiographical memories triggered by olfactory visual and auditory stimuli. *Chemical Senses*, 29, 217–24.

Herz, R.S., Eliassen, J., Beland, S. and Souza, T. (2004). Neuroimaging evidence for the emotional potency of odor-evoked memory. *Neuropsychologia*, 42, 371–78.

Hetherington, K. (2000). Museums and the visually impaired: the spatial politics of access. *The Sociological Review*, 30, 444–63.

Hudson, R. and Distel, H. (2002). The individuality of odor perception. In C. Rouby, B. Schaal, D. Dubois, R. Gervais and A. Holley (eds.), *Olfaction, Taste and Cognition,* pp. 408–20. Cambridge: Cambridge University Press.

Jenner, M. (2011). Follow your nose? Smell, smelling and their histories. *American Historical Review*, 116, 335–51.

Khan, R., Luk, C., Flinker, A., Aggarwal, A., Lapid, H., Haddad, R. and Sobel, N. (2007). Predicting odor pleasantness from odorant structure: pleasantness as a reflection of the physical world. *Journal of Neuroscience*, 27, 10015–23.

Koutsoklenis, A. and Papadopoulos, K. (2011). Olfactory cues used for wayfinding in urban environments by individuals with visual impairments. *Journal of Visual Impairment and Blindness,* 105, 692–702.

Laird, D. (1935). What can you do with your nose? *The Scientific Monthly*, 41, 126–30.

Lawless, H. T. (1991). Effects of odors on mood and behavior: aromatherapy and related effects. In D. Laing, R. Doty and W. Breipohl (eds.), *The Human Sense of Smell*, pp. 361–86. Berlin: Springer-Verlag.

Morrot, G., Brochet, F., and Dubourdieu, D. (2001). The color of odors. *Brain & Language*, 79, 309–20.

Rosenbluth, R., Grossman, E. S. and Kaitz, M. (2000). Performance of early blind and sighted children on olfactory tasks. *Perception*, 29, 101–10.

Rouby, C. and Bensafi, M. (2002). Is there a hedonic dimension to odors? In C. Rouby, B. Schaal, D. Dubois, R. Gervais and A. Holley (eds.), *Olfaction, Taste and Cognition*, pp. 140–59. Cambridge: Cambridge University Press.

Rozin, P. (1982). "Taste-smell confusions" and the duality of the olfactory sense. *Perception and Psychophysics*, 31, 397–404.

Rozin, P. and Nemeroff, C. (1990). The laws of sympathetic magic. In J. Stigher, G. Hecht, and R. Shweker (eds.), *Cultural Psychology: Essays on Comparative Human Development*, pp. 205–32. Cambridge: Cambridge University Press.

Schiffman, S. S. (1974). Physiochemical correlates of olfactory quality. *Science*, 185, 112–17.

Sobel, N., Prabhakaran, V., Hartley, C., Desmond, J., Glover, G., Sullivan, E. and Gabrieli, J. D. (1999). Blind smell: brain activation induced by an undetected airborne chemical. *Brain*, 122, 209–17.

Stevenson, R. J. (2009). Phenomenal and access consciousness in olfaction. *Consciousness and Cognition*, 18, 1004–17.

Stevenson, R. J. and Wilson, D. A. (2007). Olfactory perception: an object recognition approach. *Perception*, 36, 1821–33.

Tham, W., Stevenson, R. J. and Miller, L. A. (2009). The functional role of the mediodorsal thalamic nucleus in olfaction. *Brain Research Reviews*, 62, 109–26.

Willander, J. and Larsson, M. (2006). Smell your way back to childhood: autobiographical odor memory. *Psychonomic Bulletin and Review*, 13, 240–44.

———. (2007). Olfaction and emotion: the case of autobiographical memory. *Memory and Cognition*, 35, 1659–63.

11

The Scented Museum

Andreas Keller

The challenges and opportunities faced by artists, exhibition designers, architects, curators, and educators who consider incorporating smells in a museum exhibit are very different from the far more familiar challenges and opportunities of working with visual objects. To avoid the problems associated with using odors in museums and to successfully create a diverse and engaging multimodal experience, it is important to be aware of the fundamental differences between vision and olfaction. The goal of this chapter is to outline three fundamental differences between olfaction and vision and thereby help those who plan to incorporate odors in exhibits to make informed decisions.

The most obvious challenge of working with odors is that they are more difficult to stably position in space than visual objects. A second important difference between vision and olfaction that needs to be understood to effectively use odors is that odors, much more so than visual stimuli, have very strong effects even when they are not consciously perceived. The third peculiarity of olfaction that I will discuss here is that odors are more potent at triggering strong emotional and physiological responses than stimuli in other modalities. All these differences between olfaction and vision are differences of degree. Visual stimuli can also be difficult to control, and they often have robust subliminal effects and trigger strong emotional responses. However, being aware of these three differences will allow exhibition designers to use odors to complement visual experience in a way no other stimuli could.

SPACE AND TIME

The difference between visual objects and smells, of which many who have worked with odors are most painfully aware, is that the clouds of odor molecules that cause olfactory experiences are difficult to control in time and space. Odor clouds cannot be spatially delimited, and when there are several odor sources in a room, the odors overlap and blur and are perceived as a blend. The odor clouds are also in constant movement and cannot be tied to a specific point in space.

Because odor molecules are rapidly carried away from the object emitting them by turbulent airflow, the odor concentration close to the olfactory object—where one would want the visitors to have an olfactory experience—is often low. To fix this, one has to increase the number of odor molecules released. However, when too many odor molecules are released by the olfactory object, the airflow will no longer be sufficient to remove all of them, and odor molecules will accumulate and fill the gallery with an odor of ever-increasing intensity. The solution to this problem is to create a dynamic equilibrium in which the number of odor molecules released is high enough to create a uniform smell of the desired intensity in the room but not so high that odor molecules start to accumulate. In a dynamically changing environment like a museum gallery, this is technically very challenging. There are specialized companies that offer solutions to this problem. The German company Scentcommunication made the elegant odor diffusion machines used in The Art of Scent (1889–2012) in the Museum of Art and Design in New York. Their American competitor scentair odorized the Dinosphere exhibit at the Children's Museum of Indianapolis with the scent of rain forest and dinosaur dung.

Delivering an odor at the right time to the right place is a problem for all types of scented entertainment. An illuminating account of the failed efforts to use odors to enrich the movie theater experience can be found in Avery Gilbert's *What the Nose Knows* (Gilbert, 2008). Gilbert interviewed people who attended, in 1959, screenings of *Behind the Great Wall*, the first commercially released movie with olfactory accompaniment. After half a century, the interviewees still recalled that "the smells got all mixed up and they couldn't get them out; so it was a terrible situation," and "Your clothes reeked when you came out of this stuff that had been dumped into the air conditioning system. As I recall there was even a fine mist in the air." According to *Time* magazine, the accumulated odors were "strong enough to give a bloodhound a headache" (Gilbert, 2008, p. 160). The solution to the accumulation of odor is, of course, to use less odor. Then, however, one will have to face comments like those in the *New York Times* about the smells being "the least impressive or even detectable features of the show" and "faint and fleeting" (Gilbert, 2008, p. 163).

It is very difficult to create a uniform concentration of an odor that is stable over time in a large space. This problem is unique to the olfactory modality. In trying to tackle this problem there is a danger of either using too little odor, so that many visitors will not experience the olfactory component of the exhibit, or too much odor, which will accumulate and make the experience unpleasant. Just like when applying perfume, one should use less odor when in doubt.

PERCEPTIBLE AND SUBLIMINAL

Using less odor and thereby risking that many museum visitors will not experience the smells must seem like counterintuitive advice for those who are used to working with visual objects. A painting has to be seen to contribute to an exhibit. However, this difference in how olfactory and visual stimuli should be employed reflects the role these modalities play in a multimodal experience. Smelling is an active exploration of our environment, whereas seeing is passive and automatic. Our eyes are open as long as we are awake, whereas exploring the olfactory environment through sniffing is an active process and the sniffing is necessary to consciously perceive smells (Mainland and Sobel, 2006). There is a reason why we tell people to stop and *smell* the roses as a way of advising them to pay attention and appreciate the world around them. The smell of roses doesn't automatically draw our attention; we have to actively attend to it to be consciously aware of it (Keller, 2011). On the other hand, most of the time we do *see* the roses without stopping. We are very likely to attend to visual stimuli and become consciously aware of them, whereas we usually do not attend to our olfactory environment and are therefore often not aware of it. For a smell in a gallery to compete for our attention with a painting it has to be very strong. Unusually strong ambient smells, however, are always experienced as noxious, no matter what the smell. A better strategy than using smells that are strong enough to draw the visitors' attention to olfaction is to encourage visitors to pay attention to their olfactory environment and to let them discover the smells during their exploration of the exhibit.

Even if the odors are perceived as being very faint, they can have strong effects on the experience. In many cases it has even been shown that subliminal odors—odors at such a low concentration that they are not consciously perceived—influence mood and behavior. This is a further important difference between vision and olfaction that exhibition designers should be aware of: Odors are effective at very low concentration and even in the absence of the visitors being aware of them.

There is a large body of research investigating the effects of smells at low concentration. In a typical study, research subjects were instructed to evaluate "randomly generated computer line art." Unbeknownst to the subject, the room in which the experiment took place was scented either with lavender or with vanilla. Female subjects judged the art less favorable when they were exposed to vanilla, although only three of the ninety-three subjects reported, when they were debriefed after the experiment, that they perceived a smell (Lorig, 1992).

This result is not surprising, because subliminal odors have been shown to have profound influences on mood, behaviors, and cognitive performance (for an excellent review, see Sela and Sobel, 2010). Marketing strategists have discovered this effect, too. Headline-making studies have shown that releasing a specific odor among the slot machines on the casino floor of the Las Vegas Hilton increased the amount of money gambled in that area (Classen, Howes et al., 1994, p. 196). The British company Bodywise claimed that people who received bills treated with the odor androstenone, the smell of sweaty men, were 17 percent more likely to pay the bill than the control group that received unscented bills (Classen, Howes et al., 1994, page 196). Similarly, perfuming a small pizzeria in the Brittany region of France with lavender, but not with lemon, increased the amount of money spent on meals per patron (Guéguen and Petr, 2006). It has been rightly pointed out that studies like these need to be interpreted with care (Teller and Dennis, 2012), and the media attention is often not an accurate reflection of the quality of the research. However, the cumulative evidence shows clearly that odors that are not consciously perceived can elicit very strong responses.

Some studies have even identified cases in which an odor is *more* effective when it is not consciously perceived than when it is perceived. In one such study participants rated the likability of faces after they were exposed to an odor. The odor was either the pleasant citral (a lemon smell), the neutral anisole (anise odor), or the unpleasant valeric acid (a rancid, sweaty odor). How much the participants liked the faces was influenced by which odor they were exposed to before. However, this effect was seen only in the participants that were not consciously aware of the odors. No effect was seen in subjects that were aware of smelling an odor. In this study odors *only* had an effect when they were not perceived consciously. This suggests that with odors, less actually is more (Li, Moallem et al., 2007).

The moviegoers that watched *Behind the Great Wall* with olfactory accompaniment had to air out their clothes afterward because of the accumulation of odors in the auditorium. However, it is not necessary to use such high concentrations of odors to enrich the viewer's experience. Using odors below the detection level of most audience members would be sufficient to create a more immersive experience. A subtle smell of grass during scenes that play on a lawn or a hint of food odor during scenes that play in a restaurant may go unnoticed, but they would change the experience of watching the movie regardless.

Unfortunately, there is a practical problem with using subliminal odors in movie theaters or museum exhibits: It is difficult to get people to pay extra for odors that they cannot smell. Moviegoers that pay to experience a movie with olfactory accompaniment will be disappointed when there are no smells to experience during the movie, even when they liked the movie better than they would have liked the same movie without smells. Similarly, it is difficult to defend a budget for the olfactory component of a museum exhibit when many of the visitors will report that they did not smell anything. Using odors effectively in scented entertainment means to use them without drawing attention to them, but it is difficult to argue for the importance of something that receives no attention.

A question that arises from these considerations is if museums should announce when they are using odors in a multimodal exhibit. Announcing a scented exhibit has the effect that visitors pay close attention to their olfactory environment. This in itself can be a valuable part of the experience since it adds a dimension that is missing from most other experiences in our visuocentric society. When the visitors are actively searching for a scent they are also much more likely to consciously experience the smell. On the other hand, advertising the fact that smell is part of an exhibit creates pressure to use very high concentrations to avoid disappointing those visitors with a bad sense of smell. At these unnaturally high concentrations, smells will not have the same effects on the visitors as subtle smells have; they become just another sensation, only in a different modality.

EMOTIONS AND LANGUAGE

The responses elicited by olfactory stimuli, even by very weak ones, are of a very specific type and they are different from the responses to visual stimuli. Odors are more powerful than other stimuli at inducing emotions and at eliciting physiological and behavioral responses, but they rarely induce complex thoughts that can be verbalized (Ehrlichman and Bastone, 1992; Herz, 2002). As Trygg Engen, who pioneered the psychological investigation of olfaction, summarized it: "Functionally, smell may be to emotion what sight or hearing is to cognition" (Engen, 1982, p. 3).

The power of smells to elicit stronger responses than visual stimuli is easily demonstrated. It is difficult to make a movie that will reliably induce vomiting in the audience, but filling a movie theater with the smell of rotting corpses will have this effect. Importantly, informing the audience that the smell of rotting corpses is not "real," that it has been produced in a laboratory using synthetic chemicals, will not alter the response to the smell. This shows that we never experience an odor as representing another odor. Looking at a painting of dead bodies does not elicit nearly the same response as seeing actual dead bodies, because we are aware that the painting (no matter how realistic) is a representation. We respond to representations differently than to the thing they represent. This limits the visual experiences that can be created in a museum. Olfactory experiences, because smells in a museum *are* smells instead of merely *representing* smells, do not have this limitation.

The reason why olfaction is more closely related to emotions than vision is that olfactory information is processed in a different part of our brain than visual information. Olfactory information is processed in the limbic system, the part of the brain that is most directly involved in affective processing and the regulation of emotions (Gottfried, 2006). Visual information, in contrast, is processed most prominently in parts of the brain involved in language and abstract thought. In our evolutionary past, we used our sense of smell mainly to evaluate: to determine what to eat and who to have sex with (Stevenson, 2009). For these purposes it was important that smells elicit strong positive or negative emotions toward the source of the smell in order to induce the appropriate behavior.

Emotions are easily elicited by smells, but thoughts are much more easily elicited by visual stimuli. As the psychologist Rudolf Arnheim wrote: "One can indulge in smells and tastes, but one can hardly think in them" (1969, p. 18). Thinking is closely related to language, and it is as difficult to talk about smells as it is to think in smells. The 1,500-word review of a perfume exhibit (The Art of Scent [1889–2012]) in the *New York Times*, for example, did not discuss the olfactory experience except to say that one of the twelve perfumes smelled like cotton candy (Kino, 2012). Talking about what something smells like is the most basic way of talking about our olfactory experience, and even this most basic way of talking about smells is challenging. There are no words in the English language to describe smells in the same way in which "blue" or "green" describe colors. Instead, to talk about how something smells, we talk about the source of the odor. Things smell "flowery," "fruity," or "fishy." Furthermore, even the most familiar odors are difficult to identify when they are not experienced in their usual context. In one experiment the majority of participants was unable to name very common odors like beer, urine, roses, or motor oil (Desor and Beauchamp, 1974). Obviously, even those who couldn't name any of these odors would drink the beer but not the urine or the motor oil. This is how evolution has shaped our brain: We respond to odors correctly in many different ways, but we are not well-equipped to talk about them.

Visual stimuli activate different parts of our brain than smells, and when the two modalities are artfully combined, interesting effects can be achieved. One example of an art installation with an olfactory component was a gallery in which all the walls were covered by used $1 bills (Hans-Peter Feldmann, Guggenheim Museum New York, 2011). A reviewer of this exhibition remarked that "what sounds on paper like a conceptual stunt or a riff on Warholian materialism becomes overpoweringly physical in person, thanks to the smell of the used bills" (Rosenberg, 2011). A similar effect has been created by filling a gallery with Christmas trees that were discarded after the holidays (Klara Lidén, S.A.D. [in Klara Lidén: Pretty Vacant at Reena Spaulings Fine Art], New York, 2012). In both of these cases visual and olfactory stimuli complement each other, with the visual stimuli activating thought and the olfactory stimuli eliciting emotions. Seeing 100,000 one dollar bills pinned to the wall of a gallery results in thoughts about materialism and the role of money in the art world. Smelling a room full of money, however, is an unexpected and overpowering emotional experience. Similarly, seeing a forest of dead pines and firs in a small gallery makes the visitor think about the wastefulness of cutting down a tree to use it for a few days as decoration and then discard it. Smelling a forest of Christmas trees, on the other hand, elicits positive emotions in many who have happy childhood holiday memories that are triggered by the smell. (Triggering vivid childhood memories is another processes at which smells are better than sights; see Herz and Cupchik, 1995.)

Both the room filled with money and its smell and the room filled with Christmas trees and Christmas smell are multisensory installations that use their visual and olfactory components to engage the visitor's entire brain.

CONCLUSION

To successfully incorporate smells into a museum exhibit, the smell cannot be treated as one would treat a visual object. Instead, it is important to know the differences between vision and olfaction and recognize the limitations of odor, as well as the opportunities it presents. One limitation of odors is that they cannot easily be contained in space and time. When and where they will be experienced in an exhibition space is therefore often difficult to control. A further limitation is that our brains are not equipped to talk about what we smell in the same way in which we talk about what we see. Our culture is based on language, and experiences that are inaccessible to language, like olfactory experiences, therefore play only minor roles in our cultural institutions.

Despite these limitations, adding an olfactory component to a museum exhibit will open up an additional channel of communication between the exhibition designer and the museum visitor and add an olfactory dimension that is often missing from experiences in our visuocentric society (Classen, Howes et al., 1994) to the museum experience. Smells trigger emotions, physiological responses, and memories more efficiently than visual stimuli because they activate different parts of our brains. If we want a visitor to use all of her brain during a museum visit, odors need to be part of the experience. Furthermore, because smelling is an active perceptual process that requires attention, adding odors to an experience will result in a visitor's closer engagement and turn the passive experience into an active exploration. If odors are used with these goals in mind, then they will make a positive contribution to the overall experience of a multimodal museum exhibit.

ACKNOWLEDGMENTS

I am supported by a Branco Weiss Fellowship of the Society in Science Foundation and a NARSAD Young Investigator grant. I would like to thank Nicola Twilley and Dara Mao for comments on earlier versions of this manuscript.

REFERENCES

Arnheim, R. (1969). *Visual Thinking*. Berkeley: University of California Press.
Classen, C., Howes, D. and Synnott, A. (1994). *Aroma: The Cultural History of Smell*. London: Routledge.
Desor, J. A. and Beauchamp, G. U. (1974). The human capacity to transend olfactory information. *Perception of Psychophysics*, 16, 551–56.
Ehrlichman, H. and Bastone. L. (1992). Olfaction and emotion. In M. J. Serby and K. L. Chobor (eds.), *Science of Olfaction*, pp. 410–38. New York: Springer.
Engen, T. (1982). *The Perception of Odors*. New York: Academic Press.
Gilbert, A. N. (2008). *What the Nose Knows*. New York: Crown Publishers.
Gottfried, J. A. (2006). Smell: central nervous processing. *Advances in Oto-Rhino-Laryngology,* 63, 44–69.
Guéguen, N. and Petr, C. (2006). Odors and consumer behavior in a restaurant. *International Journal of Hospitality Management,* 25, 335–39.

Herz, R. S. (2002). Influences of odors on mood and affective cognition. In C. Rouby, B. Schaal, D. Dubois, R. Gervais and A. Holley (eds.), *Olfaction, Taste, and Cognition*, pp. 160–77. Cambridge: Cambridge University Press.

Herz, R. S. and Cupchik, G. C. (1995). The emotional distinctiveness of odor-evoked memories. *Chemical Senses,* 20, 517–28.

Keller, A. (2011). Attention and olfactory consciousness. *Frontiers in Psychology,* 2, 380.

Kino, C. (2012). *Fragrances as Art, Displayed Squirt by Squirt.* In The New York Times, New York: C37.

Li, W., Moallem, I., Paller, K. A. and Gottfried J. A. (2007). Subliminal smells can guide social preferences. *Psychological Science,* 18, 1044–49.

Lorig, T. (1992). Cognitive and "non-cognitive" effects of odor exposure: Electrophysiological and behavioral evidence. In S. Van Toller and G. Dodd (eds.), *The Psychology and Biology of Perfume*, pp. 161–72. Amsterdam, NL: Elsevier.

Mainland, J. and Sobel, N. (2006). The sniff is part of the olfactory percept. *Chemical Senses,* 31, 181–96.

Rosenberg, K. (2011). The New York Times.

Sela, L. and Sobel, N. (2010). Human olfaction: A constant state of change-blindness. *Experimental Brain Research,* 205, 13–29.

Stevenson, R. J. (2009). An initial evaluation of the functions of human olfaction. *Chemical Senses,* 35, 3–20.

Teller, C. and Dennis, C. (2012). The effect of ambient scent on consumers' perception, emotions and behaviour: A critical review. *Journal of Marketing Management,* 28, 14–36.

12

The Museum as Smellscape

Jim Drobnick

Until recently, visitors could not be faulted for thinking that the only smells found in an art museum were to be sniffed in the gift shop. Indian incense accompanied the Victoria and Albert Museum's run of The Arts of the Sikh Kingdoms (1999), and sticks scented with green tea and sandalwood celebrated paintings in the Österrichische Galerie Belvedere collection (Egon Schiele's *Sunflowers I*, 1911, and Gustav Klimt's *The Kiss*, 1908). The Philadelphia Museum of Art and the Art Gallery of Ontario offered perfumes to accompany their exhibitions of Frida Kahlo (2008) and Salvador Dali (Surreal Things, 2009), respectively. And for Le paysage en Provence, du classicisme à la modernité (2006), the souvenir shop of the Montreal Museum of Fine Arts was practically indistinguishable from the Body Shop, so replete was it with fragrant hand creams and soaps evoking southern France and its leisurely lifestyle. Besides these tie-ins to specific exhibitions, one could add a number of other more general items that engage the nose such as scented color pencils to attract young would-be artists, therapeutic essential oils for the overstressed, or aromatic teas and wines for adult diversions. By far the most popular art movements associated with scented products are Impressionism and Post-Impressionism. One can purchase, for example, a bar of chamomile and almond soap with Vincent van Gogh's *Starry Night* (1889) entombed within its clear glycerine (to provide a "gentle bathing exhibition"), herbal sachets of lavender referencing Paul Cezanne's *Le golfe de Marseille vu de l'Estaque* (1882–1885), or a candle emitting the fragrance of Claude Monet's *Bouquet of Sunflowers* (1881). On one level, these souvenirs are fun novelties and affordable luxuries that seek to capitalize on the cachet of famous artists and artworks. On another, they harbor a subtle acknowledgment

177

of aesthetics as an embodied, multisensory experience, where an appreciation of visual art is translated into the olfactory.

Hardly anyone travels to a museum to visit the gift shop, however. The profusion of objects for sale is meant to lure customers after touring an exhibition or the permanent galleries, their senses heightened even further in the store by the presence of pleasurable smells. The trend to feature scented products in museum shops is no accident. Store managers are no doubt conversant with, and eager to adopt, the burgeoning type of sensory consumerism prevalent in a wide variety of retail outlets, where scents are exuberantly incorporated into products and store environments to provide an experiential edge in branding, marketing, and value-enhancement (see Lindstrom, 2005; Hultén, Broweus and van Dijk, 2009). The shifting attitude toward smell, a sense once considered marginal and inconsequential, to something appealing and evocative is driven partly by a proven financial payoff: People like to buy things that smell nice. So it is here that olfaction enters mainstream acceptance by the museum—through the backdoor of the gift shop, so to speak, via the medium of consumerism.

One could argue that the very existence of these olfactory souvenirs posits a quasi-equivalence between scent and artwork. In the case of Monet's *Sunflowers*, the scented candle seems to literally attempt to capture the essence of the flowery painting, such that one might call it a *distilled life*, a still life that has been purified to its fragrant extract (some traditional elements of the painter's palette, after all, derive from plant products—a scent would be just another example). More interestingly, the candle performs what could be called a cross-modal aesthetic transfer from vision to scent. By converting the valuable, iconic painting into something that can be taken away and experienced within the intimacy of one's home, the candle bridges the sensory gap that tends to afflict most museumgoing: monosensory art objects being viewed by multisensory beings. The aromatic equivalent of Monet's *Sunflowers* permits a fully embodied, though virtual, imbibing of the artwork. Breathing in the painting is almost tantamount to living within it, to incorporating it within one's being, a much different experience than viewing. The point, however, is that the candle subtly implies itself as a substitute for the original painting and asserts the sense of smell as a correspondingly pleasing vehicle for aesthetics. Now that this assertion has been made, the task for institutions at present is to accept its reverse implication: As art can be translated into the olfactory, the olfactory can be translated into art.

Despite these claims, one has to be careful not to make the gift shop into too vanguard of a site; artists, after all, have been creating and installing olfactory artworks in the museum for decades, though there is just starting to be a history and theorization of this genre of work. What the gift shop does provide is a confirmation of a decided cultural shift in the sensory habitus of museumgoers in which smell is not only an accepted experience but one to be expected in a wider set of realms. In this chapter, I will examine the possibilities of olfactory art in the museum through my own curating of scent-based exhibitions and writing about artists' work over the past fifteen years. Through the use of performance, installation, object-based work, and relational projects, the exhibitions I have curated have engaged the olfactory in public sites, alternative spaces, and traditional galleries. The first, a performance art series entitled reminiSCENT (2003) (co-curated with Paul Couillard), invited audiences to "remember" the sense of smell and engage with it as both a cultural practice and a physical act. Through self-styled aromatherapy sessions, quasi-scientific experiments, intimate encounters, un-rehearsed rendezvous, and indecent appropriations of public space, the artists compelled audiences to engage with the spectrum of smell from the everyday to the abject (Drobnick, 2003, 2009). The second show, Odor Limits (2008) (co-curated with Jennifer Fisher), sought to debunk presumptions about smell as a "limited" mode of perception, one with only a rudimentary fragrant/foul range. Instead, the works in the show innovatively employed scent to gener-ate thought-provoking insights into cultural difference, spirituality, urban space, and identity, and in this sense demonstrated the capacity of scents to defy limits and exceed expectations (Drobnick and Fisher, 2008).

Other curatorial projects incorporated smell as a part of more general themes inquiring into the body, performance, public space, and multisen-soriality. Vital Signs (2001) (co-curated with Jennifer Fisher and Colette Tougas), for instance, aimed to bring attention to the significant ways in which the nonvisual senses contribute to identity, culture, and artistic practice and inquired into how the hegemonic understanding of the senses could be reconfigured. It featured works addressing the six senses, such as a forty-eight-foot mural made of marmalade, a chair with oversized arms that hugged its sitters, a broken-glass floor that one could walk barefoot on, and photographic portraits that recorded electro-magnetic auras, among others (Drobnick et al., 2001; Carter and Ovenden, 2001). Likewise, NIGHTSENSE (2009) (co-curated with Jennifer Fisher) examined the sensory hierarchy, this time in the context of a nighttime spectacle that appropriated the cityscape of the financial district in downtown Toronto. In the reduced visual world of the nocturnal carnivalesque, sight was defamiliarized to the extent that the conventional sensory economy was upended, thus permitting the other senses to be foregrounded. The works focused on generating altered sensorial states such as intoxication roused by the fumes of a pool of vodka, queasi-ness induced by a carnival ride set amid office towers, mystical experiences generated through sensory deprivation, and reverie inspired by port-a-potties outfitted with aromas associated with Lewis Carroll's *Alice's Adventures in Wonderland* (Drobnick and Fisher, 2012).

These examples of sensorial curating have several factors in common, which also apply to olfactory curating:

1. The projects were mostly commissioned, that is, the artists were invited to produce new works based on the theme and the site. If a preexisting work was selected, it was radically revised to fit the circumstances of the show.
2. The works were context-sensitive; that is, they were tailored to the specific conditions of the buildings and locations they would be situated in and to the audiences who would be experiencing them.
3. Sensory works tend to be temporary and performative—they exist for only a designated period and oftentimes change or are transformed during the time of their appearance.
4. The multisensory works in these shows required participation and involvement. One could not stand back and remain aloof from the art; one had to engage one's body in order to understand the works. In other words, the art was more fully experiential for visitors, with all of the thrills and problematics implied by that term.

In my curatorial practice, I consider olfactory artworks in much the same way as any artwork; that is, they should be meaningful on conceptual, experiential, and aesthetic levels. I would not treat scent art like a separate category of cultural practice (e.g., science or perfumery), though these aspects certainly influence artists' thinking. My curatorial focus is on works created by established artists that embody the complexity expected of any other type of artwork, such as referring to art history, making sociopolitical critiques, interrogating notions of identity, and other aesthetic investigations. As novel as smell works tend to be considered by some, they nevertheless arise out of current artworld debates and art historical trajectories, such as the rethinking of portraiture and landscape. Clara Ursitti, for instance, transformed the convention of the self-portrait by rendering it olfactively. After submitting herself to state-of-the art chemical sensors and the expert nose of olfactory scientist George Dodd, she had the elements of her odor identified and then synthesized, creating a perfume that captured her "essence," literally. *Self-Portrait in Scent, Sketch #1* (1994) contained items such as propionic acid, trimethyle amine, androstene dieneone, and skatole (Ursitti, 2006, p. 357; Drobnick, 2002a). In a similar renewal of a traditional genre, Jenny Marketou revivified landscape painting by compelling an active exploration of the olfactory environment. Rather than merely viewing a representation in the

Figure 12.1. Jenny Marketou, "Smell It: A Do-It-Yourself Smell Map" (2008), site-specific, interactive wall installation, SAV (wallpaper) on Sintra Mount, 72 x 120." Photo courtesy of DisplayCult and the Esther M. Klein Art Gallery

gallery, visitors were invited to venture into the surrounding neighborhood to note its fragrances and odors, and then return to record their impressions onto a collectively produced *Smell It: A Do-It-Yourself Smell Map* (2008) (Drobnick and Fisher, 2008).

The "medium" of scent perfectly fits the post-medium condition of the contemporary era, in which artists are no longer presumed to choose a single medium and remain with it for the entirety of their career. The modernist notion of traditional media, in which every sense possesses a unique and autonomous art form (i.e., vision is identified with painting, hearing with music), has been consistently challenged by avant-garde artists over the past 150 years who have mixed both the senses and different media in their works. With the collapse of Clement Greenberg's modernism in the late 1950s under the weight of its own logic (where, after all, could painting go once it had purged everything except flat monochromes of color?), the current post-media period began with the rise of performance, installation, video, audio art, and so on, which paved the way for ephemeral and experiential works with smell.

Olfactory artworks exemplify a post-media aesthetic in several ways: by virtue of their material range, media diversity, interdisciplinarity, and complexification of artistic identity. Scent-based artworks typically involve a number of different substances, such as organic or natural matter (flowers, dirt), technological devices (diffusers, HVAC systems), cultural and commercial readymades (incense, soap), none of which would qualify as a traditional artistic material. Olfactory artworks also tend to work across a variety of diverse media by, for instance, employing sculpture (bottles), addressing atmosphere and site (installation/architecture), involving audience participation (performance), or more directly incorporating visual, audio, linguistic, and other types of information. This is not to say that all of the elements have to work together to form a single statement (oftentimes the contrast between smell and other sensory information can be quite provocative). As opposed to synaesthesia, where all of the media combine into a greater whole, olfactory works often employ dysaesthesia, where the different media contrast with one another, thus demonstrating an interrogatory function (Drobnick, 1998). Ultimately, if one were to consider what the "medium" of smell was, it would have to be air itself, which can carry visual, auditory, tactile, and gustatory sensations, along with olfactory ones. So to try to isolate smell as a "pure" medium in the modernist vein would be a somewhat futile and unnecessary gesture.

The other two post-media characteristics of olfactory art—interdisciplinarity and complexification of artistic identity—pertain to the artists themselves. The practice of creating olfactory art is post-media in the sense that artists tend to work interdisciplinarily; they engage any number of media and techniques depending on the specific project. Unlike modernist artists who restrict themselves to a single medium in order to concentrate on its particular characteristics, olfactory artists may adopt a host of methods in order to conduct their work, such as synthesizing scents, utilizing air-conditioning apparatuses, gathering fragrant sculptural materials, conducting quasi-experiments upon visitors, employing new technologies, and so on. Finally, olfactory artists operate in a post-medium manner because their identities are often multiple—some have training as chemists, scientists, anthropologists, and perfumers besides being trained in art. This multifaceted identity is often necessary since to adequately understand and work with smell, one needs to draw from a range of fields to build a sufficient knowledge base. Collaboration offers another method to augment one's knowledge, and a number of artists productively consult with olfactory experts of all disciplines to gain specialized information and techniques.

Two fundamental motives drive artists to work with smell. On the one hand, scent provides a raw, primal sensation that is new to the visual art context. Instead of representing an object or experience, odor provides a seemingly direct and unmediated access to the real. On the other hand, the second motive recognizes that smells are redolent with personal and social significance. Smells are indelibly linked to notions of identity, place, memory, lived experience, and cultural sensibility—in other words, scents have meaning (Drobnick, 1998). Both motives have merit, though I would argue that no sensation exceeds some level of cultural reference, for the senses themselves are socially influenced. Even if a "pure" sensation existed, it still would be framed within a certain cultural context (such as the search for a way to revitalize an enervated sensorium). Despite their differences, these two motives often overlap, for smells can operate simultaneously as a sensation and a concept, as both a strategy to express intense feeling and a means to signify cultural content.

Curating scent-based artworks involves several challenges. In the following sections, I will address five general areas of concern for multisensory work in general, and olfactory work in particular, that can be summarized as institutional, critical, receptive, curatorial, and sensorial challenges. Through cases studies drawn from my writings and exhibitions, I will examine practical and conceptual issues arising from smell-based artworks.

THE DEODORIZED CUBE

A primary challenge for olfactory art is the dominant type of space available at major museums and galleries: the white cube. Such spaces are designed for the display of objects through a visual logic of white paint, geometric rooms, and even lighting to create what Rodolphe El-Khoury (2006) terms "olfactory silence." They are often inhospitable places for any kind of creative or positive olfactory experience, due to their eradication of odors and other sensory stimuli that might distract from a focused optical encounter. While a sanitized/deodorized exhibition space could bear a useful purpose for olfactory artworks in that it offers a clean slate for them to "appear," even pleasant scents can be stigmatized in the context of the white cube. For the sake of this chapter, I am considering the spaces of the museum and gallery to be interchangeable because of their shared ideological tenet of deodorization (see Drobnick, 2002b).

No space, however, is without a scent of some kind, as all indoor and outdoor atmospheres carry olfactory vestiges of human activity and natural processes. Museums are no different, notwithstanding their efforts to provide the conditions for a pure visual experience. Cleaning products can leave traces of their use, the aromas of restaurants and cafes can waft around corners, and overperfumed visitors can trail clouds through the galleries. Modifications to HVAC systems could provide artists with more flexibility in how air flows and gets refreshed but can be prohibitively expensive and require extensive engineering and bureaucratic approval, as one might expect to a basic building function. So far, I have not requested major modifications to the spaces I have curated in, other than to install the works to optimize their presentation. Given the wide range of olfactory artworks, I would argue that there is no ideal, singular space to show scent-based art. Some works respond to the preexisting scent in a space; others depend on more pristine conditions. More important is the willingness of the institution to adapt to unconventional alterations to its indoor atmosphere. Temperature, humidity, air currents, and the volume of a room are basic conditions that impact the ability of an olfactory work to achieve its proper state (de Cupere, 2013). Just as lighting needs to be flexible for various types of visual artworks, the indoor volume of air needs to accommodate different types of creatively designed olfactory experiences. That said, there are already many artists working in smell who did not wait for the proper technology or for supportive institutions. And there are many alternative spaces that seek out experimental works that disregard the supposed sanctity of the white cube.

The institutional challenges engendered by scent are not unique to this genre of art. Other types of post-media practices require accommodations by the gallery and its infrastructure, such as performance, sound art, and digital media. In the age of visual saturation, many artists feel the need to reengage with some kind of tangible experience and so create interactive, bodily works that seek to disturb the sensory calm of viewing. Some works may do this pointedly, as a critique of ocularcentrism, while others use the nonvisual senses to hybridize perception and pose alternatives to conventional visual aesthetics. Just as the silent, hushed aspect of museumgoing has been superseded by the incorporation of audio elements—a recent example involved Velvet Underground songs playing in Regarding Warhol: Sixty Artists, Fifty Years (2012) at the Metropolitan Museum of Art—other post-media practices activate more complex sensorial engagements that may require daily attention by museum staff. New media and audio art utilize equipment that needs to be turned on and monitored. For scent, maintenance can be as simple as filling up a diffuser every day, turning on a fan, or putting a handful of fragrant beads into a box.

Olfactory exhibitions should take into consideration the individuals who sit with the works during the run of the show. People can wear earplugs to tune out sound, but they cannot turn off their breathing. The physical health of attendants is an important concern, yet placing scent in a gallery can generate intolerant reactions even when relatively benign. One artist I've written about, Catherine Bodmer, wanted to disperse the scent of Bounce fabric softener in an exhibition but was prevented by the gallery attendants who worried about the potential health effects. Despite being assured that the scent carried no danger, the attendants were intransigent. The irony was that the attendants were chain-smokers. Obviously, some other agenda was at play, such as odorphobia (Drobnick, 2006, 2010). Another example of what I've called "scentsorship" involved an incident with a work by Clara Ursitti. In this case, the offended person was the gallery director herself, who made the unilateral decision to place a cut onion in front of a diffuser emitting an olfactory self-portrait by the artist (Drobnick, 2002a). Here the director felt justified in negating the artwork because of her own dislike of the smell. The onion, however, probably just compounded the odor, though it may have also domesticated the novelty of the olfactory experience of Ursitti's scentwork by masking it with a more familiar, if equally pungent, smell.

Besides presentation issues, ephemeral artworks pose difficulties for institutions with regard to their documentation, collection, and preservation. Smell is not a sense that can easily be represented in photography (as would be expected) or recorded through the use of technology, such as sound. Depending on the type of olfactory work, some forms of documentation work better than others. For performative works, a video would be useful. If actual samples of the scents are available, like those provided by Chrysanne Stathacos's "Wish Machine" (1997–2008) (in Odor Limits), audiences would be able to experience a scent beyond the circumstances of the show. For a dollar, Stathacos's machine dispensed a vial of essential oil to be taken home and utilized in the support of one's soulful aspirations. Most olfactory artworks, however, do not result in a tangible object that can be easily put into storage and, in fact, depend upon their ephemerality as a pronounced conceptual aspect. Their noncollectible nature is precisely the point. These works would have to be recreated and restaged and, then once in place, replenished as needed.

Even though ephemerality is one of the main characteristics of olfactory artworks, anything can be collected if one is creative enough. For instance, performance art is now being collected by the Museum of Modern Art, NYC. Olfactory art could be collected and archived, for example, by recording the formula for an artist's synthesized scent, or having a list of fragrant materials that could be gathered in the future, so that the work could be reconstructed. The easiest items to collect would be artist's perfumes, since they already come contained in vials or bottles. In general, however, artists tend to want to privilege the inherent qualities of smell in their olfactory artworks, and because these characteristics are experiential, difficulty in archiving and collecting will persist.

Figure 12.2. Chrysanne Stathacos, "Wish Machine" (1997–2008), digital photograph, customized vending machine, scent multiples. Photo courtesy of the artist, DisplayCult, and the Esther M. Klein Art Gallery

CRITICAL CHALLENGES

A second challenge for scent art is to develop a conceptual framework. Post-media artforms that utilize the nonvisual senses have a less established aesthetic discourse and are just beginning to be given critical attention. For instance, visual art has 2,500 years of philosophical scrutiny informing it, while an olfactory aesthetics has been only intermittently developed in the past century. A more pernicious challenge is that the nonvisual senses tend to be considered by those invested in ocularcentrism as "visceral" modalities (which is a false assumption, because vision is just as embodied as any other sense) and thus unavailable to higher cognitive or aesthetic pursuits. Yet a wide range of examples of olfactory art demonstrate that it is just as conceptual and aesthetic as any other art form.

The limited vocabulary for smell gives the impression that it is mainly a phenomenological experience, one that lies before cultural conditioning or beyond the ability of language to encompass. While some attribute this to scent's intrinsic affectiveness and emotionality (and the direct connection between olfactory neurons and the limbic system supports this rationale), my belief is that more needs to be done to develop an olfactocentric discourse. In my experience with olfactory curating, gallerygoers are more than intrigued by the exhibitions, but critics are challenged on how to address the work and often fall back upon tired stereotypes about the nonvisual senses because they do not "speak" or "represent" in the traditional ways they have been trained to identify. Bad puns abound in headlines on almost any smell-related news topic, which betrays nervousness about considering the significance of scent (recent examples include "Olfactory Art Causes a Stink" and "What's That Smell? New York Museum Calls It Art"). Smells intrinsically challenge ocularcentric thinking and the hierarchy of the senses, and so olfactory art is often subject to critical backlash. A typical ploy by those invested in the supremacy of vision is to trivialize smell by making prejudicial comparisons, such as the Mona Lisa versus dirty socks, as if such an illogical pairing meant anything. Such odorphobic responses are much rarer in the general art audience, because those interested in contemporary art are markedly more open to new experiences and perceptions, smell included. Many writers point out the lack of a terminology for smell; for curators and olfactory artists it is thus a necessity to expand and even invent the vocabulary and theory for an olfactory aesthetics.

RECEPTION AND VARIABILITY

The third type of challenge for curating olfactory artworks is the variability of smell itself, which occurs on several levels. Scents are famously subjective, to the point of being highly idiosyncratic. People form all types of personal associations and judgments about smells from the vicissitudes of their experience, which can make a "shared" language of scent seem impossible. Any smell can be imprinted with a range of emotions, depending upon the contingencies of one's life. For instance, skunk may be disgusting to many, but for those who smelled its pungency during summer drives in the countryside, it may bring about a pleasurable reminiscence. The reverse could also occur. Smelling an ostensibly "good" scent like a bouquet of roses during an emotionally trying time, such as the sickness of a loved one, could turn an oft-cherished fragrance into something to avoid. But those who consciously attend to sensory phenomena—whether smells, sounds, tastes, and so forth—can realize a broader range of meaning and a world of nuance. Every new scent experience adds to and complexifies previous ones, and so encountering olfactory art in the gallery provides a situation for reexamining smells from any time in one's olfactory memory.

Less idiosyncratic but still demonstrating variability are the positive and negative attitudes toward smells gained through socialization. Every culture privileges some scents while disdaining others. What is an acceptable household or bodily fragrance in one community could be anathema elsewhere. Even scents that are culturally acceptable in one context (garlic in the kitchen) may be deemed unacceptable in others (garlic at the office). The stigmatization of smell over the past two centuries in the West has somewhat inured many to favorable or creative possibilities. Those from non-Western cultures, however, may not be so predisposed against smell and may easily recognize its contribution to knowledge and aesthetics. Artists who address scent as a culturally loaded signifier are often confronted by differences in the audience's awareness level: those who understand the meaning of the scent, and those who may be encountering it for the first time and are uninformed of its implications. Robert Houle's installation of sweetgrass in "Hochelaga" (1992), for instance, filled the gallery with a soft, haylike scent that pleased visitors but held special relevance for those knowledgeable about First Nation politics, land claims, and medicinal traditions. More insidiously, smells that are comfortable and familiar for members of one community may elicit strong, even racist reactions by members of another (see Manalansan, 2006). "Majestic Splendour" (1997), Lee Bul's installation at the Museum of Modern Art, featured an arrangement of rotting fish covered in sequins and jewels in vinyl bags. To the artist, the decomposing odor was a common presence in

Korean cuisine, although many MoMA patrons felt otherwise and the show was prematurely taken down (it did not help that the installation was placed on the path to the museum restaurant).

The variability of each individual's sense of smell also has to be taken into account, as no two people have the same olfactory capability. For instance, everyone possesses a smell blindness to one odor or another; that is, an olfactory receptor that has been incapacitated in some way and so they cannot sense its corresponding odor. The sense of smell employs around 400 receptors, attuned to specific ranges and types of odor molecules, not all of which are functioning in every individual. By contrast, vision employs only three types of receptors. Rather than just the handful of variations that can alter visual acuity, smell offers billions of ways in which people can differ (Keller, 2012). Effectively, every nose is unique, and everyone's sense of smell is partial, because of the inherent variability in genetic makeup. Furthermore, up to 15 percent of the population experiences some type of olfactory dysfunction, due to aging, disease, injury, or congenital conditions (Herz, 2012). Nor is the average person's sense of smell uniform throughout the day. Naturally occurring hormonal cycles and respiratory rhythms can affect olfactory ability. Seasonal effects, such as winter colds, summer hay fevers, and other allergies may also impede sensitivity. No artist or museum can predict or cater to all of these contingencies to guarantee every visitor the same scent experience and so must accept that a range of responses will accompany any olfactory artwork, including the inability to perceive it.

A special case involves gallerygoers who might suffer from multiple-chemical sensitivity disorders. Institutions would be prudent to notify visitors that smells are to be present in an exhibition space. Posting a notice respects individuals with this condition and enables them to make an informed choice about whether to enter an olfactively charged atmosphere. Not all smells in olfactory artworks are synthetic, though. Organic materials, such as herbs and spices, are just as commonly used by artists (depending on concentration or intensity, organic volatile compounds may constitute as much of a danger as manufactured ones). The diversity of scent-based art precludes universalizing about the supposed risks of the genre as a whole. On another note, it would be interesting to test the legality of scent bans, in which cities like Halifax have prohibited the use of perfumed products in municipal and other public buildings, with an olfactory exhibition. Would the freedom of expression of olfactory artists take precedence over, or be censored by, such legislation?

Besides variation in the act of reception, mutability could be said to characterize the very nature of olfactory aesthetics. Unlike the bounded, defined aspects of visual artworks in a gallery, with autonomous spectators separated from the objects on view, olfactory art engages visitors intimately. If the scent is dispersed in the air of the gallery, one enters *into* the artwork, and in so doing people become immersed in its atmosphere. Olfactory artworks are also more visceral, since the act of breathing compels the absorption of airborne particles into one's inner being, where some scents will interact with a person's body chemistry and perhaps even influence their emotional state, heart rate, and other physiological functions. Inherent to an olfactory aesthetics is the gradation of scent as individuals move about a space. The intensity waxes and wanes, especially if there is a specific source, or airflow to disperse and refresh the scent. In this way, olfactory works are performative—they come and go, appear and subside, become present and then fade, with all of the vividness and ephemerality of an event. Contrary to the discrete objecthood of visual art, olfactory works manifest a level of suggestiveness because audiences are not typically trained to attend to and identify scents. Variability thus infuses visitors' contemplations as they have to answer basic questions such as "Is there a scent?" and "What scent is it?" even before asking the more demanding "Why is this scent here?" and "What does it mean?" In this case, the variability of scent adds a degree of mystery that challenges the fundamental underpinning of the aesthetic process

CURATORIAL CHALLENGES

Curating involves issues of context, choice, placement, installation, maintenance, and identification, but olfactory artworks generate new variations of these activities. Because smells are conveyed by air, and air circulates, the boundaries of olfactory artworks can exceed conventional visual and architectural features within a gallery space. The result is that two or more olfactory artworks may overlap and interfere with each other. This is most often encountered in group shows, where the preservation of a distinction between artists is crucial, but can also occur in monographic shows when multiple scent pieces can potentially compound one another. Even a scent artwork with a temporal dimension will require careful timing and airflow if the sequence of aromas diffusing over time is to be kept clear and discernable. Unfortunately, most ventilation systems in museum and gallery settings lack versatility in refreshing indoor atmospheres or directing circulation in alternative ways that artists or curators might seek.

Practically, a number of strategies can be employed. The simplest method of presenting olfactory works is to separate them into individual rooms. When too few spaces are available, techniques that can be utilized for distributing the scent include localized diffusers, individual smelling stations, boxes that open to a single visitor at a time, or smells contained in multiples that can be carried away and sniffed later. Olfactory works can also be relational (asking the viewer to create a smell map, for instance) or be imaginatively evoked by photography, sound, and video. Odor Limits, for example, featured artwork using several of these strategies. Curators can prevent the muddling of scents before they occur by being mindful of the types of works being chosen and by being sensitive to how they will be eventually positioned and installed. If an exhibition area is limited, one can, for instance, creatively repurpose the gallery's unconventional spaces, like stairs or hallways, to separate and retain the integrity of the works.

Curators also need to take into account the visitor's itinerary so that "olfactory fatigue," a perceptual numbing specific to the sense of smell, does not occur too readily. Olfactory fatigue is a more dramatic condition than the general museum fatigue phenomenon because when it occurs, the entire sense of smell virtually shuts down. To avoid this at places like perfume counters, retailers will offer a bowl of fresh coffee beans to sniff, which has the effect of revitalizing the sense of smell. For curators, addressing fatigue at the outset by factoring in a range of smells in the choice of artworks will keep visitors' noses engaged, and choreographing pauses in the exhibition itinerary permits physical as well as olfactory breathers.

Some types of artworks require maintenance to retain their fragrance, while others need to be left alone. Depending on the artist's intention, works may require daily renewal to keep the scent fresh. Replenishing Oswaldo Maciá's "Smellscape" (2006) involved refilling Plexiglas boxes with custom-made fragrance beads every day or so. Other types of works may not need any maintenance because they rely on the gradual change or dissipation of scent over time. The bed of 10,000 roses covering the gallery floor in Anya Gallaccio's "Red on Green" (1992) smelled lovely for the first week but then gave way to an odor of decay as the petals wilted and decomposed, which was essential to the work's concept. Given the spectrum of olfactory artworks, some depend upon constant refilling of the scent, others would just be set up and left to natural processes.

The identification of works—didactic panels, labels, audioguides—also should be correlated to the meaning of the work and the artist's intention. It is often the case that a "pure" olfactory artwork, consisting simply of a scent diffused into the space, can be more difficult for a general audience to perceive as art, for two reasons. One is that, because of its invisibility, visitors may not realize that an olfactory work is present or which scent in the space is actually the artwork (an attendant's perfume, or the hint of car exhaust coming through the window?). The other reason is that smell's elusiveness leaves it open to manipulation through language, as many perfume marketers know. Contextualizing elements such as labels can provide valuable clues about what is to be experienced and how visitors should react—that is, locating the scentwork, identifying its qualities, considering its aesthetic and conceptual qualities. For olfactory artworks comprising an assortment of media, identification enables the audience to know that the smell was an intended and essential component. The scent in works incorporating palpably fragrant materials, such as a bag of spices or a vat of perfume, may be too obvious to mention, but in those cases of unconventional assemblages and installations, the use of the standard phrase "mixed media" leaves the sense of smell unrecognized.

What are the optimal conditions for olfactory artworks? As more artists engage with scent, this will certainly become an issue. Since every space has some kind of scent, to some degree every olfactory artwork has to work with or against such residual odors. Some installation artists may select a site for its existing olfactory character and capitalize on an overlay or palimpsest approach, while others may seek a more immaculate environment to feature the subtlety of their work. Whatever the exhibition venue, a key curatorial concern is to protect the integrity of the artwork. In some ways, each olfactory artwork is an intervention, that is, a strategic insertion into a place with a specific conceptual and aesthetic purpose. Such a scent may draw out and comment on some aspect of the space, may elicit a contradictory or charged reaction to the expectations about the building, or set out to alter the mood of the visitor and the affect of the interior, among other intentions.

Curating scent works involves an olfactory balancing act: If smells are too subtle, the audience may miss them entirely; if too intense, they may alienate. But this is part of the perceptual experience of smell—it can be ethereally suggestive or physically impactful. In some cases an artist might seek to overpower and discomfort visitors with a confrontational smell; other artists may wish to subtly lure them or accentuate the enigmatic. The curatorial challenge is to support the intentions of the work, including installing the work to its best advantage, contextualizing it within a framework of other artworks and discourse, and inviting the audience to experience the full range of works in the show without any one smell or sensation overruling the others.

Acquiring new scent technologies, fragrance chemicals, and other olfactory products for exhibition contexts can pose another challenge. A small number of corporations perform much of the research in smell and thereby control the market in fragrance and perfumery, and these businesses operate with proprietary if not secretive mandates. That said, there are individuals in these companies who are creative in their own right and interested in working with artists, and curators can serve as liaisons to facilitate olfactory art collaborations.

If an art museum's atmosphere is to be altered, I would argue that it should be as an artist's work and part of a curatorial project, rather than as something programmed by the administration. Audiences tend to be suspicious of and annoyed at smells they cannot readily identify, especially if they are anonymously introduced. As well, ethical issues and the feeling of manipulation may arise when the purpose of the scent is not evident. Environmental fragrancing is a popular technique by retailers, corporations, and institutions to influence behavior, such as to increase shopping by consumers, regulate factory workers' production levels, or keep prisoners calm. Critics consider these functions to be instrumental, especially when they are anonymously diffused into the indoor atmosphere. However, with "named" olfactory interventions (i.e., those originating from the explicit projects of artists and curators), the purpose of scent can be inferred to be artistic, rather than instrumental, and thus the ethical issues of environmental fragrancing can be avoided. My comments here do not necessarily apply to science or nature museums, which have a different mandate toward programming related to the senses. I would, though, question the literal and instrumental nature of many of the olfactory insertions I have come across thus far in nonart venues, as well as the pedagogical value of using synthesized scents. If education is the goal, rather than just entertainment, then how are noses to be made more discerning when artificial smells trump actual ones? (see Damian and Damian, 1995; Drobnick, 2002b).

RECALIBRATING THE SENSES

Given the general anosmia of Western culture, the structured aromatic experience posed by olfactory artworks presents an opportunity to enhance the appreciation and knowledge of smell. Every encounter with an olfactory artwork also doubles as a type of sensory recalibration that prompts audiences to inquire into the significance of scent and its aesthetic potential. In this way, olfactory artworks tend to be performative and participatory; they oblige audiences to use their senses differently. To invite people into these situations, artists have devised a number of means to bring about involvement, such as using playfulness, reverie, exploration, and aspiration. Play and humor are characteristic of Peter de Cupere's work, such as *Scented02* (2009), which featured a concrete fuel station with gasoline nozzles that dispensed the smells of grass, bubblegum, and car exhaust (mixed with burnt meat and asphalt). Poetic travel informed Millie Chen and Evelyn Von Michalofski's *The Seven Scents* (2003), which had visitors reclining on the boardwalk of Lake Ontario to contemplate the watery horizon and inhale the scent of oceanic travel. Among the expected seaweed, coconut, and saltwater aromas, the artists subversively added the scents of cigarette butts, Doritos, and industrial lubricants to underscore the polluting influence of modernity and tourism upon pristine natural areas (Drobnick, 2009). An exploratory urge compelled individuals to open and sniff five garbage cans with distinctive aromas in Oswaldo Maciá's *1 Woodchurch Road, London NW6 3PL* (1994–1995), an olfactory portrait of his London apartment building and an indication of the country's cultural diversity. The five aromas that the artist found most typical of the building's intergenerational and multicultural occupants were naftalin (mothballs), olive oil, Listerine, eucalyptus, and baby powder. With this piece the artist reflected on how a sense of community can develop from a heterogeneous mix of identities, and defied the conservative rhetoric of British cultural singularity and essentialism (Drobnick and Fisher, 2008). A personal touch informed Shawna Dempsey and Lorri Millan's *Scentbar* (2003), where attendees answered a questionnaire about their fears and ambitions and were given a custom-made, therapeutic aroma to guide their self-improvement. While the scents handed out were all derived from natural sources, they referenced both aromatherapy and contemporary life. Mint and lavender formed part of the olfactory palette, along with more unconventional scents such as "light industry," "rental car," and "grandma's purse" (Drobnick, 2009). Each of these works sharpened visitors' awareness and skill in differentiating scents and exemplified the ways in which scent can analyze aspects of contemporary life.

It is important to note that all of the four projects mentioned above incorporated what are ostensibly designated "bad" smells. While it may be common sense to know the difference between a "good" and a "bad" smell, it is precisely such notions of common sense that olfactory art inevitably interrogates and critiques. Smell has often been a marginalized sense in Western culture because of the antipathy toward bad smells. A powerful strategy used by artists has been to deliberately estrange the audience with allegedly negative smells in order to address how such judgments arise. For instance, Theresa Margolles' *Vaporization* (2001) diffused the water used to wash corpses into the gallery air. A sign posted at the entranceway informed visitors of the origin of the foggy mist. While the water was sterilized and posed no health risk, its abject nature set forth a challenge: How close does one want to get to the dead? Inhaling *Vaporization*'s mist brought about a conscious connection to those who have passed away, underscoring the fact that every breath taken, whether inside or outside of the installation, contains particles of the deceased. Such proximal edginess can be found also in Clara Ursitti's dating service, *Pheromone Link* (1997–2001), in which those interested in selecting a partner must break the taboo of sniffing strangers' body odor. Dates were arranged by smelling sweaty T-shirts of potential partners (Drobnick 2010, 2000). The work of both Margolles and Ursitti recognizes how olfaction and the medium of air can be confrontational, especially in regard to assumed norms of disgust, but the works pose an opportunity to reflect on the construction and necessity of such societal normativity.

CONCLUSION

This text began with pleasurable smells in the gift shop and ended with two artists dealing with the disgusting and the taboo, a trajectory that has a deliberate objective. Smells are present in contemporary art not simply because they are enjoyable; it is because they are, to paraphrase Claude Levi-Strauss, "good to think with." Olfactory artworks utilize air as a medium and orient audiences to consider the meaning of what they sniff. For curators, the use of smells creates challenges that require mediation on several levels, as I have tried to articulate: between the artist and the institution, between the artwork and the site, between the artist and the audience, and between the artwork and notions of aesthetics, art historical traditions, and societal norms. In providing a sensorially complex encounter, olfactory artworks and exhibitions turn the museum into an animated smellscape that is pluralistic, post-media, culturally diverse, and more fully embodied.

REFERENCES

Carter, J. and Ovenden, C. (2001). Finding sense in new places: *Vital Signs* in contemporary art practice. *Material History Review*, Spring-Summer, 69–75.

Damian, P. and Damian, K. (1995). *Aromatherapy: Scent and Psyche*. Rochester, VT: Healing Arts Press.

de Cupere, P. (2013). The Use of Smell in Art, an "Olfactology" Art Research. New York: College Art Association Conference, February 16.

Drobnick, J. (1998). Reveries, assaults and evaporating presences: olfactory dimensions in contemporary art. *Parachute*, 89, 10–19.

———. (2000). Inhaling passions: art, sex and scent. *Sexuality and Culture*, 4(3), 37–56.

———. (2002a). Clara Ursitti: scents of a woman. *Tessera* 32, 85–97.

———. (2002b). Volatile architectures. In Bernie Miller and Melony Ward (eds.), *Crime and Ornament: In the Shadow of Adolf Loos,* 263–82. Toronto: YYZ Books.

———. (2003). *reminiSCENT*. Exhibition brochure. Toronto: FADO.

———. ed. (2006). *The Smell Culture Reader*. Oxford and New York: Berg.

———. (2009). Sense and *reminiSCENT*: performance and the essences of memory. *Canadian Theatre Review* 137, 6–12.

———. (2010). *Air*chitecture: Gguarded Breaths and the [cough] art of ventilation. In Patrizia di Bello and Gabriel Koureas (eds.), *Art History and the Senses: 1830 to the Present*, 147–66. London: Ashgate.

Drobnick, J. and Fisher, J. (2008). Odor limits. *The Senses & Society* 3(3), 349–58.
———. (2012). Nightsense. *Public* 45, 35–63.
Drobnick, J., Fisher, J., and Tougas, C. (2001). Vital Signs: curatorial statement. *Material History Review*, Spring-Summer, 75–76.
el-Khoury, R. (2006). Polish and deodorize: paving the city in late eighteenth-century France. In Jim Drobnick (ed.), *The Smell Culture Reader*, 18–28. Oxford and New York: Berg.
Herz, R. (2012). Presentation at Multimodal Approaches to Learning conference. New York: Art Beyond Sight and the Metropolitan Museum of Art, October 26.
Hultén, B., Broweus, N., and van Dijk, M. (2009). *Sensory Marketing*. New York: Palgrave Macmillan.
Keller, A. (2012). Presentation at Multimodal Approaches to Learning conference. New York: Art Beyond Sight and the Metropolitan Museum of Art, October 27.
Lindstrom, M. (2005). *Brand Sense*. New York: Free Press.
Manalansan, M. F. (2006). Immigrant lives and the politics of olfaction in the global city. In Jim Drobnick (ed.), *The Smell Culture Reader*, 41–52. Oxford and New York: Berg.
Ursitti, C. (2006). "Self-Portrait in Scent, Sketch #1." In Jim Drobnick (ed.), *The Smell Culture Reader*, 357. Oxford and New York: Berg.

13

Taste-full Museums

Educating the Senses One Plate at a Time

Irina D. Mihalache

In an article about "museum manners," Constance Classen (2007) wrote about the difficulty of knowing the corporeal practices of earlier eras, especially the "sensory expectations and experiences" of museum visitors. Classen's comments on "the sensory life of the early museum," which, she found, encouraged and allowed more multisensorial participation than contemporary museums, inspired my own commentaries on taste in the museum which I will develop in this chapter. If museum visits in the eighteenth century were often "informed by gustatory associations," contemporary museums such as the Art Gallery of Ontario (AGO) in Toronto and the National Museum of the American Indian (NMAI) in Washington, D.C., have great potential to transform culinary experiences into educational moments. While a formal pedagogy of taste has been the concern of famous chefs and gastronomes with roots in a French haute cuisine tradition (Parkhurst Ferguson, 2004), museums engage with the sense of taste in more informal capacities. Such new forms of engagement with taste could build on the already existing significance of food in everyday culture as a communicator of identity and play on what Barbara Kirshenblatt-Gimblett (1999) calls the "alive, fugitive and sensory" nature of taste.

While taste and its signifier, food, have been present in museums for quite some time as subjects of different works of art and artful dishes in restaurants and cafes, food's own materiality as an object with educational potential has rarely been explored. Similarly, the ability of taste to perform a pedagogical role and to inspire critical thinking has been generally overlooked in museums. This chapter is a commentary on the different ways through which food cultures, defined as complex "systems of communication" (Barthes, 2008), can be better co-opted by museums so that the overall museum experience becomes more participatory, multisensorial, and engaging for the visitor. The increased presence of food in museums in different eating spaces reflects, on one side, the popularity of food as a marker of culture and identity. Carlnita P. Greene and Janet M. Cramer agree that "we have witnessed a rise in food-focused consumption, media and culture, such that there has been what we could label a 'food explosion'" (2011). At the same time, education through food and critical engagement with the sense of taste can diversify the communicative practices of museums and accentuate the participatory nature of the museum experience. Taste is the ideal sense for an innovative participatory culture in museums because taste bridges the gap between personal experiences—each of us tastes food differently and intimately at a biological level—and collective meanings and values attached to certain regimes of taste. For example, Lisa Heldke (2008) pointed out that the consumption of "ethnic" foods is a type of cultural colonialism because "it is motivated by a deep desire to have contact with—to somehow own an experience of—an exotic Other." The taste of "other" foods, constructed as foreign or "exotic," often translates into perceptions about the cultures that produced them. Experiencing a museum through taste could increase the public's cultural sensibilities through an awareness of the role that food and its taste plays in producing stereotypes and assumptions about different cultures, including our own.

TASTE: IN AND OUT OF THE MUSEUM

The relations between food, taste, and museums have been analyzed in academic literature primarily through the lens of art and aesthetics. Locating food within the realm of critical aesthetics as a subject of numerous forms of artistic expression, from Dutch still life miniatures to feminist performative installations, reconstitutes taste as "a sense-specific art form in its own right" (Kirschenblatt-Gimblatt, 2006). In *Making Sense of Taste: Food and Philosophy*, Korsmeyer (1999) provides a philosophical investigation of the sense of taste by positioning taste in relation to its aesthetic possibilities. She asks, "Can taste experiences be legitimately considered genuine aesthetic experiences?" (Korsmeyer, 1999). The context for her question is a critical engagement with the assumption that taste occupies the lowest position in the hierarchy of senses due to the Western philosophy paradigm, which values vision as the highest intellectual sense. This ordering of the senses has been also considered problematic and unjust by David Howes, who writes that "in the West the dominant group . . . has conventionally been associated with the supposedly 'higher' senses of sight and hearing, while subordinate groups (women, workers, non-Westerners) have been associated with the so-called lower senses of smell, taste and touch" (2004). To challenge this discourse,

Korsmeyer (1999) considers how "the multiple meanings assigned to foods in visual art furnish further evidence of its aesthetic import, as do literary narratives that reflect upon the values manifest in appetite, eating, and food." Korsmeyer's arguments revolve around the development of a type of aesthetic appreciation that encompasses not only the object represented in a work of art, but also its "ethical, political, social and religious" contexts (Korsmeyer, 1999). Lisa Heldke (2011) supports this perspective, arguing that "food *does* have meanings; it connects to objects in the world in all sorts of ways . . . food is *pervasively* symbolic."

Representations of food and taste, many taking a visual form, have been present in the museum for quite a long time. Jennifer Fisher (1999) argues that "the representation of edibles has been longstanding in art works since the invention of the still life." However, Jim Drobnick (1999) writes that "cooking and perfumery belong to those ostensibly 'minor' arts, like textiles and design, accorded lesser status because of their reputed compromise by commercial, domestic and ephemeral traits." According to Korsmeyer (1999), "the very features that have seemed to disqualify taste as an object of extended philosophical interest are complexly portrayed in art. The presumption that taste and smell are closer to nature than other senses, for example, is both presented in art and challenged in the very act of its presentation." Paired with aesthetics, food has traveled throughout the history of art as a legitimate subject, which acquired symbolic and social value related to culturally constructed associations between certain food objects and ethical values. Consequently, writes Korsmeyer (1999), "many of these paintings perpetuate the role of food depictions as decorative, pleasant and enticing; but we shall find as well that food is a powerful vehicle for the expression of that which is dangerous, terrible, and abhorrent." The taste of these representations of food can only exist in the imagination of the viewer and connote different meanings, which also happen to be temporally and geographically specific. For example, Brian Cowan (2007) points out that in the seventeenth-century French courtly context, an artichoke heart included in a painting would represent a sign of luxury and sexuality. For a modern observer, the artichoke would probably take on other meanings distanced from its seventeenth-century symbolism. Representations of different foods and the invitation to imagine how they taste do provide, as Korsmeyer (1999) argues, "meaning to taste" and "invite thoughtful reflection." However, the taste of the food, from a biological perspective, remains external to the observer. The translation from the image of the food to the promise of the taste remains within the realm of the imaginary.

In the last few decades, artists have increased the participatory potential of food and taste in the museum, if we are to consider works by Janine Antoni and Barbara Smith and projects such as artist-designed temporary restaurants with clear social messages. Such works, still under the discourse and practice of art, engage the visitors' senses—especially taste—in order to point out certain types of social and political inequalities. On the reflective potential embedded in food and its practices, Kirshenblatt-Gimblett (1999) writes that "the materiality of food, its dynamic and unstable character, its precarious position between sustenance and garbage, its relationship to the mouth and the rest of the body, particularly the female body, and its importance to community, make food a powerful performance medium." Further, Drobnick (1999) comments that "the materiality of food, as opposed to its role as a nutritional and life-sustaining necessity, is a temptation for artists dealing with the politics of everyday." When food's taste can be directly experienced by the body rather than visualized and imagined, a new set of practices can be encouraged within the museum, which challenge the emphasis on sight and make the process of interpretation "reliant on circumstance and contingent on the body" (Clintberg, 2012). Reflecting on her 1969 art experiment "Ritual Meal," which invited the guests to eat a meal with a surgical theme in a surgery room setting, Barbara Smith states, "it was about ingesting the art work and being affected internally by it . . . [which is a violation] of the rules governing the way the art object is viewed. Most art happens outside the body of the viewer" (Smith qtd. in Kirschenblatt-Gimblatt, 1999). The goal of this experience was to create discomfort within the diner, a discomfort that sought to bring up a critical interpretation of the relation between art, the self, and the body. In a similar framework, Janine Antoni's works such as "Gnaw" (1992) and "Lick and Lather" (1993) play with narratives of pleasure and taste in order to challenge the relation between the self, in this case that of the artist and the artwork. Laura Heon (2001) comments on this relation:

A large cube of chocolate and a large cube of lard, each gnawed along the upper edges and corners, rest on marble pedestals in a gallery. Each cube weighed six hundred pounds before Janine Antoni gnawed them in 1992. The softer lard reveals the impressions of her nose and chin, while in the harder chocolate her teeth marks are apparent. The visible difference between the two kinds of marks reveals the different efforts each required, making the viewer viscerally aware of the extent and physicality of Antoni's effort on the paired cubes.

A similar concern to problematize the relation between the artwork, the museological space, and the body is central to the work of artists such as Dean Baldwin, who curate eating spaces as entryways into critical commentaries on social class or nationalism. Baldwin's "The Dork Porch" was on display at the Art Gallery of Ontario (AGO) in March 2010 in the Young Gallery, adjacent to FRANK, AGO's well-established restaurant. The artist intended his experiential installation to function as a temporary restaurant, where visitors could consume dishes from FRANK's menu in an alternative setting—"The Dork Porch featured roughly hewn bar stools of mismatched dimensions, strings of patio lanterns made of plastic watering cans, plywood and timber booths decorated with felt marker and ballpoint pen and a meandering copper-pipe drinking fountain" (Clintberg, 2012). This project, according to the artist, "has some curious seating that is not exactly comfortable. There's going to be a hammer and saw on site so if you break a chair, you have to fix it" (Leong, 2010). Besides fixing tables and chairs, the audience is invited to dine in the space, selecting items from FRANK's menu. Adam Clintberg (2012) argued that through this installation, "AGO audiences experienced a clash of class associations on a bodily level, through the tasting and digestion of haute cuisine in conjunction with the trailer-park visual aesthetics, smells, and tactile properties of the artist's furnishings." An art installation that claims to trouble class and ethnic divisions through space and food represents another statement for the validation of taste as an interpretative tool with both a private and public dimension—subject to the individual but crafted through a series of social and cultural processes.

While taste is the most intimate and possibly most subjective of the senses, it is also the product of social, political, and cultural discourses. Borrowing from Kant's judgments on taste, Danielle Galeggos and Alec McHoul (2006) point out that "taste as a sense . . . is based on private feelings and is restricted in scope to the individual. In universal subjectivity, or what is generally considered as 'good taste,' taste is an idea that we communicate." On the meaning of taste, Diane Ackerman (1991) writes that "taste is an intimate sense. We can't taste things at a distance," but while "the other senses may be enjoyed in all their beauty when one is alone, taste is largely social." Ackerman refers primarily to the collective experience of taste during ritualized practices of everyday life as the quality that makes taste a social sense. What makes taste an even more relevant social sense is the significant role it has in constructing identity and difference, as communications around taste and through taste inform the regimes of representation used to construct distinction and otherness. Borrowing from Pierre Bourdieu's work on cultural capital and social habitus, Roger Haden (2011) considers taste "a fundamental tool of social differentiation. Whether person, group or class, the exercise of 'personal' taste distinguishes one from another."

The ways in which individuals appreciate the gustatory qualities of a specific food are influenced by perceptions of their own identities and how these differ from others. Similarly, people often eat foods that are outside of their everyday regimes and vocabularies of taste in order to acquire identities as "foodies" or "food adventurers" (Heldke, 2003). Shun Lu and Gary Alan Fine

(1995) write about the construction of authenticity in Chinese restaurants in North America, which happens through a hybrid process of merging what is considered to be tastefully familiar to the American palate with a small dose of foreignness. As a result, "the success of an ethnic restaurant does not depend on its capacity to produce the food as consumed in the home community . . . Rather, it depends on how much the restaurant can accommodate local needs while retaining characteristics of the ethnic tradition—making it 'identifiable'" (Lu and Fine, 1995). These conclusions point toward the fact that taste—the perceptions resulting from the contact with a food or ingredient—can be educated by the self and by the larger political, social, and cultural contexts. The ability to educate taste and to conceptualize taste as a lens to raise awareness about constructions of social and cultural identities has been co-opted by Dean Baldwin in "The Dork Porch."

Baldwin's belief that a shift in the space of consumption—from impeccable design to an intentionally imperfect craftiness—will have an impact on how people taste food is a reference to the communicative and critical potential of food. The artist's desire to trouble social categories of class and social taste by providing an environment that he deems contradictory to the content of FRANK's menu is a comment on the malleable nature of food practices. However, Baldwin could have added one extra layer of interpretation by collaborating with AGO's culinary team to craft a special menu with dishes that would coincide with his aesthetics. Therefore, he could have tried to answer one question that is significant to contemporary museums in search of more participatory practices: is there a way to actually translate identity into food and taste? Pierre Bourdieu's findings in *Distinction* indicate that there are clear associations between consumption of food and belonging to a social class, but his conclusions legitimate these categories rather than contest them (see Gallegos and McHoul, 2006). For Baldwin to incorporate a gustatory component to his installation rather than borrow from FRANK's menu would have created a different set of questions about the taste of food associated with social class.

The examples above point out that the museum has been welcoming to food and taste as relevant sources of historical information and education when paired with artistic representations, and therefore legitimated through a discourse of art. Food as part of a work of art or integrated to an installation acquires a critical function within the museum, but food on its own, as an object to be critically tasted, is rarely defined as a formal pedagogical tool (there are some museums—for example, the National Museum of American History in Washington, D.C. or the Fort York National Historic Site in Toronto—that have embraced the pedagogical potential of food but these museums are exceptions). However, museums have the tools to utilize food in its everyday "raw" nature before it has been cooked into a work of art. The works by Baldwin or Antoni are addressed to a specialized audience who is willing to experiment with art and to become part of the artistic experiment. Experimental installations such as "Ritual Meal" or "Dork Porch" also have the intention to make people uncomfortable by taking them outside of their comfort zone in order to encourage critical thinking. While these are great experimentations with relevant social issues, can museums use everyday food cultures and practices to make visitors critical yet comfortable? Can tasting and eating as everyday practices be co-opted to educate and encourage visitors to think reflectively about what they eat and how their taste constructs stereotypes and ideas about other communities and cultures? Museums can become more participatory, relevant, and "matter" more if they recognize the potential taste has in education and critical thinking.

ART(ISTS) ON THE MENU: HOW DOES CULTURE TASTE?

While different in menu, design, and atmosphere, Mitsitam Native Foods Café and FRANK share their affiliation with museological culture. Located in two major museums, the National Museum of the American Indian in Washington, D.C. and the Art Gallery of Ontario in Toronto, the restaurants promise a culinary experience that mirrors the overall identity of the museum. The NMAI website informs visitors that "'Mitsitam' means 'Let's Eat!' in the Native language of the Delaware and Piscataway People. The Mitsitam Café enhances the museum experience by providing visitors the opportunity to enjoy indigenous cuisines of the Americas" (About Café and Chef, n.d.). In the preface to the Mitsitam Café cookbook, the NMAI director Kevin Gower (2010) expands on the mission of the restaurant, "divided into serving stations representing five general cultural landscapes in North and South America, the Mitsitam Native Foods Café . . . allows our visitors to experience Native cultures and indigenous foods in ways that appeal to all the senses, transcending the limits of a museum exhibition." At AGO, the restaurant plays a similar role—that of extending the museum experience through taste. However, the translation of the content and identity of the museum into the menu is not as obvious as it is in the Mitsitam Café. While NMAI is a museum about native cultures in the Western hemisphere, AGO is an art museum with a collection of more than eighty thousand objects spanning the first century to the present day. Therefore, FRANK's menu cannot rely on a geographical and culturally specific culinary heritage to be communicated through its menu. Rather than taking on a culturally specific approach, the restaurant uses "art" and "artfulness" as interpretative frameworks for its cuisine. Therefore, "the restaurant expresses culture and beauty through the art of fine dining. Warmth and vibrancy are created not only by the food or setting, but also by the energy and spark of diners who, as they enjoy their meal, reflect on their experiences of art in the galleries" (FRANK Talk, n.d.). The space itself is a work of art, authored by Frank Gehry and featuring as a centerpiece a contemporary installation by Frank Stella. Therefore, both restaurants imagine themselves as extensions of the museological space, crafting the menus to give taste to the different cultures and artistic styles on display.

It becomes clear that both museums consider their educational role within the larger context of their host institution. Further, the culinary teams at Mitsitam and FRANK work together with educators and curators in the museum to make some of the institutional goals and contents palatable. The NMAI's mission statement—"to advance knowledge and understanding of the Native cultures of the Western Hemisphere—past, present, and future—through partnership with Native people and others" (Mission Statement, n.d.)—resonates in the description of the restaurant's premise—"The Mitsitam Native Foods Cafe features indigenous food from the Western Hemisphere. Each menu reflects the food and cooking techniques from the region featured. Menus are changed with each season to reflect the bounties of that area" (Menu and Café Hours, n.d.). The emphasis on traditional recipes, some of them transmitted orally from generation to generation, on ancient techniques, and regionally specific ingredients is educational as it instructs visitors about the importance of food in different indigenous communities and about the diversity of such traditions. Gover (2010) writes that "for Native peoples, the ceremonies surrounding hunting, gathering, growing, harvesting, and cooking food were for thousands of years necessarily part of a close, intricate relationship with the land." This narrative is told in different galleries of the permanent exhibition and is performed in the restaurant—"visitors can see their tamales being made by hand and their salmon roasting on an open fire pit—both ancient techniques" (Gover, 2010). Commenting in the *Mitsitam Café Cookbook*, Nicolas I. Sandoval (2010), a Chumash Indian, reinforces the connection between communities and their land—"Native American culinary legacy tells a story of who we were, our lives, and where we are going. The buffalo recipes remind us of this perennial truth . . . the Lakota depended on *wasna* . . . made of dried buffalo meat and chokecherries, to sustain them while hunting." Therefore, the restaurant engages the sense of taste in an exploration of Native foods with a clear focus on the distinctiveness of each community, reflected in recipes and ingredients.

At FRANK, the educational mission of the menu is not as obvious in its permanent menu. FRANK's general pedagogy functions as an initiation into matters of gourmet cookery and the development of refined yet locally specific taste buds for a rather narrow audience. The "hipness" of FRANK is reflected in its highly curated space and its modern visual vocabulary, apparent in all the objects composing the space, from cutlery to menus. According to the website, FRANK is a "distinct Frank Gehry–designed space. Its casual, chic décor includes modern Danish furnishings and a contemporary installation of Frank Stellas's work" (About FRANK Restaurant, n.d.). Just as AGO presents itself as a pioneer in museum architecture, curatorial practice, and public programming, FRANK promises an equally innovative experience for diners. The discourse of newness and reinvention is central to AGO's mandate, which reads, "we will become the imaginative center of our city and province, reflecting our diverse and dynamic setting. We will enhance our international profile as a leading cultural destination and innovative partner in the celebration of art, forging a new model for art museums" (Our Mandate, n.d.).

FRANK becomes part of this discourse, which shifts to a pedagogical tone in terms of what it means to be an informed and socially conscious consumer, interested at the same time in harmony in taste and presentation. At FRANK:

> Executive chef Anne Yarymowich collaborates with her culinary team to create contemporary comfort cuisine: food that is warm and inviting, prepared with honesty and integrity. FRANK's menu showcases an exclusively Ontarian wine list and seasonal ingredients, striving to support local producers with a dedication to global concepts of sustainable farming and slow food. (About FRANK Restaurant, n.d.)

By highlighting the politics of being a good eater, FRANK's mandate seems to communicate primarily to foodies, defined by Shyon Baumann and Josee Johnson (2009) through a series of characteristics: "enthusiasm for local and organic foods . . . reflecting concern with ethical consumption . . . the growing popularity of 'ethnic' cuisine . . . widespread consumption of specialty and premium ingredients." Therefore, it can be argued that the educational scope of the restaurant is limited to "a normative ideal" of "white and relatively affluent" (Baumann and Johnon, 2009). In comparison to the Mitsitam Café, which claims to have a broader appeal by diversifying its menu according to local and collective Native traditions of communities all around the Western hemisphere, FRANK limits the access by communicating through the specialized language of gourmet cuisine. Education into matters of taste and its politics is therefore offered to those who have a preexisting cultural capital and who self-identify as foodies.

The Mitsitam culinary vocabulary is a reflection of the regional differences between different Native culinary cultures, made obvious through the geographies made palatable in the restaurant. The areas covered by the menu—the

Northern Woodlands, South America, the Northwest Coast, Mesoamerica, and the Great Plains—coincide with the cultures represented within the museum, which claims to reference "virtually all tribes in the United States, most of those of Canada, and a significant number of cultures from Middle and South America and the Caribbean" (Collections, n.d.). While the restaurant makes no concrete promises to authentic cuisine, the discourse of authenticity—defined as that which is believed or accepted to be genuine or real: true to itself (Tyler qtd. in Lu and Fine, 1995)—is present through the careful pairing of ingredients and their tastes with specific locations, which are, in turn, associated with specific communities.

The ingredients on the menus sound authentic primarily due to their specificity but are nonetheless transformed to coincide with the expectations of the Western visitor for a familiar yet slightly unfamiliar taste (Lu and Fine, 1995). For example, the description of one of the appetizers on the Northern Woodlands Fall 2012 menu reads, "chestnut stuffed goose terrine, sweet potato corn pone, wilted Brussels sprout, cider reduction" (Northern Woodlands Fall 2012 Menu, n.d.). While the corn pone—a small cake made from corn flour, salt, and milk—is a staple of many Native communities, the addition of sweet potatoes and its plating with terrine and cider reduction transform the dish for a more gourmet and modern diner. Many of the dishes commence from simple ingredients such as rice, tomatoes, or corn but are developed into complex culinary creations such as "friend yellow yucca causa, shrimp and aji peppers" (South American Fall 2012 Menu, n,d,); "persimmon cake, logon berry preserves" (Northwest Coast Fall 2012 Menu, n.d.); "budin de vegetables y tepary beans, crema poblano" (Mesoamerican Fall 2012 Menu, n.d.); or "house ground buffalo and duck burger, roasted pepper dijonaise, smoked tomatoes, aged cedar cheese" (Great Plains Fall 2012 Menu, n.d.). Gover explains this transformation—"with all the café's dishes based on indigenous American ingredients and cooking techniques, the restaurant . . . has adapted traditional foods to the requirements of a modern cafeteria . . . In this very act of adapting traditional foods and combining them in new ways, the restaurant embodies another fundamental of Native cultures: continual adaptation" (Gover, 2010).

At the Mitsitam Café, education through taste is twofold: First, the menus feature ingredients specific to each geographical area, emphasizing what is traditional to various Native communities and how Native ingredients have influenced contemporary global cooking; second, the intentional transformation of the featured dishes is positioned in relation to the adaptability of these communities, which is also a story told throughout the museum. Regardless of how much a dish and its tastes have been reinterpreted, the basic ingredients perform as cultural markers and memories of a region and its communities. Sandoval writes about one of the dishes prepared in the Mitsitam kitchen, the corn and chocolate tamales—"I know my grandmother would have found a kindred spirit in Rich Hetzler, the chef of the Mitsitam Café. His Corn and Chocolate Tamales are reminiscent of her spirit of innovation. A marriage of the ancient staple, maize, and legendary chocolate" (Sandoval, 2010). This new combination of ingredients into a hybrid dish is also a lesson into the influence of Native cuisines on contemporary North American cookery—"the combination of chocolate and maize is not new. The people of the land now known as Mexico thickened their chocolate drinks with ground maize . . . Olmec people first cultivated the cocoa tree . . . maize has its beginning in central Mexico thousands of years ago" (Sandoval, 2010). The taste of corn, an ingredient very common on the menu in dishes such as "breast of duck, dried corn & strawberry cake, red wine strawberry reduction" (Northern Woodlands Spring 2013 Menu, n.d.), "blue corn bread" (South American Spring 2013 Menu, n.d.), or "bean and corn succotash" (Northern Woodlands Winter 2012 Menu, n.d.), captures the duality of tradition-innovation presented by the restaurant and the museum as one of the main traits of Native communities.

At FRANK, the menu also embodies discourses of innovation and newness in order to reflect the overall identity of the museum, excluding any stories which could be interpreted as traditional or safe. While the Mitsitam Café is geographically and culturally located within specific geographies, promising a hint of "terroir" (see Trubek, 2008), FRANK is very loosely engaged with geography while focusing primarily on a culinary culture of gourmet and comfort. This culture, while disengaged with a specific location, is nonetheless locally focused through a discourse on ethical consumption. According to the AGO website, "a unique and cutting-edge museum dining experience, FRANK transcends visitors' expectations of gallery dining. In developing the concept and menu for this distinct restaurant, [Chef Anne] Yarymowich focused on creating 'contemporary comfort cuisine.' Drawing on regional ingredients, she sees the art experience as a major source of inspiration" (FRANK Management and Culinary Team, n.d.). Therefore, the regimes of taste cultivated by FRANK are rooted in local geographies not to promote traditional cooking, but to encourage ideologies associated with slow food and ethical eating. However, all these stories are somehow lost on the menu, which features dishes formulated in the universal vocabulary of gourmet cuisine. For example, FRANK's dinner menu features dishes such as "chevre croquette on a salad of blood orange, pickled beets, baby arugula and candied walnuts with citrus walnut oil vinaigrette" and "rosemary and roast garlic rack of lamb, pulled shank ravioli garlic chili rapini, rosemary gremolata" (FRANK Dinner Menu, n.d.). The hints of a very loose locale—ranging from Niagara to the West Coast—are present on the wine menu and in the "FRANK burger bar." The wines served at FRANK, while not exclusively from Ontario, include a variety of red, white, sparkling, and dessert wines for those supporting the local wine cultures—a sparkling wine from the Colio Estates on the Lake Erie North Shore; a chardonnay from Les Clos Jordanne in Niagara; or a merlot from Vignoble Rancourt in Niagara-on-the-Lake (FRANK Wine Menu, n.d.). Likewise, lunch guests can select from three artisanal burgers "served on soft brioche bun with housemade ketchup of the day" (FRANK Lunch Menu, n.d.). Two of the burgers incorporate the local discourse—"Ontario ground chuck and brisket burger with thick cut bacon and red onion relish" and "west coast burger, salmon burger with scallion-ginger relish" (FRANK Lunch Menu, n.d.). The ethics of cooking with local ingredients, which is meant to educate consumers about the politics of food, fades in a menu which is more universally gourmet than locally inspired.

The educational goal of the restaurant becomes more prominent in its temporary menus that coincide with special exhibitions, such as Frida & Diego: Passion, Politics and Painting. FRANK is well known for curating exhibition-inspired menus which communicate culture and identity through taste. On such occasions, the visitors are invited to understand the art displayed in the museum through taste and connect with the artists at very intimate levels. In fact, eating art-inspired dishes transforms the museum visit into a multisensory experience and the food into a keeper of visual and gustatory memories. For the recent Frida & Diego exhibition, FRANK's culinary team prepared a menu that "echoes the heat, passion and sweetness of these two famous Mexican artists" (Celebrate Frida & Diego at AGO, n.d.). Visitors could find dishes such as "Diego's pork steak" or spicy cookies in the shape of Frida's head and torso, along with a series of Frida and Diego inspired margaritas (Poplak, n.d.; Shupac, n.d.). Through food, FRANK, and by extension the AGO, educate visitors about Mexican culture by referencing a culinary vocabulary that both reinforces and challenges perceptions about Mexican cuisine.

Both the NMAI and AGO have different educational goals, which are co-opted by the restaurants in an attempt to translate culture, identity, politics, and history into palatable experiences. FRANK and the Mitsitam Café, while they differ in terms of cuisine, design and audience, represent instances that show the potential of food and taste to serve as educators for museum visitors. However, both restaurants position their menus within a larger context of foodie culture, which, as explained by Baumann and Johnston, is characterized by an enjoyment of "ethnic" dishes and ideals of ethical consumption. Further, both restaurants rely on the spectacle of food (Baumann and Johnston, 2009). At the Mitsitam Café, spectacle is displayed through the sometimes confusing combination of dishes, ingredients, tastes, and smells that bring local and national cuisines into one single space. FRANK, with its commitment to an artful display of food, is spectacular through its combination of ingredients into art-inspired dishes consumed in a highly curated space, authored by two very famous Franks. My strongest critique of both restaurants is the lack of a proper contextualization of the dishes within a political and cultural discourse, which could point out the complex histories of ingredients, many of which have traveled in time and space. For example, there is very little critical and reflective interpretation of the dishes or even awareness of the biographies of ingredients and the colonial, postcolonial, or global dimension of food consumption. This absence is especially problematic in a museum like the NMAI, which is dedicated to the culture of a historically marginalized group of communities.

CONCLUSIONS

In an effort to increase participation, museum professionals have crafted innovative approaches to opening up museological spaces to the sensorium, with an emphasis on touch, hearing, and even smell. Taste as a component of the museum experience has rarely been explored beyond the promise that the visitor would be able to savor a cup of Mexican hot chocolate to accompany the works of Frida and Diego. However, the critical aspect of tasting a certain dish as a representation of and communication about other cultures and communities has yet to be co-opted by museums. There are numerous ways in which museums can experiment with the critical aspect of tasting. Most museums already have the infrastructure to cook for their visitors, as eating spaces in various forms—restaurants, cafes, bars, bistros, food courts, food stands, even food trucks—are almost a mandatory presence in cultural institutions. But how can the pleasurable act of eating be transformed into an educational moment? Building on the examples I provided in this chapter, I would like to suggest some approaches for a more reflective incorporation of food into the educational scope of the museum.

FRANK's special menus crafted to complement certain exhibitions, such as the Frida & Diego show, and the geographically specific dishes to be consumed in the Mitsitam Café represent cultural encounters between different communities. FRANK offers churros and Mexican hot chocolate as sides to the exhibition, contributing to an extent to what Lisa Heldke calls food colonialism— "[the] strange penchant for cooking and eating ethnic foods" (2001). Similarly, Mitsitam Café offers foodies a spectacle of "ethnic" cookery by referencing in its menus culinary traditions of areas inhabited by Native communities all around the Western hemisphere. To transform the consumption of foods from other and "othered" communities into a critical reflection on the historical—primarily colonization and postcolonialism—and regimes of representation rooted in such histories, the restaurants could make visitors aware of the biographies and geographies of ingredients. Most ingredients have traveled from one space to another in the process of colonization, decolonization, immigration, or globalization. Often, the journey of food has been marked by power struggles, cultural imperialism, and political oppression. When cooked in gourmet dishes, ingredients such as corn or tomatoes lose their biographies, therefore awareness as to how such vegetables have traveled to end up on our plates could increase knowledge of such tensed histories.

Further, the educational potential of food can also be used to point out how certain ingredients and their tastes play a significant role in the social imaginary built around different cultural communities. For example, representing Frida and Diego through Mexican hot chocolate, which is spiced up with cinnamon, nutmeg, and cayenne pepper, and churros, a deep-fried street food common in many Latin American countries, equates Mexican identity with the exoticism attached to spices such as cayenne pepper or cinnamon but also misinforms about matters of cultural origins and appropriation. The churro, for example, while popular in Mexico today, was originally based on a cooking technique that the Portuguese imported from Northern China during the Ming dynasty (Cronk, n.d.). By putting the pleasure of eating before the critical potential of taste, AGO has missed an opportunity to make visitors aware of the construction of social and cultural stereotypes based on the taste and look of foods.

REFERENCES

About café and chef. Retrieved March 20, 2013 from Mitsitam Café, http://www.mitsitamcafe.com/content/about.asp.

About FRANK restaurant. Retrieved March 15, 2013 from FRANK, http://www.ago.net/frank-restaurant-contemporary-comfort-cuisine-toronto.

Ackerman, D. (1991). *A Natural History of the Senses.* New York: Vintage.

Barthes, R. (2008). Towards a psychosociology of contemporary food consumption. In C. Counihan and P. Van Esterik (eds.), *Food and Culture: A Reader*, 28–35. New York: Routledge.

Baumann, S. and Johnson, J. (2009). *Foodies: Democracy and Distinction in the Gourmet Foodscape.* New York: Routledge.

Celebrate Frida & Diego at AGO. Retrieved March 15, 2013 from Art Gallery of Ontario, http://www.ago.net/dining.

Classen, C. (2007). Museum manners: The sensory life of the early museum. *Journal of Social History*, 40(4), 895–911.

Clintberg, M. (2012). Gut Feeling: Artists' restaurants and gustatory aesthetics. *Senses & Society*, 7(2): 209–24.

Collections. Retrieved March 20, 2013 from the National Museum of the American Indian, http://nmai.si.edu/explore/collections/.

Cowan, B. (2007). New worlds, new tastes: Food fashions after the Renaissance. In P. Freedman (ed.), *Food: The History of Taste*, 197–232. Berkeley: University of California Press.

Cramer, J. M., Greene, C. P. and Walters L. M. (2011). Beyond mere sustenance: Food as communication/communication as food. In C. P. Greene, J. M. Cramer, L. M. Walters (eds.), *Food as Communication/Communication as Food*, ix–xix. New York: Peter Lang.

Cronk, L. (n.d.). Churros: A secret history. Retrieved April 30, 2013 from The Prisma, http://www.theprisma.co.uk/2011/07/17/churros-a-secret-history/.

Drobnick, J. (1999). Recipes for the cube: Aromatic and edible practices in contemporary art. In B. Fischer (ed.), *Foodculture: Tasting Identities and Geographies in Art*, 69–80. Toronto: YYZ Press.

Fisher, J. (1999). Performing taste. In B. Fischer (ed.), *Foodculture: Tasting Identities and Geographies in Art*, 29–48. Toronto: YYZ Press.

FRANK dinner menu. Retrieved March 15, 2013 from FRANK, http://www.ago.net/frank-dinner- menu.

FRANK lunch menu. Retrieved March 15, 2013 from FRANK, http://www.ago.net/frank-lunch-menu.

FRANK management and culinary team. Retrieved March 15, 2013 from FRANK, http://www.ago.net/the-frank-culinary-team.

FRANK talk. Retrieved March 15, 2013 from FRANK, http://www.ago.net/frank-talk.

FRANK wine menu. Retrieved March 15, 2013 from FRANK, http://www.ago.net/frank-wines.

Gallegos, D. and McHoul, A. (2006). 'It's not about good taste. It's about taste good': Bourdieu and Campbell's soup . . . and beyond. *Senses & Society*, 1(2), 165–82.

Gover, K. (2010). Preface. In R. Hetzler (ed.), *The Mitsitam Café Cookbook*, 1–3. Washington DC: Smithsonian.

Great Plains Fall 2012 menu. Retrieved March 20, 2013 from Mitsitam Café, http://www.mitsitamcafe.com/content/menus.asp.

Haden, R. (2011). Lionizing taste: Towards an ecology of contemporary connoisseurship. In J. Strong (ed.), *Educated Tastes: Food, Drink and Connoisseur Culture*, 237–90. Lincoln: University of Nebraska Press.

Heldke, L. (2001). "Let's eat Chinese!" Reflections on cultural food colonialism. *Gastronomica: The Journal of Food and Culture*, 1(2), 76–79.

———. (2003). *Exotic Appetites: Ruminations of a Food Adventurer*. New York: Routledge.

———. (2008). Let's cook Thai: Recipes for colonialism. In C. Counihan and P. Van Esterik (eds.), *Food and Culture: A Reader*, 327–41. New York: Routledge.

———. (2011). The extensive pleasure of eating. In J. Strong (ed.), *Educated Tastes: Food, Drink and Connoisseur Culture*, 121–57. Lincoln: University of Nebraska Press.

Heon, L. (2001). Janine Antoni's gnawing idea. *Gastronomica: The Journal of Food and Culture*, 1(2), 5–8.

Howes, D. (Ed.) (2004). *Empire of the Senses: The Sensual Culture Reader*. Oxford: Berg.

Kirschenblatt-Gimblatt, B. (1999). Playing to the senses: Food as performance medium. *Performance Research*, 4(1), 1–30. Accessed at http://www.nyu.edu/classes/bkg/issues/food-pr6.htm.

———. (2006). Making sense of food in performance: The table and the stage. In S. Banes and A. Lepecki (eds.), *The Senses in Performance*, 71–89. New York: Routledge.

Korsmeyer, C. (1999). *Making Sense of Taste*. Ithaca: Cornell University Press.

Leong, M. (2010, March 19). It's not a porch for dorks but it's a dorky porch. *National Post*. Retrieved from http://arts.nationalpost.com/author/mwleong/page/41/.

Lu, S. and Fine, G. A. (1995). The presentation of ethnic authenticity: Chinese food as a social accomplishment. *The Sociological Quarterly*, 36(3), 535–53.

Menu and café hours. Retrieved March 20, 2013 from Mitsitam Café, http://www.mitsitamcafe.com/content/menus.asp.

Mesoamerican Fall 2012 menu. Retrieved March 20, 2013 from Mitsitam Café, http://www.mitsitamcafe.com/content/menus.asp.

Mission statement. Retrieved March 20, 2013 from the National Museum of the American Indian, http://nmai.si.edu/about/mission/.

Northern Woodlands Fall 2012 menu. Retrieved March 20, 2013 from Mitsitam Café, http://www.mitsitamcafe.com/content/menus.asp.

Northern Woodlands Winter 2012 menu. Retrieved March 20, 2013 from Mitsitam Café, http://www.mitsitamcafe.com/content/menus.asp.

Northern Woodlands Spring 2013 menu. Retrieved March 20, 2013 from Mitsitam Café, http://www.mitsitamcafe.com/content/menus.asp.

Northwest Coast Fall 2012 menu. Retrieved March 20, 2013 from Mitsitam Café, http://www.mitsitamcafe.com/content/menus.asp.

Our mandate. Retrieved March 15, 2013 from the Art Gallery of Ontario, http://www.ago.net/mandate.

Parkhurst Ferguson, P. (2004). *Accounting for Taste: The Triumph of French Cuisine*. Chicago: Chicago University Press.

Poplak, L. (n.d.). One tank trip: Frida & Diego exhibit at Art Gallery of Ontario. *The Buffalo News*. Retrieved from http://www.buffalonews.com/apps/pbcs.dll/article?AID=/20121125/LIFE02/121129666/1072.

Sandoval, N. I. (2010). Introduction. In R. Hetzler (ed.), *The Mitsitam Café Cookbook*, 4–7. Washington DC: Smithsonian.

Shupac, J. (n.d.). Frida economy. *The Grid*. Retrieved from http://www.thegridto.com/culture/arts/the-frida-economy/.

South American Fall 2012 menu. Retrieved March 20, 2013 from Mitsitam Café, http://www.mitsitamcafe.com/content/menus.asp.

South American Spring 2013 menu. Retrieved March 20, 2013 from Mitsitam Café, http://www.mitsitamcafe.com/content/menus.asp.

Trubek, A. (2008). *The Sense of Place: A Cultural Journey into Terroir*. Berkeley: University of California Press.

Part IV

MUSEUM ARCHITECTURE AND THE SENSES

14

Navigating the Museum

Fiona Zisch, Stephen Gage, and Hugo Spiers

SETTING THE SCENE

A visit to a museum is generally a welcome treat. As we experience a museum our brain constructs its own internal museum of the mind to help us navigate, explore, and form the memories we live our lives by. This process is fundamentally guided by the architecture of the space and its influence on our perceptions and expectations. In this chapter we will present recent discoveries of how the brain represents and remembers space and use this understanding to create a starting point for a journey we are beginning: the relation of architecture to neuroscience.

NEURAL REPRESENTATIONS OF SPACE

The world and its underlying material substance and immaterial qualities are composed of a rich and varied assemblage of components, attributes, and interactions. In order to be able to navigate and negotiate the world, human beings are equipped with a wondrous and intricately evolved instrument, the body. This body, being a finely tuned apparatus, relies upon an array of intertwined sensory modalities, each contributing to a unified experience of the world. To form a unified cognitive sense of being and to repeatedly recognize and self-localize in a single world "out there," the brain combines and sequences sensual input in a sensible manner. Immediately aware of connecting to the world through sight, we often forget or perhaps ignore that the world exists not solely as a visible interface and that vision is not the only means we have to make sense of our surroundings.

Beyond vision, hearing, touch, taste, and smell, the brain has a sixth sense. Not extra-sensory perception but *proprioception*, the capacity to keep track of where our limbs are in space. In addition to proprioception, neurons responding to the movement of tiny stones in our inner ear (the otoliths), and hairlike cells tugged and swayed in the fluid of our semi-circular canals allow us to sense our movement relative to the gravitational pull of the earth (see e.g., Jeffery, 2008). This information allows humans to comprehend an environment through internal senses of movement and furnish it with visual and auditory information (when available) to map the space explored. Vision may be a dominant basis for the forming of internal maps of space (cognitive maps), but these maps are by no means complete—they are both filled with and strengthened by the sense of our own movement (see e.g., Massumi, 2002). The two brain systems provide converging information and, to some extent, back each other up.

The first step in understanding how the brain constructs space is to realize how the brain processes information. Our brain is composed of approximately 86 billion neurons (Azevedo et al., 2009). Each neuron sends and receives *action potentials*, which are changes in the cell's electrical charge. For example, cells in our eyes convert light into action potentials which are sent to regions of our brain involved in processing images. These processing neurons, and indeed all neurons, communicate via action potentials. A cell generating action potentials is described as firing. Neural firing can be prompted by high-level, multimodal combinations of inputs in response to environmental encouragement, such as spatial configuration, sequence, boundaries, features, or topography. Navigating an environment requires not only the processing of immediate sensory information extracted from external or internal stimuli but also matching these with internal predictions about the world and acting on the output to guide movement (see e.g., O'Keefe and Nadel, 1978). A key brain region responsible for spatial navigation is the *hippocampal formation* (see for review Spiers, 2012 and figure 14.1).

The hippocampal formation is a set of interconnected brain structures that is essential for memory and that appears highly homogenous across all mammals (see e.g., Andersen et al., 2006). Recent neuroimaging and neuropsychological observations support the assumption that the hippocampal formation is part of a core "default network" required to support episodic memory, navigation, and imagination (Buckner and Caroll, 2007). The hippocampal formation, owing to its physical appearance, is named after the Latin word for seahorse and consists of the hippocampus proper, the dentate gyrus, and the subiculum (Laveneux et al., 2002). The hippocampus proper can be divided into three main subdivisions: CA1, CA2, and CA3. CA stands for "Cornu Ammonis," derived from the Egyptian god Amun's symbol, the horns.

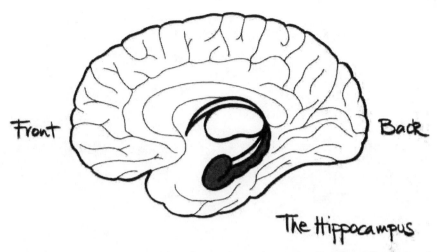

Figure 14.1. The hippocampus is an interconnected structure that lies at the center of the mammalian brain.

Due to the necessity of using invasive technologies to record from individual cells, most modern neuroscience studies hippocampal cells in rodents. After undergoing surgery and having tetrodes (sets of four electrodes which measure the electrical discharge from individual cells) implanted into its hippocampus, a rat brain can be recorded from by connecting the tetrode to a PC. Few studies have been done on humans; however, the results of such rare studies (conducted on epileptic patients who have tetrodes implanted as part of their therapy) provide evidence that rodent hippocampi behave not dissimilarly to human hippocampi, and this allows educated propositions about human spatial representation (Quiroga et al., 2005; Ekstrom et al., 2003).

Situated within the mammalian hippocampus are some of the most intriguing cell types in the brain, and one of their functions is to serve navigation and memory abilities. Many of these cells are located in the CA1 and CA3 regions and are dedicated to extracting spatial information from the world, in order to construct internal representations. Cells in the hippocampus have been named due to their spatial properties.

We will first give a brief introduction to these different cells and later revisit some of their properties as we begin our quest to explore their relation to an understanding of architectural experience. Before we begin, we offer a brief reflection. In both neuroscience and architecture exist discipline-specific distinctions and connotations among the universal terms space, place, object, boundary, and direction. Here we provide a brief summary of properties of the cells involved in processing spatial information and acknowledge that the use of terms derives from neuroscience.

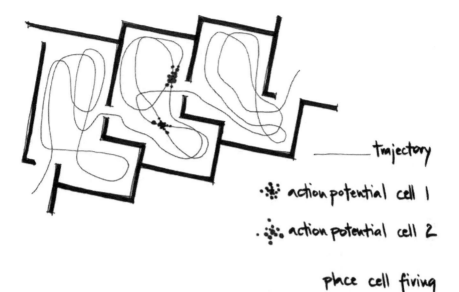

Figure 14.2. Sketch of a movement trajectory through space. Place cell 1 and place cell 2 fire in different locations along the path.

Place Cells

The first spatial cells in the hippocampal formation are *place cells* (O'Keefe and Dostrovsky, 1971). Discovered in 1971 and appropriately named, they fire action potentials only when a particular region of a space is occupied by the animal being recorded from (see figure 14.2). The specific location in the environment where a place cell fires is known as its *place field*, and this field is different for each cell. Each location in every environment is therefore represented by a unique combination of place fields. Each step of your journey to work, each place in your house, indeed every location in the world you have ever encountered is represented in your brain by the unique combination of place cells active. One question that has puzzled scientists for a while is: How do place cells know where to fire action potentials? Recent discoveries of other cells have provided insights.

Grid Cells

Grid cells in the medial entorhinal cortex fire periodically, and each cell generates multiple firing fields, which are arranged in a tessellating grid pattern across an environment (Hafting et al., 2005, and figure 14.3). Grid cells have been thought of as providing something similar to the grid divisions that divide up metric space on a cartographic map. Grid cells send action potentials

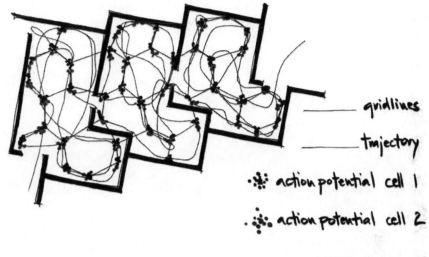

gridlines

trajectory

·※· action potential cell 1

.·※· action potential cell 2

grid cell firing

Figure 14.3.   Sketch of a movement trajectory through space. Grid cell 1 and grid cell 2 fire in different locations but exhibit the same tessellating pattern.

to place cells (Zhang et al., 2013), allowing place cells to determine how far an animal may have traveled. Several models describe how place cells may determine where to fire based on grid cell activity (see e.g., Burgess et al., 2007; Solstad et al., 2006).

Boundary/Boundary Vector Cells

Boundary cells (Solstad et al., 2008) and *boundary vector cells* (Lever et al., 2009) are cells in the medial entorhinal cortex and subiculum, respectively, which fire along or slightly offset to the boundaries of a space. It is thought that each place cell might receive information from a number of such cells, allowing it to determine how close the animal is to the different borders, thus pinpointing a specific location in space for the place cell to fire (Hartley et al., 2000).

Head-direction Cells

Grid cells and place cells provide information about locations occupied during travel, but they do not provide information about orientation. This is thought to come from neurons known as *head-direction cells,* which exist in a set of limbic brain regions, including the presubiculum and entorhinal cortex, which have been likened to an internal compass (Taube, 1998).

They fire when the head is oriented in a certain direction with respect to the environment. Head-direction cells are modulated by self-motion and by visual information.

Parietal Spatial Cells

The brain does not just form internal representations of orientation and position in the environment, it also constructs estimates of where things are relative to our body and our current viewpoint. Such cells are not found in the hippocampal formation, but in a region highly connected to it, the posterior parietal cortex of the primate brain (see e.g., Colby and Goldberg, 1999). It has been proposed that these cells provide viewpoint representations of the environment to allow action in the space and that the spatial cells of the hippocampal formation provide the map and compass to tie these views to long-term memory (Byrne et al., 2007).

A VISIT TO THE MUSEUM

Having given a brief overview of the spatial cells in the brain, we now explore how these cells might operate during a journey to a museum and ponder what may be happening in the brain of the visitor as she explores and enjoys the visit.

When going to museums, our goals and expectations are often mixed. We may follow a definite intent, such as wanting to view a specific piece of art, or we may simply wish to spend an afternoon leisurely meandering around soaking up the atmosphere. This behavior, which, for want of a better term, we call spatial, cultural, and social "browsing," is interesting from both a scientific and an architectural viewpoint. It is spatial, but it is not in the first instance spatially goal directed. It is cultural, but it relies inherently on multisensory input rather than being based uniquely in language and conventions, and it is social, as browsers often have a parallel social agenda.

Museum spaces are often described as following a narrative. The implication is that specific sets of linear experiences are created. According to Tony Bennett, display organization and thus the architectural configuration known as the *galleria progressiva* emerged after the French Revolution (Sutton, 2000). Often temporary exhibitions, there are however notable examples of permanent gallery spaces that are constructed in this way. Examples include the Picasso Museum in Paris and the Louisiana Museum of Modern Art in Humblebaek, as well as the New York Guggenheim Museum and the New York Metropolitan Museum, which combine the galleria progressiva with the other prevalent format, the *period room*. A linear approach to museum planning can offer a subtle mixture of common and individual stories to the visitor without relying on symbolic guidance cues such as signposts (Sutton, 2000).

We take it as axiomatic, from an architectural, neuroscientific, and philosophical standpoint, that the visitor through all her senses constructs the visitor experience before, during, and after the visit (e.g., Von Glaserfeld, 1996). However, unlike the radical constructivists, here we take the view that the visitor is exposed to an external physical reality that is more or less the same as the reality being experienced by other visitors at the same time. We propose that it is the intricate neural and mental construction, preconstruction, and reconstruction of sophisticated architectural environments that promotes successful navigation, while additionally eliciting sensual delight.

The past and future are immanently important both to such feelings of wonder and to navigational capacities, and we will now consider what happens in the brain before a visit.

BEFORE THE VISIT

A museum visit begins not as the visitor arrives at and enters the museum but indeed as soon as the thought of going enters her stream of consciousness. Having decided to undertake the excursion, imagination and memory take hold of her mind and her brain prepares her for the visit. The experience of a museum gallery is preconditioned by possible prior experience of the gallery, by knowledge of the gallery content, of similar gallery settings, and, increasingly, of galleries in digital representation. Even if she has never been to a specific museum, based on media or others' reports, the visitor will have an expectation of the building. Significant buildings often have a key image with which most visitors are familiar. When visitors experience the place the image was taken from, they have a memory to which they refer, regardless of their having been there before or not. Architects have been consciously aware of this since the Renaissance and it is reasonable to say that they design key moments in their buildings on this basis. The British architect Sir James Stirling is reputed to have always aimed to specifically create a place in his buildings where a key image could be taken in photographic portrait format (see e.g., Stirling and Krier, 1975).

External sources of memory underlying preexperience, such as key images, are of course shared by many visitors, but given the vast range of galleries, settings, and content any individual and personal set of preexperiences is likely to be unique. This is especially the case when we consider that preexperiences are also remembered in the context of a respective state of body and mind and of the sequence of individual life stories. The human ability to imagine the future (as the reconstructing and reconfiguring of past memories into novel assemblages) probably provides essential guidance mechanisms when traversing and browsing a museum (see e.g., Schacter et al., 2012). Original—often even fantastical—imagination is to the best of our knowledge unique to human beings. The neural basis for constructing and indeed manipulating memories which enable human imagination, however, manifest in similar ways in our mammalian relatives. We speculate that humans are able to project across larger periods in time and space and construct more elaborate novel situations than rodents. Our assumptions are based on scientific facts; for now they remain, of course, suggestions. Despite the apparent and yet to be understood differences, recent research on rodents has revealed a remarkable capacity of their neural network to "pre-play" upcoming trajectories to places in the world (see e.g., Pfeiffer and Foster, 2013). By pre-play we mean sequential activation of the cells that represent each of the places encountered on a journey in the future. As an example, imagine three place cells. The first represents the entrance to a room, the second a field in the center, and the third a field on the far side of the room. As you pass through the space, each cell fires action potentials as you enter its preferred part of the world (its place field). Intriguingly, in a quarter of a second before you set off across the room, all three cells may fire in sequence 1-2-3, much like a readout of the future path. Rat hippocampi have indeed been observed to fire in a way predictive of flexible future behavior, when trajectories between start and end of a journey are new to the animal (Pfeiffer and Foster, 2013). Extrapolating from rodent data, where pre-play is likely to act as a mechanism that guides foraging and finding, we may contemplate that such "mental time-travel" (Pfeiffer and Foster, 2013) in a prospective museum visitor can serve to generate a depository of possible sequences, which in situ can then inform her browsing behavior.

Hans Ulrich Gumbrecht refers to the future as the "horizon of expectations" (Gumbrecht, 2004) and, adopting this piece of imagery, nicely sketches how human brains may prepare a collection of likely-to-be-required operations. Having undergone this exercise, behavior which is custom tailored to each idiosyncratic situation will then be able to emerge (Foster and Knierim, 2012). As the following research shows, rest and sleep (offline periods) are especially important to planning. Memory pre-play mechanisms in hippocampal place cells appear to be most active in offline periods, giving rise to meditations about the role dreams play as simulation systems (Schacter et al., 2012). In addition to prefiring immediately before running along a trajectory, place cells in sleeping rats have been shown to briefly fire action potentials in the same order that they would if the animal were running along a familiar path (Wilson and McNaugton, 1994). This has been speculated to be, quite literally, the "stuff of dreams" (Ji and Wilson, 2008). After a visit to the museum, it is likely the visitor's hippocampus is very active replaying reruns of the experience. More controversially, recent work has argued the brain may pre-play places yet to be experienced in the future, during sleep (Dragoi and Tonegawa, 2011, 2013). This type of pre-play is thought to arise from a set of preconfigured charts in the hippocampus.

If true, it suggests that the night before the first time a museum is visited, the visitor's brain will start to simulate the next day's visit.

EXPERIENCING THE VISIT

After constructing representations and entertaining conscious and unconscious, material and immaterial forecasts of the museum visit, the visitor can begin to enjoy the unfolding journey through the space and the events that will take place within. In this section we will illustrate a succession of factors that are important both to navigation and perception of space.

The Entrance

Entrance areas to both public and private buildings are universally afforded special consideration. Museum foyers are no different and as origin points, in our subjective experience, they hold a distinct position. What happens in the hippocampus when a starting point to a journey is established? Observations show that in fact a disproportionate number of place fields are located at common starting points of rats' expeditions into testing environments (Ainge et al., 2007), as well as in "doorways" in a multiregional environment (Spiers et al., 2013). This may relate to the need for an anchor point for each experience, but more research will be required to understand this. Passing through doorways also seems to cause forgetting (Radvansky et al., 2010) and it may be that they set the "frame" for a new learning experience.

Sequence and Configuration

We will now travel to a specific linear museum to explore how the brain might process such a space. The Louisiana Museum is well known for its sophisticated design and exquisite configuration and balance of spaces (see figure 14.4). The museum as it exists today is an elegant assemblage of interlocked and interconnected pavilions and corridors of varying transparencies.

The architecture of the museum hinges on the primacy of producing flowing visitor movement through the overall exhibition space, ushering patrons from one pavilion to the next. An example of a galleria progressive, the Louisiana's arrangement is vaguely reminiscent of nineteenth-century exhibition design, which drew inspiration from urban spaces such as shopping arcades, market halls, and department stores, as well as conservatory spaces (Bennett, 1995). The aim was to create a relaxed atmosphere which, while putting the visitor on a fixed route, was also conducive to a leisurely mode of walking. The Louisiana pavilions allow visitors to stroll at a speed of their choosing, and the multiple access points along the route to the surrounding gardens serve the purpose of decentralizing viewing angles and presenting a steady succession of exit possibilities. The New York Guggenheim uses a similar principle, allowing visitors to sidestep into exhibition rooms and then return to the fixed journey on the sloping ramp.

We can now ask an interesting question. The individual spaces are connected and experienced as a flow of events, but are they part of one grid map, or do grid cells rather fire in a succession of linked submaps? Once again, data extracted from experiments on rodents can give hints and allow

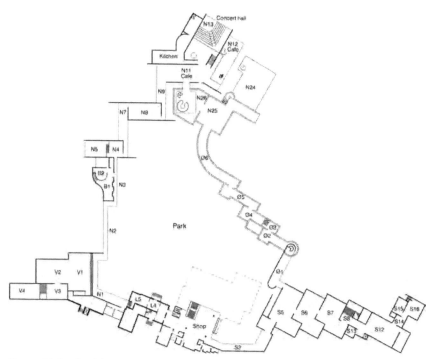

Figure 14.4.   Louisiana Museum of Modern Art—Key Plan (Level 3). Courtesy Louisiana Museum of Modern Art

reflections. In testing environments that are separated into compartments, grid and place cell map representations are veritably separated into submaps (Derdikman et al., 2009; Skaggs and McNaughton, 1996; Spiers et al., 2013). Representations are promptly reset upon entering a new space as neural firing discontinues for one space and restarts for the next. When a similar trajectory in an open field without walls is followed, no map fragmentation is observed (Derdikman et al., 2009), providing evidence for the importance of physical divisions of spaces. The overall mental map of a museum such as the Louisiana, where visitors follow one fluid linear trajectory through a succession of partitioned pavilions, probably consists of a collection of grid cell submaps based on the architectural layout, which divides the route into a succession of highly distinctive rooms and corridors. Perhaps it is the phenomenon of the doorways mentioned above that divides the route by setting a map for each space (Radvansky et al., 2010). Currently we do not know how the brain links these submaps to one another to create what we may call a "chain of submaps." What we do know is that as described above, active place cells encode spatiotemporal sequences of places; additionally, their firing is the hippocampal formation's mode of encoding transitions between events and states, often using current circumstance to predict the next stage (Alvernhe et al., 2008). In order to generate the necessary updating in the map, the hippocampus must keep note of the body's changing position in space by integrating linear and angular self-motion, which are thought to be provided by grid cell firing patterns (see e.g., McNaughton et al., 2006; Jeffery, 2008).

In the context of a museum such as the Louisiana, we may speculate that the pronounced firing sequence exhibited by place cells transitioning from pavilion to pavilion creates unique "braces" that bind each grid cell submap to its respective neighboring maps. Pondering this, an inference may be that a linear journey that is laced with salient spatial transitions between distinguishably shaped spaces, stimulates the cells in our hippocampal formation in a manner which allows for better encoding and understanding of the space. By "understanding," we mean the capacity to form a coherent internal representation of the environment. The linearization and careful punctuation of the space may lead to a strongly coherent representation. Does a strong coherent representation then produce a better sense of space and place? Representation in a linear fashion is known as linearization in psycholinguistics and, in short, describes a process by which the experience of spatial structures is transformed into a temporal succession. It has been proposed that this process promotes spatial comprehension and sense-making (Wenz, 1997). The sophisticated succession of linearly interwoven spaces at the Louisiana would thus elegantly complement the way human beings make sense of space and process it, by breaking its sequential experience down into a chronology of events. The above would thus suggest that the strong sense of space in this museum is achieved by its coherent linear representation.

Construction

In the context of museums and galleries, sense of space is desired to be a pleasurable experience. We believe that it may be the act of constructing memories of experiences in space that gives pleasure. Here we have described how movement in rats stimulates the cells in their brains and shepherds the construction of representations. The idea that pleasure is elicited by the construction process is speculative and to date there is no scientific knowledge to back this up. Pleasure responses in the brain have been explored; however, links to spatial processing have yet to be identified (see e.g., Berridge et al., 2009). The architectural speculation we make is based on an argument about the nature of an aesthetically potent environment put forward by Gordon Pask and elaborated by Stephen Gage.

Pask offers us a brief for this environment:

> With all this in view, it is worth considering the properties of aesthetically potent environments, that is, of environments designed to encourage or foster the type of interaction which is (by hypothesis) pleasurable. It is clear that an aesthetically potent environment should have the following attributes:

> It must have sufficient variety to provide the potentially controllable novelty required by a man (however, it must not swamp him with variety—if it did, the environment would merely be unintelligible).

> It must contain forms that a man can interpret or learn to interpret at various levels of abstraction.

> It must provide cues or tacitly stated instructions to guide the learning and abstractive process.

> It may, in addition, respond to a man, engage him in conversation and adapt its characteristics to the prevailing mode of discourse. (Pask, 1968)

Gage offers a hypothesis, in *The Wonder of Trivial Machines*, that the pleasure that is experienced occurs as the observer constructs an explanation for herself (Gage, 2006). Currently we still lack the scientific link between emotional feeling related to constructing and understanding a space and the spatial cell responses that map this space.

Orientation and Location

We will now return to the realm of what has been explored and ask a question of which an understanding is beginning to emerge. How is movement integrated into the grid map so that we can orient in a space? How do we know where we are—how do we self-localize?

In essence, self-localization in an environment requires two things. We need to know which environment we are in and then establish our location and direction within it. To do this, the brain connects information from multiple sensory modalities to previous knowledge (Jeffery, 2008). A process known as *path integration* relates contextual information and prominent environmental cues to velocity and angular and linear direction of self-movement to determine the present location and orientation in space (Jeffery, 2008). Head-direction cells relate the position and direction of self to environmental cues. The logical inference is that self-localization on the internal map, or in the case of a succession of spaces the sequence of submaps, is inscribed using movement, direction, and viewing angle. Let us consider an example of a cue the brain may use to extract direction information from grid and place cell interplay. One theory that has been outlined offers an explanation the role boundaries which demarcate spatial extent, such as walls, may play.

The *boundary vector model* proposes that each place cell receives information from several boundary cells, which create vectors for place cells (Hartley et al., 2000). Boundaries that are close to the animal appear to specify the location of boundary place fields, whereas more distant cues provide the additional directional information required to create vectors (Jeffery, 2008). It has further been suggested that grid cell spacing factors into metric computations within which place fields are laid down. Vector information delineating geometry of space alone may often not suffice to recognize individual spaces when shape only slightly or in fact does not provide sufficient information (Anderson and Jeffery, 2003b). Contextual information then provides sensory input—such as sound, smell, or color—to the place cells. Why does context information not appear to directly inform place cells? If it were to directly impact place cells and not be filtered through boundary cells, a single place cell's multiple place fields—in multiple environments—could not exhibit independent behavior, but would always perform in an identical manner irrespective of the environment (Anderson and Jeffery, 2003a).

Multiple Maps

Each spatial environment exists not only in immediate experience but in memory and imagination. Immediate experiences at each point in time differ, and we therefore propose the existence of a network of multiple stored spatial representations for individual spaces. Furthermore, spaces may undergo changes and thus require alteration to existing map representations (we will explore this toward the end of the chapter). All this implies that each space may be represented by a collection of temporally and sequentially separated maps, depending on circumstance and happenstance. A look at how rodent brains amass map representations and use these flexibly can help build an understanding. In its abundant memory archive, the brain accumulates maps as action patterns and can retrieve these rapidly when needed (Jeffery, 2008). Associative connections allow stored memories to be recalled from incomplete or dated versions of the original input and match these with current experience. This process is known as *pattern completion*. Its counterpart is a function called *pattern separation*, which prevents the mixing up of the memory with other memory events stored in the network. When comparing incoming information with stored representations, brain oscillations have been observed to either immediately retrieve the relevant representation or to flicker between representations, before coming to rest on one (Jezek et al., 2011). Upon imagining, remembering, or experiencing, representations will be recalled and, if necessary, be corrected and updated dynamically to elegantly include new information or exclude outdated information (Gothard et al., 1996). It is thought that it is the path integration mechanism that is updated, and when large aberrations occur, they can be accompanied by a slight delay as the internal system catches up with the external scene. Thinking of a museum visit, we may use this knowledge to reflect upon the following. The visitor, who has enjoyed many an afternoon in a museum and has accumulated a rich collection of maps and moods, knows the space well. She is therefore likely to experience surprise when she encounters novelty or discovers the unsuspected. There is little scientific knowledge about this, but could feelings of delighted surprise be connected to this process of updating and delay?

A multiple or varied map theory receives further support when we consider the following discovery. Changes in geometry, context, or a combination of both alter neural response to a spatial environment (Jeffery, 2008). This process is known as *remapping*. *Rate remapping* alters firing rates and we propose that this can create variations in the intensity of a map. *Global remapping* on the other hand, which is caused by large changes, alters the location of place fields and can also mean changes in size, shape, and firing intensity. As mentioned, we will revisit the remapping phenomenon in the final section when we consider what may happen on a return visit to the museum. Before this, we will consider one last aspect of the actual visit—how the intent of the visit may relate to its experience.

Intent of the Visit

A museum visit can follow a range of intentions. Often, visitors show browsing behavior as they move from one perceptual field to the next. The intent these visitors are following, as they browse the gallery space and its content, is foraging for experience. When rats forage for rewards, neural firing rates change significantly as the intentionality of a journey changes (Wood et al., 2000; Ainge et al., 2007; Ferbinteanu and Shapiro, 2003). Firing rates have been shown to remap depending on the type of goal or reward sought. The locations of fields remain fixed, and it is believed that rates represent variation in goal-specific encoding and thus the intention inscribed into a place field (Ainge et al., 2007). From an architectural viewpoint, perception is intimately linked to intention; intentionality of the designer who embeds it and the visitor who absorbs it (Holl et al., 1994). Phenomenal experience in architectural space merges pure sensational perception with the human inclination to conceptualize. Steven Holl writes:

> According to Brentano, physical phenomena engage our "outer perception," while mental phenomena involve our "inner perception." Mental phenomena have real, as well as intentional, existence. Empirically we might be satisfied with a structure as a purely physical-spatial entity but, intellectually and spiritually, we need to understand the motivation behind it. This duality of intention and phenomena is like the interplay between objective and subjective or, more simply, thought and feeling. The challenge for architecture is to stimulate both inner and outer perception; to heighten phenomenal experience while simultaneously expressing meaning; and to develop this duality in response to the particularities of site and circumstance. (Holl et al., 1994)

Intent in the context of meaning, specifically meaning embedded into architecture that is intellectually stimulating, is, to the best of our knowledge, exclusive to humans. For humans, intent need not always be the seeking and receiving of a specific reward aimed for, but can also mean the extraction of meaning that we discover or uncover along the way. We cannot of course equate this like-for-like to our reward-seeking rodent relatives; however, what can be observed is the highly important aspect of qualitative distinction among goals. Firing rates appear in their differences to reflect distinctions among the unique characteristics of a reward (Ainge et al., 2007). When rewards in goal locations presented in a maze differ (e.g., chocolate milk in one location, vanilla in another), these elicit different firing rate patterns depending on the flavor of the reward aimed for. The differences do not manifest once the reward is retrieved, they persist from start to finish of the journey, indicating that it is the intention motivating the pursuit and not simply the achievement of successful reward retrieval that underlies firing variation (Ainge et al., 2007).

A question still to be answered is if the intent a museum visitor is either following or uncovering is equally marked by idiosyncratic patterns and which other brain functions these might rely upon.

The Visit Ends

The visitor is now at the end of the visit, and we will offer a brief concluding observation, which fits nicely with the starting point, the entrance area.
Much like at the beginning of a journey, place fields also tend to cluster
around end points (see e.g., Gothard et al., 1996). Before leaving a museum,
humans often recap their visit mentally, and it appears that spatial neurons
follow suit. When an animal has reached the end of a run, place cells fire in
correctly timed yet reverse order and then lay down a large number of place
fields at the end (Foster and Wilson, 2006; Diba and Buzsaki, 2007). As we
reflect, the brain makes a memory of the space for its memory archive. Recalling Gumbrecht's metaphor of the future as the "horizon of expectations,"
we have now arrived at the point where the museum visit will become part of
our past, our "space of experience" (Gumbrecht, 2004).

AFTER THE VISIT

When the visitor leaves the museum the experience still lingers on her mind.
Her brain now gradually consolidates the impressions gained. The process
of consolidation refers to the storage and securing of memory traces—the
firing patterns that construct each memory—in neural networks. Contemporary neuroscience explains the accumulation of memory information as
the strengthening or weakening of synaptic efficacy between cells in brain
regions responsible for memory storage. This is referred to as *long-term
potentiation* (Bliss and Lømo, 1973) and is the persistent enhancement of
signal transmission between two neurons resulting from synchronous activity of these neurons. A stable memory is one that is deeply embedded and
can be recalled—reconstructed—over long periods of time and space. Sleep
and times of rest allow the brain to consolidate perception and experience
in a highly efficient manner and safely tuck them away in its archive. With
time the hippocampus is needed less and less to retrieve memories that can
be described without need for vivid reexperiencing (see e.g., Moscovitch et
al., 2005). During sleep and rest the hippocampus is thought to broadcast
its activity patterns to other brain regions (see e.g., Diekelmann and Born,
2010). Thus, for our museum visitor, after her trip her hippocampus will
probably be updating her internally constructed museum to other areas of
her brain for the long-term memory that will serve over decades. She may
recall the experience many years later, now drawing on other brain regions
to reconstruct the experience.

This brings us back to the beginning of our chapter and the time before the
visit, when the brain prepared and planned for the expedition.

A RETURN VISIT

The final part of our story sees the visitor return to the museum for another visit and start the next iteration of experience. Having been to the museum before, she is physically familiar with the space and her sense of the spaces— and herself in them—allows her to preimagine vividly and in detail what she may subjectively encounter (Schacter et al., 2012). The process of self-localizing and having "felt" a space, through self-motion, creates a strong foundation on which reconstruction and modified or manipulated construction can take place. What, however, happens if changes have been made to the space and can we identify different responses to different changes?

In a gallery setting, change is inevitable. A variety of scenarios is imaginable. The artwork may have been rearranged, in which case the influence of changes on spatial cells is negligible. However, changes to the space per se do have an impact. Surface textures in the space may have been altered. Small changes to the geometry of the space may have been made as temporary exhibitions come and go or pieces of art are added or (re)moved and thus necessitate changes to be made to the space that holds them. Finally, the most fundamental of all, spaces may have been redesigned completely, rendering them in essence to be perceived as novel.

Earlier we introduced the phenomenon known as remapping and outlined the differences between rate remapping and global remapping. The question of how cells remap globally from one environment to another or remap in rate when changes have been made to the same environment has fueled many a scientific experiment. In investigating rate remapping, often the effects of color, shape, or smell are tested and a number of preliminary insights have been gained (Anderson and Jeffery, 2003). As one select point of interest for a revisit of a known space, we will take a look at what may happen when the same environment undergoes contextual or minor geometric alteration and thus firing rates remap. One recent model proposes the following plausible hypothesis (Anderson and Jeffery, 2003): it may be that rate remapping is informed by a combination of geometry and context. When contextual changes are made, such as changing the color of a wall (Burgess and Hartley, 2002), what happens? First, the geometry provided by walls is assumed to not only demarcate a space, but indeed to underlie the localization of firing fields (O'Keefe and Burgess, 1996). In this role, they lay the foundation for where a firing field is located. The rate at which the cell fires upon entering the firing field is then thought be determined by context and, if this is changed, the rate also changes. In the museum, the visitor may find herself in a space she knows, but the walls have been repainted. Her place cells will fire accordingly. They recognize the space in its geometry and instantly lay down their previously acquired topographic composition of place fields. The change in color, however, promotes new firing rates and elicits a novel experience, in the knowledge that the visitor is in a familiar space; this allows spaces to be both the same and different in hippocampal representations (Fenton, 2007). Anyone familiar with the New York Guggenheim who visited the museum in 2001 or 2002 for the Brazil: Body and Soul exhibition, which was designed by Jean Nouvel, and saw the entire interior painted black, will recall vividly the peculiar experience of recognizing the space and immediately orienting within, while at the same time being exposed to a rather different Guggenheim.

What happens when minor changes are not contextual but geometric, for example if a dividing wall is moved within a space to accommodate a new exhibition setup? The overall space remains the same, yet boundary input that localizes firing fields will be altered. In this case, research has shown that those place fields that were initially informed by the wall, which has now been moved, indeed shift or stretch to accommodate the changed geometry (O'Keefe and Burgess, 1996). The walls that remain the same continue to provide input to their respective place fields and these remain fixed. Changes at times can be substantial; however, if the basic spatial layout pertinent to navigation and orientation remains fixed, a visit may thus elicit in the visitor a qualitatively different experience within a well-known space.

In our final scenario, the space has been altered to such an extent that it is now unrecognizable in every way imaginable and previously acquired navigational strategies are rendered useless. The brain will treat it as a new environment and a brand-new map is required. Old representations are discarded and the spiel between architectural space and brain can begin afresh.

WHAT LIES AHEAD

In this chapter we have outlined a brief summary of the neuroscience relevant to an understanding of how the brain constructs internal representations of space. Tentative first steps toward a conversation between architecture and neuroscience have been taken, and we hope to continue and develop the discourse. In more than one sense the journey to link these two disciplines is just beginning. At the end of this first introduction, a world of questions awaits and common ground will need to be defined. The limitations and equally affordances of technologies notwithstanding, we have myriad enquiries and ideas that invite further research. An additional limitation, of course, is the difficulty of collecting data from humans. Central to this is the degree to which we can observe the different cells in the hippocampus as they are excited when observers experience architectural spaces in real or virtual representations. Studying humans will no doubt introduce a range of unique complexities, such as sociocultural differences or the fact that human perception is not only guided by our immediate senses, but also by the human need to conceptualize, contextualize and abstract experience. The exploration of neural excitement in relation to architectural stimulation is the departing point for this journey. If technical difficulties can be overcome, however, the results could open up a range of new endeavors valuable to both the architecture and neuroscience communities. A striking challenge is the lack of understanding of how feelings, such as delight and wonder, are processed in the brain and how these interact with the spatial representations we use for memory and navigation.

REFERENCES

Ainge, J. A., Tamosiunaite, M., Woergoetter, F. and Dudchenko, P. A. (2007). Hippocampal CA1 place cells encode intended destination on a maze with multiple choice points. *The Journal of Neuroscience*, 27(36), 9769–79; doi: 10.1523/ JNEUROSCI.2011-07.2007.

Alvernhe, A., Van Cauter, T., Save, E. and Poucet, B. (2008). Different CA1 and CA3 representations of novel routes in a shortcut situation. *The Journal of Neuroscience*, 28(29), 7324–33; doi: 10.1523/JNEUROSCI.1909-08.2008.

Andersen, P. A., Morris, R., Amaral, D., Bliss, T. and O'Keefe, J., eds. (2006). *The Hippocampus Book*. Oxford: Oxford University Press.

Andersen, R. A. (2011). Inferior parietal lobule function in spatial perception and visuomotor integration. *Comprehensive Physiology*. doi: 10.1002/cphy.cp010512.

Andersen, R. A., Essick, G. K. and Siegel, R. M. (1985). Encoding of spatial location by posterior parietal neurons. *Science*, 230(4724), 456–58. doi: 10.1126/science.4048942.

Andersen, R. A. and Mountcastle, V. B. (1983). The influence of the angle of gaze upon the excitability of the light-sensitive neurons of the posterior parietal cortex. *The Journal of Neuroscience*, 3(3), 532–48.

Anderson, M. I. and Jeffery, K. J. (2003a). Heterogeneous modulation of place cell firing by changes in context. *The Journal of Neuroscience,* 23(26), 8827–35.

———. (2003b). Dissociation of the geometric and contextual influences on place cells. *Hippocampus*, 13, 868–72. doi: 10.1002/hipo.10162.

Azevedo, F. A. C., Carvalho, L. R. B., Grinberg, L. T., Farfel, J. M., Ferretti, R. E. L., Leite, R. E. P., Jacob Filho, W., et al. (2009). Equal numbers of neuronal and nonneuronal cells make the human brain an isometrically scaled-up primate brain. *Journal of Comparative Neurology*, 513(5), 532–41. doi: 10.1002/cne.21974.

Barry, C., Hayman, R., Burgess, N. and Jeffery, K. J. (2007). Experience-dependent rescaling of entorhinal grids. *Nature Neuroscience*, 10(6). doi:10.1038/nn1905

Bennett, T. (1995). *The Birth of the Museum*. Oxford and New York: Routledge.

Berridge, K. C., Robinson, T. E., and Aldridge, J. W. (2009). Dissecting components of reward: "liking," "wanting," and learning. *Current Opinion in Pharmacology*, 9(1), 65–73. doi: 10.1016/j.coph.2008.12.014.

Bliss, T. and Lømo, T. (1973). Synaptic plasticity in the hippocampus. A possible mechanism for information storage uncovered in synapses between the perforant pathway and dentate gyrus granule cells. Long-lasting potentiation of synaptic transmission in the dentate gyrus area of the anaesthetized rabbit following stimulation of the perforant path. *Journal of Physiology*, 232, 331–56.

Brun Kjelstrup, K., Solstad, T., Heimly Brun, V., Hafting, T., Leutgeb, S., Witter, M. P., Moser, E. I. and Moser, M. (2008). Finite scale of spatial representation in the hippocampus. *Science*, 321(5885), 140–43. doi:10.1126/science.1157086.

Buckner, R. L. and Carroll, D. C. (2007). Self-projection and the brain. *Trends in Cognitive Sciences*, 11(2), 49–57. doi: 10.1016/j.tics.2006.11.004.

Buhry, L., Azizi, A. H. and Cheng, S. (2011). Reactivation, replay, and preplay: how it might all fit together. *Neural Plasticity*, 2011. doi:10.1155/2011/203462.

Burgess, N., Barry, C. and O'Keefe, J. (2007). An oscillatory interference model of grid cell firing. *Hippocampus*, 17(9), 801–12. doi: 10.1002/hipo.20327.

Burgess, N. and Hartley, T. (2002). Orientational and geometric determinants of place and head-direction. In Dietterich, T., Becker, S., Ghahramani, Z (eds.), *Advances in Neural Information Processing Systems*. Vol 14, pp. 165–72. Cambridge, MA: MIT Press.

Byrne, P., Becker, S. and Burgess, N. (2007). Remembering the past and imagining the future: a neural model of spatial memory and imagery. *Psychological Review*, 114(2), 340. doi: 10.1037/0033-295X.114.2.340

Colby, C. L. and Goldberg, M. E. (1999). Space and attention in parietal cortex. *Annual Review of Neuroscience*, 22(1), 319–49. doi: 10.1146/annurev.neuro.22.1.319

Cressant, A., Muller, R. U. and Poucet, B. (1997). Failure of centrally placed objects to control the firing fields of hippocampal place cells. *The Journal of Neuroscience*, 17(7), 2531–42.

Derdikman, D., Whitlock, J. R., Tsao, A., Fyhn, M., Hafting, T., Moser, M. B. and Moser, E. I. (2009). Fragmentation of grid cell maps in a multicompartment environment. *Nature Neuroscience*, 12(10). doi:10.1038/nn.2396.

Diba, K. and Buzsaki, G. (2007). Forward and reverse hippocampal place-cell sequences during ripples. *Nature Neuroscience*, 10, 1241–42. doi:10.1038/nn1961.

Diekelmann, S. and Born, J. (2010). The memory function of sleep. *Nature Reviews Neuroscience*, 11(2), 114–26. doi:10.1038/nrn2762.

Dragoi, G. and Tonegawa, S. 2011. Preplay of future place cell sequences by hippocampal cellular assemblies. *Nature*, 469, 397–401. doi:10.1038/nature09633.

———. (2013). Distinct preplay of multiple novel spatial experiences in the rat. *PNAS*. doi: 10.1073/pnas.1306031110.

Dupret, D., O'Neill, J., Pleydell-Bouverie, B. and Csicsvari, J. (2010). The reorganization and reactivation of hippocampal maps predict spatial memory performance. *Nature Neuroscience*, 13(8). doi:10.1038/nn.2599.

Ekstrom, A. D., Kahana, M. J., Caplan, J. B., Fields, T. A., Isham, E. A., Newman, E. L. and Fried, I. (2003). Cellular networks underlying human spatial navigation. *Nature,* 425. doi:10.1038/nature01964.

Fenton, A. A. (2007). Where am I? *Science,* 315, 947. doi: 10.1126/science.1139146/

Ferbinteanu, J. and Shapiro, M. L. (2003). Prospective and retrospective memory coding in the hippocampus. *Neuron,* 40(6), 1227–39. doi: 10.1016/S0896-6273(03)00752-9.

Foster, D. J. and Knierim, J. J. (2012). Sequence learning and the role of the hippocampus in rodent navigation. *Current Opinion Neurobiology,* 22(2), 294–300. doi: 10.1016/j.conb.2011.12.005.

Foster, D. J. and Wilson M. A. (2006). Reverse replay of behavioural sequences in hippocampal place cells during the awake state. *Nature* 440, 680–83. doi:10.1038/nature04587.

Gage, S. A. (2006). The wonder of trivial machines. *Systems Research and Behavioral Science,* 23(6), 771–78. doi: 10.1002/sres.763.

Gothard, K. M., Skaggs, W. E. and McNaughton, B. L. (1996). Dynamics of mismatch correction in the hippocampal ensemble code for space: interaction between path integration and environmental cues. *The Journal of Neuroscience,* 16(24), 8027–40.

Gumbrecht, H. U. (2004). *Production of Presence. What Meaning Cannot Convey.* Stanford: Stanford University Press.

Hafting, T., Fyhn, M., Molden, St., Moser, MB and Moser, E. I.(2005). Microstructure of a spatial map in the entorhinal cortex. *Nature* 436, 801–06. doi:10.1038/nature03721.

Hartley, T., Burgess, N., Lever, C., Cacucci, F. and O'Keefe, J. (2000). Modeling place fields in terms of the cortical inputs to the hippocampus. *Hippocampus,* 10(4), 369–79.

Holl, St., Pallasmaa, J. and Pérez-Gómez, A. (1994). *Questions of Perception.* a+u Special Issue. Tokyo: a+u Publishing Co., Ltd.

Jeffery, K. J. (2008). Self-localization and the entorhinal–hippocampal system. *Current Opinion in Neurobiology 2008,* 17, 1–8. doi: 10.1016/j.conb.2007.11.008.

Jezek, K., Henriksen, E. J., Treves, A., Moser, E. I. and Moser, MB. (2011). Theta-paced flickering between place-cell maps in the hippocampus. *Nature* 478, 246–49. doi:10.1038/nature10439.

Ji, D. and Wilson, M. A. (2008). Firing rate dynamics in the hippocampus induced by trajectory learning. *The Journal of Neuroscience,* 28(18), 4679–89. doi: 10.1523/JNEUROSCI.4597-07.2008.

Laveneux, P., Suzuki, W. A. and Amaral, D. G. (2002). Perirhinal and parahippocampal cortices of the macaque monkey: Projections to the neocortex. *Journal of Comparative Neurology,* 447, 394–420. doi: 10.1002/cne.10243.

Lever, C., Burton, St., Jeewajee, A., O'Keefe, J. and Burgess, N. (2009). Boundary vector cells in the subiculum of the hippocampal formation. *The Journal of Neuroscience,* 29(31), 9771–77. doi: 10.1523/JNEUROSCI.1319-09.2009.

Massumi, B. (2002). *Parables for the Virtual: Movement, Affect, Sensation,* revised. Durham, NC: Duke University Press.

McNaughton, B. L., Battaglia, F. P., Jensen, O., Moser, E. I. and Moser, M. B. (2006). Path integration and the neural basis of the "cognitive map." *Nature Reviews Neuroscience*, 7(8), 663–78. doi:10.1038/nrn1932.

Moscovitch, M., Rosenbaum, R. S., Gilboa, A., Addis, D. R., Westmacott, R., Grady, C., and Nadel, L. (2005). Functional neuroanatomy of remote episodic, semantic and spatial memory: a unified account based on multiple trace theory. *Journal of Anatomy*, 207(1), 35–66. doi: 10.1111/j.1469-7580.2005.00421.x.

O'Keefe, J. and Burgess, N. (1996). Geometric determinants of the place fields of hippocampal neurons. *Nature*, 381, 425–28.

O'Keefe, J. and Dostrovsky, J. (1971). The hippocampus as a spatial map: Preliminary evidence from unit activity in the freely-moving rat. *Brain Research*, 34, 171–75. doi: 10.1016/0006-8993(71)90358-1.

O'Keefe, J. and Nadel, L. (1978). *The Hippocampus as a Cognitive Map.* Oxford and New York: Clarendon Press.

Pask, G. (1968). *A comment, a case history and a plan.* Cybernetic Serendipity exhibition.

Pfeiffer, B. E. and Foster, D. J. (2013). Hippocampal place-cell sequences depict future paths to remembered goals. *Nature* 497, 74–79. doi:10.1038/nature12112.

Quirk, G. J., Muller, R. U. and Kubie, J. L. (2008). The firing of hippocampal place cells in the dark depends on the rat's recent experience. *The Journal of Neuroscience*, X7(6), 2008–17.

Quiroga, R., Quian, Reddy L., Kreiman, G., Koch, C. and Fried, I. (2005). Invariant visual representation by single neurons in the human brain. *Nature*, 435(23). doi:10.1038/nature03687.

Radvansky, G. A., Tamplin, A. K., and Krawietz, S. A. (2010). Walking through doorways causes forgetting: Environmental integration. *Psychonomic Bulletin & Review*, 17(6), 900–904. doi: 10.3758/PBR.17.6.900.

Rivard, B., Li, Y., Lenck-Santini, P. P., Poucet, B. and Muller, R. U. (2004). Representation of objects in space by two classes of hippocampal pyramidal cells. *J. Gen. Physiol,* 124, 9–25. doi: 10.1085/jgp.200409015.

Schacter, D. L., Addis, D. R., Hassabis, D., Martin, V. C., Spreng, R. N. and Szpunar, K. K. (2012). The future of memory: remembering, imagining, and the brain. *Neuron,* 76. doi: 10.1016/j.neuron.2012.11.001.

Skaggs, W. E., McNaughton, B. L., Wilson, M. A. and Barnes, C. A. (1996). Theta phase precession in hippocampal neuronal population and the compression of temporal sequences. *Hippocampus*, 6, 149–72.

Snyder, L.H., Grieve, K. L., Brotchie, P. and Andersen, R. A. (1998). Separate body- and world-referenced representations of visual space in parietal cortex. *Nature* 394, 887–91. doi:10.1038/29777.

Solomon R. Guggenheim Museum, *Past exhibitions.* Accessed June 2013, http://pastexhibitions.guggenheim.org/brazil/.

Solstad, T., Moser, E. I. and Einevoll, G. T. (2006). From grid cells to place cells: a mathematical model. *Hippocampus*, 16(12), 1026–31. doi: 10.1002/hipo.20244.

Solstad, T., Boccara, C. N., Kropff, E., Moser, M. B. and Moser, E. I. (2008). Representation of Geometric Borders in the Entorhinal Cortex. *Science*, 322(5909), 1865–68. doi: 10.1126/science.1166466.

Spiers, H. J. 2012. Hippocampal Formation. In: V.S. Ramachandran (ed.) *The Encyclopedia of Human Behavior*, vol. 2, pp. 297-304. Academic Press

Spiers, H. J., Hayman, R. M. A., Jovalekic, A., Marozzi, E. and Jeffery, K. J. (2013). Place field repetition and purely local remapping in a multi-compartment environment. *Cerebral Cortex*, in press. doi:10.1093/cercor/bht198.

Stirling, J. and Krier, L. (ed.) (1975). *James Stirling: Buildings and Projects 1950-1974*. Oxford: Oxford University Press.

Sutton, T. (2000). *The Classification of Visual Art: A Philosophical Myth and Its History*. Cambridge: Press Syndicate of the University of Cambridge.

Taube, J. (1998). Head direction cells and the neurophysiological basis for a sense of direction. *Progress in Neurobiology,* 55(3), 225–56. doi: 10.1016/S0301-0082(98)00004-5.

The Lousiana Museum of Modern Art. (2012). *The Architecture*. Accessed March 2012, http://www.louisiana.dk/uk/Menu/Visit+Louisiana/The+museum+and+architecture/The+architecture.

Vanderwolf, C. H., Kramis, R., Gillespie, L. A. and Bland, B. H. (1976). Hippocampal rhythmic slow activity and neocortical low-voltage fast activity: relations to behavior. *The Hippocampus*. doi: 10.1007/978-1-4684-2979-4_3.

Von Glaserfeld, E.(1996). *Radical Constructivism, A Way of Knowing and Learning*. London: Falmer Press.

Wenz, K. (1997). *Raum, Raumsprache und Sprachräume: zur Textsemiotik der Raumbeschreibung*. Tübingen: Gunter Narr Verlag.

Wilson, M. and McNaughton, B. (1994). Reactivation of hippocampal ensemble memories during sleep. *Science*, 265(5172), 676–79. doi: 10.1126/science.8036517.

Wishaw, I. Q. and Vanderwolf, C. H. (1973). Hippocampal EEG and behavior: Change in amplitude and frequency of RSA (Theta rhythm) associated with spontaneous and learned movement patterns in rats and cats. *Behavioral Biology*, 8(4), 461–84. doi: 10.1016/S0091-6773(73)80041-0.

Wood, E. R., Dudchenko, P. A., Robitsek, R. J., Eichenbaum, H. (2000). Hippocampal neurons encode information about different types of memory episodes occurring in the same location. *Neuron,* 27(3), 623–33. doi: 10.1016/S0896-6273(00)00071-4.

Zhang, S. J., Ye, J., Miao, Ch., Tsao, A., Cerniauskas, I., Ledergerber, D., Moser, M. B. and Moser, E. I. (2013). Optogenetic dissection of entorhinal-hippocampal functional connectivity. *Science*, 340(6128). doi: 10.1126/science.1232627.

15

Museum as an Embodied Experience

Juhani Pallasmaa

Our technologized consumer culture of today is a world of uncontested vision. The primacy of the eye among the human senses was already established by the ancient Greek philosophers, and in the tradition of Western thinking, vision has even been closely associated with knowledge and truth: "the eyes are more exact witnesses than the ears," Heraclitus argued, and vision has, indeed, been considered as the measure of truth (Levin, 1993,1). Today, in everyday life, as well as the technological and scientific worlds, the hegemony of the eye has been further strengthened through countless technical inventions. Even architecture, which should fundamentally create multisensory settings for various human situations, has been regarded primarily as an art form of the eye in accordance with Le Corbusier's famous credo, "Architecture is the masterly, correct and magnificent play of masses brought together in light" (Le Corbusier, 1959, 31).

Knowing this historical development, it is not surprising to observe that the sense of vision has also dominated museum and exhibition designs throughout the era of modernity. Artworks are seen as individual and independent aesthetic objects with a special "aura," and they are exhibited to their best advantages in visually "neutral" settings. Neutrality has usually been thought of as an overall whiteness, smoothness, and even illumination of surfaces. It is evident that the modernist preference for whiteness is an aesthetic choice with hidden moralistic tones and often far from any objective perceptual neutrality. The moral dimension of the modernist preference for whiteness is well expressed in Le Corbusier's surprising argument: "Whiteness is extremely moral. Suppose there were a decree requiring all rooms in Paris to be given a coat of whitewash. I maintain that that would be a police task of real stature and a manifestation of high morality, the sign of a great people"

(Le Corbusier, 1925, 192). Any museum space frames the exhibited objects in particular ways, and the space projects characteristics and qualities on the work of which we are usually not conscious.

During the past three or four decades, the ideal of art museum design has been the evenly lit and immaterial "white cube." However, this ideal of the white and shadowless space has not been as forcefully applied in the design of museums for other purposes than art, such as historical, anthropological, and archeological museums. In these contexts, objects and exhibits have usually been woven into the fabric of a contextual narrative, instead of emphasizing the perceptual autonomy of the displayed pieces. Use of materials, textures, colors, and contrasts of illumination, as well as nonvisual modes of communication in nonart museums, has usually introduced multisensory experiences and a distinct sense of reality instead of an ambience of artificiality, detachment, and isolation. It is thus thought provoking to realize that even the finest art museums back in history were rarely, if ever, white spaces, or devoid of the tactile presence of materials and the *chiaroscuro* of shadows in their spaces, surfaces, and structures. In the case of premodern art, the sense of distinct artistic realm was achieved by means of forceful framing and pedestals that detached the art pieces from the utilitarian world.

The idea of the white, featureless exhibition space is clearly a modernist conceptual and aesthetic preconception and prejudice. At the same time, this ideal also reflects a distinct psychological and sociological understanding of the institution of art and its relationship to the normality of life. Yet, artworks are born in the lived world of the artist's studio, and their forceful detachment from a sense of gravity, orientation, materiality, and natural light, as well as the other sense modalities, when displayed in a museum is thus surprising and questionable. The extremely chaotic studio of Francis Bacon, with mountains of paint, rags, paper, publications, and so forth on the floor, exemplifies the perceptual distance between the spaces in which artistic works are made and displayed.

In my view, a museum space should mediate the psychological and perceptual situation between the object and the viewer, and create a sense of intimacy and specific reality appropriate for the work. The ideal museum space needs to enhance and focus perception, activate and sensitize the senses of the visitor, and facilitate an intense dialogue between the exhibits and the viewer. A museum and exhibition design can greatly facilitate the presence and special features of the exhibits and make them address our entire existential sense through the activation of all our sensory channels. The most important single aspect in a museum space is surely illumination, which directs attention and creates spatial rhythm and scale as well as hierarchy. But we do not experience works of art merely visually; we grasp their material, sensory, and symbolic being in "the flesh of the world," to use a notion of Maurice Merleau-Ponty. As he describes it: "My body is made of the same flesh as the world [. . .] this flesh of my body is shared by the world"; and, "The flesh (of the world or my own) is [. . .] a texture that returns to itself and conforms to itself" (Merleau-Ponty, 1992, 248 and 146). We experience even paintings in a multisensory manner, and sense sounds, tactile qualities, smells, temperatures, and so forth as "ideated sensations" in the visual phenomena themselves, as Bernard Behrenson suggested (Montagu, 1986, 308).

In fact, every great piece of art is an entire world, not a singular object, and it opens up multisensory connections with the world. "We come to see not the work of art, but the world according to the work," as Maurice Merleau-Ponty argues (McGilchrist, 2010, 409).

A sensitive museum and exhibition design uses all the means of preconceptual and embodied nonverbal communication by turning the experience into silent theater in which the space, the objects, and the viewer are in constant, although mostly unconscious, interaction and dialogue. As the philosopher John Dewey taught us in his book *Art as Experience*, the artistic dimension is an experiential and imaginative quality projected or recreated by the viewer him/herself. A great museum and exhibition addresses the visitor primarily emotionally, not solely intellectually. A memorable museum visit is an exploration and discovery in which the visitor's body movements, sensory experiences, associations, recollections, and imaginations contribute to the overall effect beyond what is explicitly presented and expressed. An exhibition turns into a personal experience grasped through embodied sensation instead of offering intellectualized information or mere visual stimuli. Due to the existential, multisensory, and embodied nature of the experience, the exhibited works become part of us forever.

The function of exhibition design is to create an appropriate atmosphere for a sensitized encounter with the works, themes, or information in question. In my view, the task of exhibition design is to mediate between the given space, the exhibits, and the viewer, and to "amplify" or heighten the presence of the exhibits by projecting an ambiance that resonates with the character and essence of the exhibition. In the following, I will show images of a few of my own exhibition designs and explain the intentions and psychological logic of the various aspects of design.

When designing an exhibition of a Finnish graphic artist, Pentti Lumikangas, in the Helsinki City Art Hall in 1977 (figure 15.1), I felt that hanging the white graphic prints on the white walls of the exhibition space would make them disappear, or dissolve, in the immateriality of the large white walls. As the theme of the majority of the displayed graphic works was

242   *Juhani Pallasmaa*

Figure 15.1.   Penti Lumikangas

fantasy architecture, frequently based on historical architectural settings, I
decided to hang all the prints on thick, blocklike walls painted in dark gray
and brown earth colors, placed in the exhibition spaces away from the white
walls. These walls were arranged in symmetrical configurations in order to
create an association with architectural ruins. These "ruins" gave the rather
immaterial prints on white paper a heightened presence and "amplified" their
architectural themes, as well as a sense of time and historicity. Protective
glass sheets, fixed with special metal units at a 50-millimeter distance from
the prints, created an appropriately intimate space for the artworks without
using conventional framing.

In an exhibition of Renaissance Art in the Wäinö Aaltonen Museum in
Turku in 1991 (figure 15.2), I faced a similar problem as in the exhibition of
the graphic works; the pieces of Renaissance art on loan from Florence were
of rather small size and would easily have appeared insignificant in the over-

Figure 15.2.   Renaissance art

whelmingly large museum rooms. By hanging the paintings on backgrounds raised a few centimeters from the wall surfaces and painting these backgrounds with characteristic Renaissance colors, the valuable but small pieces of art were experientially "enlarged" in relation to their setting. Lights placed next to the works created an illuminated space of intimacy for each work and further focused the viewer's attention by turning the relative emptiness of the museum space into a positive perceptual and emotive amplifier; emptiness turned into a feeling of value and authority.

The 1987 exhibition on wood in Finnish architecture, design, and art, entitled The Language of Wood (figure 15.3), juxtaposed wooden objects of daily use, decoration, design, and high art all the way from the timeless peasant past to contemporary culture without giving any immediate identifications as to the age, function, or author of the objects. Utilitarian objects, such as farming tools and household implements, were thus shown next to objects of today's high design and abstract art. The objects were displayed in accordance with their formal, aesthetic, and material qualities, not their type (art or nonart, utilitarian or decorative, for example) or age. The total elimination of identifying explanations activated the viewer's aesthetic judgement, and set the displayed objects in a silent and emotive dialogue with each other,

Figure 15.3.   Animal Architecture

and this air of mystery evoked strong recollections and associations. Precise descriptions of the objects were revealed only in the exhibition catalogue. The simple psychological arrangement heightened the aesthetic and emotive experience, as the viewers were required to deduct the essence of the exhibited objects themselves by deploying their own memories and imagination instead of simply reading labels; withholding information served the purpose of personal emotive encounter.

An exhibition titled Behind the Mask at the Museum of Finnish Architecture in 1990 (figure 15.4) presented the settings of life, architecture, and objects of everyday use, as well as ritual objects of the Dogon people living in the Bandiagara Canyon in Mali, Africa. The walls of the exhibition space

Figure 15.4. Behind the Mask

were inclined either outward or inward and painted in earth colors, to evoke distant associations with the landscape of the African desert canyon where the Dogon people live. To suggest further contextual associations of the hot desert, the floor of the exhibition space was covered with ten centimeters of sand. Sound sources, such as voices of chickens running between imaginary mud huts, activated by the visitor's movements, projected another level of sensory illusion. However, all these experiences and associations were highly abstracted not to create the feeling of a cheap stage setting, but to evoke an emotive and unconscious background atmosphere for the viewing of the individual exhibits and to transport the viewer mentally into the African context.

The exhibition Animal Architecture at the Museum of Finnish Architecture in Helsinki in 1995 (figure 15.5), presented constructions made by numerous animal species, from fish to insects, birds to primates. To focus the visitor's attention on the exhibits, drawings, and texts, the space was darkened, and only the exhibition items were directly illuminated; the smallest specimen (insects and their cases) were only one centimeter in size. In addition to samples of animal constructions, the exhibition included sixteen live animal communities that continued to work on their constructions during the entire exhibition period of four months. Several films on animal building activities were shown on small screens set in the dark exhibition blocks next to photographs and drawings to add a further illusion of real life. As an unexpected psychological effect, the live elements also projected a sense of life onto the inanimate exhibits.

The floor of the exhibition space was covered by ten centimeters of sand, with the intent that walking in the soft sand would create a sensory illusion of being outdoors rather than on the second floor of an urban museum building. The slight difficulty of walking on the soft and uneven surface helped to focus the visitor's sense of reality into the imaginative world of the subject matter. Discontinuous soundtracks of various sounds of nature and animal life were played in the space at very low volumes in order to activate the sense of hearing and to enhance imagination.

The Sámi Lapp museum and Northern Lapland Visitor Centre in Inari was opened in 1998 (figure 15.6). The project, designed in collaboration with interior architect Sami Wirkkala and funded by the European Union and the Finnish Ministry of Education, was luckily scheduled so that the permanent exhibition was largely designed before the design development of the museum itself.

The main theme of the permanent exhibition presents survival strategies of nature and Sámi Lapp culture at the northern edge of life. As the most emotive aspect of the Nordic world is the dramatic alternation of seasons, the

Figure 15.5. Language of Wood

Figure 15.6. Sámi Lapp Museum

annual cycle of the year was taken as the basic structuring idea. The exhibition presents this annual cycle circumferentially through twelve sections of the space for the twelve months (three months on each one of the four walls of the square space).

The radial direction presents causalities and interactions between nature, traditional culture, and contemporary life. Each month, depicted on the peripheral walls, shows a gigantic backlit photograph of a landscape with numerous small exhibits installed in the depth of the backlit wall, from plants, insects, rodents, and birds to the winter nest of a bear. The setting with its various inserts was sketched for the photographer, who searched an appropriate natural location in Lapland for the depiction of each one of the twelve months. The huge photographs create a continuous horizon line in order to suggest a singular landscape around the space; as the visitor turns around 180 degrees, the course of a full year is experienced.

The central area of the exhibition hall, depicting Sámi culture, is on an elevated floor so that the images of nature can be seen as an emotive background or context across the wall blocks surrounding the raised floor. When viewed from the outer corridor, the wall blocks present aspects of the survival strategies of nature, and strategies of traditional Sámi culture when seen from the raised inner floor. Shared exhibits between the two contexts are placed in recesses; these exhibits have a different message depending on from which side of the block they are viewed. The central floor area depicts contemporary culture, which is usually detached from dependence on nature or traditional ways of life. The gigantic backlit photographs set in the floor were photographed outdoors in natural settings from the top of a crane after the displayed objects (including a skimobile and a live reindeer) that had left their traces on the ground and snow had been lifted away. In the final exhibition situation, the displayed objects were placed back on their places in the highly illusory photographic enlargement of the ground in full scale. The combined effect of high illusion and extreme abstraction is psychologically surprising.

The annual cycle is emphasized psychologically by illumination and general color schemes, which vary from the bright illumination and greenery of the summer through the multicolored autumn to the darkness and whiteness of winter, and further to the reemergence of light, color, and life in the spring.

The movements of the visitor activate a number of soundtracks that either give an added sense of life to the local exhibits or introduce sounds (such as wind, thunder, or large birds flying across the space) that unify the scene and guide the visitor to observe the entirety of the space instead of the details.

The exhibition concept is fully spatial in the sense that every position and direction in the exhibition space has a specific meaning and role in the manner of a spatial crossword puzzle. The main psychological strategy of the design was to avoid the linearity of pedagogic exhibitions and turn the visit into an unpredictable walk through nature, which reveals different aspects of the countless, partly hidden, exhibits at each visit. The success of this intention is proved by the fact that the exhibition has remained unaltered for fifteen years, and many of the guests of a ski resort forty kilometers away revisit the exhibition every year.

REFERENCES

Le Corbusier. (1959). *Towards a New Architecture*. London: The Architectural Press.
———. (1925). *L'art decoratif d'aujourd'hui*. Paris: Editions G. Grès et Cie.
Levin, David Michael, ed. (1993). *Modernity and the Hegemony of Vision*. Berkeley and Los Angeles: University of California Press.
McGilchrist, Iain. (2010). *The Master and His Emissary*. New Haven and London: Yale University Press, p. 409.
Merleau-Ponty, Maurice. (1992). The intertwining—the chiasm. In Lefort, Claude (ed), *The Visible and the Invisible*. Evanston, IL: Northwestern University Press.
Montagu, Ashley. (1986). *Touching: The Human Significance of the Skin*. New York: Harper & Row.

16

Architectural Design for Living Artifacts

Joy Monice Malnar and Frank Vodvarka

The architectural challenges associated with the design of museums in the Western tradition are not significantly different from those encountered in architecture generally: aesthetics, program, and structure. In this paradigm, the architect determines the aesthetic outcome (form and context) desired, the development of the interior spaces that will house the artifacts and associated aspects of exhibition, and a structural system that best expresses that outcome. These factors remain fairly constant, even though buildings of course have varying functions such that we can easily distinguish between the hospital and museum. While this list suggests that there is a procedural order to the process of combining these aspects into a single built artifact, these facets can be—and usually are—approached as quasi-separate considerations. Thus changes often occur once the structure largely becomes the responsibility of an engineering firm, and the precise nature of the interior spaces becomes the responsibility of a professional exhibition firm specializing in display programming, leaving only the (original) aesthetic intent to the architect. To this often-volatile mix one might add the additional concerns of client self-identity and budget. But however the situation evolves, the artifacts themselves tend to be seen as fixed objects whose location and display will be governed by the visual needs of a controlled, semi-fixed audience. This paradigm is reinforced by the use of closed display units, flow planning, and ever-present security personnel.

In her book, *Destination Culture: Tourism, Museums, and Heritage*, Barbara Kirshenblatt-Gimblett (1998, 57) takes this a step further: "The partiality so essential to the ethnographic object as a fragment is also expressed in the fragmentation of sensory apprehension in conventional museum exhibitions." She points out:

The European tendency has been to split up the senses and parcel them out one at a time to the appropriate art form. One sense, one art form. We listen to music. We look at paintings. Dancers don't talk. Musicians don't dance. Sensory atrophy is coupled with close focus and sustained attention. All distractions must be eliminated—no talking, rustling of paper, eating, flashing of cameras. Absolute silence governs the etiquette of symphony halls and museums. Aural and ocular epiphanies in this mode require pristine environments in which the object of contemplation is set off for riveting attention. . . . In contrast with conventional exhibitions in museums, which tend to reduce the sensory complexity of the events they represent and to offer them up for visual delectation alone, indigenous modes of display, particularly the festival, present an important alternative.

In large measure, this paradigm results from the static view Western society takes of historic and cultural artifacts, and the limited interaction that is expected to occur between object and viewer. Even on those rare occasions when some thought is put into a sensory interaction with objects beyond the purely visual, it is usually by virtue of setting up a sensory-specific application, as in museums dedicated to touch or sound. In the course of research for *New Architecture on Indigenous Lands* (Malnar and Vodvarka, 2013), we have experienced a different paradigm, in large degree the result of a purposeful, even causal relationship between artifact and individual. We found that Native peoples in Canada and the United States (the subjects of our book) seldom like the term "museum" at all, as it implies a place of static, visual displays that offer no interaction beyond controlled viewing, and—most importantly—implying that the culture that produced these artifacts is no longer extant.

In the film *Box of Treasures* (1983), Gloria Cranmer Webster ('Namgis), former curator of the U'mista Cultural Centre, expresses this when she points out: "A lot of those people who have read about us think we all died, that we disappeared because we were the vanishing races those early white people said we were. And when you look at museum exhibits in a lot of places it is as if we were gone. There is no reference to us still being here, still being alive, and we are." Later in the film, Elder Agnes Alfred ('Namgis) says: "This place on the beach that you call a museum, we have not had such a thing among our people. It is like a storage box, like a box of treasures the old people used to have." In an email correspondence to Nancy Marie Mithlo (Chiricahua Apache) (2004, 754), Gloria Cranmer Webster confirms this crucial distinction with the following statement: "U'mista was never meant to be a museum. Wouldn't we have called it that, if that's what it was going to be? Our Board of Directors said, at the time we incorporated as a registered society, 'We're not building a museum. Museums are for white people and are full of dead things'" (Mithlo, 2004, 754).

Thus, "cultural center" or "research center" are the preferred terms, although they are still less than entirely appropriate, suggesting that these are specialized places where one goes to experience cultural aspects no longer found outside the center. The argument here is that unlike the descendents of Euro-American culture, who have severed a continuous relationship to their own ancestors—and thus freely place their artifacts in funereal isolation—Native peoples feel an intense connection to all who have gone before. In their view, Western museums by contrast do little to bring people together.

Indeed, it is arguable that the concept of promoting social identity and cohesion through design has been fading in Euro-American culture for a very long time, with the result that estrangement itself has been raised to the status of aesthetic value. The difference between Western and indigenous ways of understanding the built world is made clear in the evaluation criteria put forward by a Native organization, the Center for American Indian Research and Native Studies: "CAIRNS believes that the evaluation of projects that provide services to Native communities should include four dimensions—spatial, social, spiritual, and experiential—that conceptually define traditional Native communities." That this is a quite different set of design priorities from the Western model is no accident and is nowhere better reflected than in the structures that house artifacts and their attendant cultures.

This is certainly the guiding concept behind the U'mista Cultural Centre in Alert Bay, British Columbia, home of the Kwakwaka'wakw Potlatch Collection. Alert Bay, a village on Cormorant Island (located between Vancouver Island and the mainland), was peopled by the Nimpkish Band, who moved there to work in a fish saltery in the 1870s. The U'mista Cultural Centre was designed by Henry Hawthorn, of Hawthorn Mansfield Towers Architects, with an extension by Marshall Fisher Architects, and direction from council members of the Kwakwaka'wakw. The center was built to house the spectacular masks and ceremonial dress associated with the potlatch ceremony—items that are still used today—and provide a ceremonial space.

Those hosting a potlatch give away useful items like food, blankets, and coppers (worked ornamental mediums of exchange). In return, the hosts enhance their reputation and social rank, their prestige increasing with the sheer generosity of the potlatch. The ceremony was outlawed in Canada in 1885, and shortly afterward in the United States. In both cases, this was the result of instigation by missionaries and government bureaucrats who thought it a profligate and uncivilized custom that made assimilation of the locals difficult (Fisher, 1977, 207). In Canada, the laws against potlatching were later expanded to include guests who participated in the ceremony, and, for that matter, anyone who encouraged the celebration of such a festival. In 1921, the Canadian government raided a large potlatch given on Village Island, arresting forty-five people and confiscating a wide range of ceremonial items—many of which were later sold.

In 1967, the Kwakwaka'wakw initiated efforts to regain these items. The Canadian Museum of Civilization agreed to return objects located in their collections provided appropriate facilities were built to house them. Hence the building of the U'mista Centre, a space in which the architect had to balance standard museum practice against the broader needs of the locals in such a way as to satisfy both. The actual space in which the costumes are displayed—and where ceremonies are held—is in the form of a Wakashan structure, whose western wall is adorned with traditional imagery that can be seen from a distance by approaching boats (figure 16.1).

It has been observed that "there were two kinds of wealth in the Northwest cultures: material and hereditary. The material wealth of the potlatch gifts, masks, canoes and homes was replaceable and therefore could be given away. The wealth of clan affiliation and status, embodied in the songs, myths, dances and crests, was owned by right of inheritance and could not be either given away or sold" (Carr, 1993). Thus the latter aspect constituted the real wealth of society, while the former was transferrable. Nonetheless, on the surface of it, the copious gift-giving was an incomprehensible largesse, an affront to the values of Euro-American culture, which is nothing if not ma-

Figure 16.1.   U'mista Cultural Centre, 1980. Photo by Frank Vodvarka

terially acquisitive. Moreover, the things thought to be worth the most by Western standards were the very objects given away.

While objects are commonly regarded as those things perceptible to our senses, they also are things to which action, thought, or feeling is directed, or something that on being perceived excites a particular emotion. Thus objects are the tangible, sensory repositories of experience and involve both self-confirmation and social communication. Russell W. Belk points out that to view relationships between people and their possessions as Cartesian fails to account for the power and mystery inherent in many of these relationships. Cartesian rationality, he says, has sought to demystify the role of possessions in our lives, leading us to believe that they are devoid of magical powers and blinding us to their "mystery, beauty and power" (Belk, 1991, 17). In his conception, the rational and measurable benefits of material goods are secondary to their magical function. The myth of rational possession—so central to the basis of Western culture—fails because "it denies the inescapable and essential mysteriousness of our existence" (Belk, 1991, 18). Among the Kwakwaka'wakw, these possessions act as continuous mediators, as their meaning is shared ideologically and functionally, making them particularly powerful social arbiters.

From the ferry, the U'mista Centre—designed in 1980—provides only a limited suggestion of the impressive and varied façades and totems that characterized the entire village's past appearance. The ceremonial entrance is located on a windowless façade oriented toward the water. Located above the door, near the peak of the gable is a centrally placed, carved head of a raven. The highly three-dimensional straight beak projecting outward stands in strong contrast to the stylized thunderbird and whale painted on the flat wall planks by artist Doug Cranmer (Hereditary Chief of the 'Namgis Nation). The weathered gray cedar planks provide a large surface for the bold, black-lined paintings of the thunderbird's feathers and the whale's internal bones drawn to communicate with pride the heritage of the community when seen from a great distance. There is no hint from the outside that this simple, single-story building, with a low double-pitched roof, is supported by a massive post and beam system significantly larger than necessary for mere structural support. The diameter of the structural elements remains constant whether the beam is spanning a short distance or the full length of the room. This was perhaps originally done for labor-saving purposes, but as present inheritors of a Euro-American tradition used to viewing minimal structures designed by engineers for mathematical efficiency, it provides an unfamiliar proportional relationship.

Today this building contains the family-owned ceremonial regalia—masks, baskets, and coppers—seized by the authorities and has been used to celebrate significant family events and provide cultural training for their children. The display is cleverly conceived. The Kwakwaka'wakw labored for a long time to reclaim these artifacts, and it was decided that they should be displayed in the U'mista Big House just as they would be seen in a potlatch, not behind glass. In Olin's documentary film, Cranmer Webster explains, "The feeling some of us had was these pieces when they had been returned had been locked up for so long in a strange place that it seemed wrong to lock them up again."

This arrangement provides a more intimate encounter with the masks; in particular, it allows natural materials such as animal skins, cedar bark trimming, and natural dyes to be experienced in multisensory terms. These masks are very much alive—and immediately accessible—to the community. The display room also serves as stage, for the masks and costumes reveal their meaning in their ritual use. Given that these are private community events, the understanding of how the masks come to life, moving to the rhythmic sound of the drums, rattles, and voices, is best comprehended in the film the Kwakwaka'wakw produced, *Box of Treasures,* and the easily accessed film (on YouTube) produced by the Aboriginal Tourism Association BC and filmed within the U'mista Cultural Centre.

When Johnpaul Jones (Choctaw/Cherokee) was retained to design the Southern Ute Tribal Museum and Cultural Center in Ignacio, Colorado, he intended the building to relate the history of the Southern Utes in such a way that it both resonates with the tribe and educates visitors. Located on the bank of the Los Piños river, it is intended to emphasize the connection of the Southern Utes to the eagle, the tribe's sacred symbol, and their "circle of life" belief. Jones and his project manager, Bruce Arnold, worked on the museum over a seven-year period, during which time they held dozens of meetings with members of the tribe. Jones (2010) notes that it took the better part of a year to gain the trust of the elders on the museum board: "And one day they handed us this little pamphlet, and they said, design the building around this. And the pamphlet was all about their circle of life philosophy. That's what we want our building designed around, they said. And that's what we worked with." The new 52,000-square-foot, state-of-the-art center houses the tribe's existing collection of more than 1,500 artifacts and provides space for tribal gatherings. The two wings adjacent to the central cone contain an education wing with arts and crafts classrooms, a multimedia room, and library, and a museum wing with permanent and temporary exhibit rooms. The south wing also contains a dance room where ceremonial regalia is donned for traditional ceremonies, while the semi-enclosed space in front of the entrance is used for larger, community-wide dances.

Figure 16.2. Southern Ute Cultural Center and Museum, 2011. Photo by Frank Vodvarka

The Southern Ute expressed a tremendous concern to make sure that their culture and tradition was personified with integrity through a modern, yet timeless sacred symbol of the eagle: "The arms of the building are symbolic of the wings of an eagle poised for flight. The eagle and the circle of life are both key influences on the building's design and layout" (Southern Ute Cultural Center & Museum, n.d.). Upon approach, a sense of the building's main components are apparent (figure 16.2).

The wings of the building spread outward in a grand gesture to welcome the Southern Ute people and their visitors into the circular, communal gathering space defined on the east by the shade arbor. Dramatically centered in the façade is a fifty-two-foot-tall, truncated conical atrium resembling wickerwork, which provides a welcoming focal point. It also suggests other aspects of Ute culture like tipis, basketry, shawls, and drums. Specifically, the shape was designed to evoke elements of Southern Ute experience, including the wickiup—the traditional domestic structure—and the later tipi typical to the lower elevations, while the lattice refers to basketry and the interior is designed to look like the head of a tightly pulled drum (Gamache, 2008). The overlapping lattice was thought of as a woven shawl, and where it parts it draws attention to the location of the main eastern-facing entry. The soaring atrium is supported by a vertical assembly of pitch pine logs held together at the top by a steel band. While a complicated engineering feat, the central supporting element also expresses the strength gained through the social aspect that binds the tribe together, which according to Jones is based on the knowledge that "a bundle of sticks is stronger than a single stick"(Jones, 2012).

Jones (2010) describes the symbolic aspects of its design: "It has twelve wood columns that run around the central part, and those are tied to the twelve months of the year. And then it's laid out on the cardinal directions, and also in respect of the equinoxes and the solstices, because this tribe did a lot of things related to those events . . . So those important events and directions are very strongly established inside that form." The multiple curves of the wings, latticework, and atrium reflect the Southern Utes' "circle of life" ways and beliefs, and are carried into the welcoming hall, where a central skylight contains a circle of glass. The skylight is divided into four quadrants, each filled with one of the four colors of the Southern Ute: yellow (representing the east—springtime and infancy), red (south—summer and youth), black (west—fall and adulthood) and white (north—winter and old age), colors that may be seen reflected below. Mary Nowotny (2011, 45), media coordinator for the center, further explains that this "represents components of Ute life as well as the four worlds of many indigenous people: the natural world, the earth, its plants and the cycles of the solstice and equinox; the animal world that shares messages with mankind; the spirit world, in which all things are alive; and the human world, where knowledge is transferred." While the central column of the atrium draws all together, it is the skylight "that is the point from which all areas of the building radiate" (Southern Ute Cultural Center & Museum, n.d.).

To address the traditional respect the tribe has for the land and its concern for the environment, the semicircular, first-floor turf roof is practical: "Planted with special grasses, it insulates in winter and summer, while passive solar gain in winter provides natural interior warmth." But it also becomes an "evolving part of the life of the museum" (Southern Ute Cultural Center & Museum, n.d.). The lattice, while visually relating to basket weaving, also serves a necessary function in mitigating the heat buildup in the central glass atrium. Acting as a woven shawl wrapped around the body, the protective aluminum slat-wrapping provides protection from the hot summer rays of the sun (Jones, 2012).

The surrounding landscape is as important as the building. The landscape at the entry point was designed to resemble the Southern Ute's native lands in the Rocky Mountains. All of the plants are native to the region and represent a wide variety of elevations. Also critical, and represented on the edge of the courtyard, is a reference to water; in his meeting with various Ute groups, a high school student said: "We are mountain people, so you should have a little stream, a little meadow stream as a welcoming and greeting thing" (*Southern Ute Cultural Center Museum: Building a Dream*, n.d.).

Paths wander through the landscape, allowing visitors to appreciate the historical, physical dichotomy of the Southern Ute's origin. Arnold sees the main idea as people being reminded that this is a Southern Ute place, and that these ancient peoples have been here for all time and will continue to be here for all time. The overriding theme, according to Arnold (Gamache, 2008), is responsiveness to the client: "It's important that they see themselves in it and that they can sit inside their ways and beliefs in the museum." The result is a building that concretizes the Southern Ute's philosophies while devoting space to caring for their treasured family artifacts, photographs, and stories, but with an area equal in size devoted to celebrating their living culture.

The idea of a center for the housing, use, and creation of cultural materials has found an interesting incarnation at the Poeh Center–Pueblo of Pojoaque, in New Mexico.

The Pueblo of Pojoaque—*Po-suwae-geh*, or "Water-drinking place," in Tewa—has long been considered the cultural center for the Tewa people. Pojoaque was a stopping place for travelers, and known for its rich cultural and artistic traditions, especially as seen in its polychrome pottery, stone carving, and basket making. Planning for a cultural center and museum really began in 1987 as the concept of Governor George Rivera, who saw such a center as a means of cultural preservation, but perhaps more importantly, revitalization. By 1993 sufficient monies had been raised as to make possible plans for a permanent facility, to be named the Poeh Center, *Poeh* meaning "traditional pathway" in Tewa.

The Tribal Council took the unusual step of forming their own construction company, Pojoaque Pueblo Construction Services Corporation (PPCSC), which was chartered to work on a variety of commercial construction projects throughout the state, and to utilize the profits for the construction and maintenance of the Poeh Center (Honoring Nations Award, 2000). Nycha Leia Zenderman (1996, 235) explains that the final design is the result of professional design expertise blended with ideas from individuals in the Pueblo itself and was "directly inspired and informed by the architectural design principles of Pojoaque's ancestors, the Anasazi, and from the surviving architecture of the Northern Pueblos . . . " This derivation did not preclude the incorporation of contemporary structural techniques and mechanical systems, as Pueblo culture has always been attuned to practical possibilities. The four-story tower, signifying the four worlds of the Tewa, is a striking expression of adobe construction perhaps possible only on tribal lands where local building codes do not apply. That is, its height would normally not be permitted in adobe, despite several of the pueblos historically being even taller (figure 16.3).

The cultural center occupies a three-acre site on land donated by the Pueblo of Pojoaque. Phase I of the project was completed in 1996, comprising classrooms, pottery, jewelry, and sculpture studios, and workshops in a 7,560-square-foot facility. By 2002, Phase II was complete, which houses the center's administrative offices and museum in an 18,966-square-foot structure. The project is ambitious: When complete, the center will comprise the Poeh Museum itself, an art sales gallery, a museum collections research space, and classrooms. It may also include a children's museum, a library and

Figure 16.3. Poeh Cultural Center and Museum, 2002. Photo by Frank Vodvarka

archive research center, a theater, and even a café that focuses on traditional foods and their cultural role (George Rivera, pers. comm.). By placing each function in separate buildings, the end result will closely resemble a traditional Pueblo village. Traditional materials—adobe brick and local wood—have been used in the center's construction, and incorporated training programs in the traditional construction methods (Facilities. Poeh Center, n.d.). It is in fact a point of pride that the facilities have been built in the traditional pueblo architectural form, as they feel that pueblo architectural design and building techniques are as important as the other traditional arts the center is reviving (Poeh Center Presentation, 2000).

The interior of the Poeh Center is visually intriguing, with ceiling beams made from spruce, pine, and Douglas fir in an alternating pattern of thin to thick log diameters in order to ensure an even appearance. Rivera points out that the ceiling in each room is different, a consequence of financial necessity that wound up having aesthetic appeal. The very thinness of the wood actually has a historical basis—the wood-carrying capacity of horse-drawn carts. McHorse, Jr. (Rivera et al., 2010) noted that the floors were made of local flagstone, dung, mud, and wood but also pointed out: "We want to try to maintain our traditional building styles but by the same token the functions of this facility require a high degree of sensitivity to climate control and security, so we had to incorporate that without changing the type of structures we have in the southwest."

There are some unconventional methods connected with the center; for one thing, there are few specific references to what you will see in the exhibits. Instead, the Elders were asked how they would want to be represented. Rivera (2010) explains:

> When we go through the exhibit you will see it is a little unusual. There are no labels at all. You can get a headset and listen to some of the Elders speaking about the way of life in the pueblos but it is not specific, saying that this is what that sculpture represents. It is more about being in these little environments that we created, and interpreting it and getting a feeling in yourself . . . We don't want another museum that just puts labels on everything.

Another anomaly concerns the running water in the midst of the permanent exhibits, which are arranged by seasons. Rivera (2010) explains: "everybody said we can't have water in the exhibit, that we could do fake water. But that wasn't going to cut it for us. We had to have this element. It is critical for our exhibit to have water flowing through it. All the pueblos are built around rivers and creeks."

The Poeh Center is the sum of many parts, and the "museum" display areas are not necessarily the most significant; in fact it is arguable that in terms of maintaining culture, the studios are more important. And the studios—of which there are several—are indeed impressive, as they are designed with care and integrity (figure 16.4). The massive stone column that dominates the jewelry studio was cut from the nearby mountains, and the huge wooden beam is fitted to the stone with great care. Governor Rivera is a noted sculptor, and it was he who hollowed the stone column so as to allow the beam to fit into its concave embrace. (Governor Rivera's work—heroic bronze sculpture—may be seen in the Smithsonian in Washington, D.C. The fact of an artist serving as political figure is not unusual in Pueblo culture; the Governor of the Zuni Pueblo creates jewelry.) Again, as with the importance of real water in the exhibition, the integrity of the stone is maintained; unlike typical construction of our day the column is solid and not faced with thin slices of veneer. While in the Tewa language, there is no word for "art," the Poeh Cultural Center and Museum has devoted the majority of buildings to places where the "creative impetus that evokes both experimentation and a sense of timelessness that has defined the transmission of knowledge among [their] Pueblo people both in the past and in the future" can take place.

The Huhugam Heritage Center of the Gila River Indian Community in Chandler, Arizona, was designed by Donald J. Stastny, of StastnyBrun

Figure 16.4.   Poeh Cultural Center Jewelry Studio, 1996. Photo by Frank Vodvarka

Architects Inc. with David N. Sloan (Navajo) of D. Sloan Architects. It is a unique building that becomes one with the surrounding five mountain ranges. It has, as a part of its design, its own earthen berm suggestive of the lip on a southwestern water jar, or olla, but also the ubiquitous earthen works common to Native North America. The inside of the berm is stepped in the manner of Huhugam agriculture terraces. The Huhugam Heritage Center serves two functions: as venue for the archaeological collections recovered as part of the Bureau of Reclamation's Central Arizona Irrigation Project; and the need for a cultural center for the community. Specifically, the facility contains the Gila River Indian Community's archaeological and ethnographic collections and Tribal Archives, as well as a library and reading area, and a museum with exhibit support functions. The architects worked closely with the Gila River Indian Community to create a sixty-eight-acre campus of buildings that speaks of the local community's respect for the land and water, a seamless integration of structure and landscape (figure 16.5).

Sloan (2010) describes the process:

We [Stastny and Sloan] started working with the Bureau of Reclamation in partnership with the tribe. Then we went through many visioning sessions with the community. We worked with the two tribes, the Pima and the Maricopa, and

Figure 16.5. Huhugam Heritage Center, 2004. Photo by Frank Vodvarka

you had to understand their history. What we tried to do was to provide a lot of visual information on boards, and we would talk about the landscape. Elders would come in and recognize their images, they'd recognize their history, and then they would begin to tell their stories about that.

The visuals, Sloan (2010) believes, were crucial: "if you create a lot of visual imagery for the community, it really starts people talking together, especially discussion between the elders and the youth, and then the tribal leaders. A lot of times they're not in a context like that where they are able to express and flow their ideas to one another. That's when that consensus-building starts . . ." Don Stastny echoes the importance of client interaction when he says: "In the case of Huhugam, we spent a good deal of time out in the community . . . David [Sloan] has the sensitivity to understand and respect what other native cultures believe—and he and I are very careful to not dig into areas that the community may not want to share" (Don Stastny, pers. comm.).

The center's functions have been divided among a number of buildings that are separate, yet joined peripherally to the central court. The central outdoor area is based on the "ball courts" used by the Hohokam people, so-called on the assumption that they are a northern corollary to the Mesoamerican phenomenon found in Mexico and Central America. In any event, the "ball court" at the Huhugam Heritage Center is used for music and dance on a regular basis. The trellised, ethnobotanical gardens, based on the community's relationship with desert plants, was designed by McCormack Landscape Architects. Brian McCormack (Nez Perce), one of only three licensed Native American Landscape Architects in the United States, was the main landscape consultant on the project. The site's interpretive signage tells the stories of the Huhugam in their own words in regard to the use of the plant species.

The Vision/Program/Concept Design, as it evolved, clearly portrayed the Huhugam on their own terms and recognized the traditional relationship between the people, the land, and the sky. "Discussion revolved around the feeling and smell of the buildings, the textures, and the sunlight, as well as the shapes of architecture and the materials used for building. Historic and symbolic thoughts were shared with regard to basketry, pottery, the Casa Grande, calendar sticks, forms and textures" (StastnyBrun et al., 1998, 8). Other elements that were to act as inspiration included the sacred number four with regard to directions, life transitions, seasons, and colors, but also such symbols as animals, legends, artifacts, patterns, and the like. What is striking about this long list of items is the sensory aspect of many of them, and the stress on symbolic concerns, as neither is customarily found in early stages of Western design programming.

These two parameters led, according to the architects, to an analysis of the project's organization and layout, with seminal elements like east-facing entries, cardinal points, and such. The environment—and especially water—had to be considered in terms of location, appearance, and smell (StastnyBrun et al., 1998, 8). No matter how clever the design, or efficient the programming, a failure in these areas would have produced an alien (and alienating) building. "The importance of the land, water, flora and fauna will also be paramount in the landscape design. The modern-day descendants of the Huhugam have stressed the importance of water and plants. . . . They represent many things for the people, such as comfort, security, etc." (StastnyBrun et al., 1998, 16). The design also had to take into account the difference between rectilinear and curvilinear shapes in building structure and landscape.

The interior of the center serves the functions of housing a permanent collection of Huhugam artifacts generally, with specific spaces for modern Pima and Maricopa objects, and changing exhibitions of works that relate to the area. Part of the permanent collection is devoted to the Breazeale Basket Collection purchased by the Gila River Indian Community and consisting of eighty-four Pima baskets. The collection is unique because many of the weavers can be identified and because they have named some of the designs. All the spaces have in common an attention to light and materials.

The design also points to what would be a stunning direction in Native American architecture in the Southwest, again raising the question of unique approaches generally. In response to our query, Stastny stated the situation succinctly:

Is there a new tribal architecture emerging? I would hope so, but if it is coming, it is coming very slowly. Probably the number of Native American architects and landscape architects has a lot to do with it. There is a danger to thinking that native architecture can be achieved in casinos or by painting symbols on walls. It has to come from creating architecture and sites that tell stories, that provide places to gather and teach, that incorporate ceremony and procession—and most of all, give the native people a voice. (Stastny, pers. comm.)

In these places, artifacts are housed that either are still in general use, or have associated spaces that allow for ceremonial practices directly connected with these objects.

NEW APPROACHES: RECOMMENDATIONS
FOR ARCHITECTS AND CURATORS

Ironically, Native Americans—as a condition of artifact retrieval from various authorities and institutions—have often had to call their own centers "museums" and conform to museum standards. Yet it is entirely common that the square-footage provided for making artifacts and performing ceremony exceeds that reserved for artifact display. Architectural design difficulty proceeds from having to use technologically sound—yet symbolically correct—materials, a modern aesthetic that hearkens to a particular worldview, and an interactive system of spaces that accommodates both a multisensory understanding of objects and their actual purpose in ritual and ceremony. The resulting building must be authentically a part of its milieu such that it is regularly used for rituals both mundane and extraordinary, rather than exist as a specialized part of a larger, and often disinterested, culture. On Native lands it is required that the architect have a far more holistic view of the design process, and be involved in every step of the building's construction. The result is a fully sensate building at one with its site and culture quite different from the usual Western museum experience.

What can Western design take from the Native American experience? That depends on the degree to which we embrace our own history, its ideas and artifacts. Certainly, the Native view of building could be of tremendous value as instruction to a generation of contemporary Euro-American architects that the cultural meaning that has largely been lost in Western design is something worth regaining. Sean Robin (1995, 8) refers to this when he says: "We also expect that non-Native communities will continue to learn the lessons that can be generalized from indigenous experience and culture."

Another, even deeper problem is alluded to in these types of discussions— the sort of mind/body separation that has been central to our self-view in Western culture. In his discussion of the Navajo Universe, Gary Witherspoon (1977, 151) comments that given the Western predilection for seeing the world in dualities, it is "not surprising that art would be divorced from the more practical affairs of business and government and the more serious matters of science, philosophy, and theology. In the Navajo world, however, art is not divorced from everyday life, for the creation of beauty and the incorporation of oneself in beauty represent the highest attainment and ultimate destiny of man." Thus, he points out, "The Navajo experience beauty primarily through expression and creation, not through perception and preservation" (1977, 151). While it would be in error to assume that the Navajo view absolutely prevails among Native Americans, it is common. Witherspoon (1977, 152) concludes by noting that the Navajo find it incomprehensible that we have more art critics and consumers than art creators and see art as marginal rather than integrated. Small wonder the Western concept of the museum is seen as an aberration.

In her article, "'Red Man's Burden': The Politics of Inclusion in Museum Settings," Nancy Marie Mithlo (2004, 746) discusses "the complexities involved in Indian/non-Indian relations in museums." Her research and experiences with the inclusion of indigenous artifacts in Western museum settings has led her to conclude that "both Indigenous knowledge and Western knowledge systems can be interpreted as subjective enterprises with restricted codes. Museum mandates to collect and preserve are not universal standards but particular norms associated with specific embedded social histories." In another insightful article by Mithlo, "No Word for Art in Our Language?: Old Questions, New Paradigms," (2012, 113) she explains:

> From one perspective, the "no word for art" descriptor indicates an Indigenous rejection of how Native arts are perceived in non-Native contexts such as museums, cultural centers, galleries, and scholarly texts—contexts that imbue fine arts with the Western values of individualism, commercialism, objectivism, and competition, as framed by an elitist point of reference. A rejection of the term "art" is then a rejection of Western culture as capitalist, patriarchal, and, ultimately, shallow, one that does not value the central principles of Indigenous identity, such as land, language, family, and spirituality. A refusal to be co-opted into a more narrow definition of what is an intrinsically more holistic enterprise is also a refusal to be named. It is an effort toward self-determination.

Thus the application of Western museum standards involves ideology, as well as the more prosaic considerations of practical display—a seemingly insurmountable design obstacle.

Notwithstanding, it is indeed possible for architects to successfully design on Native lands. The question really is: How do designers—Native and non-Native alike—make provision for a client whose cultural modalities are significantly different from their own? What become the controlling factors in creating a new and innovative design paradigm? We believe there are four key considerations: first, the attitude of the designers; second, the nature of their education; third, the source of the project's financing; and fourth, the degree of client control over the project (regardless of funding source). While the latter two lie beyond the scope of this chapter, the others are critical. The first refers to the willingness of the designer to listen and sensitively respond to the client's unique set of expectations, which—while time-consuming—is critical to the result. Second, the education of architects is, by virtue of their academic institutions and licensing, almost exclusively Western, a situation producing mixed results at best.

Every culture develops its own sensori-symbolic formula, suggesting that it is necessary to evolve a flexible design typology both specific and overarching. Such a formula might include the following elements: first, a determination, by virtue of an inclusive, specific research, of the relative value placed on the senses in order to design buildings that will perceptually resonate with a particular culture; second, the need to identify the symbolic, spiritual, and mythological concerns—and their spatial manifestations—that local cultures consider appropriate and necessary; third, the development of a new way of thinking about the appropriate functions of cultural space, from the ceremonial to the evocative; fourth, the importance of prior consensus in the group who will be the building's primary occupants; and last, the creation of a design that represents a larger social ethos, as it will house the integrative activities and objects of an entire peoples.

There are, of course, always the prosaic issues, which in Native culture often involve materials that need to be locally available, inexpensive, and easily manipulated by the community. Maintenance must be considered no matter the building's type, and technical installations requiring specialized skills probably should be avoided in remote areas. Any designer would be wise to listen to local residents in regard to long-standing practices vis-a-vis weather and topographic conditions—as well as traditional ways of ameliorating them.

The architect Daniel Glenn (Crow) (2001, 147) offers us an inclusive description of the extant approaches to indigenous design, which basically fall into three categories—iconographic, naturalistic, and cosmological. The first attempts to express the culture through the built expression of emblematic icons; the second is an approach in which architects design buildings to express the spirit of nature; and the third seeks a spiritual design, in which the universal worldview of a tribe is used to inform the tectonics and siting of structures. Here the cosmology of the tribe is a primary tool in generating the form of the building. As for architecture's final form, Glenn (2001, 144) concludes: "First, a participatory process directly involving tribal members is vital in determining the nature of a culturally specific design. Second, critical determinants of form can be drawn from traditional tribal architecture and artifacts without necessarily being derivative of the form of those artifacts." The most vital element, however, is to recognize the fundamentally different way in which Native peoples regard the nature of culture itself; for them, a successful cultural center—or, if one insists, museum—is that which engages and reinforces the social bond.

REFERENCES

Belk, R. W. (1991). The ineluctable mysteries of possessions. In Floyd W. Rudmin (ed.), *To Have Possessions: A Handbook on Ownership and Property*, pp. 17–56. Corte Madera, CA: Select Press.

Box of Treasures (1983). DVD. Directed by Chuck Olin. © U'mista Cultural Society. Vancouver, BC: Moving Images Distribution.

Carr, M. H. (1993). A conservation perspective on the wooden carvings of the Pacific Northwest coast. Paper presented at the Nineteenth Annual Conference of the Graduate Conservation Training Programs in North America, State University College at Buffalo, Art Conservation Department, April 15–17, 1993. http://cool .conservation-us.org/coolaic/sg/wag/1993/WAG_93_carr.pdf.

Center for American Indian Research and Native Studies. http://www.nativecairns .org/Evaluating.html (accessed August 2, 2011).

Facilities. Poeh Center. http://www.poehcenter.com/center/poeh-cultural-center/ facilities.html (accessed February 21, 2010).

Fisher, R. (1977). *Contact and Conflict: Indian-European Relations in British Columbia, 1774-1890*. Vancouver: University of British Columbia Press.

Gamache, S. (2008). Southern Ute museum connects with the land. *Seattle Daily Journal of Commerce*, August 26. http://www.djc.com/news/ae/11203979.html?id =11203979&printmode=true.

Glenn, D. J. (2001). Towards a new tribal architecture: designing the Little Big Horn College campus plan. In Hormuz Batliboi (ed.), *Paradoxes of Progress: Architecture and Education in a Post-Utopian Era*, pp. 144–49. Washington DC: ACSA Press.

Honoring Nations Award: 2000 Honoree Poeh Cultural Center. The Harvard Project on American Indian Economic Development. http://www.hpaied.org/images/re-sources/publibrary/Poeh%20Center%20Sustaining%20and%20Construction%20 Legacies.pdf.

Huhugam Heritage Center. http:// www.huhugam.com/collections.htm (accessed March 1, 2010). The Center's website is no longer online but can be accessed from the Internet Archive Wayback Machine site: http://archive.org/web/web.php.

Jones, J. (2010). Interview by Joy Monice Malnar and Frank Vodvarka. Tape recording. April 1. Jones & Jones Architects, Landscape Architects, Planners, Seattle, WA.

———. (2012). Indigenous Design: Ancient Gifts—Verbal Gifts—Emerging Gifts. Lecture at the School of Architecture, University of Illinois at Urbana-Champaign, Champaign, IL. October 29.

Kirshenblatt-Gimblett, B. (1998). *Destination Culture: Tourism, Museums, and Heritage*. Berkeley: University of California Press.

Malnar, J. M. and Vodvarka, F. (2013). *New Architecture on Indigenous Lands*. Minneapolis: University of Minnesota Press.

Mithlo, N. M. (2004). "Red Man's Burden": the politics of inclusion in museum settings. *American Indian Quarterly*, 28(3/4), 743–63.

———. (2012). No word for art in our language?: Old questions, new paradigms. *Wicazo Sa Review*, 27(1), 111–26.

Nowotny, M. (2011). Native places. *National Museum of the American Indian* 12,(2), 40–46.

Poeh Center Presentation. (2000). Harvard University's Honoring Nations 2000 Award. St. Paul, Minnesota, September 27. http://www.poehcenter.com/center/ poeh-cultural-center/harvard/pdf/presentation.pdf (accessed June 17, 2009).

Rivera, G., Lujan, V., McHorse, Sr., J. C. and McHorse, Jr., J. C. (2010). Interview by Joy Monice Malnar and Frank Vodvarka. Tape recording. May 5. Poeh Center, Santa Fe, NM.

Robin, S. (1995). From the Editor. In the *Indigenous Planning Newsletter* 1(1). American Planning Association, June.

Sloan, D. (2010). Interview by Joy Monice Malnar and Frank Vodvarka. Tape recording. May 4. David N. Sloan Architects, Albuquerque, NM.

Southern Ute Cultural Center & Museum. http://www.succm.org/feature (accessed June 9, 2011).

Southern Ute Cultural Center & Museum: Building a Dream. [n.d.]. DVD. Played in library during opening day ceremonies of Saturday, May 21, 2011.

StastnyBrun Architects, Inc., David N. Sloan & Associates, and McCormack Landscape Design. (1998). Gila River Indian Community Huhugam Heritage Center, Vision/Program/Concept Design.

Tradition & Experimentation. (2006). Poeh Cultural Center and Museum. http:// www.poehmuseum.com/Tradition_Experimentation.html (accessed January 24, 2013).

U'mista: Courtesy Aboriginal Tourism Association BC. [n.d.]. Video clip, uploaded May 18, 2010. Museum of Anthropology. http://www.youtube.com/ watch?v=PndL5fHnK04.

Witherspoon, G. (1977). *Language and Art in the Navajo Universe*. Ann Arbor: The University of Michigan Press.

Zenderman, N. L. (1996). Poeh Center: A statement by Pojoaque Pueblo. In Krinsky, C.H., *Contemporary Native American Architecture: Cultural Regeneration and Creativity*, pp 233–35. New York: Oxford University Press.

Part V

FUTURE MUSEUMS

17

Multisensory Memories

How Richer Experiences Facilitate Remembering

Jamie Ward

This chapter will focus on how memories are constructed and retrieved using information from different senses. A key concept is the idea that memories consist of a constellation of different attributes (sensory, emotional, verbal, etc.) that are distributed throughout the brain but bound together in different hubs that represent objects, concepts, and events. Retrieving a memory involves reinstating this pattern (i.e., creating a whole given a constituent part). Encoding an event using different senses leads to a more distributed memory pattern across the brain, although this, in itself, is not a guarantee of more efficient remembering. The latter depends on the extent to which the constituent parts can be meaningfully integrated together (e.g., based on prior experience and knowledge) versus being arbitrarily associated, and the extent to which the initial conditions at learning are reinstated at remembering. The chapter also considers individual differences in mental imagery and unusual perceptual experiences (synaesthesia) and the extent to which this is linked to better, or worse, memory. Finally, implications of the scientific findings are discussed with respect to the real-world setting of museums.

MEMORY FORMATION AS FEATURE BINDING

Learning and memory are functions that the whole brain participates in. Our experiences of the world change the way that neurons interconnect with each other and this, in turn, changes their responsiveness to future events. Thus, a stimulus that has recently been encountered (e.g., a sound or object) will tend to be responded to faster on a subsequent encounter (a phenomenon termed "repetition priming"). This happens because the brain's coding of that stimulus has been changed in some way (e.g., by making its response more selectively tuned or more synchronous, Gotts, Chow et al., 2012). When two things are presented together (e.g., a sound and an object), then the responsiveness of each item is changed but, moreover, their responsiveness to each other is also changed (Albright, 2012). That is, an association between the two is formed. In neural terms stimuli that "fire together, wire together." So encountering the sound again will make the object more available, for instance, by bringing it consciously to mind or by enabling a faster response to it (a phenomenon termed "associative priming").

Our memories can be thought of as constellations of different kinds of information that are bound together in this way (e.g., McClelland, McNaughton et al., 1995; Rissman and Wagner, 2012). A memory for a familiar object, such as a banana, consists of different kinds of information associated together: visual features (its color), nonvisual features (smell, taste), and features that are shared between several senses (size and shape). Other kinds of information would also be linked to this, such as factual information (e.g., where they grow), its name ("banana"), and its function (eat it). Collectively, this would constitute the semantic memory for a banana. Semantic memories can be thought of as stable, time-invariant, decontextualized memories of the world. However, the lay notion of "memory" has a more specific meaning, corresponding to events in particular times and places. These contextualized memories are referred to in psychology as episodic memories (the term "autobiographical memory" is effectively interchangeable with this). Episodic memories enjoy a special status in psychological research, just as they do in lay notions of memory, because of their experiential quality. To experience an episodic memory is to partially reconstruct the patterns of sensory, conceptual, emotional, and contextual details that were initially present during the event itself (e.g., see Rissman and Wagner, 2012). For this reason, recollecting episodic memories is sometimes described as a form of "mental time travel" (Wheeler, Stuss et al., 1997). Interestingly, the more a situation of remembering resembles the specific learning situation, the easier it is to remember. That is, the easier it is to reconstruct the patterns of sensory, conceptual, emotional, and contextual details. This powerful psychological law is named "transfer appropriate processing" or TAP for short (Morris, Bransford et al., 1977).

Figure 17.1 illustrates the general principle that has been described so far: namely, memories are constructed by binding different kinds of information together. Perceptual representations of objects (e.g., their basic shape), semantic knowledge, and episodic memories are all types of memory but differ in terms of the nature of their content. They also differ in terms of the regions of the brain that support them. Regions in the medial temporal lobes, such as the hippocampus, have a particularly important role to play in more complex memories (episodic and semantic memories) because they receive inputs from regions throughout the brain specialized for different kinds of information (e.g., from different senses [Quiroga, Kraskov et al., 2009]). They may also be well equipped to support this kind of memory because of the type of computation they perform which enables them to separate out the features of a new event from existing, similar memories. These medial temporal lobe structures are often considered to form an "index" that links together the different features of an event (McClelland, McNaughton et al., 1995). Whether this indexing is needed initially to create the memories (consolidation) or is additionally to support remembering later on remains debated (e.g., Frankland and Bontempi, 2005; Moscovitch, Rosenbaum et al., 2005). In contrast, regions in other parts of the brain do not have as rich a pattern of inputs but can, nevertheless, bind certain kinds of information together. For instance, there are specialized regions for shape perception within the inferior temporal lobe that bind together information from touch and vision to form a perceptual memory for the shapes of objects (Amedi, von Kriegstein et al., 2005). Other regions may bind together smell and taste to create flavor memories for food (e.g., Small, Voss et al., 2004), and so on. That is, the kind of memories that different brain regions can support depends on their pattern of inputs (in addition to the kinds of computation they perform).

A concrete example of how the brain can store parts and wholes in separate systems is given by an influential study of Luck and Vogel (1997). This

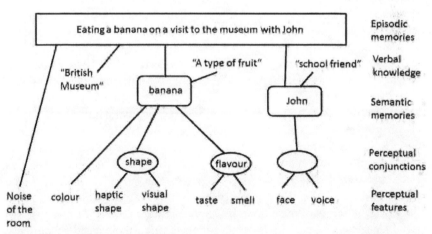

Figure 17.1. Information from different senses can be bound together at different levels in an approximately hierarchical fashion. Binding together in memory, say, a taste and a smell may rely on different regions of the brain (associative "hubs") than binding together a sound and a color.

study presented participants with an array of simple visual material to hold in mind in so-called working memory, which denotes a storage component for things *actively* held in mind. In one version, they presented arrays of different colored squares (with the arrays varying in size from two to six). In another version they presented arrays of different line orientations. In both cases, memory deteriorates when holding in mind more than four features. The interesting comparison was when conjunctions of features had to be remembered (i.e., an oriented and colored line). Even though the conjunction involves holding twice as many features in mind, it was found that memory performance was not halved but remained constant; that is, around four feature conjunctions could be remembered. They even extended this finding to a quadruple feature condition: sixteen features distributed across four objects can be retained as accurately as four features distributed across four objects. The explanation is that the capacity limitations stem from different kinds of memory representation (features versus objects). Our memory for objects does not consist merely of our memory for the features that comprise those objects but are themselves represented as whole, discrete entities.

RETRIEVING WHOLES FROM PARTS

The view introduced above is that the features comprising complex memories are distributed in specialized systems of the brain but bound together in "hubs" that enable particular kinds of information to be combined, with structures such as the hippocampus acting as a central hub receiving information from all different senses. Within this framework, memory retrieval involves reactivating this pattern of features. Broadly speaking, memory retrieval can be done in two different ways. First, it could be triggered by encountering one of the elements making up the event (e.g., seeing an object; smelling a smell). This is referred to as bottom-up retrieval of memory associations. Alternatively, it can be triggered based on top-down demands. For instance, answering a question such as "when was the last time I visited a museum?" may trigger various contextual associations (e.g., places I have recently visited on vacation) which then, in turn, may lead to retrieval of specific features of the event (e.g., what was seen). In both instances, memory retrieval can be construed as retrieving the whole from a constituent part, but the two situations differ in terms of the nature of the cueing part.

Evidence from the neurosciences supports this basic model of memory retrieval. Gottfried et al. (2004) investigated associative memory between smells (e.g., roses) and objects (e.g., images of a helmet or cabinet) using brain imaging (fMRI; functional magnetic resonance imaging). During the encoding phase, participants were asked to construct a narrative linking the smell and object together. At testing, participants were presented with just visual objects and were asked to determine whether the object had been seen previously (old items) or not (new items). A comparison between the two conditions revealed that brain regions linked to olfactory perception were activated by visual objects that had previously been associatively linked to it. In a similar study, Nyberg et al. (2000) presented participants with either multisensory (visual words paired with environmental sounds, such as a dog bark) or unisensory stimuli (visual words only) to remember. At testing, only the visual words were presented but—nevertheless—those words previously associated with auditory stimuli led to activity within regions of the brain dedicated to auditory processing (i.e., auditory cortices). Multisensory memory retrieval (relative to unisensory) was also related to brain activity in the hippocampal region, which may serve to bind these components together.

Activation of previously encountered wholes, given a part cue, is also found at the level of individual neurons recorded in the brain of animals who have, for instance, been trained that an arbitrary stimulus from one sense (e.g., vision) is predictive of a stimulus in another (e.g., audition, touch). Brosch, Selezneva, and Scheich (2005) recorded neuronal activity from monkeys who had learned to pair visual stimuli with subsequent sounds. Neurons in the auditory cortex responded to visual stimuli that had been associated with sounds but not other kinds of visual stimuli. Similar findings have been found in neurons located in regions of the brain dedicated to touch perception (primary somatosensory cortex): these neurons respond to visual stimuli that have been previously paired with tactile stimuli (Zhou and Fuster, 2000). These findings fit well within the framework described thus far—that is, that presenting different stimuli together changes their future responsiveness to each other. However, there remains a puzzle as to how this pattern of brain activity should be interpreted. One interpretation of these findings is that brain regions traditionally considered as "visual," "auditory," or "tactile," should no longer be considered as such but should instead be considered as multisensory in nature (albeit having a bias toward one particular sense). The alternative viewpoint is to argue that a neuron in "auditory" cortex that responds to associated visual stimuli remains essentially "auditory" in character but now responds not only to real sounds but also to implied sounds (i.e., sounds implied by association to previous visual stimuli). In other words, the neuron's response encompasses both auditory perception and (visually elicited) auditory imagery (Albright, 2012). In summary, we do not yet have a full understanding of how to link these interesting neuroscience observations with the subjective content to imagery and memory.

THE ROLE OF SEMANTIC CONGRUENCY
IN MULTISENSORY MEMORY

The studies of Nyberg et al. (2000) and Gottfried et al. (2004) involved arbitrarily paired stimuli from different modalities (e.g., smell of rose plus sight of a helmet; seeing the word "table" plus hearing the bark of a dog). However, certain types of pairing may be particularly prone to co-occur together in natural environments (e.g., tastes and smells invariably go together, as do faces and voices), and we have preexisting, learned, semantic multisensory associations (e.g., we know what a dog sounds like and looks like). These preexisting associations between sounds and appearance of objects facilitate subsequent episodic remembering. Murray et al. (2004) presented a continuous stream of visual images that participants had to categorize as old or new (i.e., according to whether they had been previously presented in the stream of images or not). The initial presentation was either visual only (e.g., an image of a gun) or audiovisual and semantically congruent (e.g., an image of a gun and a "bang" sound). Memory for images was better when it had previously been paired with its semantically associated sound. This effect depended on rapid brain activity within a multisensory region involved in object recognition (the lateral occipital complex, LOC) rather than the hippocampus. This suggests that, when audio and visual features are semantically congruent they can bind together at an object-level of multisensory processing. When they are arbitrary (as in Nyberg et al., 2000) they may bind together at an event-level of multisensory processing (e.g., in the hippocampus). In the Nyberg et al. (2000) study the arbitrarily associated multisensory events were no better remembered than the unisensory events (with a trend for them to be worse), whereas in the Murray et al. (2004) study the meaningfully associated multisensory events were better remembered. Subsequent studies have confirmed that multisensory encoding of events only leads to a benefit in performance when the features of the event can be meaningfully integrated (e.g., because they correspond to the same object), but not when multisensory features are mismatching or arbitrary (Lehmann and Murray, 2005; Thelen, Cappe et al., 2012). Meaningful integration can be regarded as a kind of "deep level of processing" that follows another basic psychological law, namely that deeper encoded memories are generally remembered better. In psychology this notion is referred to as Levels of Processing (LOP) in short (Craik and Lockhart, 1972).

Comparable findings have been demonstrated in the domain of face-voice associative memory. Von Kriegstein and Giraud (2006) taught groups of participants to associate voices with either faces or names. The sound of a person's voice and their visual appearance are not arbitrary but, instead, is related to reliable mediating factors such as their size, age, and gender. However, the link between the sound of a person's voice and their name is more arbitrary (with gender providing some constraint). Participants found it easier to learn to recognize unimodal voices after being previously paired with faces than with names (see also O'Mahony and Newell 2012). The face-voice advantage was also found to other baseline measures involving arbitrary associations to objects rather than people, specifically between ring tones and cell phone names or ring tones and cell phone images. This face-voice advantage was linked to greater neural coupling of activity between regions involved in face recognition and voice recognition. Similarly, studies using well-known voices show that speaker recognition (i.e., voice only) activates face-processing regions of the brain (von Kriegstein, Kleinschmidt et al., 2005): that is, reinstating a whole from a part. A link between face and voice is, arguably, one of the earliest learned specific audiovisual associations. The mother's voice is learned prenatally and, within days of birth, the familiar voice enables rapid association with the mother's face (Sai, 2005).

These congruency effects are not just found for complex stimuli such as faces and objects but can be found for basic perceptual learning tasks. Shams and colleagues (Seitz, Kim et al., 2006; Kim, Seitz et al., 2008) trained participants on a difficult visual motion task in which they had to detect, from an array of dots moving in different directions, whether there was more movement to the left or right. During training they were shown visual stimuli only, congruent audiovisual stimuli (the sound moved in the same direction as vision), or incongruent audiovisual stimuli (the sound moved in the opposite direction as vision). The main test condition consisted only of moving visual stimuli (i.e., no sounds). It was found that the congruent audiovisual training lead to significant benefits relative to the other two conditions (which did not differ from each other). One might imagine that the best learning would be in the visual-only condition because the test itself was visual-only. This was not so: the presence of meaningful audio during training improves performance on a purely visual test.

MENTAL IMAGERY, SYNAESTHESIA, AND MEMORY

Strategies that involve the use of visual imagery are known to benefit memory performance. For instance, memory performance for verbal material is likely to be enhanced when additionally encoded as a mental image (Paivio, 1969). This has previously been explained in terms of Paivio's dual coding theory: namely that storing information in multiple codes (visual and verbal) is beneficial to memory. Concreteness and imageability of word stimuli (i.e., the extent to which the meaning of a word is linked to sensory experience) are beneficial to memory performance and this lends further support to the theory (for a review see Paivio, 1995). These observations relate closely to the previously described literature in which remembering, say, a gun is more likely if it has been both seen and heard. However, in those studies both sensory components were perceived whereas in these studies one (or more) component is merely imagined. Similar brain processes are known to support both perceiving and imagining (e.g., Kosslyn, Ganis et al., 2001), so this is perhaps not entirely surprising.

More complex mental images can be used to support more impressive feats of memory. For instance, the "method of loci," which was first noted by the ancient Greeks, involves memorizing arbitrary sequences by placing each element in the sequence along landmarks on a familiar route (e.g., from home to work). Using this method, people with "normal" levels of memory ability can train themselves to remember, say, the sequence in a shuffled pack of playing cards (O'Brien, 2001).

Although the use of mental imagery is known to benefit memory (for at least some kinds of stimuli), the evidence that individual differences in the vividness of mental imagery is related to differences in memory ability is weaker. People with high visual imagery perform better on tests involving the learning of arbitrary word pairs (Rossi and Fingeret, 1977). They also re-call more pictorial details from previously presented images (Hänggi, 1989). However, others have argued that increased memory in tests such as this is enhanced by general relational coding between items rather than imagery it-self (Marschark and Surian, 1989). It has also been argued that individual dif-ferences relating to imagery may depend more on whether an individual tends to make use of imagery strategically rather than its vividness per se (Ernest and Paivio, 1971; Cohen and Saslona, 1990). Finally, more vivid imagery (and more habitual use of imagery) is sometimes linked to significantly worse memory. Heuer, Fischman et al. (1986) examined memory for colors based on either long-term experience (e.g., the color of a New York police car) or short-term exposure (holding in mind a color to match it to a set of possible colors). People with better visual imagery were less accurate at recalling the exact color. The explanation is that their good imagination may lead them to accept a wider range of answers as plausible.

In addition to considering individual differences in imagery, this section will conclude by considering another interesting individual difference in perception—synaesthesia. For people with synaesthesia, stimuli (such as words or music) are associated with perceptual experiences such as colors or flavors (Ward, 2013). For instance, "Tuesday" may be pink and "7" may taste of sherbet. However, these are not learned associations due to exposure to arbitrary pairings in the environment (e.g., colored alphabet books [Rich, Bradshaw et al., 2005]) but are, instead, internally derived as a result of subtle functional and structural differences in the brains of people who have synaesthesia (Rouw, Scholte et al., 2011). In many respects they resemble mental images; for instance, they are created by the brain rather than sensory organs and are not confused with reality. However, unlike most mental images they are often externally projected and, by definition, they are always elicited. Whereas most mental images can be controlled (e.g., switched off, swapped color) this is not true of synaesthetic percepts (e.g., if "Tuesday" were pink then it would always and inevitably be pink). Within the framework outlined in this chapter, we can say that the stimulus/concept "Tuesday" has an additional feature bound to it (pink) and whenever that stimulus/concept is encountered then the feature is both retrieved and experienced.

Having synaesthesia leads to enhanced performance on many tests of memory (Rothen, Meier et al., 2012). If words are perceived as colored then these synaesthetes are better at recalling word lists (Radvansky, Gibson et al., 2011). If time (e.g., days, months) is perceived visuo-spatially, then these synaesthetes are better at recalling the details of an event from a time cue (Simner, Mayo et al., 2009). However, the memory advantages are not just found for stimuli that trigger extra perceptions. They can be found in certain other domains too. For instance, synaesthetes who experience color have better memory for colors (Yaro and Ward, 2007). This is the opposite result to people with high imagery (Heuer, Fischman et al., 1986). This suggests that synaesthesia is not the same as standard forms of high imagery even if synaesthetes, as a whole, tend to be visual thinkers (Barnett and Newell, 2007).

FROM THE LAB TO THE MUSEUM

From the evidence above, what concrete guidelines could be provided to practitioners attempting to create a multisensory museum? The following advice stems from the evidence above:

1. The extent to which information from different senses can be meaningfully integrated is of primary importance for subsequent remembering.
2. The actual amount of information is of less importance and the brain is quite capable of avoiding "sensory overload," provided the sensory information is not conflicting.
3. Imagery and imagination can improve remembering, although this can depend on what is to be learned and the imagery abilities of the individual.

REFERENCES

Albright, T. D. (2012). On the perception of probable things: neural substrates of associative memory, imagery, and perception. *Neuron* 74(2), 227–45.

Amedi, A., K. von Kriegstein, et al. (2005). Functional imaging of human crossmodal identification and object recognition. *Experimental Brain Research* 166(3-4), 559–71.

Barnett, K. J. and F. N. Newell (2007). Synaesthesia is associated with enhanced, self-rated visual imagery. *Consciousness and Cognition* 17, 1032–39.

Brosch, M., E. Selezneva, et al. (2005). Nonauditory events of a behavioral procedure activate auditory cortex of highly trained monkeys. *The Journal of Neuroscience* 25, 6797–806.

Cohen, B. H. and M. Saslona (1990). The advantage of being an habitual visualizer. *Journal of Mental Imagery* 1, 101–12.

Craik, F. I. M. and R. S. Lockhart (1972). Levels of processing: A framework for memory research. *Journal of Verbal Learning and Verbal Behaviour* 11, 671–84.

Ernest, C. H. and A. Paivio (1971). Imagery and sex differences in incidental recall. *British Journal of Psychology* 62(Feb), 67–72.

Frankland, P. W. and B. Bontempi (2005). The organization of recent and remote memories. *Nature Reviews Neuroscience* 6, 119–30.

Gottfried, J. A., A. P. R. Smith, et al. (2004). Remembrance of odors past: Human olfactory cortex in cross-modal recognition memory. *Neuron* 42(4), 687–95.

Gotts, S. J., C. C. Chow, et al. (2012). Repetition priming and repetition suppression: A case for enhanced efficiency through neural synchronization. *Cognitive Neuroscience* 3(3-4), 227–59.

Hänggi, D. (1989). Differential aspects of visual short- and long-term memory. *European Journal of Cognitive Psychology* 1, 285–92.

Heuer, F., D. Fischman, et al. (1986). Why does vivid imagery hurt color memory? *Canadian Journal of Psychology* 40, 161–75.

Kim, R. S., A. R. Seitz, et al. (2008). Benefits of stimulus congruency for multisensory facilitation of visual learning. *Plos One* 3(1).

Kosslyn, S. M., G. Ganis, et al. (2001). Neural foundations of imagery. *Nature Reviews Neuroscience* 2, 635–42.

Lehmann, S. and M. M. Murray. (2005). The role of multisensory memories in unisensory object discrimination. *Cognitive Brain Research* 24, 326–34.

Luck, S. J. and E. K. Vogel (1997). The capacity of visual working memory for features and conjunctions. *Nature* 390(6657), 279–81.

Marschark, M. and L. Surian. (1989). Why does imagery improve memory? *European Journal of Cognitive Psychology* 1, 251–63.

McClelland, J. L., B. L. McNaughton, et al. (1995). Why there are complementary learning systems in the hippocampus and neocortex: Insights from the successes and failures of connectionist models of learning and memory. *Psychological Review* 102, 419–57.

Morris, C. D., J. D. Bransford, et al. (1977). Levels of processing versus transfer appropriate processing. *Journal of Verbal Learning and Verbal Behavior* 16, 519–33.

Moscovitch, M., R. S. Rosenbaum, et al. (2005). Functional neuroanatomy of remote episodic, semantic and spatial memory: a unified account based on multiple trace theory. *Journal of Anatomy* 207(1), 35–66.

Murray, M. M., C. M. Michel, et al. (2004). Rapid discrimination of visual and multisensory memories revealed by electrical neuroimaging. *NeuroImage* 21, 125–35.

Nyberg, L., R. Habib, et al. (2000). Reactivation of encoding-related brain activity during memory retrieval. *Proceedings of the National Academy of Sciences of the United States of America* 97(20), 11120–124.

O'Brien, D. (2001). *Quantum Memory Power*. Nightingale Conant.

O'Mahony, C. and F. N. Newell. (2012). Integration of faces and voices, but not faces and names, in person recognition. *British Journal of Psychology* 103, 73–82.

Paivio, A. (1969). Mental imagery in associative learning and memory. *Psychological Review* 76, 241–63.

———. (1995). Imagery and memory. *The Cognitive Neurosciences.* M. S. Gazzaniga. Cambridge: MIT Press.

Quiroga, R. Q., A. Kraskov, et al. (2009). Explicit encoding of multimodal percepts by single neurons in the human brain. *Current Biology* 19, 1308–13.

Radvansky, G. A., B. S. Gibson, et al. (2011). Synesthesia and memory: color congruency, von Restorff, and false memory effects. *Journal of Experimental Psychology-Learning Memory and Cognition* 37(1), 219–29.

Rich, A. N., J. L. Bradshaw, et al. (2005). A systematic, large-scale study of synaesthesia: Implications for the role of early experience in lexical-color associations. *Cognition* 98, 53–84.

Rissman, J. and A. D. Wagner. (2012). Distributed representations in memory: insights from functional brain imaging. *Annual Review of Psychology* 63, 101–28.

Rossi, J. S. and A. L. Fingeret. (1977). Individual differences in verbal and imagery abilities: Paired-associate recall as a function of stimulus and response concreteness. *Perceptual and Motor Skills* 44, 1043–49.

Rothen, N., B. Meier, et al. (2012). Enhanced memory: Insights from synaesthesia. *Neuroscience and Biobehavioral Review*.

Rouw, R., H. S. Scholte, et al. (2011). Brain areas involved in synaesthesia: A review. *Journal of Neuropsychology* 5, 214–42.

Sai, F. Z. (2005). The role of the mother's voice in developing mother's face preference: Evidence for intermodal perception at birth. *Infant and Child Development* 14(1), 29–50.

Seitz, A. R., R. Kim, et al. (2006). Sound facilitates visual learning. *Current Biology* 16(14), 1422–27.

Simner, J., N. Mayo, et al. (2009). A foundation for savantism? Visuo-spatial synaesthetes present with cognitive benefits. *Cortex* 45(10), 1246–60.

Small, D. M., J. Voss, et al. (2004). Experience-dependent neural integration of taste and smell in the human brain. *Journal of Neurophysiology* 92, 1892–1903.

Thelen, A., C. Cappe, et al. (2012). Electrical neuroimaging of memory discrimination based on single-trial multisensory learning. *Neuroimage* 62(3), 1478–88.

von Kriegstein, K. and A. L. Giraud. (2006). Implicit multisensory associations influence voice recognition. *Plos Biology* 4(10), 1809–20.

von Kriegstein, K., A. Kleinschmidt, et al. (2005). Interaction of face and voice areas during speaker recognition. *Journal of Cognitive Neuroscience* 17, 367–76.

Ward, J. (2013). Synesthesia. *Annual Review of Psychology* 64.

Wheeler, M. A., D. T. Stuss, et al. (1997). Toward a theory of episodic memory: The frontal lobes and autonoetic consciousness. *Psychological Bulletin* 121, 331–54.

Yaro, C. and J. Ward. (2007). Searching for Shereshevskii: What is superior about the memory of synaesthetes? *Quarterly Journal of Experimental Psychology* 60, 682–96.

Zhou, Y. D. and J. M. Fuster. (2000). Visuo-tactile cross-modal associations in cortical somatosensory cells. *Proceedings of the National Academy of Science, USA* 97, 9777–82.

18

The Secret of Aesthetics Lies in the Conjugation of the Senses

Reimagining the Museum as a Sensory Gymnasium

David Howes

Western philosophers and psychologists have debated whether the blind are capable of aesthetic experience. The eighteenth-century *philosophe* Denis Diderot held that the blind have no direct knowledge of aesthetics: "when [a blind man] says 'that is beautiful,' he is not making an aesthetic judgment, he is simply repeating the judgment of one who can see . . . Beauty is only a word for the blind" (Diderot quoted in Morgan, 1977: 33). The early-twentieth-century psychologist Géza Révész similarly held that the blind lack an aesthetic sense. He found that blind persons were neither able to accurately identify nor judge the aesthetic value of a series of sculpted busts. This led him to conclude that "we have to deny absolutely the ability of the blind to enjoy plastic works aesthetically" (Révész, 1950: 219)

The question to be explored in this chapter is whether these judgments are attributable to a lack or deficiency on the part of the blind, or a deficiency in the conventional Western definition of the aesthetic, and the protocols of the institutions that enforce that definition. In the first section, it will be shown that the fault lies with the definition and the institution, particularly in their modern incarnation. In origin, the meaning of the term *aesthetic* and the institution of the museum were far less exclusively tied to the visual than they are at present. In the next section, two case studies are presented of how the experience of the aesthetic is produced in non-Western cultures—specifically, the Shipibo-Conibo and the Navajo. These cultures' art forms are of interest because they are not beholden to the ideology of "the aesthetic gaze" and can thus help us to start imagining the aesthetic otherwise than by reference to "eyesight alone" (Jones, 2008). In the concluding section, building on the cross-cultural and cross-modal research that has gone before, a theory is advanced of the secret of aesthetics. It is suggested that the secret of aesthetics

285

lies in the conjugation of the senses. It is the combination (not the isolation) of the modalities that is key. The implications of this new *intermodal* definition of the aesthetic are then drawn out, first for the practice of art history and, then, for the practice of Art Education for the Blind.

The message of this chapter is that the best way to imagine the museum of the future is by delving into the museum's origins and by exploring how aesthetic experience is structured across a range of cultures.

THE INVENTION AND SUBJUGATION OF AESTHETICS

The concept of "aesthetics" was coined by the philosopher Alexander von Baumgarten in the mid-eighteenth century. It is derived from the Greek *aisthesis*, meaning sense perception. For Baumgarten (1750), aesthetics had to do with the perfection of perception and only secondarily with the perception of perfection, or beauty. That is, the aesthetic was rooted in the body, rather than the object, and turned on the disposition to sense acutely. It was also rooted in the body in the sense that it was to remain separate from reason: Baumgarten saw aesthetics as a "science of the lower cognitive power" (sense perception) in contradistinction to "the higher cognitive power" (reason). Its object was to grasp the "unity-in-multiplicity of sensible qualities" but not reduce that unity to arid rational formulae (Gregor, 1983: 364–65; Howes, 2010)

It did not take long for Baumgarten's wondrous definition to be drained of its sensory plenitude and subjugated. In the *Critique of Judgment* (1790), the philosopher Kant refined Baumgarten's definition to the point where it came to stand for "disinterested" contemplation and judgment. The Kantian paradigm continues to dominate the discourse of aesthetics to this day. The field of aesthetics is limited to the appreciation of the formal relations intrinsic to a work of art and is supposed to be divorced from any consideration of that work's content. Robert Redfield offers the following analogy by way of specifying the proper object of aesthetics:

> Art . . . is like a window with a garden behind it. One may focus on either the garden or the window. The common viewer of a Constable landscape or a statue by St. Gaudens focuses on the garden. Not many people . . . "are capable of adjusting their perceptive apparatus to the windowpane and the transparency that is the work of art." (Redfield, 1971: 46 quoting Ortega y Gasset)

The implication of this analogy is that it is only the uncommon viewer, or art connoisseur, capable of training his or her gaze on the windowpane itself, and capable of seeing the arrangement of forms and colors in itself, who is able to enjoy a pure aesthetic experience and exercise the proper form of judgment.

It is important to note how this construction deflects attention from the focus on intersensory relations that was given in Baumgarten's concept of aesthetics as the perception of "the unity in multiplicity of sensible qualities." The idea of a windowpane effectively silences any input from the nonvisual senses, which are deemed to constitute so many distractions (except in the case of it being a concert that is the object of attention, in which case it would be sight that needs censoring). Consider the following passage from a Harold Osborne essay on "The Cultivation of Sensibility in Art Education":

> In the appreciation of a work of art we concentrate attention exclusively upon a selected region of the presented world. When listening to music we shut out so far as possible the sounds of our neighbours' coughing, the rustle of programmes, even our own bodily sensations. When reading a poem, looking at a film or watching a stage play we tend to be imperceptive and unmindful of sensations from outside. But within the chosen sector we are alert to the intrinsic qualities of the sense-impressions imparted rather than to their practical implications and we are alert to the patterned constructs formed by the relations in which these intrinsic qualities stand to each other . . . This is perception for its own sake, and represents the kernel of truth in the traditional formula "disinterested interest." (Osborne, 1984: 32; see further Elkins, 2000: xi)

It should be noted that the aesthetic sensibility of which Osborne speaks is not only something that is cultivated by the viewer from within, it is also instilled in the viewer from without. The protocols of the museum, as of the concert hall, impose all sorts of restrictions on the viewer or listener's senses, with the result that these institutions function as spaces for the production of "single sense epiphanies" (Kirshenblatt-Gimblett, 1998)—visual or aural but not both, and certainly not olfactory, gustatory, tactile, or kinaesthetic. But things were not always this way, not at the beginning.

THE MUSEUM AS SENSORY GYMNASIUM

Barbara Kirshenblatt-Gimblett has observed that the museum is "a school for the senses and . . . its sensory curriculum has a history." Her observation is amply borne out by the work of Constance Classen (2005, 2012), Fiona Candlin (2010), and Helen Rees Leahy (2012). As Classen relates, based on her study of seventeenth- and eighteenth-century travelers' accounts, early public museums like the Ashmolean in Oxford and the Tower of London,

> retained many characteristics of the private collections on which they were based. The museum tour led by a curator matched the house tour that might be offered by a host. The curator, as gracious host, was expected to provide

information about the collection and offer it up for handling. . . . The museum
visitors, as polite guests, were expected to show their interest and goodwill by
asking questions and by touching the proffered objects. (2012: 138)

And touch them they did: unscrewing a knob, caressing a statue, and generally hoisting, brandishing, and fingering objects to ascertain their weight,
texture, or temperature, and thereby verify the evidence of their visual appearance alone. Visitors put things to their ears, such as seashells, or shook
them, such as a petrified egg, to hear the yolk rattle. There are also accounts
of visitors sniffing objects and even tasting some exhibits (particularly
popular in this connection were Chinese bird's nests and Egyptian mum-
mies). Such olfactory and gustatory exploration makes sense given that
smell and taste are chemical senses and therefore the only means by which
to ascertain the chemical composition (or "essence") of an item in the days
prior to laboratory testing.

Multimodal interaction with museum exhibits was thus the norm in the
early museum. This was mandated by contemporary scientific practice which
held, in the words of empirical philosopher Robert Hooke, that "ocular in-
spection" must be accompanied by the "manual handling . . . of the very
things themselves" (quoted in Classen, 2012: 141). But it was also prompted
by other notions, like the notion of "annihilating time and space" and entering
into direct contact with the original creator of some treasure through touching it, or the lingering notion that contact with extraordinary objects, like a
"unicorn's horn," could give one a "supernatural boost" (much like contact
with religious images and relics in centuries past).

All this changed in the nineteenth century with the emergence of what
Tony Bennett has called the "exhibitionary complex." The use of the nonvisual senses came to be seen as coarse, uncivilized, and even as potentially
damaging to the exhibits (in the case of touch) as objects came to matter more
than people with the spread of bourgeois values. Most seriously, the notion
took root "that touch had no cognitive or aesthetic uses and thus was of no
value in the museum, where only cognitive and aesthetic benefits were to
be sought" (Classen, 2012: 145). The cumulative result was that all that the
museum visitor could now expect "was to have a clear, well lit view of the
objects on display" (Classen, 2007: 907).

Alongside the demotion of the proximity senses there was the progressive
inculcation, through "prestigious imitation," of new ways of walking and looking, talking and sitting. As Rees Leahy brings out in *Museum Bodies*, learning
how to stand at the "correct" distance from an artwork, walking at a pace that is
neither too fast nor too slow, and knowing what to "feel" (without touching, of
course) are corporeal techniques that must be mastered if a museum visitor is to

display the requisite degree of cultural competence—and no one wants to look like a boor. The normative practices of attentive viewing and self-restrained comportment, which were the corollary of "the *institution* of the artwork as an object of contemplation" (Rees Leahy, 2012), resulted in the interposition of more and more distance between the average museum visitor and the work of art, whether there were physical barriers (a glass case, a rope) or not.

Throughout the modern period there nevertheless remained an elite class of individuals who were permitted to handle art—namely, connoisseurs, curators, and private collectors. These men, for they were typically men, and men of independent means at that, enjoyed a monopoly on handling art and were thus uniquely positioned to acquire and exercise the skills of identification and authentication that went with their station in society (Candlin, 2010: 101). However, the privilege enjoyed by the connoisseur and curator came under attack in the twentieth century due to its association with private ownership, when museums and their collections were supposed to belong to the public. In an extraordinary about-face, as debates about access raged in the 1970s and 1980s, expert object handling would fall into desuetude and, "tactual provision," first for the blind or partially sighted visitor and increasingly for "underrepresented audiences" (prisoners, hospital patients, and other disadvantaged groups) would become the new norm. Indeed, many museums have introduced touch tours, handling sessions, and handling tables as a matter of course.

Conservation remains an issue, perhaps even more of an issue now than previously, and the negotiations over access provision between the conservation and education branches of the museum can be quite protracted. Furthermore, with increased physical access to collections a whole new set of issues has arisen, which have to do with access to the *social and cultural significance* of objects—dimensions which cannot be accessed by handling alone, experts say (Candlin, 2010: 120). How is the sense of things to be sensed? Enter anthropology.

AESTHETICS IN CROSS-CULTURAL PERSPECTIVE

In many non-Western cultures, the aesthetic does not constitute an autonomous realm but is rather an aspect of everyday life and/or ritual practice, and the senses are not separated from each other but rather combine in specific ways to achieve specific purposes, such as healing (Howes and Classen, 2014). Two case studies in cross-cultural aesthetics are presented below. Each case discloses a slightly different manner of conjugating the senses.

HEALING ARTS OF THE SHIPIBO-CONIBO

Consider the highly intricate, geometric designs of the Shipibo-Conibo Indians of Peru, with their delicate traceries (for an illustration, see Gebhart-Sayer, 1985: 158; Howes, 1991: 7). These designs—which are said to originate in the markings of the cosmic serpent, Ronin—are woven into textiles, incised on pots and houseposts, painted on faces, and even recorded in folios (see Illius, 2002). However, their foremost use is in the context of Shipibo-Conibo healing rituals.

The Shipibo-Conibo understand medicine to be an art, literally, and their healing practices place a premium on synaesthesia in contrast to contemporary Western medical practice, which is more geared to the anaesthetization of the patient.

> One important condition of [Shipibo-Conibo] therapy is the aesthetically pleasing [*quiquin*] environment into which the shaman and the family place the patient. He is carefully surrounded by an ambience designed to appease both the senses and emotions. Visible and invisible geometric designs, melodious singing, and the fragrance from herbs and tobacco smoke pervade the atmosphere, and ritual purity characterizes his food and each person with whom he has contact. The patient is never left alone in the mosquito tent during the critical time of his illness. This setting induces in the patient the necessary emotional disposition for recovery. But how is this indigenous concept of aesthetics [*quiquin*] to be understood? (Gebhart-Sayer, 1985: 161)

The Shipibo-Conibo term *quiquin*, which means both aesthetic and appropriate, is used to refer to pleasant auditory and olfactory as well as visual sensations. Let us follow how the shaman operates with *quiquin*-ness on these three sensory levels—visual, auditory, and olfactory—and how they are "synaesthetically combined to form a therapy of beauty, cultural relevance, and sophistication" (Gebhart-Sayer, 1985: 162).

At the start of a healing session (there will be five such sessions in all), the shaman, under the influence of the ayahuasca hallucinogenic vine, sees the body of the patient "as if with an X-ray machine." A sick person's visual body pattern appears "like a very messy design," or mixed-up pile of garbage, and its pathological aura has a vile stench that is the mark of the attacking spirits (*nihue*) causing the illness. The healing ritual involves both the restoration of a healthy visual body pattern and the neutralization of the pathogenic aura through life-enhancing fragrance.

The shaman begins by brushing away the "mess" on the patient's body with his painted garment and fanning away the miasma of the attacking spirits with his fragrant herbal bundle, all the while blowing tobacco smoke.

He then takes up his rattle and beats a smelling rhythm: The air is now "full of aromatic tobacco smoke and the good scent of herbs." Following this, the shaman, still hallucinating, perceives whole "sheets" of luminescent geometric designs, drawn by the Hummingbird spirit, hovering in the air, which gradually descend to his lips. On reaching his lips the shaman sings the designs into songs. At the moment of coming into contact with the patient, the songs once again turn into designs that penetrate the patient's body and, ideally, "settle down permanently." However, the whole time the healing design is being sung onto the body of the patient, the *nihue* will "try to ruin the pattern by singing evil-smelling anti-songs dealing with the odor of gasoline, fish poison, dogs, certain products of the cosmetic industry, menstrual blood, unclean people, and so on" (Gebhart-Sayer, 1985: 171), and thereby smudge or contaminate it. This is why it may take up to five sessions for the design to come out "clear, neat, and complete," and the cure to be finished. (If the design does not settle down permanently, the patient is unlikely to recover.)

Another strategy commonly employed by the evil *nihue* to prevent the cure from taking is to seek out the shaman's medicine vessel, which contains all his design songs, and pry the lid off it. This causes the therapeutic power of the songs to escape. "This power is imagined as the fragrance of the design songs or the aromatic gas fizzing from fermenting yucca beer" (Gebhart-Sayer, 1985: 172). The design songs thus have an olfactory dimension, in addition to their visual one, as their power is understood to reside in their fragrance.

The synaesthetic interrelationships of the designs, songs, and fragrances used in Shipibo-Conibo healing rituals are nicely brought out in the following lines from a shamanic healing song:

> The (harmful) spirit pneuma
> swirling in your body's ultimate point.
> I shall tackle it right now
> with my fragrant chanting.
> [. . .]
> I see brilliant bands of designs,
> curved and fragrant . . .

> (Gebhart-Sayer, 1985: 172)

An important point to note here is that, whereas we perceive these designs as visual abstractions, the Shipibo-Conibo perceive them as matrices of intersensory perception, since these geometric designs are at the same time musical scores and perfume recipes. They resonate in each of the senses at once. They are not simply addressed to the eye.

THE FEEL OF PAINTING AMONG THE NAVAJO

Navajo sandpaintings have long been admired in the West as an ingenious, "primitive" form of visual art. However, as in the case of the Shipibo-Conibo design songs, sandpaintings are created by the Navajo for purposes of healing rather than aesthetic display. Sandpainting is the English term for a type of design executed by Navajo shamans. This design consists of iconic images of Navajo "holy people" created from dry colored pigments sprinkled on the sandy floor of the Navajo ceremonial house, or *hogan*. The chants sung by the shaman as he works call on the holy people to enter their representations in the sand.

A sandpainting is created to restore health or wholeness to an ailing member of the community. When the sandpainting is finished and alive with sacred power, its role is not yet completed. The patient must enter the ceremonial house and sit on the painting, or, in other words, integrate his or her own being with the sacred order manifested in the design. The shaman transfers the positive energy of the painting and the integrity of the sacred order it manifests to the patient by rubbing sand from the different parts of the picture onto the patient's body. After the ritual is finished the sandpainting is swept away (Gill, 1982: 63).

While the importance of the sandpainting for the Navajo lies in its ability to channel healing power and to affirm Navajo cosmological beliefs, it has primarily been appreciated by Westerners as an exotic counterpart to a Western painting (Witherspoon, 1977: 152). From this perspective the sandpainting becomes something to see and not something to feel. This change in sensory priorities results in dramatic violations of the Navajo ritual rules according to which the sandpainting was originally created. (The Navajo notion of sitting on a painting, of course, dramatically violates Western protocol.) In order to make the sandpainting a proper object for the Western eye it must be made more visually accessible. Within the Navajo hogan, one would only have a dim side view of the painting, for there would be no way to see the design in its entirety from above. In order to "rectify" this, Westerners have tried several approaches. One is to photograph the sandpainting looking down from the hole in the hogan's roof—a viewpoint that the Navajo themselves would never adopt, as this hole is believed to be the entry point for the spirits. Another is to have the Navajo create sandpaintings on canvasses covered with glue. When the glue dries the canvas can be lifted upright and the sandpainting can be mounted on a wall, just like a "real" painting (Parezco, 1983: 31, 39).

Not only do such practices alienate Navajo sandpaintings from their original sensory and cultural context, they also contravene the Navajo tradition that sandpaintings must be swept away by sundown of the day in which they are made. The goal is to feel the sandpaintings, to integrate their power into one's own body, and then to scatter them to the winds, not to try to preserve them indefinitely as visual objects. Blindness, in fact, was held to be the punishment for looking at the sacred symbols for too long (Parezco, 1983: 38, 48).

SENSORY SELECTION IN THE EVOLUTION OF WESTERN ART

Western artists have, occasionally, derived inspiration from their exposure to the artistic creations of non-Western cultures. One of the most famous examples of such cultural borrowing (and concomitant transformation of primitive craft into fine art) is Pablo Picasso's *Les demoiselles d'Avignon* (1907). This work, from Picasso's Cubist period, stands at a critical juncture in the evolution of Western art, since it broke so decisively with the tradition of linear perspective vision that had dominated Western painting for centuries. As John Berger remarks: "For the Cubists, the visible was no longer what confronted the single eye, but the totality of possible views taken from points all around the person (or object) being depicted" (Berger, 1972: 39). It is apparent from the masklike faces of two of the figures in *Les demoiselles d'Avignon* that a major impetus behind Picasso's experimentation with multiperspectival vision was the ostensibly multiperspectival design (or "proto-Cubist morphology") of the African tribal masks and other sculptures that he encountered during his visits to the Musée Trocadéro at a critical stage in his work on the "demoiselles d'Avignon" project (Rubin, 1984). The question arises of whether Picasso would ever have developed multiperspectival vision to the extent he did had it not been for the jolt to his visual system that he got from his exposure to these masks due to their having become objects of cross-cultural consumption.

Cultural border-crossing was also the impetus behind Jackson Pollock's invention of "color field" or "action painting." Pollock was deeply influenced by his exposure to Navajo works of art, both as a youth and in many subsequent trips to the Southwest from his base in New York. He took the practice of painting on an unstretched canvas on the floor, instead of an easel, from the Navajo: "On the floor I am at ease. I feel nearer, more a part of the painting, since that way I can walk around it, work from the four sides and literally be 'in' the painting. This is akin to the method of the Indian sand painters of the West" (quoted in Witherspoon, 1977: 175–76). "Like Navajo artists," Witherspoon (1977: 177) writes, "Pollock tried to express forcefulness, energy, and motion without the loss of order, balance and control." His canvases thus come across as "energized surfaces" and have the same temporary quality as

a sandpainting (i.e., they do not age well, much to the chagrin of those curators charged with conserving them).

Both of these momentous mutations in the evolution of Western art may
be analyzed as a product of the *selective* appropriation of non-Western
techniques of representation—that is, of cultural borrowing (though "borrowing" is perhaps too benign a word). The appropriations in question
were selective in the sense that Pollock elided the tactility and dynamic
symmetry of Navajo sandpainting in the process of converting it into his
own unique style, while Picasso captured the plasticity but effaced the
rhythmicity of African tribal art. (In African cultures, masks are for dancing, not displaying, and their apparently "distorted" morphology is rooted in
the rhythms of African culture, not simply their look [see Howes, 1991: 20,
n. 6].) Thus, while the incorporation of non-Western elements into Western
art has contributed significantly to the development of new artistic styles, it
has not done much to expand the sensory repertoire of Western art works,
or alter their mode of display within the museum.

SENSING A PAINTING

It is unlikely that a Western art historian would gain much insight from trying
to listen to a painting by Picasso, or feel a canvas by Jackson Pollock, though
an African carver might be capable of doing so in the case of a Picasso, and
a Navajo sandpainter might succeed in doing so in the case of a Pollock. This
would be consistent with the sensory dispositions of their respective cultures
of origin. More to the point, it would scarcely occur to a Western art historian to engage in such a cross-sensory analysis of a painting, because there is
nothing in the art historian's training that would dispose them to adopt such
a multimodal approach to the appreciation of a canvas. Painting is, after all,
a branch of "visual culture," not "aural culture" nor "haptic culture"—or so
it is supposed. However, the falsity of this supposition should already be
apparent from the cross-cultural perspective on aesthetics that we have been
developing in this chapter. The practice of rubbing a patient with the grains of
a sandpainting among the Navajo, or the fragrant design songs of the Shipibo-
Conibo, represent examples of crossing sensory borders in the arts. The key
to the appreciation of each of these art forms lies in learning how to combine—or better, *conjugate*—the senses in a culturally appropriate manner.

These examples could be multiplied from outside the tradition of Western
art, but also from within. As Constance Classen has shown in *The Color of
Angels* (1998), the key to comprehending the art of the Symbolists, Surreal-
ists, and Futurists lies in attending to the interplay of the senses in their work.

And one need not stop at the Futurists, for it emerges that the trend toward abstraction that came to define much twentieth-century art is best understood from a multimodal perspective. For example, it would appear that it was the aspiration to create "visual music" that provided the impetus behind many of the earliest (and still finest) expressions of "non-representational" art, such as Wassily Kandinsky's *Fugue* (1914) or Georgia O'Keefe's *Blue and Green Music* (1921) (see Brougher et al., 2005). Thus, in art appreciation, as in most things in life, two senses are better than one. To grasp the inner sense of a Kandinsky or an O'Keefe, it behooves the art historian to develop a good ear as well as a discerning eye.

Of course, most abstract art consists of so many patterns on a windowpane and there is no music, much less a garden, behind it (to refer to Redfield's analogy). Nevertheless, I would submit that the multimodal approach we have been elaborating here has far more to commend it than does the conventional unimodal approach of "looking at pictures"—or worse still, looking at things in the world as one would look at a picture. Consider *How to Use Your Eyes*. This treatise, by James Elkins, professor at the School of the Art Institute of Chicago, consists of thirty-two chapters dedicated to teaching us "how to look" at manmade and natural objects ranging from postage stamps to sunsets. Elkins' approach is profoundly revealing, but at the same time curiously stultifying insofar as the nonvisual senses are concerned. "For me," Elkins writes,

> looking is a kind of pure pleasure—it takes me out of myself and lets me think only of what I am seeing. Also, there is a pleasure in discovering these things. It is good to know that the visual world is more than television, movies, and art museums, and it is especially good to know that the world is full of fascinating things that can be seen at leisure, when you are by yourself and there is nothing to distract you. Seeing is, after all, a soundless activity. It isn't talking, or listening, or smelling, or touching. It happens best in solitude, when there is nothing in the world but you and the object of your attention (Elkins, 2000: xi)

In view of the case studies discussed in this essay, we have to deny absolutely the ability of Professor Elkins to enjoy plastic works aesthetically.

The last sentence deliberately echoes Géza Révész's pronouncement concerning the aesthetic capabilities of the blind quoted at the beginning of this essay. We can now perceive how Révész's judgment (like Elkins' "pure pleasure") is predicated on a narrow, visualist definition of the aesthetic, which is simply not tenable from the cross-cultural perspective elaborated here. The aesthetic is not to be defined one sense at a time (for painting, for music, for architecture, etc.). Rather, the aesthetic arises at the *intersection* of the senses, as we have come to understand through delving into the original meaning of this concept in Baumgarten's work, along with our own brief investigations into the varieties of aesthetic experience across cultures. And aesthetic experience is, in principle, open to anyone, whatever their particular complement of senses might be. One need not be sighted to enjoy a Shipibo-Conibo geometric design, since its inner sense is equally accessible through its accompanying song and fragrance. A similar point is made by neuropsychologist Oliver Sacks in "The Mind's Eye: What the Blind See" (2004), where he discusses the cases of John Hull who, on falling blind, "shift[ed] his attention, his center of gravity, to the other senses" and became a "whole-body seer"; the case of the blind biologist Geerat Vermeij, who has been able to "delineate many new species of mollusk, based on tiny variations in the shapes and contours of their shells"; and Sabriye Tenberken who, though she has been blind for twenty years, "continues to use all her other senses, along with verbal descriptions, visual memories, and a strong pictorial and synesthetic sensibility, to construct 'pictures' of landscapes and rooms, of environments and scenes, pictures so lively and detailed as to astonish her listeners" (Sacks, 2004: 26, 28, 32). In all these cases, blindness is no barrier to having an aesthetic experience.

THE MULTIMODAL VISION OF ART EDUCATION FOR THE BLIND

The multimodal approach to art appreciation advocated here is consonant with the philosophy of Art Education for the Blind (AEB), which has made it its mission to render the classics of Western art accessible to the visually impaired.

Consider the following scenario. The visitor to a contemporary art museum who stands in front of an abstract painting is faced with much the same predicament, whether sighted or blind. Neither is able to perceive anything through the windowpane of the painting. However, while it may not be possible for either party to perceive anything beyond the surface of the painting, much could transpire in the space *in front* of the painting. For example, a tactile model of the painting could be provided for the visitor to touch, so they might feel the relationships between the figures or forms. A verbal description and/or clip of music could be supplied for them to hear. Another possibility would be for the visitor to assume the same poses as each of the figures (or other elements) in the painting—to dance the painting, as it were. In this way the visitor would internalize the relations kinaesthetically. In the case of blind visitors, a docent would help position their limbs and guide them through the motions.

All of the above strategies (and more) were discussed at the Art Beyond Sight conferences I have attended—testimony to the extraordinary inventiveness of those who involve themselves in art education for the blind. Interestingly, it was reported by one delegate at the 2008 conference that sighted visitors found their experience of a painting to be enriched when they were able to simultaneously view and explore a painting manually with the aid of a tactile model. This strategy helped focus their attention on aspects of the work that they might otherwise have missed and also compelled them to spend longer in front of a work and thus come to appreciate it more. The point here is that the experience of a painting need not be mediated by sight alone, as if its visual surface were the only sensory dimension that mattered. The painting itself may represent a transposition of an auditory or tactile experience into a visual one (as in the case of a painting by Kandinsky or a Navajo sandpainting), and even if it doesn't, there is no intrinsic reason not to enlist other sensory channels in one's perception of it by constructing a multisensory model of its topology in the intervening space between the painting and the perceiver.

Art Education for the Blind has produced various kits (both in box form and online) to enable the visually impaired to experience the masterworks of Western art through nonvisual channels. Consider their rendition of Marcel Duchamp's *Nude Descending a Staircase, no. 2* (1912). In the tactile diagram devoted to this painting in *Art History Through Touch and Sound, European Modernism: 1900–1940* (Art Education for the Blind, 1999), Duchamp's work has been broken down into a composition of raised lines of varying thickness, areas of raised dots of varying size, and areas of cross-hatching, and so on, to convey a sense of the interlocking planes and directionality of the painting. The perceiver grasps the structure and movement of the painting through running his or her fingertips over its surface, guided by the narrative on the accompanying audiocassette. At one point on the cassette, a staccato melody is heard, which aptly conveys the machinelike motion of the figure in the painting. It will be appreciated how the tactile and sonic dimensions of this rendition would appeal to the Navajo shaman and African carver, confirming impressions they would already have taken from the painting, consistent with the sensory dispositions of their respective cultures to feel and hear before seeing. In the case of the blind or sighted Western perceiver of this work, the tactile and sonic cues would serve as an alternative mode of entering into its composition. The Shipibo-Conibo shaman would likely demand more, however, for this rendition lacks an olfactory track. It should not prove too difficult to add one, though, since Duchamp was notoriously fascinated by scent (see Drobnick, 2005). One could study some of the smellworks he created to develop an appreciation for his olfactory style, and then create a smell track for *Nude Descending* based on the results of that analysis.

The next work I, personally, would like to see AEB render in "multimodal vision" (if such a phrase be permitted) is the Spanish Surrealist artist

Remedios Varo's painting *The Creation of the Birds* (1958). Varo's painting is the one of the finest examples I know of the conjugation of the senses, or crossing sensory borders in the arts. (I had the privilege of being allowed by Varo's widower to use *Creation of the Birds* on the cover of the book *Sensual Relations* [Howes 2003].) In the painting, an owllike figure sits at a desk with a canvas spread out before her. In her left hand she holds a prism that focuses a moonbeam (streaming into the chamber through the window over her left shoulder) onto the canvas. In her right hand there is a paintbrush that is attached by a cord to the violin suspended from her neck. A tube (which enters the chamber from the window over her right shoulder) is attached to an alchemical vessel, which appears to be converting the fragrant night air sucked in by the tube into the color pigments on her pallette. The bird she paints is lifting off the canvas, while two other birds have already taken flight and escape (back) into the night through yet another window (see further, Kaplan 1988; Classen 1998: 133–37).

The mode of presentation of Varo's painting, with its emphasis on engaging all the senses, is consonant with its content, which is about the creation of birds as living beings, not simply their depiction as specimens the way, say, John Audubon painted them. (In fact, Audubon worked from dead specimens). *The Creation of the Birds* is a painting which, like music, is supposed to fill the air, rather than remain a windowpane. To fulfill its vocation would therefore involve rather more than hanging it in a gallery. The gallery would need to be reconfigured as a sort of sensory gymnasium, in place of the conventional "white cube" or mausoleum. In particular, the gallery would need to be equipped with a smell track keyed to the color scheme of the birds' plumage, and a soundtrack that blends the chirping of the birds with the strands of a violin melody, and an air conditioning system that evokes the flutter of the birds' wings. That is what Varo's painting wants, and also what Art Education for the Blind wants for all of us, sighted and unsighted alike.

ACKNOWLEDGMENTS

This chapter is based in part on research carried out for "The Sensory Museum" project, which was funded by a grant from the Social Science and Humanities Research Council of Canada (no. 410-2007-2038). Part of this chapter was previously published in *Empire of the Senses: The Sensual Culture Reader* (ed. David Howes 2004) from Berg Publishers, an imprint of Bloomsbury Publishing Plc. It is used with the permission of the publisher. The section on the healing arts of the Shipibo-Conibo is derived from my essay "The Aesthetics of Mixing the Senses" (n.d.), which is an Occasional

Paper of the Centre for Sensory Studies. See http://www.centreforsensory studies.org/occasional-papers/.

REFERENCES

Art Education for the Blind. (1999). *Art History Through Touch & Sound, A Multi-sensory Guide for the Blind and Visually Impaired. European Modernism: 1900-1940*. Louisville: American Printing House for the Blind.

Bennett, T. (1995). *The Birth of the Museum: History, Theory, Politics*. London: Routledge.

Berger, J. (1972). *Ways of Seeing*. London: BBC.

Brougher, K., Mattis, O., Strick, J., Wiseman, A. and Zilzcer, J. (2005). *Visual Music: Synaesthesia in Art and Music Since 1900*. London: Thames & Hudson,

Candlin, F. (2010). *Art, Museums and Touch*. Manchester: Manchester University Press.

Classen, C. (1993). *Worlds of Sense: Exploring the Senses in History and Across Cultures*. London and New York: Routledge.

———. (1997). Foundations for an anthropology of the senses. *International Social Science Journal*, 153, 401–12.

———. (1998). *The Color of Angels: Cosmology, Gender and the Aesthetic Imagina-tion*. London and New York: Routledge.

———. (2005). Touch in the early museum. In C. Classen (ed.), *The Book of Touch*, 275–86. Oxford: Berg.

———. (2007). Museum manners: The sensory life of the early museum. *Journal of Social History* (Summer): 895–914

———. (2012). *The Deepest Sense: A Cultural History of Touch*. Champaign, IL: University of Illinois Press.

Classen, C. and Howes, D. (2006). The museum as sensescape: western sensibilities and indigenous artifacts. In E. Edwards, C. Gosden and R. Phillips (eds.), *Sensible Objects*, 199–222. Oxford: Berg.

Classen, C., Howes, D. and Synnott. A. (1994). *Aroma: The Cultural History of Smell*. London and New York: Routledge.

Drobnick, J. (2004). Volatile effects: olfactory dimensions of art and architecture. In D. Howes (ed.), *Empire of the Senses: The Sensual Culture Reader*. Oxford: Berg.

———. (2005). *Olfactory Dimensions of Modern and Contemporary Art*. Ph.D. dis-sertation, Concordia University.

Elkins, J. (2000). *How To Use Your Eyes*. New York: Routledge.

Gebhart-Sayer, A. (1985). The geometric designs of the Shipibo-Conibo in ritual context. *Journal of Latin-American Lore*, 11(2), 143–75.

Gill, S. (1982). *Native American Religions: An Introduction*, Belmont, CA: Wadsworth.

Gregor, M. J. (1983). Baumgarten's Aesthetica. *Review of Metaphysics*, 37, 357–85.

Howes, D., ed. (1991). *The Varieties of Sensory Experience: A Source Book in the Anthropology of the Senses*. Toronto: University of Toronto Press.

———. (2003). *Sensual Relations: Engaging the Senses in Culture and Social Theory*. Ann Arbor: University of Michigan Press.

———, ed. (2004). *Empire of the Senses: The Sensual Culture Reader*. Oxford: Berg.

———. (2006a). Scent, sound and synesthesia: Intersensoriality and material culture theory. In Christopher Tilley, Webb Keane, Susanne Küchler, Michael Rowlands and Patricia Spyer (eds.), *Handbook of Material Culture*, 161–72. London: Sage.

———. (2006b). Cross talk between the senses. *The Senses & Society*, 1(3), 381–90.

Howes, David. (2010). Hearing scents, tasting sights: toward a cross-cultural multi-modal theory of aesthetics. In Francesca Bacci and David Mellon (eds.), *Art and the Senses*, 161–82. Oxford: Oxford University Press.

Howes, D. and Classen, C. (2014). *Ways of Sensing: Understanding the Senses in Society*. London: Routledge

Illius, B. (2002). *Una ventana hacia el infinito: arte shipibo-conibo*. Lima: Instituto Cultural Peruano Norteamericano.

Jones, C. (2008). *Eyesight Alone: Clement Greenberg's Modernism and the Bureaucratization of the Senses*. Chicago: University of Chicago Press.

Kant, Immanuel. (1790, 1987). *Critique of Judgment*, translated by W. Pluhar. Indianapolis, IN: Hackett Publishing Co.

Kaplan, J. A. (1988). *Unexpected Journeys: The Art and Life of Remedios Varo*. New York: Abbeville Press.

Kirshenblatt-Gimblett, B. (1989). *Destination Culture*. Berkeley: University of California Press.

Marinetti, F. (1989). *The Futurist Cookbook*, translated by Suzanne Brill. New York: Bedford Books.

———. (2005). Tactilism. In C. Classen (ed.), *The Book of Touch*. Oxford: Berg.

Morgan, M. J. (1977). *Molyneux's Question: Vision, Touch and the Philosophy of Perception*. Cambridge: Cambridge University Press.

Osborne, H. (1984). The cultivation of sensibility in art education. *Journal of Philosophy of Education*, 18(1), 31–40.

Parezco, N. J. (1983). *Navajo Sandpainting: From Religious Act to Commercial Art*. Tucson: University of Arizona Press.

Redfield, R. (1971). Art and icon. In Charlotte Otten (ed.), *Anthropology and Art*, 74–92. New York: Natural History Press.

Rée, J. (2000). The aesthetic theory of the arts. In P. Osborne, (ed.), *From an Aesthetic Point of View*. London: Serpent's Tail.

Rees Leahy, H. (2012). *Museum Bodies*. Aldershot: Ashgate Publishing.

Révész, G. (1950). *Psychology and Art of the Blind*, trans. H. A.Wolff. London: Longman, Greens and Co.

Rubin, W. (1984). Picasso. In W. Rubin (ed.), *Primitivism in 20th Century Art: Affinities of the Tribal and the Modern*, vol. I, 241–333. New York: Museum of Modern Art.

Sacks, O. (2004). The mind's eye: what the blind see. In D. Howes, (ed.), *Empire of the Senses*. Oxford: Berg.

Witherspoon, G. (1977). *Language and Art in the Navajo Universe*. Ann Arbor: University of Michigan Press.

19

Multisensory Mental Simulation and Aesthetic Perception

Salvatore Maria Aglioti, Ilaria Bufalari, and Matteo Candidi

Our perception of the world is driven by the integration of the information processed by our different sensory systems: vision, audition, touch, taste, and smell (Fetsch et al., 2013). However, far from being exclusively determined by the external world (bottom-up variables), perception is strongly modulated by our previous knowledge, understanding, and internal predictions/expectations (top-down variables: Vartanian and Kaufman, 2013). For example, our "perception" of eating an apple is not only determined by the unique firmness, redness, and eating. The influence of top-down variables on single-sensory experience and multisensory integration is fundamental when recalling personal memories (representing objects of the world when they are no longer present: mental imagery) as well as when internally simulating and, accordingly, understanding the physical and mental states of other individuals (Gallese, 2007).

Top-down modulation may be even more important for the perception of aesthetics: the human ability to feel and sense objects in the world and assign them a positive or negative value along a continuum between beauty and ugliness. Put another way, appraisal of beauty and ugliness may depend on both the physical experience of the object being judged and the internal cognitive/emotional *reaction* based on prior life experiences. Similar psychological processes likely apply to appraisal of objects of art.

Theories of embodied cognition suggest that perception, mental imagery, and aesthetic appraisal are inherently related to the physical body. Thus, aesthetic appraisal and appreciation likely depend on our bodily sensations and the way we use our body to interact with objects and individuals (Aglioti et al., 2012). Under these theories, aesthetic appreciation is intimately linked to the human body and its physical sensations as engendered by an object itself, and internal memories of similar sensations as engendered by prior objects and experiences. For example, exposure to a unique sculpture may cause the body to feel certain physical sensations similar to those felt in a previous, unrelated situation, such as curling up in a soft blanket by a warm fire or drinking a cold beverage too fast. Although engendered by different objects/situations, these similar physical sensations likely trigger similar neural networks and, accordingly, may be intimately integrated at a neural level. Therefore, perceiving the ineffable properties of art objects may lead to changes in bodily feelings that mirror effable properties of physical objects or bodily sensations.

SIMULATION AND EMBODIMENT

According to standard cognitive theories, higher-order mental processes (such as the ability to read and understand another individual's actions and/ or intentions) are activated independent of specific sensory systems (termed "amodal" activation) and are driven by neural systems largely unrelated to sensory and motor networks (Pylyshyn, 1984; Fodor, 1983). Mounting evidence, though, suggests that these higher-order mental processes may, in fact, rely on and be driven (in part) by physical senses and sensory networks (Barsalou, 2008). The bodily instantiation of cognitive operations is called "embodiment," and the internal reproduction of others' mental and emotional states is called "simulation" (Gallese, 2007).

Philosophers and cognitive neuroscientists who embrace embodied cognition theories posit that many features of cognition and higher-order mental processes are made up of experiences of the physical body and actions of an agent. Even apparently abstract operations, such as semantics and syntax, may be composed of bodily sensation, may be reflected in changes of body representation, and may be considered embodied (Lakoff and Johnson, 1999). Similar mental representations of unique physical sensations between individuals may underpin linguistic and sensorimotor processes. Support for this simulation account of language processing comes from studies on action simulation and posits that the automatic and rapid reactivation of the sensorimotor copy of an action is crucial for understanding its meaning. Put another way, in order to understand the word "up," one must activate the neural networks responsible for processing the physical sensation of moving up (whether via jumping, using an elevator, ascending in a hot air balloon, or anything similar).

Physiological support for embodied theories, particularly with regards to movement and motor cognition, is provided by the striking finding that neurons within a monkey's brain that fire when the monkey performs a specific movement (motor execution) are also activated when said monkey watches a *different* monkey perform a similar movement (motor observation: Rizzolatti and Craighero, 2004). Several studies suggest this pattern is also present in humans; namely, similar neural regions activate both when one performs an action and when one observes another perform a similar action (Mukamel et al., 2010; Rizzolatti and Craighero, 2004). Moreover, neural resonance with observed actions had been suggested by functional neuroimaging methods like fMRI (Kilner et al., 2009) and by noninvasive brain stimulation procedures like repetitive transcranial magnetic stimulation techniques (Avenanti et al., 2013). Beyond watching another perform an action, similar brain activation has been seen when people *hear* the sounds associated with a specific motor action (Aglioti and Pazzaglia, 2011) and when people simply *imagine* another performing a specific motor action (Fourkas et al., 2006; 2008; Bufalari et al., 2010). These results suggest that simulation is multisensory in nature, utilizing vision, sound, and likely other sensory modalities.

Simulations linked to interactions with the world and other individuals (known as *action resonance*) are intimately linked with aesthetics. Think for example of the notion of *Einfühlung,* or aesthetic empathy introduced by Theodore Lipps (1903) to indicate the experiences of individuals while contemplating pieces of artwork, and to the domain of intersubjectivity as inherently linked to an inner imitation process (Di Dio and Gallese, 2009; Freedberg and Gallese 2007). A key consequence of this view is that art appreciation is inherently sensorimotor. Put another way, the experience of art may rely intimately on unique physical and motor sensations and the internal (covert) activation of neural networks responsible for these physical and motor sensations.

In sum, recent cognitive neuroscience research supports embodied cognition theories, according to which virtually any type of experiential knowledge is grounded in the brain's systems for perception, action, and affect (Barsalou, 2008). Although strong forms of grounded cognition might not grasp the complexity of the issue of whether cognition is necessarily embodied, and how it is reflected in sensorimotor activations (Mahon and Caramazza, 2008), studies suggest that higher-order cognitive processes, such as understanding others' intentions from observing their actions, emotions, and sensations, may trigger the automatic *simulation* of the others' states as reflected in neural activity within the sensory, motor, and emotional circuits of the onlooker's brain (Barsalou, 2008; Keysers et al., 2010).

MULTISENSORY PERCEPTION, MENTAL IMAGERY IN DIFFERENT SENSORY MODALITIES, AND SIMULATION

The traditional view that sensory inputs in a given modality (visual, auditory, tactile-proprioceptive, gustatory, olfactory) are processed along isolated sensory-specific streams is now considered somewhat obsolete (Spence and Parise, 2012). It makes perfect sense that in our daily life, our sensory systems interact continuously to process objects, people, and places. A common example of this is the change in taste when one's sense of smell is altered by a cold. The notion that we analyze the world according to inherently multisensory rules applies also to seemingly disparate senses. The case of well-known audiovisual illusions, like the McGurk or ventriloquist effects, speaks in favor of the frequent occurrence of multisensory interaction and integration. Studies indicate that brain regions previously considered to be specialized for various aspects of visual processing are also activated during passive tactile or active haptic tasks (Sathian et al., 1997; Costantini et al., 2011). Although each sensory channel might use unique brain regions to perform the initial analysis of a stimulus, the ultimate *evaluation* of said stimulus requires activity in sensory independent brain regions associated with the determination of value and reward. As such, multisensory integration is fundamental for achieving a full appreciation of a given stimulus (Jacobsen, 2010; Freedberg and Gallese, 2007; Lacey et al., 2011).

Humans not only perceive the external world but can also represent it via mental imagery, a function that makes possible quasi-perceptual experiences occurring in the absence of external stimuli, likely central to inventive and creative thinking. Mental images are fundamentally influenced by emotions, and it is not surprising that thinking with images is at the very core of artistic cognition (Arnheim, 1969). That the ability to generate mental images is closely linked to artistic training is suggested by studies in which students with training in studio art were better at producing mental images than untrained novices (Pérez-Fabello et al., 2007).

One fundamental distinction between perceiving and imagining is that while sensory input is crucial for the former, it is absent in the latter. Importantly, mental images are not necessarily mere recall of previously perceived objects, people, or events. Mental images can be created by combining and modifying stored perceptual information in novel ways, allowing for individuals to "see with the mind's eye" or "hear with the mind's ear" (Moulton and Kosslyn, 2009). Unlike perceptual aftereffects (e.g., auditory distortion occurring after prolonged auditory stimulation) or hallucinations, mental images can be called up in one's own mind as a result of a voluntary act and are, thus, at least partly under conscious control. Think, for example, of expert musicians who can recall at will a given piece of music. Although imagery is inherently a private affair, the contents of which are entirely subjective and thus difficult to study objectively, the advent of functional imaging has allowed researchers to investigate changes in neural activity during different forms of sensory and motor imagery (Albright, 2012). The existence of specific neurons that fire when one "imagines" has been directly demonstrated in the human brain (Kreiman et al., 2000).

While most of the classical studies of mental imagery were performed in the visual and auditory domain, there is evidence to suggest one can form olfactory, gustatory, and somatosensory images and, thus, have the experience of "smelling, tasting and feeling with the mind's nose, tongue and skin" (McNorgan, 2012). It is also worth noting that one can form mental images specifically concerning the actions of other individuals. Functional imaging studies indicate a certain degree of overlap between perceptual and imagery processes in both sensory and motor domains (McNorgan, 2012). The overlap, however, is not complete. Studies in brain damaged patients indicate, for example, that visual imagery deficits can occur *independently* from deficits of visual perception (Moro et al., 2008). Also, deficits of visual imagery typically occur without any related deficit in auditory, tactile, gustatory, olfactory, and/or motor imagery (Moro et al., 2008). In sum, multisensory integration is of great importance for both perception and imagery. It is worth noting that, while visual imagery is an ability largely shared by many individuals, mental imagery linked to other senses may be acquired or strengthened only through effortful learning (e.g., proprioceptive imagery in tennis players is stronger than in non-sports players: Fourkas et al., 2008).

EMBODIED AND "EMBRAINED" BEAUTY AND ART

Combining philosophical and psychological concepts, experimental aesthetics attempts to reduce the possible lexical ambiguities inherent to the complexity of the topic. While "aesthetic preference" is used to refer to the degree to which people *like* a particular stimulus or not, how much they prefer it to another, or how they rate its beauty, "aesthetic judgment" is used to refer to the assessment someone does of the aesthetic or *artistic value* of a certain stimulus (McWhinnie, 1968). Thus, one can place a positive aesthetic judgment on a piece of art whilst not maintaining an aesthetic preference for it.

The experimental approach to aesthetics has also to take into account the issue of the impact of subjectivity and objectivity on perception and appreciation of art. The Kantian Universalist approach to aesthetics suggests the existence of invariants that can be scientifically explored (Conway and Rehding, 2013) and supports the objectivist theories of beauty. These theories maintain that aesthetic experience depends on general qualities of a stimulus such as symmetry, balance, complexity, and order (Jacobsen et al., 2004). Research inspired by objectivist theories is based on the attempt to find predictive mathematical formulae that describe the possible relation between certain attributes of an artistic stimulus and individuals' evaluative reactions to them. Although attractively simple, this approach does not take into account emotional, sensual, or any other subjective dimensions of art (Conway and Rehding, 2013). Conversely, the notion of individual variation in aesthetic preference is at the basis of subjectivist theories, which posit that beauty "is in the eye of the beholder" and is largely based on the interplay between individual tastes and preferences and experiential and cultural factors (Zajonc, 1968). In keeping, scholars have long acknowledged that aesthetic experience is exquisitely human, is present in virtually all cultures, and is influenced by historical, evolutionary, and adaptive (e.g., the need to find suitable mates) variables (Jacobsen, 2010).

The strength and ubiquity of aesthetic preference in humans seem to indicate that this phenomenon plays a sociocultural role in addition to its fundamental personal role. While group-based dynamics certainly play a role in shaping our sense of what is beautiful and ugly, individual differences in personality, neural anatomy, and psychology have attracted increasing attention in recent years as well. Aesthetic experience implies that viewing a valued object induces sensory, intellectual, and emotional gratification or repulsion. Thus, when studying what we *feel* when experiencing objects of positive and negative aesthetic evaluation, societal and cultural influences as well as individual dispositions must be taken into account. The combination of all these influences may shape not only the psychological (individual taste), but also the physiological (changes in the body) and neural (changes in the brain) response to a piece of art.

Exploring the mechanisms underlying the various reactions to art is at the core of neuroaesthetics (Ishizu and Zeki, 2011; 2013). In recent years, researchers interested in this newly developed cognitive neuroscience domain have focused on the analysis of the bodily and neural activity associated with feelings of pleasure or displeasure generated by either cognitive or sensual interaction with a wide variety of objects (which may be thought of as "art" objects). The theoretical framework of this discipline derives from the notion that aesthetics can be explored and ultimately understood by referring to the principles of the organization and functioning of the brain. The pioneers in the field started by drawing parallels between the concerns and techniques of artists, on one side, and the organization of the visual brain on the other (Zeki, 1999; Ramachandran and Hirstein, 1999). Additionally, important insights into visual arts have come from comparing the work of a given artist before and after damage to the visual system (Chatterjie, 2004; Blanke and Pasqualini, 2011) or to the brain in general (Cantagallo and Della Sala, 1998).

Most neuroimaging studies have focused on brain activity induced by aesthetic appreciation through the visual sensory system, though an increasing number of studies are being conducted which aim at investigating brain activity induced by aesthetic appreciation through nonvisual sensory modalities (Brown et al., 2011). Brown et al. (2011) looked at a number of existing studies exploring brain activation associated with positive aesthetic appreciation of stimuli across four different senses (vision, olfaction, gustation, audition) and found that although each sense activates unique, sensory-specific brain regions, the right anterior insula—a brain region crucial for the evaluation of one's own visceral and internal state—is commonly activated, regardless of which sense is being explored. From this, it has been suggested that the insula may be involved in objective beauty representation (Di Dio et al., 2007) by determining if a given object of aesthetic appreciation will satisfy or oppose our homeostatic needs, regardless of the sense used to perceive the stimulus. In addition, Ishizu and Zeki (2011) found that the orbitofrontal cortex—a brain region involved in emotion and reward processing—plays a common role in the aesthetic appreciation of visual and auditory stimuli. The activity in this region correlates with the subjective experience of beauty intensity (the more beautiful one finds a stimuli, the more active this brain region will be). Since at least two complex and separate brain regions may be responsible for the essence of aesthetic experience, the model of a single neural locus for aesthetic appreciation does not seem tenable.

Particularly relevant to the notion of embodied and embrained aesthetics are studies focusing on human bodies as objects of aesthetic experience. Since the body plays a fundamental role in social interaction, distinct features of its aesthetic appreciation include both personal and interpersonal/communicative dimensions. Undeniably, the body is the medium for the expression of many forms of art, ranging from dance to tattoos. Explicit and implicit perception and appreciation of bodies along the like/dislike aesthetic dimension is a fundamental adaptive process that has previously been suggested to be the precursor of attractiveness and the beauty/ugly perceptive and perceptuoaffective dimensions (Thornhill and Gangestad, 1999).

That the perception of human bodies has a great importance for humans is also highlighted by the presence of a large but rather specific cortical network dedicated to its representation (Berlucchi and Aglioti, 2010). This network includes unique brain regions that activate in the visual presence of specific bodily or facial features; such as the extrastriate body area (which activates when looking at or visually imagining a human body) (Urgesi et al., 2007a; Urgesi et al., 2007b; Downing et al., 2001) or the fusiform face area (which activates when looking at or visually imagining a human face). In keeping with the notion that our perception and representation of the world is inherently multisensory (Pascual-Leone and Hamilton, 2001) is that the extrastriate body area also activates when perceiving body shapes by tactile exploration (Costantini et al., 2011). An intuitively appealing idea is that the activation of visual brain regions during haptic perception reflects visual imagery (Sathian et al., 1997): When feeling an object, one naturally "visually" imagines what it might look like. Therefore, the link between tactile perception and visual imagery has to be taken into account when considering multisensory integration as a tool for improving aesthetic appreciation. The extrastriate body area has been shown to be more active during observation of dancing body stimuli that are rated as the most beautiful (Calvo-Merino et al., 2008) and the most difficult to physically reproduce (Cross et al., 2011). Also, inhibition of the extrastriate body area activity reduced perceived beauty of body images (Calvo-Merino et al., 2010). Tellingly, an opposite pattern of results was obtained after inhibition of ventral premotor cortical activity, suggesting that appreciation of the beauty of the body is inherently sensorimotor in nature (Calvo-Merino et al., 2010). It is also worth noting that specific and inherent aspects of the body, such as the movement implied by body stimuli, are coded in sensorimotor regions (e.g., the somatosensory cortex and the ventral premotor cortex) that are known to be involved in the vicarious experience of what is observed in others (embodied simulation: Gallese, 2007; Avenanti et al., 2007; Keysers et al., 2010).

The idea that *rewarding* aspects of a stimulus are part of its aesthetic appraisal is also proposed within the framework of the embodied simulation theory of aesthetic perception (Freedberg and Gallese, 2007). Di Dio and Gallese (2009) conceptualized the relation between perception, emotions, reward, and aesthetic evaluations, suggesting that perception of art pieces might activate different forms of embodied simulation (internally representing and experiencing what is observed in others), which, in turn, might trigger aesthetic pleasure and aesthetic appraisal. These two forms of reactions can be related to emotional and cognitive aspects of aesthetic experiences.

In the embodied simulation theory of aesthetic perception, two different aspects of a perceived art piece might be embodied in the sensorimotor system: the intrinsic content of the stimulus (such as what the subject is doing in a particular painting) and the visible traces of the artist's creative gestures (such as the stroking utilized to paint said subject). These aspects could ultimately induce a form of empathy with the observed art piece. Freedberg and Gallese (2007) speculated that viewing artwork may activate neural movement programs associated with the way the artwork was produced (internally mimicking brush strokes or sculptural motions), and that aesthetic empathy and, thus, aesthetic pleasure may stem from body resonance between the body of the observer and the body of the artist imagined ("simulated") during the act of creating the artwork (Calvo-Merino et al., 2010). This line of reasoning developed from the consideration that the features most closely related to the artist's movements may be discerned from the painting style, such as Pollack's sweeping color drips or Monet's confined color daubs (Dutton, 2009). A recent study explored the possible influence of the relationship between the hand movements supposedly performed by the artists and those performed by the observers on their aesthetic evaluation of paintings. Paintings in two styles, stroking (as practiced by van Gogh) and pointillism (as practiced by Seurat), were shown to participants who were asked to physically perform similar and dissimilar hand movements while providing ratings of their appraisal of stroking and pointillism paintings (Leder et al., 2012). The results showed increased aesthetic appreciation during physical movements congruent with respect to the painting style, supporting the notion that a sensorimotor matching between the actions of the onlooker and the model (the artist in this case) may strengthen the tendency to appreciate art pieces.

In a similar vein, observing abstract paintings that convey strong information about the movements of the artist activate the corresponding neuro-cognitive representations in the observer and may possibly play an important role in aesthetic appreciation of art (Umiltà et al., 2012). Interestingly, parts of the brain known to be involved in motor action simulation also play a role in aesthetic appreciation, as suggested by a recent brain imagining study that showed increased activity in these brain regions when subjects listened musical rhythms they preferred as opposed to musical rhythms they did not prefer (Kornysheva et al., 2010). Even more striking is that experimental alteration of activity in these brain regions (through noninvasive brain stimulation) actually changed the aesthetic evaluation of the rhythms (Kornysheva et al., 2011).

LEARNING TO PERCEIVE AND APPRECIATE ART AND THE FUTURE OF AESTHETICS EDUCATION

The term *neuroplasticity* indicates the ensemble of changes in brain and behavior in reaction to physiological and pathological changes in the environment. Not thirty years ago, neuroscientists believed the brain was largely unchangeable—that neuroplasticity could only occur within specific time windows (critical periods). Today, neuroscientists recognize the brain is constantly changing and reorganizing, across the entire lifespan. Relevant to the present chapter is that neural signatures of plasticity can be found not only in comparatively simple systems (the motor or somatosensory cortex: Pernigo et al., 2012; Lenggenhagger et al., 2012) but also in more complex, higher-order cognitive and affective systems (Klimecki et al., 2012). Similarly, it has been demonstrated, for example, that emotional, sensory, and motor systems can be modulated by higher-order cognitive variables, such as feelings of belonging to a social group (e.g, political or racial: Avenanti et al., 2010; Azevedo et al., 2013; Liuzza et al., 2011).

Modifications of an individual's aesthetic appreciation during the lifespan and changes in social taste (fads) indicate that the sense of art appreciation undergoes similar plastic changes—yet very little work on whether and how the sense of aesthetics can be changed has been performed in psychology and neuroscience. The question of how art preferences may change over time is at the very root of any attempt to provide brain-based information on aesthetics education. The increasing number of studies on this topic highlights its importance. For example, based on the notion that the human body and its movement can induce powerful aesthetic experiences, Orgs and collaborators (2013) have recently demonstrated that exposing participants to postures and dynamic body stimuli increased their liking of the same stimuli.

As to the importance of multisensory simulation with regards to aesthetic perception and appreciation, it may be worth considering the case of Giorgio de Chirico (an Italian painter influenced by the metaphysical movement of Surrealism), who emphasizes strange, eerie scenes mainly set in open spaces, such as Italian piazzas. Many of de Chirico's works evoke a sense of dislocation between past and present, between the individual subject and the space he or she inhabits. Although it has been argued de Chirico suffered from migraines, Blanke and Landis (2003) discuss the possibility that de Chirico's artistic production might instead have been influenced by morbid manifestations of temporal lobe epilepsy that may affect the function of the temporo-parietal junction, a crucial integrative region where bodily perceptions are matched with orientation in space and time. Under this assumption, de Chirico's work is, in essence, a reflection of his sense of his own body and its physical movements through the world.

The transition from the notion that vision is the only way to truly perceive art to the concept that multisensory integration is essential for aesthetic appreciation is occurring not only in the most advanced art and museum experiences (Lacey and Sathian, 2013; Candlin, 2010) but also in neuroscience and technology research. One of the most promising and powerful tools is the creation of immersive virtual reality (IVR) environments. Psychology and neuroscience research in the last twenty years has demonstrated that people tend to respond realistically to events and situations in IVR (Sanchez-Vives and Slater, 2005). Thanks to IVR, it has been possible to simulate social situations difficult or impossible to create in physical reality. In particular, the combination of psychology, neuroscience, and IVR approaches has allowed for the comparing the reactivity of people in real versus virtual worlds (Slater et al., 2013). Very simple experimental manipulations can induce changes in the way in which the world and the self are perceived (Maselli and Slater, 2013). For example, it is possible to induce the feeling that a white participant is embodied in a black-

skinned avatar, and this experience has been shown to reduce the implicit prejudice against the different ethnic group (Peck et al., 2013). IVR can also generate the feeling of being in a different place remote from where one is actually
located and create a sort of hyper-reality, where the virtual world is *more* real
than the real one. The implication of this tool for education is straightforward
(as highlighted by several articles in the issue of the journal *Science* of April
19, 2013 specifically dedicated to this topic). It has been shown, for example,
that learning scientific concepts in IVR has a number of advantages over "real
world" learning in acquiring scientific concepts and it was, thus, recommended
that the two modalities of learning are combined (de Jong et al., 2013).

Such a combination of virtual and real is likely to be even more important
when considering art and aesthetics. Once acknowledged that multisensory
perception is necessary for mapping the self to a piece of art, one can imagine
a number of scenarios whereby artistic understanding and appreciation can
be enhanced, such as running the hands along the contours of Michelangelo's
David. Although these scenarios may be impossible in the real world, immersive virtual reality may allow one to experience the combined feeling of
seeing and touching a masterpiece (figure 19.1).

Figure 19.1.   Virtual aesthetics.   Reliving at will the situations of aesthetic appreciation may allow each individual to experience the encounter with the object of art at
perceptual, motor, and emotional levels. Courtesy of Gaetano Tieri

An important project specifically dedicated to the use of immersive virtual reality for museums has been developed in the last decade (Roussou, 2001). Using state-of-the art technology, researchers are trying to implement virtual reality displays and computer-generated interactive experiences, to allow visitors to travel through space and time without stepping out of the museum building. All the advantages of virtual reality, namely the potential to transcend the physical location of the built environment, the illusion of being in the projected world, and being surrounded by images and sound have been implemented. Moreover, simulated interactions (e.g., traveling in an ancient city and having the feeling of knocking on doors or entering buildings) were implemented.

Even more relevant is the pure-form museum project, where concepts derived from haptic perception and IVR are combined to allow visitors, either sighted, blind, or visually impaired, to virtually touch sculptures which, for obvious security reasons, cannot be touched in traditional museums (Carrozzino and Bergamasco, 2010). Since most of this work is still in its infancy, a strong increase is expected in the near future.

THE BRAIN AT THE MUSEUM

Relevant to the notion of embrained and embodied aesthetics developed in this chapter is that perception and imagery of physical human actions triggers neural activity in multisensory integration and action-related brain areas. Such a pervasive effect turns out to be important when attempting to understand the emotional and neural counterparts of art appreciation. The implementation of simulation of the sensorimotor states induced by an art piece may directly link the observer to the artist and the piece of art. This type of empathetic link may be at the very basis of the drive we may (or may not) feel toward specific objects of art.

In this perspective, brain studies may inform education to art by indicating the importance of simulation for the aesthetic experience. In particular: i) while passive exposure to an object can trigger some degree of simulation, active processes (such as those underlying mental imagery) are fundamentally important for appreciating art; ii) the enrichment that can be obtained thanks to IVR needs to be complemented by the active effort to simulate experience; iii) simulation of mental imagery implies that all senses, not just vision, and physical action are involved in artistic understanding and aesthetic appreciation. As such, the sensuous interaction with an object that underlies the (re)living of aesthetic experiences will benefit from multisensory integration and motor imagery.

ACKNOWLEDGMENTS

The authors' research was financially supported by VERE project, FP7-ICT-2009-5, Prot. No. 257695.

REFERENCES

Aglioti, S. M., Minio-Paluello, I., and Candidi, M. (2012). The beauty of the body. *Proceedings Lyncei* Academia, 23, 281–88.

Aglioti, S. M., and Pazzaglia, M. (2011). Sounds and scents in (social) action. *Trends in Cognitive Science,* 15(2), 47–55.

Albright, T. D. (2012). On the perception of probable things: neural substrates of associative memory, imagery, and perception. *Neuron,* 74(2), 227–45.

Arnheim, R. (1969). *Visual Thinking.* Berkeley and Los Angeles: University of California Press.

Avenanti, A., Bolognini, N., Maravita, A., and Aglioti, S. M. (2007). Somatic and motor components of action simulation. *Curr Biol.,* 17(24), 2129–35.

Avenanti, A., Candidi, M., and Urgesi, C. (2013). Vicarious motor activation during action perception: beyond correlational evidence. *Front Hum Neurosci.,* 7, 185.

Avenanti, A., Sirigu, A., and Aglioti, S. M. (2010). Racial bias reduces empathic sensorimotor resonance with other-race pain. *Curr Biol.,* 8; 20(11), 1018–22.

Azevedo, R. T., Macaluso, E., Avenanti, A., Santangelo, V., Cazzato, V., and Aglioti, S. M. (2012). Their pain is not our pain: Brain and autonomic correlates of empathic resonance with the pain of same and different race individuals. *Hum Brain Mapp.,* July 17.

Barsalou, L. W. (2008). Grounded cognition. *Annu Rev Psychol.,* 59, 617–45. Review.

Berlucchi, G., and Aglioti, S. M. (2010). The body in the brain revisited. *Exp Brain Res.,* 200(1), 25–35.

Blanke, O., and Landis, T. (2003). The metaphysical art of Giorgio de Chirico. Migraine or epilepsy? *Eur Neurol.,* 50(4), 191–94.

Blanke, O., Ortigue, S., Landis, T., and Seeck, M. (2002). Stimulating illusory own-body perceptions. *Nature,* 419(6904), 269–70.

Blanke, O., and Pasqualini, I. (2011). The riddle of style changes in the visual arts after interference with the right brain. *Front Hum Neurosci.,* 5, 154.

Botvinick, M., and Cohen, J. (1998). Rubber hands "feel" touch that eyes see. *Nature,* 391(6669), 756.

Brown, S., Gao, X., Tisdelle, L., Eickhoff, S. B., and Liotti, M. (2011). Naturalizing aesthetics: brain areas for aesthetic appraisal across sensory modalities. *Neuroimage,* 58(1), 250–58.

Bufalari, I., Sforza, A., Cesari, P., Aglioti, S. M., and Fourkas, A. D. (2010). Motor imagery beyond the joint limits: a transcranial magnetic stimulation study. *Biol Psychol.,* 85(2), 283–90.

Calvo-Merino, B., Jola, C., Glaser, D. E., and Haggard, P. (2008). Towards a sensorimotor aesthetics of performing art. *Conscious Cogn.*, 17, 911–22.

Calvo-Merino, B., Urgesi, C., Orgs, G., Aglioti, S. M., and Haggard, P. (2010). Extrastriate body area underlies aesthetic evaluation of body stimuli. *Exp Brain Res.*, 204(3), 447–56.

Candlin, F. (2010). *Art, Museums and Touch*. Manchester: Manchester University Press.

Cantagallo, A., and Della Sala, S. (1998). Preserved insight in an artist with extrapersonal spatial neglect. *Cortex.*, 34(2), 163–89.

Carr, L., Iacoboni, M., Dubeau, M. C., Mazziotta, J. C., and Lenzi, G. L. (2003). Neural mechanisms of empathy in humans: a relay from neural systems for imitation to limbic areas. *Proc Natl Acad Sci USA*, 100(9), 5497–502.

Carrozzino, M., and Bergamasco, M. (2010). Beyond virtual museums: experiencing immersive virtual reality in real museums. *Journal Of Cultural Heritage*, 11(4), 452–58.

Chatterjee, A. (2004). The neuropsychology of visual artistic production. *Neuropsychologia*, 42(11), 1568–83.

Conway, B. R., and Rehding, A. (2013). Neuroaesthetics and the trouble with beauty. *PLoS Biol.*, 11(3), e1001504.

Costantini, M., Urgesi, C., Galati, G., Romani, G. L., and Aglioti, S. M. (2011). Haptic perception and body representation in lateral and medial occipito-temporal cortices. *Neuropsychologia*, 49(5), 821–29.

Cross, E. S., Kirsch, L., Ticini, L. F., and Schütz-Bosbach, S. (2011). The impact of aesthetic evaluation and physical ability on dance perception. *Front Hum Neurosci.*, 5, 102.

de Jong, T., Linn, M. C., and Zacharia, Z. C. (2013). Physical and virtual laboratories in science and engineering education. *Science*, 340(6130), 305–8.

Di Dio, C., and Gallese, V. (2009) Neuroaesthetics: a review. *Curr Opin Neurobiol.*, 19(6), 682–87.

Di Dio, C., Macaluso, E., and Rizzolatti, G. (2007). The golden beauty: brain response to classical and renaissance sculptures. *PLoSONE* 11, e1201.

Downing, P. E., Jiang, Y., Shuman, M., and Kanwisher, N. (2001). A cortical area selective for visual processing of the human body. *Science*, 293, 2470–73.

Dutton D. (2009). *The art instinct*. Oxford: Oxford University Press.

Fetsch, C. R., Deangelis, G. C., and Angelaki, D. E. (2013). Bridging the gap between theories of sensory cue integration and the physiology of multisensory neurons. *Nat Rev Neurosci.*, 14(6), 429–42.

Fodor, J. (1983). *The modularity of mind: An essay on faculty psychology*. Cambridge, MA: MIT Press.

Fourkas, A. D., Avenanti, A., Urgesi, C., and Aglioti, S. M. (2006). Corticospinal excitability during first and third person imagery. *Experimental Brain Research*, 168, 143–51.

Fourkas, A. D., Bonavolontà, V., Avenanti, A., and Aglioti, S. M. (2008). Kinaesthetic imagery and tool-specific modulation of corticospinal representations in expert tennis players. *Cerebral Cortex*, 18, 2382–90.

Freedberg, D., and Gallese, V. (2007). Motion, emotion and empathy in esthetic experience. *Trends Cogn Sci.*, 11(5), 197–203.

Gallese, V. (2007) Embodied simulation: from mirror neuron systems to interpersonal relations. *Novartis Found Symp.*, 278, 3–12; discussion 12–19, 89–96, 216–21.

Ishizu, T., and Zeki, S. (2011). Toward a brain-based theory of beauty. *PLoS ONE*, 6:e21852.

———. (2013). The brain's specialized systems for aesthetic and perceptual judgment. *Eur J Neurosci.*, 37(9), 1413–20.

Jacobsen, T. (2010). Beauty and the brain: culture, history and individual differences in aesthetic appreciation. *J Anat.*, 216(2), 184–91.

Jacobsen, T., Buchta, K., Köhler, M., and Schröger, E. (2004). The primacy of beauty in judging the aesthetics of objects. *Psychol Rep.*, 94(3 Pt 2), 1253–60.

Keysers, C., Kaas, J. H., and Gazzola, V. (2010). Somatosensation in social perception. *Nat Rev Neurosci.*, 11(6), 417–28.

Kilner, J. M., Neal, A., Weiskopf, N., Friston, K. J., and Frith, C. D. (2009). Evidence of mirror neurons in human inferior frontal gyrus. *J. Neurosci.*, 29, 10153–159.

Klimecki, O. M., Leiberg, S., Lamm, C., and Singer, T. (2012). Functional neural plasticity and associated changes in positive affect after compassion training. *Cereb Cortex.*, June 1.

Kornysheva, K., von Anshelm-Schiffer, A. M., and Schubotz, R. I. (2011). Inhibitory stimulation of the ventral premotor cortex temporarily interferes with musical beat rate preference. *Hum Brain Mapp.*, 32(8), 1300–310.

Kornysheva, K., von Cramon, D. Y., Jacobsen, T., and Schubotz, R. I. (2010). Tuning-in to the beat: Aesthetic appreciation of musical rhythms correlates with a premotor activity boost. *Hum Brain Mapp.*, 31(1), 48–64.

Kreiman, G., Koch, C., and Fried, I. (2000). Imagery neurons in the human brain. *Nature*, 408(6810), 357–61.

Lacey, S., Hagtvedt, H., Patrick, V. M., Anderson, A., Stilla, R., Deshpande, G., Hu, X., Sato, J. R., Reddy, S., and Sathian, K. (2011). Art for reward's sake: visual art recruits the ventral striatum. *Neuroimage*, 55(1), 420–33.

Lacey, S., and Sathian, K. (2013). Please DO Touch the Exhibits! Interactions between visual imagery and haptic perception. This volume.

Lakoff, G., and Johnson, M. (1999). *Philosophy in the Flesh: The Embodied Mind and Its Challenge to Western Thought.* New York: Basic Books.

Leder, H., Bär, S., and Topolinski, S. (2012). Covert painting simulations influence aesthetic appreciation of artworks. *Psychol Sci.*, 23(12), 1479–81.

Lenggenhager, B., Pazzaglia, M., Scivoletto, G., Molinari, M., and Aglioti, S. M. (2012). The sense of the body in individuals with spinal cord injury. *PLoS One*, 7(11), e50757.

Lenggenhager, B., Tadi, T., Metzinger, T., and Blanke, O. (2007). Video ergo sum: manipulating bodily self-consciousness. *Science*, 317(5841), 1096–99.

Lipps, T. (1903). *Psychologie des Schönen und der Kunst* [Psychology of beauty and the arts]. Hamburg, Germany: Verlag Leopold Voss.

Liuzza, M.T., Cazzato, V., Vecchione, M., Crostella, F., Caprara, G. V., and Aglioti, S. M. (2011). Follow my eyes: the gaze of politicians reflexively captures the gaze of ingroup voters. *PLoS One,* 6(9), e25117.

Mahon, B. Z., and Caramazza, A. (2008). A critical look at the embodied cognition hypothesis and a new proposal for grounding conceptual content. *J Physiol Paris.,* 102(1-3), 59–70.

Maselli, A., and Slater, M. (2013). The building blocks of the full body ownership illusion. *Frontiers in Human Neuroscience,* 7, 83.

McNorgan, C. (2012). A meta-analytic review of multisensory imagery identifies the neural correlates of modality-specific and modality-general imagery. *Frontiers in Human Neuroscience,* 6, 285.

McWhinnie, Harold J. (1968). A review of research on aesthetic measure. *Acta Psychologica,* 28(4), 363–75.

Moro, V., Berlucchi, G., Lerch, J., Tomaiuolo, F., and Aglioti, S. M. (2008). Selective deficit of mental visual imagery with intact primary visual cortex and visual perception. *Cortex,* 44(2), 109–18.

Moulton, S. T., and Kosslyn, S. M. (2009). Imagining predictions: mental imagery as mental emulation. *Philos Trans R Soc Lond B Biol Sci.,* 364(1521), 1273–80.

Mukamel, R., Ekstrom, A., Kaplan, J., Iacoboni, M., and Fried, I. (2010). Single-neuron responses in humans during execution and observation of actions. *Curr. Biol.,* 20, 750–56.

Orgs, G., Hagura, N., and Haggard, P. (2013). Learning to like it: Aesthetic perception of bodies, movements and choreographic structure. *Conscious Cogn.,* 22(2), 603–12.

Pascual-Leone, A., and Hamilton, R. (2001). The metamodal organization of the brain. *Prog Brain Res.,* 134, 427–45.

Peck, T., Seinfeld, S., Aglioti, S. M., and Slater, M. (2013). Putting yourself in the skin of a black avatar reduces implicit racial bias. *Consciousness and Cognition* (in press).

Pérez-Fabello, M. J., Campos, A., and Gómez-Juncal, R. (2007). Visual imaging capacity and imagery control in fine arts students. *Percept Mot Skills.,* 104(3 Pt 1), 815–22.

Pernigo, S., Moro, V., Avesani, R., Miatello, C., Urgesi, C., and Aglioti, S. M. (2012). Massive somatic deafferentation and motor deefferentation of the lower part of the body impair its visual recognition: a psychophysical study of patients with spinal cord injury. *European Journal of Neuroscience,* 36(11), 3509–18.

Preston, S. D., and de Waal, F. B. (2002). Empathy: Its ultimate and proximate bases. *Behavioral Brain Science,* 25(1), 1–20; discussion 20–71.

Pylyshyn, Z. W. (1984). *Computation and Cognition: Toward a Foundation for Cognitive Science.* Cambridge, MA: MIT Press.

Ramachandran, V. S., and Hirstein, W. (1999). The science of art: A neurological theory of aesthetic experience. *Journal of Consciousness Studies,* 6(6–7), 15–51.

Rizzolatti, G., and Craighero, L. (2004). The mirror-neuron system. *Annu Rev Neurosci,* 27, 169–92.

Roussou, M. (2001). Immersive interactive virtual reality in the museum. Proceedings of TiLE–Trends, Technology & Design in Leisure Entertainment (CD–ROM). London: Aldrich.

Sanchez-Vives, M. V., and Slater, M. (2005). From presence to consciousness through virtual reality. *Nat Rev Neurosci.*, 6(4), 332–39.

Sathian, K., Zangaladze, A., Hoffman, J. M., and Grafton, S. T. (1997). Feeling with the mind's eye. *Neuroreport*, 8(18), 3877–81.

Sforza, A., Bufalari, I., Haggard, P., and Aglioti, S. M. (2010). My face in yours: Visuotactile facial stimulation influences sense of identity. *Soc Neurosci*, 5(2), 148–62.

Slater, M., Rovira, A., Southern, R., Swapp, D., Zhang, J. J., Campbell, C., and Levine, M. (2013). Bystander responses to a violent incident in an immersive virtual environment. *PLoS One*, 8(1), e52766.

Spence, C., and Parise, C. V. (2012). The cognitive neuroscience of crossmodal correspondences. *Iperception*, 3(7), 410–12.

Thornhill, R., and Gangestad, S. W. (1999). Facial attractiveness. *Trends in Cognitive Science*, 3(12), 452–60.

Umiltà, M. A., Berchio, C., Sestito, M., Freedberg, D., and Gallese, V. (2012). Abstract art and cortical motor activation: an EEG study. *Front Hum Neurosci.*, 6, 311.

Urgesi, C., Calvo-Merino, B., Haggard, P., and Aglioti, S. M. (2007a). Transcranial magnetic stimulation reveals two cortical pathways for visual body processing. *Journal of Neuroscience*, 27, 8023–30.

Urgesi, C., Candidi, M., Ionta, S., and Aglioti, S. M. (2007b). Representation of body identity and body actions in extrastriate body area and ventral premotor cortex. *Nat. Neurosci.* 10, 30–31.

Vartanian, O., and Kaufman, J. C. (2013) Psychological and neural responses to art embody viewer and artwork histories. *Behav Brain Sci.*, 36(2), 161–62.

Zajonc, R. B. (1968). Attitudinal effects of mere exposure. *Journal of Personality and Social Psychology*, Monograph Supplement, 9, 1–27.

Zeki, S. (1999). Inner vision: an exploration of art and the brain. Oxford: Oxford University Press.

Zentgraf, K., Munzert, J., Bischoff, M., and Newman-Norlund, R. D. (2011). Simulation during observation of human actions—theories, empirical studies, applications. *Vision Res.* 22; 51(8), 827–35.

20

Islands of Stimulation

Perspectives on the Museum Experience, Present and Future

Rebecca McGinnis

Why do museums matter? Why do we need them when we can see works of art online? What is important about the space of the museum? As a museum educator at The Metropolitan Museum of Art in New York I see every day the extraordinary power of the galleries—rather than the lecture hall or the classroom—as places for multilayered and holistic learning and enjoyment. My argument in this chapter is that the sense of sight is only one of many modalities through which the museum is experienced. The perspective of visitors who are blind and partially sighted, a group often excluded or marginalized by art museums, is significant in drawing attention to the richness of experience beyond the visual that a museum visit can offer. In the first half of this chapter, then, I will draw on interviews with visitors who are blind and partially sighted, who speak of the value of being in the gallery space, in the presence of original works of art.

In the second section, I move on to consider briefly a few current ways of thinking about the gallery experience that are suggestive for future programming and curation. These move beyond traditional paradigms of education, in which experts share wisdom about works of art to a largely passive audience. Instead, these approaches are responsive to the individual interests and abilities of visitors, and are therefore more inclusive than traditional practices. As earlier chapters have demonstrated, multisensory experiences around works of art enrich all visitors' understanding: To touch, to smell, to hear is often as important as to see a material object. Experiencing things through different senses can be mutually reinforcing. Our conceptual understanding of multisensory experience has been greatly enhanced by recent findings in the fields of cognitive psychology and neuroscience. These often reinforce what museum educators have long intuitively understood. However, insights about the physiology underlying the visitor's museum experience can help us to incorporate multisensory opportunities more effectively into pedagogical practice. These scientific perspectives take us beyond traditional concepts of the five senses to allow us to think, for example, about situated cognition—how the position of our bodies in space, in an environment, shapes our thinking. We think differently because we are in a particular space, with particular people, doing particular things, and seeing particular objects. Rather than hearing from experts, the museum visitor can now be encouraged to engage in co-creation of knowledge in the galleries. Finally, in being more responsive to the needs and interests of visitors, new possibilities for the museum are emerging. Our experience in the museum need not be solely intellectual or aesthetic: rather, the museum can be a place for contemplation and calm reflection, and for understanding our own emotions and motivations. Mindfulness, the idea of being fully present in the moment, is a concept with enormous potential for the museum in the new landscape of the twenty-first century, moving beyond the five senses.

PART I

A Visit to the Met: A Sensory Experience

I will begin by considering the unique qualities of the museum within the built environment, using examples from two research projects conducted at the Metropolitan Museum in 2011 that focused on visitors who are blind or partially sighted. One aim of these research initiatives was to explore the significance for visitors of experiencing the physical space of the museum's galleries (Hayhoe, 2012). Why do people who cannot see, or who see very little, come to the museum, often encountering—and overcoming—many barriers along the way? Why not experience art via the museum's website, using assistive technology, or through descriptions in books? What compels people to return again and again to this place, and what do they gain from the experience? What do their responses tell us about the experience of cultural environments for others?

The anthropologist Daniel Miller gave the title to his recent book on material culture a single word: *Stuff* (Miller, 2010). The Metropolitan Museum of Art is a storehouse of more stuff than most of us could readily imagine. Its two-million-square-foot building spanning four city blocks comprises many additions that engulf the original structure erected in 1880, and houses over two million objects, tens of thousands of which are on view at any given time. The museum's collections span global cultures and all periods from the earliest manmade objects to contemporary art: It is a universal survey museum (Duncan and Wallach, 1980). The range of materials and object sizes encompasses vast stone and wood sculptures, Maori canoes, and even the facade of a nineteenth-century bank, but also tiny coins and jewels, and even digital art, which has no physical form at all. In 2013, over six million people visited this enormous edifice.

Why is the Metropolitan Museum one of New York's top tourist attractions? There are many different reasons, but most in some way revolve around being in the presence of all that stuff. In *The Social Work of the Museum*, Lois Silverman describes the multiple roles of museum galleries replete with culturally significant artifacts. She notes that "As people engage with objects and each other, museums become containers and catalysts for personal growth, relationship building, social change, and healing" (Silverman, 2010, xi).

Museum galleries can be magical places of discovery, offering access to new ideas and previously unknown objects, fostering learning and engagement. However, this transformative experience can be tempered by more mundane challenges and distractions, for visitors with and without disabilities, especially in large and popular museums like the Metropolitan. Fifty percent of the Met's visitors are in the museum for the first time, so they face the barrier of unfamiliarity, whatever their degree of ability or disability. Crowds, lines, poor acoustics, tired feet, lack of seating, orientation, and navigation difficulties can all contribute to a less-than-ideal museum experience. Add to these mobility challenges, the lack of expectation that art will be accessible, and the prospect of being stared at or even reprimanded while looking closely at or touching a work of art, and you might indeed wonder why a person who is blind or partially sighted would want to partake in this public and communal encounter with art in museum galleries.

Throughout any visit to the Metropolitan Museum, the senses are assailed by multifarious sights, sounds, smells, textures, temperatures, even tastes. The visitor enters the museum from busy Fifth Avenue. The imposing front steps are designed to impress and even intimidate—they create a physical, social, and psychological barrier. As you ascend, you are surrounded by the wafting mingled scents of hot dogs and pretzels from food carts on the plaza in front of the museum. In the Great Hall, olfaction shifts to the sweet smell of flowers from the five enormous arrangements flanking the hall in niches and in the center of the round information desk in the middle of the hall. The large open space with a high triple-domed ceiling, marble floor, and stone walls creates an echoing acoustic that magnifies the sound of milling visitors speaking dozens of languages.

The Visit beyond the Visual

Leaving that cacophony behind, let's now consider what is important and enjoyable about being present in the museum's galleries surrounded by works of art for visitors with varying degrees of visual disability, as opposed to at home, in a library, or online. The reflections of visitors who are blind or partially sighted reveal deep connections to the physical space of the museum and the importance of engaging with works of art in that space, an experience they often describe with the term "looking" even when more than one sense is involved.

One congenitally legally blind visitor who is an avid museumgoer reported:

I've found that looking at art online and in books is interesting, but not very exciting. It's so exhilarating being in the museum environment amongst the works of art. I'm like a child in a toy store—feeling so thrilled and excited to be there! The colors in the actual works of art are so vibrant and buoyant when viewed in the museum gallery setting. Nothing can compare to that experience!

She continued:

I love hearing people around me talk about the artwork. Also, having a tour guide describe the works of art . . . helps to make the art come alive. It enables me to make sense of shapes and colors that might otherwise be something my eyes couldn't discern. . . . my spirits get so uplifted when I'm in a museum setting. I feel chills going up my spine when surrounded by famous works of art! This feeling lasts for hours after leaving the museum—isn't that amazing and wonderful?!

This visitor participates in programs regularly, including those engaging with art in the galleries through touch and description and those focusing on art making. She attends Seeing through Drawing, the Museum's drawing class for adults who are blind or have low vision. She says: "Both activities [looking and drawing] are important to me. Drawing in the galleries is a relatively new experience for me. I'm shy about the public watching me create a drawing. That said, looking at a sculpture and drawing my rendition of it is very relaxing" (Anonymous visitor, interview with author, The Metropolitan Museum of Art, January 14, 2012).

She reflected on her experience at another museum that lacked the authenticity of a gallery experience: "Many years ago, [another museum] used to have tours for blind visitors in a conference room to view replicas. I told the staff that this was very boring and that the colors in the posters didn't resemble the colors in the actual paintings. Thankfully, the museum stopped doing tours in that manner." In his famous essay of 1936, "The Work of Art in the Age of Mechanical Reproduction," Walter Benjamin discussed the phenomenon of the "aura" of the individual work of art, and the way it was threatened by photomechanical processes of reproduction (Benjamin, 1969). Clearly, despite the extreme diversification and sophistication of alternate means of delivery for the visual image, from cinema and television and DVD to Google image or the Met's website, the experience of the original work of art has lost none of its mystique. Indeed, the museum environment seems only to enhance the mysterious auratic qualities attached to the "original." Perhaps the temple-like architectural spaces, and the careful regulation of behavior by the Museum's security staff, create the sense of a ritual among museum visitors—a sacred rite for a secular age.

Another visitor, who is eighty and has been severely visually impaired for ten years, has been visiting the Met for over fifty years. She has visited museums since she was a child—and sighted—and she remembers seeing many paintings. Since becoming blind, she still attends films and lectures at the museum as well as programs for people who are blind or partially sighted, including Verbal Imaging tours of popular exhibitions. These are descriptive tours with an educator that visitors can request for any part of the museum. She describes herself as someone who can get around in the museum environment with help, even though she cannot see the details of things around her, and she chooses to make the effort to come to the museum, traveling via subway. "I've always loved European paintings . . ." she explains. "I like portraits more than anything else, but I love all paintings" (Anonymous visitor, interview with Simon Hayhoe, The Metropolitan Museum of Art, August 2011).

Despite warnings about the crowds, the dark and dramatically lit galleries, and the sometimes loud soundscape in the exhibition, she requested a Verbal Imaging tour of the summer 2011 blockbuster exhibition of the work of fashion designer Alexander McQueen, Savage Beauty, visited by over 660,000 people during its four-month run. She wanted to experience the space as well as to learn about McQueen's career and have his works described to her. She said afterwards: "I like to have an emotional connection, especially with music . . . I love good music . . . even going through there [referring to the exhibition soundtrack of loud punk and other rock music playing in the galleries]."

Despite proclaiming herself a lover of art, she said she did not use the Internet at all either for art or general browsing, giving her disability as a reason. She preferred to face the physical obstacles of a physical museum visit to those presented by a virtual visit. Ultimately the physical presence of the object, rather than merely access to a fine reproduction of it, is sufficiently powerful to make it worth overcoming many barriers to reach and enter the museum.

A couple who are regular consumers of Verbal Imaging tours at the Metropolitan, both of whom have congenital and almost total blindness, are also lifelong museumgoers. (One said that when he was younger "I would almost live in museums, all day long," and he studied fine art at university.) Despite their enduring connection to art and museums, they request descriptive tours based on their interests in specific countries and historical periods, rather than on aesthetic preferences. In fact, one admitted that he often didn't fully understand the works of art in front of him. He added: "[When I was young] I used to come here. In those days I would come to a museum and look at a painting, but I could not really tell what [was there] because I didn't have [a guide to describe it to me]." Last summer the couple requested four Verbal Imaging tours focusing on works of El Greco and Goya. These were compelled by an interest in Spanish history rather than a preference for the paintings themselves, prompting detailed discussions with the educator about the history of Spain along with descriptions of the paintings. One recalled of *View of Toledo* after a tour: "It's strange, [when the painting] was described . . . that was fine . . . , but all the time I'm thinking more about the painter himself" (Anonymous visitor, interview with Simon Hayhoe, The Metropolitan Museum of Art, August 2011).

Despite the emphasis on history rather than the works of art themselves, the couple chose to make the trips to the museum, viewing paintings in the galleries and discussing them with an educator, eschewing the potentially more comfortable option of learning about Spanish history at home through books or online. The cultural value they attached to being in the museum environment was beyond that held for the art alone. To be in the museum galleries, in the presence of these historical artifacts that acted as windows to another time, elicited an intellectual rather than an aesthetic appreciation, but the space of the gallery was central to this experience. Together, making the pilgrimage to the museum and standing in front of El Greco's *View of Toledo* as they discussed its visual qualities and the cultural and historical context of its creation comprised the complete experience for them.

These examples make clear that the museum environment and not just the nature of the collections displayed within it, is a significant factor in the success of museum visits, and the desire to return for people with little or no vision. These visitors reported that the sensory, social, intellectual, and aesthetic benefits derived from a museum visit outweighed the substantial difficulties encountered in reaching the museum.

PART II

The Multisensory Museum Space and the Visitor Experience: The Museum Education Perspective

The words of visitors with varying degrees of visual disability to the Metropolitan Museum attest to the impact of the museum visit for one particular group of people who you might consider especially disenfranchised from the art museum. Now we broaden our exploration and consider how museums are thinking about the visitor experience today, how they are reinventing themselves by crafting different types of spaces and experiences with new goals in mind. These reconstructions of the visitor experience offer food for thought for designers of these spaces now and in the future.

Before we look at where museums are going, let's see where they have come from. The earliest museums were highly exclusive, private places for an elite few. These private cabinets of curiosities of the Renaissance demonstrated the collector's control over nature, organizing, categorizing, and presenting a collection of objects from the arts and sciences to a select few. By the late nineteenth century, common definitions of "museum" had broadened to include education and public service as primary functions. Museums were seen as institutions whose function was not only to educate, but also to socialize and to civilize. While education was paramount to the nineteenth-century museum, in the twentieth century, museums prioritized preservation, interpretation, and scholarly inquiry, sometimes relegating the visitor experience to an institutional by-product.

So what is the role of museums in today's technology-driven, fast-paced society? We can acquire *information* about art online, so what's so special about going to see it in the *space* of the museum? In the twenty-first-century museum, *experience* is paramount. Stephen Weil, longtime deputy director of the Hirshhorn Museum (Washington, D.C.), believed that the ultimate goal of museums is to improve people's lives. In his 2002 collection of essays, *Making Museums Matter*, he described the evolution of museums from primarily collections-based to more education-focused places, asserting that museums have changed "from being *about* something to being *for* somebody" (Weil, 2002, 28). Journalist Kenneth Hudson summed up this shift in the UNESCO magazine *Museum International*: "The most fundamental change that has affected museums during the [past] half century . . . is the now almost universal conviction that they exist in order to serve the public" (Hudson, 2003, 43).

In the twenty-first century, museums are more than just institutions in the public service; they are places for social interaction as well as engagement with art; places for finding out about oneself as well as discovering other cultures and times. This new emphasis on a shared and even jointly constructed cultural experience positions museums to play significant roles in their communities and shifts agency from the curator to the visitor. With this new dialogic relationship as museums embrace their communities as partners and diversify their activities, we see the first step toward inclusion as opposed to mere accessibility. And museum design must continue to evolve in order to accommodate and promote this new vision.

Contemporary Theory and Future Directions for the Museum

Many chapters in this book have explored how we experience museum environments and understand museum objects through all our senses. These might include not only the traditional five senses, but many others as well, including kinesthesia and proprioception (senses relating to the body's movement and location), and the sense of balance, time, and direction. The fields of cognitive psychology and neuroscience continue to offer advancements in our understanding of multisensory experience and to challenge our preconceptions. For example, recent developments in cognitive science are revealing how cognition is not solely a process of the mind, but rather, of the interplay between our minds, bodies, and the environment. We are learning that cognition is embodied, meaning that it takes place not just in our brains and minds but in our whole bodies (see Anderson, 2003; Lakoff and Johnson, 1999). This revolutionary shift in the way we understand mental processes also suggests that the environment is not just a backdrop to or potential distraction from learning, but rather an integral part of it. That is, cognition is also situated (see Robbins and Aydede, 2008). Our thinking and the knowledge we create is "in part a product of the activity, context, and culture in which it is developed and used" (Seely Brown, Collins and Duguid, 1989, 32). We are all well aware of the impact of a place on emotion and memory—memories, too, are situated by our sensory and physical perception—and now we add cognition and learning. This new understanding of mental processes may help to explain why the blind and partially sighted visitors quoted earlier in this chapter choose to come to the museum repeatedly to learn about art even when they cannot see it at all or as well as they might in an enlarged image at home: the environment is integral to their thinking and learning. It also opens up potential avenues in museum education for all visitors, by suggesting the importance of conducting programs in the gallery space among works of art—an auratic environment—in preference to the lecture hall or classroom.

Knowledge is in part created by the environment, but people are a crucial part of that environment in museums and therefore of our knowledge creation. Twenty-first-century art museums are places for shared experiences, for looking at and discussing art with others, for making art with others, for other social activities. Experiential and social learning is replacing the one-way museum lecture. Museums are not imparting knowledge from on high but rather sharing in its construction, co-creating meaning with their visitors. The lines between "education program" and going to the café, the shop, and even the website are blurring more and more. Agency on the part of the visitor becomes an important component of a successful museum experience. In *The Participatory Museum*, Nina Simon describes three key reasons why museums seek to engage in co-creation with their visitors:

1. To give voice and be responsive to the needs and interests of local community members
2. To provide a place for community engagement and dialogue
3. To help participants develop skills that will support their own individual and community goals (Simon, 2010, 263)

The definition of community is crucial here. Rather than implying the group that traditionally attends art museums, it can be expanded to refer to underserved communities, whose ethnic, socioeconomic, educational, or geographic position may have effectively excluded them from museums hitherto.

Finally, museums are increasingly identifying themselves as places for health and well-being. We know about the impact of the environment on patients in hospitals (see Dijkstra et al., 2006), but museums, too, can offer health benefits to their audiences. Museum provide social, mental, and physical stimulation, all known to be good for cognitive functioning, contributing to better memories and better brain health generally. Met Escapes, the Met's program for people with dementia and their caregivers, is designed to encourage all three forms of exercise: participants look at, discuss, and make art with others, and they walk considerable distances over the course of a gallery tour.

Some museums are promoting the well-being and health of their visitors by incorporating Mindfulness practices derived from Buddhist traditions into their programming. Mindfulness techniques help people to focus attention and awareness on the present moment. Since Dr. John Kabat-Zinn founded the Mindfulness-Based Stress Reduction program at the University of Massachusetts in 1979 (Center for Mindfulness in Medicine, Health Care, and Society at UMass Medical School, 2013), there has been growing interest and evidence to support the therapeutic benefits of Mindfulness practices, including stress reduction, pain management, and overall enhancement of mood and well-being (see Hölzel et al., 2011; Marchand, 2012; Shapiro, Oman, Thoresen, Plante, and Flinders, 2008).

Mindfulness and meditation sessions for both visitors and staff are appearing at museums around the country, from the Frye Art Museum in Seattle and the Hammer Museum in L.A. on the west coast to the Rubin Museum in New York. Museums are spaces for active engagement, but activity can also be inward-looking, reflective, and insightful. Being present in the moment is essential to experiencing and appreciating art, and can reduce stress levels and clear the mind. There is great promise in mindfulness and other practices encouraging well-being for museums to remain relevant and responsive to the demands of an aging and increasingly fast-paced society.

I conclude with a quote from a former participant in the Met Escapes program, for people with dementia and their families and care partners, which sums up the enduring importance of the museum space to him and his family. He attended with his father. He wrote to us a year after his father died, reflecting on what the museum experience meant to both of them:

> those visits were islands of stimulation, a touchstone of sorts that enriched our lives well beyond those few hours within your walls. Dad came to look forward to them. And though I miss them, I have his artwork, my memories, and the photographs I took when we wandered the galleries after our sessions. Robert Frank's photographs or Walker Evans's postcards, whatever we saw was another welcome surprise. Which is what art should be.

REFERENCES

Anderson, Michael L. Embodied cognition: A field guide. *Artificial Intelligence* 149, no. 1 (September 2003), 91–130.

Benjamin, Walter. The work of art in the age of mechanical reproduction. In Walter Benjamin, *Illuminations: Essays and Reflections*, edited by Hannah Arendt, translated by Harry Zohn, 217–51. New York: Schocken, 1969.

Center for Mindfulness in Medicine, Health Care, and Society at UMass Medical School. Last modified June 4, 2013. http://www.umassmed.edu/cfm/stress/index .aspx.

Dijkstra, Karin, Marcel Pieterse, and Ad Pruyn. Physical environmental stimuli that turn healthcare facilities into healing environments through psychologically mediated effects: systematic review. *Journal of Advanced Nursing* 56, no. 2 (October 2006): 166–81. Originally published online.

Duncan, C., and A. Wallach. The universal survey museum. *Art History* 3 (1980): 448–69.

Hayhoe, Simon. Viewing paintings through the lens of cultural habitus: A study of students' experiences at California School for the Blind and the Metropolitan Museum of Art, New York. *Space, Place & Social Justice in Education*, Manchester Metropolitan University. Manchester. February 13, 2012.

Hölzel, Britta K., Sara W. Lazar, Tim Gard, Zev Schuman-Olivier, David R. Vago, and Ulrich Ott. How does mindfulness meditation work? Proposing mechanisms of action from a conceptual and neural perspective. *Perspectives on Psychological Science* 6, no. 6 (November 2011): 537–59.

Hudson, Kenneth. The museum refuses to stand still. *Museum International* 50, no. 1 (February 4, 2003): 43–50.

Lakoff, George, and Mark Johnson. *Philosophy in the Flesh: The Embodied Mind and Its Challenge to Western Thought.* New York: Basic Books, 1999.

Marchand, W. R. Mindfulness-based stress reduction, mindfulness-based cognitive therapy, and Zen meditation for depression, anxiety, pain, and psychological distress. *Journal of Psychiatric Practice* 18, no. 4 (July 2012): 233–52.

Miller, Daniel. *Stuff.* Cambridge: Polity Press, 2010.

Robbins, Philip, and Murat Aydede, eds. *The Cambridge Handbook of Situated Cognition.* Cambridge: Cambridge University Press, 2008.

Seely Brown, John, Allan Collins, and Paul Duguid. Situated Cognition and the culture of learning. *Educational Researcher* 18, no. 1 (January-February 1989): 32–42.

Shapiro, Shauna L., Doug Oman, Carl E. Thoresen, Thomas G. Plante, and Tim Flinders. Cultivating mindfulness: effects on well-being. *Journal of Clinical Psychology* 64, no. 7 (2008): 840–62.

Silverman, Lois H. *The Social Work of Museums.* New York: Routledge, 2010.

Simon, Nina. *The Participatory Museum.* N.p.: Nina Simon CC Attribution-Non-Commercial, 2010.

Weil, Stephen. *Making Museums Matter.* Washington DC: Smithsonian Institution, 2002.

21

The Future Landscape of 3D in Museums

Samantha Sportun

The three-dimensional (3D) digitization of collections opens up a world of possibilities for museums and cultural venues, some of which have been tried and tested, and others we haven't yet imagined. These three-dimensional interventions do and will take place in virtual space, on the gallery, and outside cultural venues offering new and exciting forms of access and engagement.

Touching objects in museums is generally not encouraged, as it can put the object at risk, but there is still a desire to have this interaction with objects. It is well known that making collections available for visitors to handle and touch (physically or virtually), through the provision of object-handling sessions (Pye, 2007) tactile displays, and with technology such as haptics, benefits all visitors, as the sense of touch connects the visitor to the object and its story (Candlin, 2010). These developments also recognize the need to make collections accessible to the visually impaired and those with physical disabilities. (As outlined on the website http://www.euroblind.org/working -areas/access-to-culture/nr/205.)

Museums are beginning to establish the use of handling collections and the accessioned objects that get used tend to be robust enough to be routinely touched or handled; the fragile, potentially dangerous, or particularly rare objects do not get used in these sessions. As a result, these objects remain unavailable to the visitor and become completely inaccessible to the visually impaired unless there is some form of audio description or a replica.

Digital technologies are providing a shift in the way we engage with material culture. There is a universal drive to digitize collection records and documents—written, photographic, video and sound—as this has huge implications for sharing collections more extensively between cultural organizations and with the public.

3D SCANNING AND 3D DIGITAL DATABASES AND ARCHIVING

3D digital forms can be created using CAD (computer-aided design) software; however, 3D scanning (using laser or structured light) produces the most accurate record of an artifact (see figure 21.1). This technology has the advantage of being noncontact and so can be used to record the most fragile or the largest of objects. There are different types of scanners depending on the scale

Figure 21.1. Probos™ haptic kiosk being used by member of Blind Veterans UK. Scan of predynastic hippo bowl imported and displayed alongside other scans in three-dimensional room. All solid features can be felt including walls and floor. The ball stylus is held in the fingertips. Courtesy of Freeform Studios

of projects; some are designed for scanning buildings and landscapes, and others have sub-micron scanning capabilities manufactured for the electronics industry. The commercial use of scanning and 3D printing/rapid prototyping has expanded exponentially, driving the technology to become more efficient and cost effective. This, coupled with expanding computing power, makes a 3D digital resource for museums a more realistic proposition.

Once captured, the 3D digital scan of the museum artifact is the starting point for many different forms of outputs and manifestations. With the use of intelligent software the scanned object can be explored from all angles; altering parameters such as lighting conditions can reveal details that are invisible to the naked eye (see figure 21.2). Fragments of objects or assemblages can be reunited, large objects compared side by side, or tool markings superimposed from different objects. If an object has been X-rayed or scanned using a technology such as magnetic resonance imaging, there is also the possibility to investigate the inside of the object as well as the outer surface (Metallo and Rossi, 2011). The possibilities are endless and would provide unprecedented access to collections, especially as the information could be accessed remotely from the museum.

Software to manipulate and display 3D data is becoming more intuitive and not solely the reserve of software developers. As a digital record, it has the advantage that it can be shared cheaply and efficiently across continents and there can be immediacy to the sharing of this information over the Internet, which allows many more individuals to be involved with the same set of data.

Figure 21.2. Actual size nylon replica of predynastic hippo bowl before patination. Courtesy of Freeform Studios

The importance of high-resolution digital scanning has been recognized in the cultural sector for some time. Scans can be used to monitor deterioration caused by neglect, vandalism, and environmental factors. If an artifact becomes damaged after scanning, the loss can be recreated both in a digital form and as a physical duplicate. It is important for museums to engage the public with the care of collections, and this type of physical evidence can be used to enhance understanding of the challenges that face material culture in every country. If this can be achieved with striking graphics and three-dimensional reconstructions as well as physical replicas that can be used in public programs, it will have more of an impact.

As an example, if an object is actively deteriorating, an accurate copy can be made to replace the original. One of the earliest examples of this process occurred in 2000, when two fragile Roman marble reliefs were scanned and replaced with marble replicas in the front facade of the Garden Temple at Ince Blundell Hall, Merseyside (Fowles, 2000). This issue of replacing originals with a replica can be controversial; however, in this case the original reliefs were at risk and after removal were rehoused in a museum-controlled environment, which has stabilized them for the foreseeable future. Since that early demonstration of the technology, there have been many more high profile projects, such as the scanning and reproduction of Tutankhamen's tomb (http://www.factum-arte.com/eng/conservacion/tutankhamun/tutankhamun_en.asp) and the famous prehistoric Altamira limestone cave in Spain, both sites having closed because of negative effects from tourism. The replica Altamira cave is housed in a purpose-built museum for the public (Donelan, 2002) to enjoy while ensuring that the original is preserved. On a smaller scale, many museums now have objects recreated from scans used in handling displays, outreach, or education programs.

To make the information available to the public, 3D scans need to be stored in a database that is intuitive, and the quality of the rendered scan should be enticing enough to capture the visitor's imagination. Digital information is being added daily to museum databases, but presently most museum databases are not constructed to host large amounts of three-dimensional data. There are practical implications for museums and galleries wanting to embed 3D scans in documentation tools, including cost, protection of data, training, and organizational challenges such as providing safe access for the objects whilst scanning. To scan some objects in three dimensions can also present physical and logistical challenges. In 2008 University College London looked at how a database using 3D scans might function in the form of their ECurator project (http://www.ariadne.ac.uk/issue60/hess-et-al). There is still much work to be done to produce intuitive searchable and shared digital databases that would integrate with museums' existing collection databases, but it is an exciting prospect and would be a valuable tool.

An ideal scenario would be to scan every object in the collection, which is a journey that the Smithsonian has embarked on to create an unprecedented digital resource (http://blogs.smithsonianmag.com/aroundthemall/2013/02/from-pyenson-lab-when-is-a-museum-specimen-the-real-deal/); it does, however, have to be recognized that at this point in time many institutions still have backlogs of collection records to digitize. This can be due to lack of staff, expertise, or budgets; however, the benefits are clearly extolled by organizations such as JISC (Joint Information Systems Committee), which is a government charity funding digital innovation within education and research (http://www.jisc.ac.uk/#).

A number of museums and galleries around the world are beginning to accumulate a 3D resource of scans. There have been experiments in sharing and exhibiting 3D data, one of which was the Museum of Pure Form (http://www.pureform.org/). In 2004 a collection of sculpture, both existing and newly commissioned, were scanned. Installations of the artworks were created and visitors used new technology that allowed them to physically interact with the 3D digital forms, such as stereo vision, virtual cave technology, and haptics.

HAPTICS

Haptics is the ability to experience touch with computers and is becoming an important element in many digital devices, the most common form being the physical vibration that users feel when playing video games. Haptics technology started emerging in the late 1950s/early 1960s, with scientists such as Ralph Mosher (1962–1964, who used the technology as a component in his robotic systems and exoskeletons (GE Pedipulator) (http://cyberneticzoo.com/?p=2108). It was not until recently that the technology has been affordable, practical in size, and capable of believable sensory feedback. The technology has been utilized in the field of teleoperation and robotics, and recent applications include surgical training and 3D clay modeling for artists and designers.

Traditionally, human interactions with computers have been predominantly visual, using text, data, or imagery on screen. The keyboard or mouse is used to input and manipulate this data on a two-dimensional plane and there is no physical response relayed back to the user as a result of those actions. Haptics can provide both touch (tactile) and motion (kinaesthetic) feedback and can simulate physical properties, such as the weight of an object. The user can feel friction, texture, or resistance and the haptic hardware conveys those properties back to the user who can sense what is happening on the screen. Haptic interfaces come in many forms, such as touch mice, gloves, styluses, and joysticks. A common arrangement uses an articulated stylus to link a person's fingers to a computer interface. The Phantom haptic device (SensAble) was created by J. Kenneth Salisbury and Thomas Massie at the Massachusetts Institute of Technology and has a pen (stylus) or a fingertip thimble that acts as an interface.

In 2012 a haptic system was created at Manchester Museum, by technology provider Christopher Dean (Touch and Discover Systems) in consultation with a visually impaired user group (Henshaws, Society for Blind People). The group selected objects that would be inaccessible to them once displayed within a case and too vulnerable to be used routinely on a handling table. Features were specifically introduced into the interface that would help the visually impaired user locate the object and the additional contextual information. This enables a self-guided exploration of the object through touch that doesn't need to be facilitated and can exist remotely from the museum. A series of three-dimensional "examination" rooms were created that allow the user to explore the objects' history, manufacture, and use. The use of spatial sound within the 3D space is another important feature, which not only gives clues to the material qualities of the objects (which resonate when tapped), but also gives the visually impaired user the ability to locate the object within the three-dimensional space. The haptic interface captures the imagination of all types of museum visitors who are intrigued by the sensory feedback, and children are naturally drawn to using the computer device and become quickly comfortable with moving the stylus freely in space, exploring and looking closely at objects they would not necessarily engage with. There is still much to be done to make this a truly intuitive, rewarding experience, but there is enormous potential for it to provide a playful learning experience (http://www.museumsandheritage.com/advisor/news/item/2804).

TOUCH-ENABLED REPLICAS

A further project at Manchester Museum that involves the sense of digital touch is the Stela of Hesysunebef project, Unlocking the Story. A nylon replica has been printed from a scan of the limestone stela (~1600BC), which has a very complex narrative based on family relationships, status, and religious beliefs. This story remains silent to the majority of visitors and only a small percentage with specialist knowledge have the ability to interpret it. Intelligent sensors have been embedded in the replica, which are triggered by touch. The sensors have been strategically placed to allow the visitor to interrogate themes, symbols, and narratives in a self-guided exploration. The visitor can feel the surface of the stela (which has been hand-colored to look like the original), sensing the carved lines and triggering sound and picture files which relate to the information of the carved detail, whether hieroglyphics, objects, or the characters. These images and sound files play out on a screen and speaker close to the replica relief. This is a prototype; however, the technology has the capability to tell an artifact's hidden story using the physical clues that are present on the object.

Facsimiles of artifacts have existed for thousands of years; the best works of art and design have always been copied, cast, and emulated and used as an aid for teaching; museums' extensive plaster cast collections are evidence of this practice. Scan data can be used as a source for producing tangible products in the form of replicas. Currently, very accurate replicas can be made of things ranging from building complexes, sculptures, dinosaurs, and turtles to Greek helmets, and produced to a scale that can be assembled on a desk. Conversely, a microscopic organism or feature on an object that can only be seen on a scanning electron microscope can be enlarged to fit into the palm of a hand. Once an object is scanned, the scale and material of the copy can be selected and reproduced in anything from chocolate to monumental stone, with traditional casting sometimes being part of the process. The hand of a craftsman or artist is usually involved in finishing the form from both types of manufacturing processes if it is to imitate the original patina of the object.

3D REPLICAS

Hard copies are mostly produced using two different methods. Rapid prototyping is an "additive" process, combining layers of material or powder to create a solid object. The other method is CNC milling machine (computer numerical control), which drives a machine tool to selectively remove material from a solid block. The nature of 3D printing allows it to create objects with complicated internal features that are difficult to manufacture by other means. There are scanners available that will capture accurate colour and texture and will give the digital scan excellent resolution; however, when the results are printed the quality can still be variable. As the price of 3D printing machines falls, this opens up the possibilities for prints to be used more experimentally in educational institutions and the domestic market.

This technology has implications for the whole museum and gallery sector, as there is the possibility of an endless supply of good quality replica 3D objects that can be shared, sourced from the very finest example of artifacts that reside in our museums and galleries. Hard-wearing surrogates can be used on handling tables, in outreach sessions, or attached to permanent handling displays, making the collection available to the visually impaired or those that cannot make the journey into the museum due to economic or geographical limitations. Engagement develops around the use of collections and new activities will be created with the increased availability of 3D prints of objects that are either confined to cases or in store (http://www.wired.com/design/2012/10/scanathon/). The objects used in teaching sessions could be downloaded and printed in the classroom or examined in touch-enabled kiosks similar to the one that is on the gallery at Manchester Museum (there is currently a portable version of the system that is used in outreach sessions and can be taken to schools and hospitals). In time, 3D scans could be downloaded remotely, as we now download books, and exchanged and examined.

HACKING 3D DIGITAL DATA

Collections have always inspired generations of artists, designers, and schoolchildren; an extension of making the information available online through the database is allowing the public and developers to have access to the raw data, for the growing "hack" or "mash-up" scene. Mash-ups reuse, repurpose, and assimilate existing data, art, or content to create original works (see http://www.3Dprinter.net/mashing-up-museum-art-at-the-met).

Amateurs and professionals alike are working with collections using open source software and freely available data to create exciting new narratives, designs, and works of art, which exist in the real world as well as online. There are some associated risks with allowing data to become freely available because of it being used in the production of forgeries. There are ways of mitigating this risk and they need to be considered.

AUGMENTED REALITY

Augmented reality is another exciting area of technology that can utilize scan data, which can be introduced into real or virtual environments. Placing them within historical context can enhance museum displays by explaining the use and significance of objects (Wojciechowski et al., 2004). The three-dimensional form is suspended like a ghost in front of real contextual material on the gallery or alongside other relevant virtual data. Until recently this technology has largely been confined to tablet computers and phones; however with Google releasing their highly anticipated smart glasses, this will remove the barrier of the handheld device and heralds the arrival of a more spontaneous interaction with these three-dimensional virtual forms and the ability to move them through gesture control (http://www.kinecthacks.com/top-10-best-kinect-hacks/).

These new technologies do not replace the unique experience of seeing or holding a real object, but they can greatly enhance our understanding and enjoyment of their stories. They can make collections universally available and relevant to a more diverse audience, generating new forms of engagement.

Finally, before we understand the implications or the possibilities of the new 3D, Skylar Tibbits from MIT heralds the advent of 4D printing:

> The big idea is to create objects that can change after they are printed, making them self-adapting. The act of printing is no longer the end of the creative process but merely a waypoint . . . What we're saying here is, you design something, you print it, it evolves. (http://www.wired.co.uk/news/archive/2013-02/27/4d-printing)

REFERENCES

Candlin, F. (2004). Don't touch! Hands off! Art and blindness and the conservation of expertise. *Body Society* 10(1), 71–90. http://eprints.bbk.ac.uk/775/2/Candlin2004 .pdf.

———. (2010). *Art, Museums and Touch*. Manchester: Manchester University Press

Chatterje, H., ed. (2008). *Touch in Museums*. Oxford and New York: Berg.

Donelan, J. (2002). Researchers digitize a cave-art gallery. *Computer Graphics World* 25(3). http://www.cgw.com/Publications/CGW/2002/Volume-25-Issue -3-March-2002-/Making-Prehistory.aspx#.UTMzTTfd6So.

Dudley, S. (2012). *Materiality matters. Experiencing the displayed object*. University of Michigan Working Papers in Museum Studies Number 8

Fowles, S. (2000). The Garden Temple at Ince Blundell: a case study in the recording and non-contact replication of decayed sculpture. *Journal of Cultural Heritage* 1(Supplement 1), 89–91.

Giachristis, C. (2008). *The Use of Haptic Research Touch in Museums*. Oxford and New York: Berg, 75–90.

ICOM. (1991). *Museums without Barriers*. London: Routledge.

Metallo, A., and Rossi. V. (2011). The future of three-dimensional imaging and museum applications. *Curator the Museum Journal*. http://www.curatorjournal.org/archives/562.

Onol, I. (2008). Tactual explorations; A tactile interpretation of a museum exhibit through tactile art works and augmented reality. In *Touch in Museums*, 91–106. Oxford and New York: Berg.

Paterson, Mark. (2007). *The Senses of Touch: Haptics, Affects and Technologies*. Oxford and New York: Berg.

Pye, Elizabeth. (2007). *The Power of Touch*. Walnut Creek, CA: Left Coast Press.

Stone, Robert. (2001). *Haptic Feedback: A Potted History, From Telepresence to Virtual Reality*. Proceedings of the First International Workshop on Haptic Human-Computer Interaction. London: Springer Verlag.

Weisen, M. *(2008)*. How accessible are museums today? In *Touch in Museums, 243–53*. Oxford and New York: Berg.

Wojciechowski, R., et al. (2004). Building virtual and augmented reality museum exhibitions. Proceedings of the ninth international conference on 3D Web technology. *Web3D* 1(212). doi: 10.1145/985040.985060.

Zimmer, R. (2008). Touch technologies and museum access. In *Touch in Museums, 150–62*. Oxford and New York: Berg.

22

Technology, Senses, and the Future of Museums

A Conversation with Nina Levent, Heather Knight, Sebastian Chan, and Rafael Lozano Hammer

This chapter on potential uses of technology to enhance sensory museum experiences takes the form of a conversation between Art Beyond Sight's Nina Levent, curator Sebastian Chan, artist Rafael Lozano Hammer, and roboticist Heather Knight. **Sebastian Chan** is the director of digital and emerging media, Smithsonian, Cooper-Hewitt, National Design Museum. Sebastian is well known for his strategic perspective on the use of cutting-edge technologies in cultural institutions. **Rafael Lozano Hammer** is an electronic artist, who uses large technology such as search lights, robotic sensors, and surveillance networks to create performances and interactions that involve the whole body, amplify one's sensory presence, and create performances that are poetic, evocative, and critical. His main interest is in creating platforms for public participation. His large-scale interactive installations have been commissioned for events such as the Millennium Celebrations in Mexico City, the Cultural Capital of Europe in Rotterdam, and the UN World Summit of Cities in Lyon (2003). Recently Rafael was the subject of a solo exhibition at the San Francisco Museum of Modern Art. **Heather Knight** runs Marilyn Monrobot Labs, which creates socially intelligent robot performances and sensor-based electronic art. She is founder and director of the Robot Film Festival and Cyborg Cabaret, as well as a doctoral candidate at Carnegie Mellon's Robotics Institute.

Technology is changing the way we think about museums. We have access to a lot of museums' content on the web even before we go to museums. We bring our personal technology in museum spaces and use our mobile devices to navigate the space and the content of the museum. Robotic installations, sensors, and real-time data enable museums to think differently about creating personalized, multisensory experiences and learning opportunities. Machines, robots, and augmented experiences have a potential to amplify our physical and sensory realities. Being a trusted public space and a trusted source of information, museums have a potential to transform the technologies that are used for commercial and surveillance purposes elsewhere. Technologies, on the other hand, might have potential to aid museums in redefining their unique place in public life.

WHAT MIGHT THE FUTURE MUSEUM
LOOK LIKE IN TWENTY YEARS?

Nina Levant (NL): We see a number of emerging technologies used in museums already, augmented reality, games, 3D printing, and robotic installations to name a few. Some of these technologies are truly innovative and experimental as used by artist and designer, and some are consumer technology trends pushing their way into the galleries. What role will technology play in transforming the future of museums?

Sebastian Chan (SC): Museum visitors' demographics are broadening, on one hand. On the other hand, we're starting to see more spectacular entertainment venues—theme parks and cinema among them. Such spectacular immersion is becoming normalized, so that other leisure activities also have to scale up to compete. We're also starting to see this immersive technology in the hotel lobbies. Even boutique shopping is becoming more experiential: You're starting to see projection walls and touch-based shopping experiences. So museums are starting to think about how we can create interactive experiences using some of these consumer technologies. In recent times with the trend toward blockbuster exhibits, there's a more multisensory approach to exhibition design; museums are really engaging experience designers. The exhibit design is really beginning to happen more theatricality.

At the higher end of such museum immersion experience is the Museum of Old and New Art (MONA) in Tasmania, Australia. It is in my opinion the most exciting museum of art in the world at the moment. MONA has done a full experience design in their building, from getting on a ferry to coming into the lobby and then descending down into darkened galleries. It is an exciting alternative to going up into a white cube sort of experience.

Similarly, the Tate's new underground galleries known as the Tanks (three enormous underground concrete cylinders, former oil tanks) are successfully merging the theater with the museum experience. These are pointers toward much more performative and performed museum experience, and technology underpins all of that experience design, really—even when the technology is invisible—from lighting design to computer-based experiences, and importantly, visitor tracking.

NL: How can technology change our experience of interacting with a museum object or exploring a work of art? Is there room for new technology to facilitate an emergence of a new kind of museum? Can robots and other interactive technologies change our perception of what museums have to offer?

Rafael Lozano Hammer (RLH): The most important thing for the future museums, especially art museums, to overcome is an endemic attitude of paternalism and condescension toward the public. I believe that sadly, many museums—and it's not just museums, it's the curators and the directors and the press and the artists themselves—have this attitude that the public should just be counted, so it's good for metrics and statistics; how many people visited the show and how many went to the gift shop?

But smart museums are taking a much more experimental approach to the way that they're showing the artworks. So a good example would always be the Tate, where the curators have gone beyond the division of chronology, or ethnic and geographic assignation. They have mixed up the artworks in a way that sets up creative tensions, which are extremely purposeful and important. I would like to see more of that type of curating. I want museums to understand that the visual arts are performing arts, that painting and sculpture are closer to theater, closer to performance art, closer to music than unfortunately they were designed to present. So if you start thinking about visual art as having these performative qualities, you will show it differently. You will learn from the sophisticated vocabulary of theatrical presentation. And in so doing you will allow the public to have a fuller, more participatory experience.

Heather Knight (HK): Often museums put the works on display as if attendees are worshippers visiting a temple. We can disrupt this traditional hierarchy in various ways, but in the museum of the future, one of the most impactful instigators will be robotics. People come to be inspired, experience, socialize, learn, enjoy, or even create. Technological work can move, sense, and respond to interaction partners in their environments. Visitors need not be subjugated when they can be courted, encouraged, or provoked. The installations themselves can have personalities that engage, or accoutrements that play off the data of the weather that day. For example, we might place semi-humanoid robots in museum spaces: They can roam the galleries, changing the social patterns of visitors like a group of people facing the wrong way in an elevator. A robotic sculpture can take inspiration from mirroring visitors' motion, improvising around visitors' undulations like a jazz pianist. The odd mix of familiar and unrecognizable that robots so uncannily populate can disrupt and provoke our social patterns. The museum itself becomes a more playful installation, worshipers and worshipped now indistinguishable.

VISITOR DATA AND PERSONALIZED MUSEUM EXPERIENCE

NL: The technology is also enabling us to have more knowledge than ever about visitor behavior, visitor preferences, museum trajectories, and pace of visits. Often what we are finding out is not what we expect. We know more about how diverse and unique the needs of different groups of museum visitors are. Museums are hard-pressed to meet the learning, entertainment, and social needs of visitors who range from elementary school students to college professors, from seniors to teens who are blind. Could technology solve some of the problems around providing experience that's both learning and entertaining and highly personalized?

SC: There is a trend and desire to create galleries and information experience that is responsive to what visitors do, either one-on-one, or as a group or aggregated through time. There is a sense that a museum might learn more about visitors as people move through it. We already know from the audience research that visitors don't traverse our galleries in a linear way. Technologies now allow us to play with that understanding more and better. The other thing I like about getting real-time visitor data is that you get a chance to show a visitor things she or he didn't think about. It's not about being responsive, it's also about saying: "Oh, you really liked this, but you overlooked that."

Colleagues at the Dallas Museum of Art, who have just rolled out their new virtual membership system, found through their data collection that there was one visitor who was coming back daily. They thought the guy must have gamed our system. It turned out he was a schoolteacher who stopped at the museum on his way from work every day to think about his lessons for the next day. The museum has been inspiring his work. This was not visible, until the Dallas Museum brought in this technology platform. There were people who come in for very different purposes, and I think that's awesome. The question then becomes how do you redesign your galleries and redesign your whole museum experience to accommodate more of the types of users that you want.

ROBOTS AND THE FUTURE MUSEUM

NL: Could you reflect on the current trends in robotics and where you see robots in museum environments in ten to twenty years? Do you see robots becoming a part of museum infrastructure? How can robots and robotic tech-nology be integrated in museum galleries to enhance the experience, help to discover new meaning, facilitate discovery and learning? Or perhaps help assist visitors through the galleries?

HK: It's impossible to discuss the impact of robots in museums in isolation from the potential impact of robotic technologies in everyday society. In the same way that most attendees now carry smartphones in their pockets, one day robots assisting older people or kids will accompany their companions into our public spaces. Embodied machines will be present in entertainment, autism therapy, and language education. Autonomous vehicles might even drop the visitors off at the museum door. Artists will be able to create new installations that particularly address their rising presence.

Within the museum, robots can transform the overall environment or be installations themselves. There are a couple of ways I could see robots used in museum galleries. One idea would be to assist with creating museum narra-tives, for people to explore, either actively, as a literal tour guide, or indirectly as a catalyzer to social behavior. Imagine a robot that lays bread crumbs for visitors to follow, helping to tell the story through words, sounds, objects. There could be playful and curious robotic boxes, covered in bright-colored fur, with a desire for attention and curiosity. They might lead or follow visi-tors on their wanderings or aid in a scavenger hunt, collecting bones at certain museum objects along the way.

Each art piece or museum object could be partnered with a robotic label that beckons passersby when it is feeling neglected or when it knows of a visitor's particular interest in a subject. These roboticized plaques would be animated through motion, attracting your attention and highlighting layers of museum object information. Research shows that we are strongly influenced by robots in our physical space; we have a visceral reaction to moving ob-jects. As soon as we see something traverses space with intention, we ascribe it social characteristics. These robots would grab the attention of children or adult visitors. I envision bringing such robots into museum spaces and incor-porating them into our shared spaces skillfully, for example by incorporating known principles of social psychology for smooth integration.

Another idea is to create a robot that is an attendee itself, equipped with strong opinions and natural motions. I imagine a humanoid-looking robot that walks around the galleries and observes works of art, spending a lot of time in front of some works, just a few moments in front of others. This machine's persona might be that of an art expert or art historian. We are social creatures, we react to robots viscerally, placing them within our known social schema of friendliness, dominance, interest, and importance. We feel viewed, accom-panied, judged, or responsible. Such reactions to a robot impersonating an art critic is markedly different from that of an art history app on your phone. People might be curious about his choice or critical of his taste, but he would not be a persona who is easily ignored.

TECHNOLOGY, ART, AND SENSORY INTERACTION

NL: Artists bring technology into museums, sometimes to entertain, sometimes to poke fun or pose serious questions. On occasion they "rehabilitate" technology that is otherwise used for surveillance, commercial, or military purposes. Can museums compete with other venues as entertainment centers? What technology could art museums offer in ten to twenty years that will be worth the effort of traveling across town to get to it as opposed to getting in front of the screen?

RLH: Art museums can offer two simple things: The first one comes from American composer Frederic Rzewski, whose composition "Coming Together" from 1971 underlined the joy, power, and complicity of people congregating from disparate realities. As simple as that idea is, that's why it's so strong: There will always be this need for us to assemble and experience in the company of others.

The second important thing museums can offer is something called in the entertainment industry "location-based entertainment," which is the idea of experiences that people could not get at home because of scale, or cost, or concept. A lot of my work is based on the sense of immersion, for example. "Pulse Room" is a work of art that is an array of 300 blinking light bulbs, which literally represent the heartbeats of people who visit the show. As more people participate the heartbeats get recycled. An experience like this is based on a very intimate biometric that is amplified to take on a more architectural presence: One heartbeat by itself is of little aesthetic interest, but your heartbeat together with the heartbeat of another 300 people creates a very interesting pattern.

Along the lines of Derrick de Kerckhove's notions of connected intelligence, I like to think about "connectivity" in a museum space, rather than the populist and problematic notion of "collectivity." Connectivity is this idea that there is this moment where disparate places and experiences actually get in touch. So in a project like "Pulse Room," through the measurement of your biometrics, which typically is associated with either medical or surveillance control, we create a connective space, which we hope is poetic and critical. And as people walk around the light bulbs they get an experience, which is in terms of scale is very different than what they can get at home. But, in terms of symbolism it's also tremendously different because the light show itself is

Figure 22.1. Rafael Lozano-Hemmer, "Pulse Room," 2006. Musée des Beaux-Arts du Québec, Quebec City, Québec, Canada, 2008. Photo by Antimodular Research

made out of hundreds of people who have participated. This idea of coming together is materialized in a piece like that.

HK: An eternal motivation of art is understanding ourselves, exploring meaning, intelligence, love, and nihilism. I have been thinking about machines on stage and in film settings, and specifically about storytelling with robots. Most times when we use robots to narrate a story it is not about robots but about humans. They are mechanical foils for human experience. I think robotic works of art can expose us to unexpected angles of ourselves, highlighting some part of our existence. We recognize ourselves in robots.

Astroboy of Japanese manga books is a robot without human flaws, and he teaches humans how to be better creatures. However, as a creator of robots I recognize that creating robots that remind us of ourselves is a daunting task. Our flaws and foibles are some of the most difficult attributes to recreate in robots. Humor is hit or miss. Creativity is limited in scope. Friendship and love are poor approximations. And each time a technologist claims to have solved the problem, we slide our scale a notch deeper.

SC: The discussion of technology in museums on one end is led by artists and at the other end should be contextualized by science museums. The science museums have really struggled with doing an exhibit about the Internet or exhibits about surveillance. Art museums shouldn't be the only place where these technologies are questioned and talked about.

MUSEUM OBJECTS AND COLLECTING IN THE DIGITAL AGE

NL: The notion of exhibits without physical objects, or collecting digital works of art, raises a number of questions. Historically, museums tend to be possessive about the collections; after all, they are the reason for museums' existence. Museums also tend to take pride in the fact that they provide an authentic experience. How do you see technology changing the relationship between the public and a museum object?

SC: I think there's an interesting tension between objects and theatricality. Helen Whitty at the Powerhouse Museum in Sydney did this fabulous series of exhibits with a children's book author. The children's book author would pull out some strange objects from the collection and write fictional labels for those objects, and later the museum would provide the real ones as well. But it was about immersing children and visitors in this exploration of possibilities: "What if this is something else? What if this is a magical device?" It made you look at the object in a new way and see the objects as props for storytelling, which they are really. So, we get a sense of objects as having multiple interpretations, multiple lives, and technology allows those multiple lives to be revealed. Particularly video designers are playing with the narrative, in which a story occurs in this space and time, but the time is not linear. The technologies to create nonlinear stories are becoming better, and museums are the obvious place for such storytelling to occur.

RLH: My relationships with museums and the notion of collecting has evolved. My work used to involve solely interventions that transform a public space with an eccentric platform for participation and lasted for a few weeks. I grew up thinking about museums as mausoleums, with the Douglas Crimp text that was so influential. But then I realized that in fact the contemporary situation is nothing like the Douglas Crimp, but rather the opposite. Today, museums are not letting artworks have an honorable death; they keep them alive, artificially, through restoration and preservation and quotation. I thought of this kind of desire for collection for having especially a pedagogical or didactical, chronological representation of culture as quite toxic and vampiric. But as soon as I started working with commercial galleries I changed my tune and decided that my work could in fact be added to a museum collection so long as it had a vibrant and open attitude toward the art. And most museums today, unless they're extremely conservative, have understood that art is not just an object, it's a process, it's an event, it's a performance. In general, how I justified my inclusion in collections like the Tate or Museum of Modern Art in New York, is by talking not so much about preservation, but perpetration of the cultural act. The idea that the artwork itself is aware and it is living and that what it needs is to be re-performed into the future.

FUTURE MUSEUM VISITORS AND SENSORY EXPERIENCES

NL: With the proliferation of digital and web-based experience, museums are concerned with cultivating new audiences and giving them experiences that will draw visitors back to their spaces again and again. . . . I am often asked, "Why should I make an effort to visit a museum when I can see its collection and learn so much about them on my computer?" How can museums draw visitors to their actual spaces and inspire repeat visits? What on-site experiences can technology offer that are meaningful and distinct from the museum's web content?

SC: In twenty years' time there will be a number of museums that survive on mainly tourism. But outside of those I think the ones that will do best will be the museums that can engender a need for repeat visitations. Museums could be a place where you can spend time. That's all about experience design, service design, and architecture that invite people to stay, rather than invite people to come and move on. I think that's been very interesting looking at some of the working designers who I know in the UK, who will go for a day and sit in a museum and do their work because they want to be inspired by the objects around. Not necessarily any particular object, but the whole environment.

When it comes to technology, museums are often behind the curve that is popular culture and are not able to effectively play in the technology space. But there are some examples of using technology in museums in a way that pushes the whole field further forward. The climate change exhibit at the Maritime Museum in London is great example of such design. It was an interactive exhibit with no objects. It is interesting that the Maritime Museum would launch the new gallery for museum objects with no objects. United Visual Artists, famous for providing stage visuals to Massive Attack and Chemical Brothers, was hired to create enormous exhibition that would give visitors a taste of what it's like to travel to the Arctic. They created an amazing experience, in which a visitor was walking around with a UV torch that triggered interactive experiences. The gallery was darkened and you were walking through this projected landscape experiencing the effect of the shrinking polar caps. The interactivity of the exhibit was done really through sound. It was all about the spatial arrangement of sound and the commissioning of a British poet to create a multistranded poem out of scientific reports and data and ship logs that would give the visitors an experience of traveling through the North Pole, and the experience of shrinking ice caps. It was high tech and it was elegant.

HK: I think a great museum experience is a visceral experience; an experience of an augmented self is still an embodied, visceral experience. I know of current augmented reality projects where researchers seek to reanimate ancient buildings in China. Using your phone's camera and the results of their program, you would be able to overlay full buildings on the images of ruins from any angle. The resulting experience is a whole-body walk through an ancient city. Mars rovers are often talked about as extensions of ourselves. Is there a difference between our traveling to space and participating in the travel through these extensions of ourselves? This is very exciting for us in the field of robotics to see how we can expand our senses through using machines.

Robots can play a similar role in a museum context. They have the additional advantage of embodiment, which uniquely embeds itself in our psychology as compared with screen-based interfaces. Though their natural motions and behaviors, robotic installations can facilitate reactive, visual, and participatory experience. Technology can manipulate people's behavior, coaxing strangers to meet or friends to come out of their shells. They can act very much like a great host or successful party planner. A robot has the advantage of not being human itself, so people can misbehave and not feel judged, relaxing into playfulness. Imagine an installation that gives the viewer a feeling of superpowers.

Conclusion

Multisensory Art Museums and the Experience of Interconnection

*Elisabeth Axel and Kaywin Feldman,
in conversation with artists and curators*

A multisensory experience of artwork allows for visceral intimacy in ways that sometimes seem forgotten in today's museum. The relevance of together thinking through the possibilities for the multisensory museum is universal; it extends beyond the necessity of making art institutions accessible to people with disabilities and on to the possibility of creating immersive experiences for all visitors. Truly we each navigate our need to connect with the world and with one another using our own individual sets of sensory as well as cultural tools, none exactly the same as our neighbors'. We learn and interact idiosyncratically, some more or less active, contemplative, visual, auditory, or tactile in our strengths and challenges of engagement. Museum-visiting, a predominantly social experience, provides the perfect opportunity for people to connect not only with others but at the same time with their own senses. This chapter documents a conversation between several artists and curators whose practices consider the potential for increasing opportunity for connecting with artwork and through artwork. Collectively they imagine a new future for museums.

Elisabeth Axel is the founder of Art Beyond Sight and Art Education for the Blind, dedicated to making the arts and culture accessible to people with various disabilities, including those who are blind or have low vision. She is co-chair of Project Access, a national initiative to make cultural institutions accessible to all. **Kaywin Feldman** is the director and president of the Minneapolis Institute of Arts, past president of the Association of Art Museum Directors, and vice president of the American Alliance of Museums. A scholar of seventeenth-century Dutch and Flemish art, she has become known for balancing popular and experimental art exhibitions. **Yukio Lippit** is professor of the history of art and architecture at Harvard University, and his work as scholar and curator is primarily focused on premodern Japanese painting. His recently curated exhibition Colorful Realm: Japanese Bird-and-Flower Paintings by Itō Jakuchū at the National Gallery of Art was one of the museum's most visited exhibitions of all time. **Ann Hamilton** is known around the world as an artist whose immersive, site-specific installations engage many modes of sensory experience. Her recent installation "the event of a thread" at the Park Avenue Armory combined billowing fabric, readings, sound, live pigeons, and giant swings in which participants could float through the space and interact with one another. **Peter Sellars** is a world-renowned theater, opera, television, and film director, and professor of world arts and cultures at the University of California at Los Angeles, where he teaches Art as Social Action and Art as Moral Action. **Julián Zugazagoitia** is the director of The Nelson-Atkins Museum of Art in Kansas City, where his Art Tasting series presents casual conversation with curators over wine about objects in the museum's collection to the public. **Frederick John Lamp** is the Frances and Benjamin Benenson Foundation Curator of African Art at the Yale University Art Gallery. His expertise in developing innovative strategies for the display of African art has been developed through art historical scholarship informed by interest in dance and performance. **Lawrence Rinder** is the director of the Berkeley Art Museum and Pacific Film Archive at the University of California, Berkeley. For the 2007 exhibition Shahrokh Yadegari: Through Music, Rinder curated for the Judah L. Magnes Museum in Berkeley a sound piece combining singing in Hebrew, Farsi, and English with classical Persian and electronic music that was installed to give new context to the Magnes Collection. **Jan-Lodewijk Grootaers** is the curator of African art and the head of the department of arts of Africa and the Americas at the Minneapolis Institute of Arts. A recent exhibition at the MIA, iAfrica: Connecting with Sub-Saharan Art, featured a vitrine visitors could turn themselves, sound stations, a virtual lamellophone (thumb piano), and opportunities to smell works of art. The exhibition tested the usefulness of contextual sensory and written information in enriching visitors' understanding of African art.

THE MULTISENSORY ART MUSEUM

Elisabeth Axel (EA) and Kaywin Feldman (KF): How do you envision that considering all of the senses, beyond sight, could help to improve art and museums?

Yukio Lippit (YL): Sensory experience is fundamentally synesthetic, involving multiple senses at the same time. Arguably the traditional museum display/experience does not even engage sight in any meaningful sense. Anything that fully engages the senses will engage the mind and lead to new forms of empathy and understanding of artworks/artifacts created in a different world from ours. Many artworks presupposed very specific conditions of encounter: the cave, the temple, or the ritual moment. Some were products of systems of thought that had a great deal to say about how we experienced the world through our senses, like certain kinds of Buddhist philosophy, which explored, to the most intensive degree possible, the nature of how our senses took in, and sometimes constructed, the illusory world.

Ann Hamilton (AH): We think and feel through all our senses. All experience is embodied, even when we privilege our eyes over our feet. How we pay attention to all the qualities of experience will affect how long we linger. The longer we linger will affect how we think and how we think will increase our capacity to respond. The felt experiences of spaces, sound, light, temperature, and smell, have everything to do with what and how we think.

EA and KF: What role do you envision the multisensory museum can play in changing our definitions of connection, connectivity, and community?

Peter Sellars (PS): Art is here to prove that our wholeness is actually based on every part of our lives being completed by someone else. That in fact none of us are capable of doing anything alone, ever. None of our perceptions are deep enough until we're sharing them with someone else and someone else is completing our understanding, our thought, our point of view.

Art offers us the chance to meet within our differences. And in fact it is the one thing that encourages us all to say, "Well, I see something different here." Actually it's the one place where our difference is affirmed, rather than being a drawback, a negative, something we have to hide.

YL: Meaningfully exploring the cultural production of the past can generate an empathy and understanding of experiences and worldviews other than our own. This is the greatest value of museums and cultural knowledge—to take us outside of our own subjectivity.

THE ARTISTS' ROLE IN CREATING MULTISENSORY ART EXPERIENCE

EA and KF: What role can artists play in transforming museum spaces and experiences toward including senses other than vision?

Frederick Lamp (FL): Art museums are historically oriented toward the final product, and the tautology between the roles of artists and the roles of museums has not always been obvious. In fact, the very idea of "activity" somehow seems to be incompatible with the passivity expected in the hushed gallery where one receives art through sight. Touch is forbidden. Sound is frowned upon and rarely is included in the installation. Smell is anathema. And taste would be unthinkable. Yet many artists today address any number of the five senses. Obviously the objects in the art museum are of high value—essentially priceless—and cannot be violated. Traditionally, artists are sometimes invited into the museum to give talks—often separate from the art spaces in an auditorium, but sometimes in the art galleries themselves. What about asking artists to interact with the objects? This was done successfully by Fred Wilson at the Maryland Historical Society, where he created, in effect, an installation piece, transforming the objects themselves and their meanings by each particular replacement, violating each piece intellectually without destroying it.

AH: Rather than purpose built, some of the most successful exhibition spaces have been former industrial spaces that have involved artists heavily in their design and renovation. Former social histories and an architecture that is specific, but doesn't call attention to itself, work in a recessive way. Perhaps it allows the same for visitors. For many in my generation, Dia [Art Foundation] remains one of the most important. The design of their spaces and history has been tied closely to their unique collaboration with artists.

YL: Artists have already been playing an important role in transforming gallery spaces since the 1960s, and this role can certainly be expanded to include more traditional museum exhibition spaces in the future. This is especially true of those involved in artistic practices centering around sound art, environmental art, and space-making. The important thing is to involve artists at the outset as curators of the space, working in close conjunction with the curator of the exhibition, and to have them explore how best to set off the space-time conditions and cultural value of art objects, without turning the exhibition into an occasion to create a separate artwork that drowns out the specificity of the works on display.

FL: At Yale University we have invited artists into the Art Gallery to create work that somehow responds to the material arts on view, sometimes directly reflecting the art, sometimes independent, yet causing the audience to see the arts in a different way. Reggie Wilson, the choreographer, has set pieces within particular galleries, changing the way the art would be seen and the way the dance would be seen in separate contexts, bringing both movement and sound. Students from the School of Drama have set sound pieces onto particular works of sculpture in one instance, and light and sound pieces onto whole collections of sculpture in another instance. These performance pieces laid upon existing sculpture sometimes worked to explore the meanings of the sculptures, but some simply used the existing art as a core on which to build an independent art form, yet causing the visitor to view the original art form in a different way through multisensory stimulation.

Obviously, performance art and installation art in the art museum are one way to dissolve the divide between process and product. Artists and sculpture, painting, and other material arts should be invited more often to work in the art-filled galleries themselves, to alleviate the disconnect that the visitor has between the finished work of art and the complex strategies, contemplation, struggle, fabrication of materials, technique, resolution and failure, and human effort that constitute a time-based art of which the finished work is only evidence.

Lawrence Rinder (LR): Berkeley Art Museum/Pacific Film Archive's L@TE Friday evening performance series introduced multisensory experience into the museum by introducing music, dance, film, and other performance works. One of the factors that makes this series especially radical is its siting in the museum's central atrium which is, by nature of the building's unique design, open to every one of the museum's exhibition galleries, which spiral around and above it. As a result, visitors to the gallery exhibitions hear music being played in the atrium and can, if they choose, gaze down at the performances from the overhanging balconies. Furthermore, we intentionally undermine the formal, static conventions of performance spectatorship by locating the performances in ways that encourage audience movement during the events themselves . . . We do not enforce silence during performances, so a certain degree of ambient sound is generally present, conveying an informal, dynamic atmosphere . . . When the museum is filled with hundreds of visitors, simultaneously looking at art, listening to music, and walking around, it is tremendously energizing and inspiring.

SENSORY APPROACHES AND EXPERIENCE OF TRADITIONAL AND CONTEMPORARY ART

EA and KF: How can a multisensory approach to exhibitions affect how we experience art?

PS: What we're talking about is sight and insight. And art is here not to say what something looks like but to say what something feels like and to take you not into the visible world but into the invisible world and to begin to be comfortable with the invisible world. And when we're talking about listening we're talking about deep listening. Deep listening is listening to everything that is unspoken. Just slowing down and having to really create a zone of attention. Deep attention. Which is what a work of art is all about. Slow down, and start listening more deeply, and looking more deeply. Start to move with more awareness. Start to actually begin to taste. For me this is what art is about. Becoming skillful in looking deeply, listening deeply, responding deeply, moving deeply, moving with grace, moving with understanding. Actually tasting the world—taste obviously brings every part of your being into life.

AH: The challenge is always what kind of experience is possible—not how do you fill it in, but how do you allow it to be open.

FL: Curators in many fields are coming to see the "white box" as inadequate for the understanding of the object, especially in the ritual arts of the Third World, but also in Western arts, obviously in ancient and medieval, but even in the contemporary. . . . The original context often had to do with a larger form of art in which the museum object is simply a fragment, and the performance of larger scope including enmeshed multisensory factors. Often this original context included such aspects as sound, movement, audience involvement with the object, sometimes involving manipulation and a tactile sense, a sense of space or theatrical staging, a sense of timing, strategic lighting to effect the proper sensory reading, and important olfactory elements contributing to the understanding of the work.

Postmodern and postcolonial thought argues for understanding through bodily experience, the somatic (awareness within the body as opposed to the mind), the proprioceptive (perception through one's own bodily responses) with a distrust of the taxonomies especially perfected in the past century.

Julián Zugazagoitia (JZ): Museums normally engage all of the senses because as visitors we are participants; we arrive at any experience incapable of separating sight, smell, sound, and so forth. I think of the Getty Villa in Malibu, and upon the approach the botanical gardens—the floral aroma that fills the air cannot be extricated from the memory. On the other side, you go through the galleries of the Louvre and the cracking of the floor, the imperial grandeur of the galleries remind you that the initial function of the building was a palace, engaging all the senses in that experience.

Nevertheless, museums have never totally focused on the overall sensory experience. What I think artists today can do, as well as museum professionals, is design an environment with that heightened awareness in mind; that the works of art are displayed in surroundings that contributed to their understanding, exaltation, and appreciation.

EA and KF: Could you reflect on the relationship between object and experience in museums?

AH: We extend our hands in touching [and] what we do not know becomes known. It is always reciprocal, but a museum protects objects from the damage of our touch and so has the challenge to find ways we can touch with our eyes. How to invite tactility and haptic experience into the museum in a way that is complex and not didactic is a challenge, but addressing this challenge will keep objects—removed from their social context—alive to our contemporary experience.

The felt experience of an object has as much to do with the atmosphere and landscape of the exhibition design as the object itself. We can walk past something or be stopped dead in our tracks . . . great exhibition design offers us solitude with an object, but also experiences, information, sometimes startling juxtapositions and, perhaps most importantly, opens us up to something we didn't know before. It changes our perception of time, allows us to take time, and, like touch, we are motivated and changed by the exchange.

FL: Contextualization of the object in the art museum ought to address the entirety of the art form itself in all its integration and the history of the specific object from conception to material fact, and beyond, to ownership and audience. The problem of translation in the museum gallery is paramount. African art in performance, for example, may require the space of the entire village, incorporating the architecture, the plazas, the walkways and streets, as well as the hot sun of mid-day or the dim gray of dusk, hundreds of viewer-participants, the cacophony of competing groups of dancers, polyphonic singers, and multiple-meter drummers, the billowing dust from under stamping feet, and five or six hours of duration. Obviously, all this cannot be brought literally into the museum gallery—and should not, for the risk of exoticizing and trivializing something of deep significance. But it should be acknowledged, suggested, and in some ways represented in museum interpretation where possible, if only for a few objects to highlight the difference between the full art form and the museum fragment.

Jan-Lodewijk Grootaers (JLG): Art museums are silent places for looking. This is the case in part because art museums are the secular temples of the late nineteenth and early twentieth centuries. Sacred places that stimulate intense, exalted looking, to the exclusion of the other senses . . . The opposite of the temple, to a certain extent, is the marketplace: crowded, rowdy, and smelly. A few installations back, the Tropenmuseum in Amsterdam had part of its Africa display reorganized as a West African market, with heaps of plastic fruits and veggies, piles of pots and colorful textiles, and noises in foreign tongues coming out of speakers. It did not work for me and felt completely disconnected with the actual collection . . .

So how does one clarify the multisensory nature of African art without falling into the marketplace trap, and without implicitly reinforcing the stereotype that African art is less civilized, more sensorial, and therefore requires special treatment that, again, sets it apart? The underlying question is how one should deal with context. One wants to get away from the referential representation of context to one that is experiential—from the typical period room or, more appropriately in the context of African art, the diorama (with the hut, the savanna grass, the painted sunset) to something else. Any exhibition is a collage, a new whole made up of several, disparate fragments, and any object removed from its original context has become a fragment. Interactive technology can place an African sculptural fragment, say a mask, in an environment of other fragments from Africa, coming from other sources and appealing to other senses: the sounds, smells, light, and kinesis referred to at the beginning. This would create a multisensory experience. A possible drawback, however, would be the danger of not getting closer to Africa and African art at all, but instead expanding our experience of American technology.

PS: All of our actions are offerings, and that is one of the things missing in museums. In India the Hindu statues, of course, would be every single day dressed, painted, given incense, reclothed, and given food, candles. And the entire experience is not a bronze statue, the entire experience is a living being. We're beholding our most divine selves. And of course, in India, the tradition is Darshan, which is the statue sees us. It's not us looking at the statue, it's the god beholding us. And that beautiful image of reciprocity, that beautiful image of this is the shared space where we see our divine selves, and our divine selves behold us, where we see ourselves whole, resplendent, shining, surrounded by flames, surrounded by joy in a state of unbelievable peace, calm, balance, secret mastery, and deep compassion. In order to open the statue we need to make an offering, to activate the art. Because the art is just sitting there, the art is an object until we activate it, until we offer our prayer, until we offer our incense, until we offer our buttermilk, until we cover it with flowers, until we dress it again today, until we give everything we have to give and then it receives us, opens and sees us, and offers a blessing. And that idea that we activate the art and then the art activates us, that's the energy, the reciprocity.

And all of these works of art are not objects, they're immersive experiences. Almost every object in the museum is a ritual object and is meant to engage in ceremony. The piece of wood was not meant to be in a display case; that piece of wood was meant to invite the spirits, that piece of wood was meant to be part of the fire, that piece of wood was meant to float on the ocean, that piece of wood was meant to be active. These objects are meant to create experiences and these experiences are the key to each of our own infinity.

POSSIBILITIES FOR THE FUTURE

EA and KF: What type of experience or interactivity is missing in art museums today?

LR: Art making. Some museums do provide art-making opportunities for children but rarely for all-ages audiences and rarely on a drop-in basis. Believing that art making positively impacts audiences' experience of art and their ability to understand new creation, we have planned an all-ages, drop-in art-making space in a central location of our new downtown Berkeley building. We are also currently working on an experimental exhibition that will include several art-making studios (for clay, textile dying, print and book making, and sound recording) and which will be located in the museum's galleries. Works made in these studios, both by visiting artists as well as the general public, will be presented subsequently as part of the evolving exhibition. Through these approaches we hope to celebrate and encourage creativity, participation, and collaboration, and to instill a deeper appreciation of art.

[In general the design of museum buildings for the future should reflect the increasing trend of visitor participation and interaction by] creating informal spaces for music, dance, and other performances; creating spaces for participatory art making; creating cozy reading nooks; creating moveable, modular furniture to encourage sociability and interaction.

PS: We need to take the museum from a place of a prison for art where all these things are locked up looking a little sad. Or a hospital for art, where you know, you're not allowed to bring in any plants, it's extremely sanitized, and of course the art was not created in sanitized conditions at all, but quite the opposite. And so what we have to do is once again pollute these places, make a mess, make a set of rituals, activate ourselves, and activate the art.

The kind of experience or interactivity we need in art museums is the kind of experience that makes us reach below the surface.

EA and KF: What kind of art museum or gallery would you want to visit or see built by 2020?

FL: Art museums have a long way to go before curators and directors are willing to introduce the more ephemeral aspects that have been left behind when the objects were collected. But technology allows us today to isolate sound and smell, and exhibits can approximate the tactile with touchable displays. These should not be seen as separate "educational" experiences, but rather essential experiences to the understanding of the art. . . . As in the original contexts of art, contributing sensory experiences sometimes are syncretic, contributing to a unified meaning, but just as often they are not, and they need not be to be justified in a museum display.

JLG: I imagine a display of African masks, each artwork being doubled by an exact copy that is offered to the visitors and can be worn before the face or put over the head. Invited to lie on a bench and fasten the mask, the visitor gets connected to micro-processors that instantly create an alternate reality: (S)he is projected into the performance arena of the mask, able to live it both as a dancer and a spectator and experiencing all the sensory stimuli that go with it, understanding the meaning of the words and songs, capable of joining in, and so on. During the experience the visitor stays put and remains quiet.

I would enjoy this type of submersive experience in other galleries of the museum, too.

JZ: In an age of information, one where we can access information and reproduction of works digitally from anywhere in the world, the museum is irreplaceable. Embracing the potential of a full immersion and site specificity could enhance the experience and count it among the greatest of accomplishments.

Index

361

About the Contributors

Salvatore Maria Aglioti, neurologist, neuropsychologist, and social neuroscientist, is a full professor of social neuroscience at Sapienza University of Rome. His research focuses on the neural bases of corporeal awareness in healthy, brain-damaged, and spinal cord-injured people and on the intersubjective aspects of action and empathy. He directs the Cognitive Social and Affective Neuroscience Laboratory and international PhD program in cognitive social and affective neuroscience (http://w3.uniroma1.it/cosan/). His research is conducted at the Department of Psychology (Sapienza University) and at the IRCCS Fondazione Santa Lucia, Rome (http://w3.uniroma1.it/aglioti/).

Claude Alain graduated from the Université du Québec à Montréal in 1991. He then moved to the VA Medical Center at Martinez, California, for his postdoctoral training, where he worked with Dr. David Woods until 1996. Dr. Alain is currently a senior scientist at the Rotman Research Institute at Baycrest Center for Geriatric Care and professor in psychology at the University of Toronto. He has received several awards, including a Canadian Institutes of Health Research Scholarship and the Premier Research Excellence Award from the government of Ontario. His research is in the field of cognitive neuroscience and focuses on the brain processes supporting auditory scene analysis. Dr. Alain is using a combination of neuroimaging techniques (e.g., EEG, MEG, and fMRI) to investigate which, and how, different brain areas work together during auditory scene analysis.

Stephen Arnott graduated from the University of Toronto in 2005. He completed his postdoctoral training at the University of Western Ontario, where he worked with Dr. Mel Goodale until 2008. Dr. Arnott is currently an adjunct scientist at the Rotman Research Institute at Baycrest Center for Geriatric Care. He has received several awards, including the Canadian Institutes of Health Research Doctoral award. His work seeks to understand auditory processing in the human brain, with a special focus on its multisensory interactions with visual brain areas.

Elisabeth Salzhauer Axel is the founder and president of Art Beyond Sight (ABS), formerly Art Education for the Blind (AEB), a nonprofit organization founded in 1987. During this time she also served for fifteen years as the senior lecturer and curriculum developer at the Whitney Museum of American Art. Elisabeth presents nationally at conferences such as the American Association of the Museums and the National Art Educators Association. She is the editor-in-chief of AEB's *Art History Through Touch and Sound*, a unique multisensory art encyclopedia. Drawing on the organization's methodology and expertise, Elisabeth coedited another publication: *Art Beyond Sight: A Resource Guide to Art, Creativity, and Visual Impairment*. Considered authoritative for professionals in this field, this publication was copublished with the American Foundation for the Blind. Elisabeth has trained staff and educators in art education and accessibility issues at notable institutions such as the Smithsonian Institution, Los Angeles County Museum of Art, Museum of Modern Art, John and Mable Ringling Museum, Birmingham Museum, and California School for the Blind, to name a few. She has served on the board of directors of United Jewish Appeal Leadership Development Division; the Associated Blind, a housing and rehabilitation facility; and the Mayor's Office for the Handicapped (now the Mayor's Office for Disabilities).

Francesca Bacci is curator of special projects at the Museum of Modern and Contemporary Art of Trento and Rovereto (MART). She trained as an art historian and restorer at the University of Udine, where she received her laurea in preservation of the fine arts. She completed her PhD in history of art, as well as a Curatorial Certificate, as a Fulbright Fellow at Rutgers University (USA). She has taught university courses for Oxford University, Oxford Brookes, Rutgers University, and Harvard University. Her main research interests focus on late-nineteenth- and early-twentieth-century European art, early photography, the psychology of art, curatorship, and the public experience of art. Bacci has collaborated on research and exhibition projects with the Guggenheim Museum (Venice and New York City), the Brooklyn Museum of Art (New York City), the Centre Pompidou (Paris), the Musée Rodin (Paris), and the MART Museum (Rovereto). With David Melcher, she is the editor of *Art and the Senses*.

Ilaria Bufalari, is a post-doctorate in cognitive neuroscience in the Department of Psychology, Sapienza University of Rome. Her research focuses on the neural correlates and the psychosocial variables that influence body representations, self-identity illusions, and social interactions (with particular emphasis on empathic processes). Her research activity combines brain-imaging and stimulation techniques with personality measures.

Matteo Candidi, psychologist and cognitive neuroscientist, is assistant professor in the Department of Psychology, Sapienza University of Rome. His research focuses on the neural correlates of visual and motor body representations in healthy individuals studied in realistic social contexts. He studies the influence of personality and cultural variables on the kinematics of interpersonal communicative behaviors and on the neural correlates of visuo-motor simulative processes through brain stimulation methods.

Antonino Casile received a laurea degree in computer engineering (summa cum laude) from the University of Pisa, Italy, and a PhD in computational neuroscience (summa cum laude) from Scuola Superiore S. Anna, Pisa, Italy. The focus of his research is the investigation of the influences of motor processes on both low- and high-level perception. For his research he uses psychophysical, theoretical, brain-imaging, and neurophysiological techniques.

Seth Cluett is an artist, perfomer, and composer whose work ranges from photography and drawing to video, installation, concert music, and critical writing. His "subtle . . . seductive, immersive" (Artforum) soundwork has been characterized as "rigorously focused and full of detail" (e/i) and "dramatic, powerful, and at one with nature" (The Wire). Boomcat described his 2011 CD Objects of Memory on the Line Imprint as a "beautifully tremulous and thoughtful exploration in electro-acoustic sound." Cluett has published articles for the Pew Center for Arts and Heritage, *BYPASS*, *Shifter*, *The Open Space Magazine*, *Leonardo Music Journal*, *306090*, *Earshot*, and the *Journal of the Acoustical Society of America*, and his work is documented on Errant Bodies Press, Line, Sedimental, and Winds Measure Recordings. The recipient of grants and awards from Meet the Composer, The Foundation for Contemporary Arts Emergency Fund, and the Andrew W. Mellon Foundation, he has presented work internationally at venues such as MassMoCA, The Kitchen, GRM, Palais de Tokyo, FRAC Franche-Compté, STEIM, and Dundee Contemporary Arts. Cluett holds both an MFA in electronic arts from Rensselaer Polytechnic Institute and a PhD from the composition program at Princeton University, where he completed a graduate certificate in media and modernity studies; in the fall of 2012 he joined the faculty of Contemporary Arts at Ramapo College of New

Jersey, where he teaches courses in audio engineering as well as electronic and experimental sound practices.

Jim Drobnick is a critic, curator, and associate professor of contemporary art and theory at OCAD University, Toronto. He has published on the visual arts, performance, the senses, and post-media practices in recent anthologies such as *Art, History and the Senses* (2010) and *Senses and the City* (2011), and the journals *Angelaki, High Performance, Parachute, Performance Research*, and *The Senses & Society*. He edited the anthologies *Aural Cultures* (2004) and *The Smell Culture Reader* (2006), and recently cofounded the *Journal of Curatorial Studies*. He is a cofounder of DisplayCult, a curatorial collaborative that produced *Odor Limits* (2008), *MetroSonics* (2009) and *NIGHT-SENSE* (2009) (www.displaycult.com). He is working on an upcoming book on smell in contemporary art.

Stephen Gage studied at the Architectural Association, where he was influenced by the work of Cedric Price and Gordon Pask. On graduating, he worked with a UK government research group and taught at Bournemouth College of Art. He went on to work with Stephen Mullin, who had started his own practice after being lead assistant to Cedric Price, and then became a partner in a design and build practice in California.

Upon his return to the United Kingdom in 1973, Professor Gage was invited to run a Design Unit at the AA together with Ranulph Glanville, where he taught until 1993. In 1973 he also joined the Douglas Stephen Partnership. Professor Gage started teaching at the Bartlett in 1993, where he led Diploma Unit 14, the Bartlett Interactive Architecture Workshop, became the director of technology in the School of Architecture, and reengaged with theoretical research that is ongoing. He now leads a Research Cluster in the MArchGAD program and coordinates the written component of the program. He has been an external examiner at The University of the Arts and the University of Liverpool and is part of the RIBA architectural course's validation panel.

Professor Gage is interested in the way that the technology of building relates to the external environment. His other area of research comes from a long-standing interest into the time-based aspects of architecture that relate to human occupation and building use and takes forward an early interest in cybernetics and building brief writing. This has also led to an interest into the ways that buildings might "put on" performances to entertain and enlighten their occupants.

Melissa Harding is a science educator at Phipps Conservatory and Botanical Gardens (Pittsburgh, Pennsylvania), creating and teaching school field trip programs, seasonal camps, and related programming in the science education and research department. She is also the department's online outreach coordinator; she writes and edits the Phipps Science Education and Research blog. She holds a BS in environmental science from West Virginia Wesleyan College and has been working in the field of environmental education for six years. Before coming to Phipps, Melissa spent four years as the regional outdoor recreation coordinator for the Pennsylvania Department of Conservation and Natural Resources, facilitating urban youth outreach and education through recreation programming. She has also taught for the Audubon Society of Western Pennsylvania, the Outdoor Classroom, and Shaver's Creek Environmental Center. Melissa is currently the southwest regional director for the Pennsylvania Association of Environmental Educators and a mentor for PAEE's Environmental Education Certification Program. She has also served on the North American Association of Environmental Education's E-STEM Blue Ribbon panel, helping to determine commonalities and priorities across the most successful and innovative STEM programs incorporating environmental education.

David Howes is professor of anthropology at Concordia University, Montreal, and the director of the Centre for Sensory Studies. He holds three degrees in anthropology and two degrees in law. His main fields of research include sensory anthropology, culture and consumption, constitutional studies, and the anthropology of law. Howes has conducted field research on the cultural life of the senses in the Middle Sepik River region of Papua New Guinea, northwestern Argentina, and the southwestern United States. He recently concluded an anthropological study of the sensory life of things in the Pitt Rivers Museum, Oxford, and has just embarked on a new media art project in collaboration with colleague Christopher Salter, called "Mediations of Sensation." Howes's research in law has focused on the elaboration of a methodology for resolving cases that are products of the increasing mixity and friction of cultures brought on by transnational migration. In place of using culture as a defense, he advocates the development of a cross-cultural jurisprudence. He has also conducted a study of the cultural underpinnings of the Canadian and U.S. constitutions (www.canadianicon.org). Howes is the editor of *The Varieties of Sensory Experience* (1991), *Cross-Cultural Consumption* (1996), and *Empire of the Senses* (2004); the co-author with Constance Classen and Anthony Synnott of *Aroma: The Cultural History of Smell* (1994); and the author of *Sensual Relations: Engaging the Senses in Culture and Social Theory* (2003). His latest book is *The Sixth Sense Reader* (2009). He is the co-convenor of the Sensory Studies website (www.sensorystudies. org). See further www.david-howes.com.

Andreas Keller works as a research associate at the Rockefeller University where he investigates the causes and consequences of the variability of human odor perception. In addition, he is a graduate student in the philosophy department at the Graduate Center of the City University of New York, where he is writing a thesis on the role of olfaction in the philosophy of mind. He also sometimes organizes exhibitions of olfactory art and builds interactive odor art pieces.

Simon Lacey, PhD, is a senior research associate at Emory University. His research interests include multisensory processing, in particular object recognition and representation, and grounded cognition. He has recently coedited *Multisensory Imagery* (2013).

Dr. **Alvaro Pascual-Leone** serves as the associate dean for clinical and translational research at Harvard Medical School and has directed the Clinical Research Center Program of Harvard Catalyst since 2012. Previously, he served as program director (2001–2012) at the Harvard-Thorndike GCRC at BIDMC. Pascual-Leone is an HMS Professor of Neurology and an internationally recognized pioneer in the field of noninvasive brain stimulation, where his contributions span from technology development, through basic neurobiologic insights from animal studies and modeling approaches, to human proof-of-principle and multicenter clinical trials. His clinical research using transcranial magnetic stimulation (TMS) has been fundamental in establishing the field of therapeutic noninvasive brain stimulation, securing FDA approval for TMS in depression and human cortical mapping, and opening up a growing number of applications in clinical neuroscience. He is a dedicated mentor, recognized with a K24 NIH award and various distinctions, including the Daniel Federman Outstanding Clinical Educator Award from Harvard Medical School. He directs an intensive mini-fellowship in noninvasive brain stimulation at HMS that has trained more than 300 people in the past ten years. He continues to work as a cognitive neurologist.

Nina Levent, PhD, is the executive director at Art Beyond Sight (ABS). She is an art historian and also serves as assistant professor at the New York Academy of Art. Levent is a coeditor of *Art Beyond Sight Resource Guide*, a definitive resource on art, creativity, and visual impairment; the principal art historical advisor for AEB's *Art History Through Touch and Sound* multisensory encyclopedia; and the editor of the *Handbook for Museums and Educators* and of AEB's *Teachers' Resource*. Levent has lectured on accessibility and multisensory learning at museums and conferences around the world. She has trained docents and educators at many museums, including Whitney Museum of American Art, Brooklyn Museum, Buffalo's Albright-Knox Art Gallery, and Baltimore's Walters Museum of Art, Baltimore Museum of Art, and Jewish Museum of Maryland. Levent has worked with classroom educators in New York and Seoul, South Korea. She is one of the principal organizers of Art Beyond Sight: Multimodal Approaches to Learning, an international conference that has been taking place every two years at the Metropolitan Museum of Art in New York since 2005. Currently Levent is the lead investigator on the Multi-Site Museum Accessibility Study, a research project that involved major art museums such as SFMOMA; Guggenheim; Museum of Fine Arts, Houston; National Gallery of Art, Washington, D.C.; Brooklyn Museum; and Indianapolis Museum of Art, as well as a number of small museum sites. She is also the principal on the Disability and Inclusion Curriculum for Museum Studies, a university curriculum development project that involved Georgetown University, Arizona State University, University of Washington, University of the Arts, and Cooperstown Graduate School. She received her PhD from the Humboldt Universitat in Berlin.

Joy Monice Malnar, AIA, is associate professor of architecture at the University of Illinois at Urbana-Champaign and a licensed architect. She teaches architectural design studios and a seminar on our sensory response to the built environment. She received her M.Arch. from the University of Illinois at Chicago. Her professional experience includes employment at Whitaker Associates and Skidmore, Owings, and Merrill. She co-authored, with Frank Vodvarka, *The Interior Dimension: A Theoretical Approach to Enclosed Space* and *Sensory Design* and has given presentations at conferences in Singapore, Sydney, Seoul, and at the Canadian Centre for Architecture in Montreal. For the last five years, she has been traveling to reservations throughout North America to interview those involved in designing the successful buildings constructed to support the cultural component of tribal programs. Her third book with Frank Vodvarka, *New Architecture on Indigenous Lands*, was published in 2013.

Carrie McGee is the associate educator for community and access programs in the Department of Education at The Museum of Modern Art. She is responsible for developing programming for visitors with disabilities and in collaboration with community-based organizations. She also teaches gallery and studio programs and trains museum educators. In 2009, Ms. McGee co-authored *Meet Me: Making Art Accessible to People with Dementia*. She also teaches a seminar at the museum for medical students from Columbia University College of Physicians and Surgeons and serves on the board of directors of the Global Alliance for Arts & Health.

D. Lynn McRainey is the Chief Education Officer/Elizabeth F. Cheney Director of Education at the Chicago History museum, where she leads a highly creative department in designing interpretive programs and resources to expand and diversify audiences. She has chaired several teams for institutional advancement, including a visioning committee, audience strategic planning, and currently a team to redefine the museum as a family destination. She was lead educator/project director on the exhibition "Sensing Chicago" that received an Honorable Mention from the Excellence in Exhibitions competition (2007 AAM annual meeting) and was project director for "Imagining Lincoln and Juarez," a non-narrated audio tour for high school students that received the Gold MUSE Award for Audio Tour (2010 AAM annual meeting). Lynn served on the editorial advisory board and was guest editor for the *Journal of Museum Education*. She is coeditor and chapter author of *Connecting Kids to History with Museum Exhibitions*. She has been a guest instructor for the Leadership in Museum Education program at Bank Street College of Education and delivered the keynote presentation at the Museum and Gallery Services Queensland, Australia 2007 state conference. With more than twenty-five years of experience in museum education, Lynn has worked at art, history, and children's museums. She has received fellowships from the Smithsonian Institution and the National Endowment for the Humanities and participated in the Getty Leadership Institute program "Museum Leadership: The Next Generation." Lynn has an MA in art history and a BA in American studies from the University of Virginia.

Irina D. Mihalache is an assistant professor of museum studies at the iSchool at the University of Toronto. Before her move to the University of Toronto, Irina was a post-doctoral fellow in the Department of Global Communication at the American University of Paris. Irina received her PhD in communication from the School of Journalism and Communication at Carleton University and her MA in French studies from New York University. Irina researches restaurants in museums as alternative spaces for education, bridging the gap between food studies, museum studies, and cultural studies. She is also interested in the display of food and food cultures in exhibitions and museums. Further, Irina explores representations of men in the kitchen by focusing on performances of masculinity on different Food Network shows. Also, she focuses on the curatorial practices around the display of everyday objects in cultural institutions, especially in post-Communist countries. Irina has published on topics including postcolonial food cultures in France, restaurant identity in museums, and taste and display in museums.

Juhani Pallasmaa is a practicing architect and professor emeritus of the Helsinki University of Technology. He has held several visiting professorships, including at the Catholic University of America in Washington, D.C. (2011); University of Illinois at Urbana-Champaign (2010); Washington University in St. Louis (1999–2004); University of Virginia (2002); and Yale University (1993). He has also been director of the Museum of Finnish Architecture (1978–1983) and rector of the Institute of Industrial Arts, Helsinki (1972–1974). He teaches and lectures around the world. He has published more than forty books including *Encounters 1* (2005/2012) and *Encounters 2* (2012); *The Embodied Image* (2011); *The Thinking Hand* (2009); *The Eyes of the Skin* (1996, 2005, 2012); *The Architecture of Image: Existential Space in Cinema* (2001, 2007); and *Animal Architecture* (1995).

Francesco Pavani trained as a neuropsychologist and in experimental psychology at the Univerisity of Bologna (Italy) and the University College London (UK), before moving to the University of Trento (Italy). He is currently associate professor at the Department of Psychology and Cognitive Science of the University of Trento and member of the Center for Mind/Brain Sciences. The focus of his research interest is multisensory perception, particularly in the domain of sensory deprivation and reafferentation (e.g., deafness and cochlear implantation) and in body perception.

Richard V. Piacentini is the executive director of Phipps Conservatory and Botanical Gardens (Pittsburgh, Pennsylvania). He is past president, treasurer, and Green Buildings and Landscapes Committee founding chair of the American Public Gardens Association and is recipient of multiple awards, from local to international, including the Living Future Hero Award from the International Living Future Institute and U.S. Green Building Council Individual Leadership Award for an NGO for his work directing the green transformation of Phipps's facilities and operations, including the opening of the first LEED-certified visitor's center in a public garden; the first LEED-certified greenhouses (LEED Platinum EBOM); construction of the Tropical Forest Conservatory, the most energy-efficient structure of its kind in the world; and the Center for Sustainable Landscapes, a net-zero energy and water building designed to meet the Living Building Challenge, LEED Platinum and SITES certification for landscapes. Piacentini received a bachelor's degree in pharmacy from the University of Rhode Island, an MS in botany from the University of Connecticut, and an MBA from Virginia Commonwealth University. He currently is a member of the boards of the International Living Future Institute and the Waldorf School of Pittsburgh, and serves on the Mission and Community Needs Committee for Magee-Womens Hospital.

Francesca Rosenberg is the director of Community, Access, and School Programs at The Museum of Modern Art. In her eighteen years at MoMA, she and her team have won national and international respect for their efforts to make the museum accessible to all. Most recently, MoMA received awards from the Alzheimer's Association; American Association of Museums; and Museums and the Web for its efforts on behalf of people with dementia. In 2007, Ms. Rosenberg received the Ruth Green Advocacy Award from the League for the Hard of Hearing and, in 2002, was recognized as the Community Leader of the Year by Self Help for the Hard of Hearing. Ms. Rosenberg is a founding member of the Museum Access Consortium and currently serves on its steering committee. She is the co-author of *Meet Me: Making Art Accessible to People with Dementia* and *Making Art Accessible to Blind and Visually Impaired Individuals.*

Krish Sathian, MD, PhD, FANA, is professor of neurology, rehabilitation medicine and psychology at Emory University, and medical director of the Emory Center for Systems Imaging. He is also the executive director of the Atlanta VAMC Rehabilitation R&D Center of Excellence for Visual and Neurocognitive Rehabilitation. His research interests include somatosensory and multisensory perception, the neural basis of metaphor, and novel approaches to visual and neurological rehabilitation. He has published extensively in these areas, and his research is funded by the NEI, NSF, and VA. He was the recipient of Emory University's Albert E. Levy Faculty Award for Excellence in Scientific Research in 2001. He is a member of a number of professional societies, a fellow of the American Neurological Association, and current president of the American Society of Neurorehabilitation.

Dr. **Hugo Spiers** is interested in how our brain constructs representations of the world and uses them to navigate, imagine the future, and remember the past. His research group uses brain imaging, neuropsychological testing, virtual reality, eye-tracking, and single cell recording as methods to understand brain function and spatial cognition. He gained his PhD at the UCL Institute of Cognitive Neuroscience in the research group of Neil Burgess and John O'Keefe. After post-doctoral fellowships at the MRC Cognition and Brain Sciences Unit in Cambridge (with Kim Graham) and the Wellcome Trust Centre for Neuroimaging (with Eleanor Maguire), Dr. Spiers was awarded a Wellcome Trust Advanced Training Fellowship to learn single unit recording. His research group has received funding from the Wellcome Trust, BBSRC UK, and the James S. McDonnell Foundation, USA.

Sam Sportun has an undergraduate degree in fine art (sculpture) and an MA in the conservation of historical and archaeological objects from Durham

University. She is currently collection care manager/senior conservator at Manchester Museum. Previously she ran the Sculpture Conservation Department at National Museums Liverpool, where she worked for thirteen years and where she developed her interest in scanning and replication technology. She has an interest in 3D digital technologies and how they can be used to make collections more accessible, and recently completed an MA in creative technologies at Salford University.

Molly Steinwald is the director of science education and research at Phipps Conservatory and Botanical Gardens (Pittsburgh, Pennsylvania). She holds a BS in biology from the University of Dallas, an MS in ecology from Purdue University, and is a current PhD candidate in zoology at Miami University (Ohio), conducting environmental psychology research on how people relate to nature in the built environment. She is a visiting scholar at the University of Pittsburgh Center for Learning in Out-of-School Environments, a fellow with the Fine Outreach for Science program at Carnegie Mellon University, and an affiliate of the International League of Conservation Photographers, a project-driven organization made up of many of the top nature photographers in the world. Molly has fifteen years of teaching experience at the undergraduate and graduate level to science and nonscience majors and formal and informal educators, in topics including ecology, molecular biology, anatomy, plants-people interactions, photography, and communicating science; and she has taught in classroom, field, zoo, and online settings. Additionally, she has more than ten years of research experience in topics including animal behavior, conservation genetics, and plant community composition, and she has conducted fieldwork in desert, woodland, and coastal habitats around the United States. She is an internationally recognized photographer and a frequent invited speaker on human-nature interaction and environmental outreach to nontraditional and underserved audiences.

Richard J. Stevenson gained an MSc and DPhil in experimental psychology at the University of Sussex, UK, in 1993. He then worked for the Commonwealth Scientific and Industrial Research Organisation in Sydney, Australia, studying flavor perception. Following a further period of postdoctoral study at the University of Sydney, he became a lecturer in psychology at Macquarie University in 1998. He is currently professor of experimental psychology at Macquarie University, with a central interest in the psychology of eating, including all of the senses involved in flavor, and especially smell.

Luca Francesco Ticini got a laurea degree in biological sciences from the University of Trieste, Italy, and a PhD in neural and behavioral sciences from the International Max Planck Research School, University of Tuebingen, Germany. His research interests focus on the neuroscientific approach to the study of aesthetics, known as neuroaesthetics. He is scientific advisor for numerous artistic and scientific initiatives and he is president of the Italian Society of Neuroaesthetics, "Semir Zeki" (www.neuroestetica.org).

Frank Vodvarka is professor of fine arts at Loyola University Chicago. He teaches design, color theory, and the American experience in the University Honors Program. He received his MFA from the University of Chicago. His exhibition record includes shows in Australia, Belgium, Botswana, South Africa, and Zimbabwe, as well as in the United States. He co-authored with Joy Monice Malnar *The Interior Dimension: A Theoretical Approach to Enclosed Space* and *Sensory Design* and has given presentations at conferences in Singapore, Sydney, Seoul, and at the Canadian Centre for Architecture in Montreal. For the last five years he have been traveling to reservations throughout North American to interview those involved in designing the successful buildings constructed to support the cultural component of tribal programs. His third book with Joy Monice Malnar, *New Architecture on Indigenous Lands*, was published in 2013.

Salomé Voegelin is an artist and writer based in London. She is the author of *Listening to Noise and Silence: Towards a Philosophy of Sound Art*, 2010. Other writings include "Ethics of Listening" in *the Journal of Sonic Studies*, Vol. 2, 2012; a chapter on durational radio for the forthcoming book *Magic Spaces—25 years of Kunstradio, Austria*; and "Listening to the Stars" in *What Matters Now? (What Can't You Hear?)*, 2013. Her composition "Moving Stones" is part of the award-winning compilation "Autumn Leaves" by Gruenrekorder. Most recently her work has been included in SOUND-WORKS at the ICA (Institute for Contemporary Arts) London. Voegelin is a reader in Sound Arts at the London College of Communication, University of the Arts London. www.salomevoegelin.net soundwords.tumblr.com.

Jamie Ward is professor of cognitive neuroscience at the University of Sussex, UK. His main research focus is on typical and atypical interactions between the senses and how this multisensory processing affects cognitive functioning (in domains such as memory, language, and social cognition). He is particularly well known for his research on synaesthesia, in which "extra" sensations are experienced in addition to those that normally occur. He has written extensively on this topic in addition to writing leading textbooks in the field (*The Student's Guide to Cognitive Neuroscience and Social Neuroscience*) and acting as editor-in-chief for the journal, *Cognitive Neuroscience*.

Fiona Zisch has a master's degree in architecture from the University of Innsbruck, Austria. She is a freelance architect and a researcher in Dr. Clemens Plank's Architecture and Neurophilosophy group at the University of Innsbruck, where she also teaches architectural design. Fiona is currently working on a transdisciplinary PhD at UCL under the supervision of Prof. Stephen Gage and Dr. Hugo Spiers. Fiona is interested in how the mind and brain represent and structure spatial experience and what role memory—past and future—and association play. Her research focuses on mind, body, and environment interaction and perception. She is especially interested in new technologies and how the virtual and actual relate to and implicate architecture in light of the digital lifeworld.